PARAMEDIC PROTOCOLS

NOTICE

Medicine is an ever-changing science. As new research and clinical experience broaden our knowledge, changes in treatment and drug therapy are required. The author and the publisher of this work have checked with sources believed to be reliable in their efforts to provide information that is complete and generally in accord with the standards accepted at the time of publication. However, in view of the possibility of human error or changes in medical sciences, neither the author nor the publisher nor any other party who has been involved in the preparation or publication of this work warrants that the information contained herein is in every respect accurate or complete, and they are not responsible for any errors or omissions or for the results obtained from use of such information. Readers are encouraged to confirm the information contained herein with other sources. For example and in particular, readers are advised to check the product information sheet included in the package of each drug they plan to administer to be certain that the information contained in this book is accurate and that changes have not been made in the recommended dose or in the contraindications for administration. This recommendation is of particular importance in connection with new or infrequently used drugs.

PARAMEDIC PROTOCOLS

RICHARD E. J. WESTFAL, M.D., F.A.C.E.P.
Associate Director
Department of Emergency Medicine
Saint Vincent's Hospital
New York, New York
Associate Professor
Department of Emergency Medicine
New York Medical College
Valhalla, New York

McGRAW-HILL

HEALTH PROFESSIONS DIVISION
New York   St. Louis   San Francisco   Auckland
Bogotá   Caracas   Lisbon   London   Madrid
Mexico City   Milan   Montreal   New Delhi
San Juan   Singapore   Sydney   Tokyo   Toronto

McGraw-Hill

A Division of The **McGraw-Hill** Companies

This book was set in Goudy by V & M Graphics, Inc.

The editors were Gail Gavert and Peter J. Boyle; the production supervisor
was Richard Ruzycka; the cover designer was Patrice Sheridan.
Special thanks to Ossining Volunteer Ambulance Corps for their assistance
in photographing the cover art.
Malloy Lithographing, Inc. was printer and binder.

This book is printed on acid-free paper.

Library of Congress Cataloging-in-Publication Data

Westfal, Richard E. J.
    Paramedic protocols / Richard E. J. Westfal.
      p.   cm.
    Includes bibliographical references.
    ISBN 0-07-069318-8
    1. Medical emergencies—Handbooks, manuals, etc. 2. Emergency
medical technicians—Handbooks, manuals, etc. 3. Medical protocols—
Handbooks, manuals, etc.   I. Title.
    [DNLM: 1. Emergency Medical Services—standards. 2. Clinical
Protocols. 3. Emergencies. 4. Emergency Medical Technicians—
standards.   WX 15 W527p 1996]
RC86.8.W474 ~~1996~~ 1997
616.02'5—dc20
DNLM/DLC
for Library of Congress   96-23226
                                      CIP

For my loving and always supportive wife, Debbie,

and for my Chairman and dear friend, Eduardo

ABBREVIATED CONTENTS

CONTENTS

SECTION II

UNIQUE ADULT PROTOCOLS

SECTION III

STANDARD PEDIATRIC PROTOCOLS

SECTION IV

UNIQUE PEDIATRIC PROTOCOLS

S E C T I O N   V

APPENDICES

CONTENTS

CONTRIBUTORS

Grateful acknowledgment is made to the following EMS systems and administrators, without whose help this book would not have come to fruition:

BIRMINGHAM, ALABAMA
Birmingham Fire & Rescue Service Dept.
1808 Seventh Avenue North
Birmingham, AL 35203

Chief F. E. Wilks

ANCHORAGE, ALASKA
Anchorage Fire Dept./EMS Division
1301 East 80th Street
Anchorage, AK 99518

Mr. Harvey Huyett
Deputy Chief

PHOENIX, ARIZONA
St. Lukes Medical Center
1800 East Van Buren
Phoenix, AZ 85006

John V. Gallagher III, MD

SCOTTSDALE, ARIZONA
EMS Division
8430 East Indian School Road
Scottsdale, AZ 85251

Craig S. Laser, RN, BSN, CEN

ANAHEIM, CALIFORNIA
Anaheim Fire Department
500 East Broadway
Anaheim, CA 92805

Janice Turner, RN,
EMS Coordinator

FREMONT, CALIFORNIA
Regional Medical Systems
2529 Grant Avenue
San Leandro, CA 94579

Jeanne Lalich, RN
Director of Medical QA & Ed.

LOS ANGELES, CALIFORNIA
EMS Agency
5555 Ferguson Drive, Suite 220
Commerce, CA 90022

Samuel J. Stratton, MD
Medical Director

SACRAMENTO, CALIFORNIA
American Medical Response
Northern California Training Institute
5255 Elkhorn Blvd.
Sacramento, CA 59842

Chris Thos. Ryther, BS, NREMT-P
Field Training Coordinator

SAN FRANCISCO, CALIFORNIA
Dept. of Public Health
Paramedic Division
2789 25th Street, Room 200
San Francisco, CA 94110

Marshal Isaacs, MD
Medical Director

SAN MATEO, CALIFORNIA
Health Services Agency
EMS
225 West 37th Avenue
San Mateo, CA 94403

Jean Duncan, EMT-P

SANTA ANA, CALIFORNIA
Santa Ana Fire Department
1439 South Broadway
Santa Ana, CA 92707

Mr. James Dalton
Battalion Chief

SAN JOSE, CALIFORNIA
American Medical Response West
PO Box 50001
San Jose, CA 95150

Martha G. Libby, EMT-P
Director QI and Education

COLORADO SPRINGS, COLORADO
EMS
1400 East Boulder Street
Colorado Springs, CO 80909

Marilyn J. Gifford, MD
Director

DENVER, COLORADO
EMS/Paramedic Division
777 Bannock Street
Denver, CO 80204-4507

Earl Wm. Hall, MS, EMT-P
Senior Analyst

NEW HAVEN, CONNECTICUT
City of New Haven Fire Dept.
Training Academy
PO Box 374
New Haven, CT 06502

Lt. William Seward III, EMT-P
EMS Coordinator

JACKSONVILLE, FLORIDA
Jacksonville Fire Rescue Dept
107 North Market Street
Jacksonville, Florida 32202

Capt. Fred Johnson
QA Officer

TAMPA, FLORIDA
Tampa Fire Dept. Rescue Division
808 East Zack Street
Tampa FL 33602

Catherine Carrubba, MD
Medical Director

COLUMBUS, GEORGIA
Columbus EMS
1905 Third Avenue
Columbus, GA 31901

Mr. James R. Bloodworth
Training Officer

SAVANNAH, GEORGIA
Medstar Ambulance Services
PO Box 23917
Savannah, GA 31403-3917

Frank E. Davis, MD
Medical Director

STATE of HAWAII
Dept. of Health
EMS Systems Branch
3627 Kilauea Avenue, Room 102
Honolulu, HI 98616-2317

Ms. Donna Maiava
Chief

CHICAGO, ILLINOIS
Chicago FD Bureau of EMS
121 N. Lasalle Street, Room 105
Chicago, IL 60602

Max D. Koenigsberg, MD
Project Medical Director

ROCKFORD, ILLINOIS
Fire Department
204 South First Street
Rockford, IL 61104

Mr. Marty Vuttera
District Chief

EVANSVILLE, INDIANA
Mercy Ambulance
522 N.W. First Street
Evansville, IN 47708

Mr. Lee Turpen
Quality Assurance Coordinator

INDIANAPOLIS, INDIANA
IEMS
Wishard Memorial Hospital
Indianapolis, IN 46202-2859

Roland McGrath, M.D.
Medical Director

DES MOINES, IOWA
Iowa Dept. of Public Health
EMS, Lucas State Office Building
Des Moines, IA 50319-0075

Mr. Christopher Atchison
Director of Public Health

STATE OF KANSAS
Board of Emergency Medical Services
109 S.W. Sixth Street
Topeka, KS 66603-3805

Mr. Robert McDaneld
Administrator

WICHITA, KANSAS
Sedgwick County EMS
PO Box 607
Wichita, KS 67201

Mr. Dennis Mauck
Assistant Director

LEXINGTON, KENTUCKY
Division of Fire & Emergency Services
219 East Third Street
Lexington, KY 40508

Mellayne R. Myers, MD
Medical Director

NEW ORLEANS, LOUISIANA
New Orleans Department
EMS Division
1700 Moss Street
New Orleans, LA 70119

Ms. Dawne Orgeron
EMS Administrator

STATE OF MARYLAND
MI EMS
636 West Lombard Street, Room 106
Baltimore, MD 21201

Mr. Andy Trohinis

BOSTON, MASSACHUSETTS
Metropolitan Boston EMS Council
5 New England Executive Park
Burlington, MA 08103

Mr. William J. Schneiderman
Executive Director of MBEMSC

DETROIT, MICHIGAN
Detroit Fire Department
EMS Division
900 Merrill Plaisance
Detroit, MI 48203

Mr. Gary N. Kelly
Assistant Superintendent

FLINT, MICHIGAN
Genesee County Medical Control Authority
702 S. Ballenger Highway
Flint, MI 48532-3803

Michael Jule, MD
Co-director
John Walker, MD
Co-director

MINNEAPOLIS, MINNESOTA
Community Health Department
525 Portland Avenue South
Minneapolis, MN 55415

Mr. John Urback
Program Supervisor

SAINT PAUL, MINNESOTA
Dept. Of Fire & Safety Services
100 East 11th Street
Saint Paul, MN 55101

Mr. David Huisenga
EMS Chief

KANSAS CITY, MISSOURI
Kansas City FD/EMS
1734 East 63rd St., Suite 510
Kansas City, MO 64110

Jack Campbell, MD
Medical Director

SAINT LOUIS, MISSOURI
EMS
2634 Hampton Avenue
Saint Louis, MO 63139

Mr. Robert Hardy III
Chief

LAS VEGAS, NEVADA
Department of Fire Services
500 N. Casino Center Blvd.
Las Vegas, NY 89101-2986

Mr. Eric Cheese
Paramedic

RENO, NEVADA
Regional EMS Authority
450 Edison Way
Reno, NV 89502-4117

Rodney Dyche, NREMT-P
Field Supervisor

ALBUQUERQUE, NEW MEXICO
Albuquerque Fire Department
724 Silver Avenue, S.W.
Albuquerque, NM 87102

Chief Michael Fox
EMS Commander

NEW YORK, NEW YORK
NYC EMS
55-30 58th Street
Maspeth, NY 11378-1190

Lorraine Giordiano, MD
Medical Director

Dario Gonzalez, MD
Medical Director of Training

CHARLOTTE, NORTH CAROLINA
Mecklenburg County
Emergency Medical Services
618 N. College Street
Charlotte, NC 28202

Laura T. Bowers, BSN, EMT-P
Training Officer

DURHAM, NORTH CAROLINA
Emergency Medical Services
3643 N. Roxboro Street
Durham, NC 27704

Mr. J. M. Tezai
Director

AKRON, OHIO
Akron Fire Department
146 S. High Street
Akron, OH 44308

Mr. Patrick M. Caprez
District Chief
EMS

COLUMBUS, OHIO
Division of Fire
739 W. Third Avenue
Columbus, OH 43212

David P. Keseg, MD
Medical Director

OKLAHOMA CITY, OKLAHOMA
EMSA
1111 Classen Drive
Oklahoma City, OK 73106

Peter A. Maningas, MD
Medical Director

EUGENE/SPRINGFIELD, OREGON
Central Training
Dept. of Public Safety
710 McKinley Street
Eugene, OR 97402

John Mackey, MD

PORTLAND, OREGON
Health Department
426 S.W. Stark Street, 9th Floor
Portland, OR 97204

Mr. Roy R. Kallas
EMS Administrative Secretary

PHILADELPHIA, PENNSYLVANIA
Fire Department
240 Spring Garden Street
Philadelphia, PA 19123-2991

Otis N. Tyler, ADC
Director of EMS

PITTSBURGH, PENNSYLVANIA
University of Pittsburgh Medical Center
230 McKee Place, Suite 500
Pittsburgh, PA 15213

Vincent N. Mosesso, Jr., MD
Assistant Medical Director

MEMPHIS, TENNESSEE
Memphis Fire Department
65 S. Front Street
Memphis, TN 38103-2498

Mr. Larry W. Youngman
Supervisor

NASHVILLE, TENNESSE
Tennessee Dept. of Health
Division of Emergency Medicine
287 Plus Park Blvd.
Nashville, TN 37247-0701

Mr. Steven White
Director of EMS

ARLINGTON, TEXAS
Life Star Ambulance Service
601 E. Main Street
Arlington, TX 76010

Ms. Deb Silkwood
Chief Operating Officer

AUSTIN, TEXAS
Emergency Medical Services
517 South Pleasant Valley
Austin, TX 78741

Edward M. Racht, MD
Medical Director

DALLAS, TEXAS
Fire Department
EMS
2014 Main Street
Dallas, TX 75201

Maxie Bishop, RN, EMT-P
EMS Training Coordinator

HOUSTON, TEXAS
EMS
410 Bagby, Suite 300
Houston, TX 77002

Paul E. Pepe, MD
Director

NORFOLK, VIRGINIA
Tidewater EMS Council, Inc.
855 West Brambleton Avenue
Norfolk, VA 23510

J. Stephen Huff, MD
Chairman

SEATTLE, WASHINGTON
Seattle Medic One
325 Ninth Avenue
PO Box 359727
Seattle, WA 98104

Chief Michael Brooks
EMS Administrator

WASHINGTON, DC
EMS Bureau
1923 Vermont Avenue, N.W.
Room 201 South
Washington, DC 20001

Wayne Moore, MD
Medical Director

MILWAUKEE, WISCONSIN
Milwaukee County EMS
8700 West Wisconsin Avenue
Box 204
Milwaukee, WI 53226

Ronald G. Pirrallo, MD
Medical Director

FOREWORD

In 1966, the National Academy of Sciences and the American Medical Association published a joint report entitled *Accidental Death and Disability: The Neglected Disease of Modern Society*. This report, and the legislation and funding programs that followed, launched the development of the United States Emergency Medical Services (EMS) system, which has become the most comprehensive network of its kind in the world. Emergency Medical Technician (EMTs) and paramedics (EMT-Ps) rather than physicians or nurses provide prehospital treatment in our country. These skilled individuals are highly specialized technicians who function legally as agents of their Medical Director to provide emergency care for acutely ill or injured patients in a wide range of clinical settings.

Prehospital providers function as the "eyes, ears and hands" of a physician who is typically based at a remote hospital. In the early days of contemporary EMS, paramedics had to obtain a direct physician order by telephone or telemetry radio for every advanced life support (ALS) intervention. Individual physician variation in orders made it difficult for large numbers of paramedics to anticipate the next order when treating a critical patient. In an effort to ensure consistency and to improve the efficiency of prehospital providers, in the 1970s many systems began to create written protocols for patient management.

The first protocols typically permitted paramedics to perform only a minimal number of critical interventions based on "standing orders" (e.g., defibrillation, CPR, initial airway management). Physician contact and direct orders were required early in the intervention sequence. In the 1980s and early 1990s, most progressive EMS systems began to move away from direct physician orders (the "Mother, may I?" approach) in favor of "off-line" or "indirect" medical control using protocols and standing orders. This strategy frees paramedics to act much more promptly in a rapidly changing emergency. It also requires sophisticated protocol development, more intensive initial training of paramedics, continuing education, and, most of all, a program of continuous quality improvement. By defining the standard of care expected of everyone in the system, patient care protocols provide a foundation for consistent, high quality, efficient, effective EMS patient care.

How does an EMS system develop a set of high quality, scientifically sound, operationally feasible protocols? How many specific protocols should there be? How should they be designed and written? Who should be involved in their design and development? Who needs to approve them? Although each of these questions (and many more) need to be answered based on the unique characteristics of the local EMS system, it is possible to identify common denominators in protocol development.

The process of new protocol development and revision of existing protocols is just as important as the end product itself. The process should be fair, easily understood, widely participatory, and dynamic. If possible, each proposed new protocol should be scrutinized and commented on by representatives of all EMS personnel who might be affected by its implementation. Common steps that need to be taken to develop and revise effective protocols include:

Step 1. Identify the need for a specific new protocol or revision of an existing protocol.

Any individual (e.g., field provider, dispatcher, administrator, physician) involved in the EMS system should be allowed to suggest the need for development or revision of a specific patient care protocol. The system's continuous quality improvement process may identify the need for a standardized approach to a particular problem, or may uncover weaknesses in an existing protocol or procedure. Introduction of new technology or pharmaceuticals often necessitates development of new protocols.

Step 2. Assemble a representative committee or task force to develop the protocol.

This step is the most important element to assure scientific validity and operational feasibility. Ideally, the group should include a medical control physician, or a physician intimately familiar with prehospital care and the targeted injury or illness, several prehospital providers at various levels of certification (representing all providers potentially affected by the new protocol), a system administrative or operational representative (for issues such as costs of program implementation and effect on existing system programs), and a secretary. Additionally, if the committee has access to "experts" on a particular topic, they should be included in protocol development. By assembling a representative committee, the final protocol will reflect a consensus of those disciplines involved in patient management.

Step 3. Review existing literature and protocols.

The first step in creating any new protocol is to review existing scientific knowledge pertaining to protocol content. This can be accomplished in several ways including a search of computerized databases, review of scientific articles, investigation of professional organization policy statements, and now, perusal of the many superb sample protocols contained in this book.

Step 4. Develop the protocol.

The protocol format should be consistent with the design of other current protocols and should clearly identify actions based on symptoms or assessment. High quality protocols usually identify a point at which mandatory contact with a base station physician (or on-line direct medical control) is desirable or necessary. One should also decide whether each protocol is designed to be an absolute patient management document, a guideline that should usually be followed, or merely a suggestion for a specific approach to patient care. Circumstances that may have implications on the use of the protocol, such as loss of radio contact or prolonged transport times, should be covered in the development of the protocol. Once developed, the protocol should be submitted to the appropriate individuals and groups for final approval. Whenever feasible, it is usually a good strategy to have representatives from the approving entities involved in development of the protocol from the beginning (e.g., if the Medical Control Board in the system must approve all protocols, it is wise to have one or more members of that board on the protocol development task force).

Step 5. Implement the protocol.

Protocol implementation requires education of all members of the EMS system, periodic review of the new materials, and continuous quality improvement monitoring to identify problems. Members of the committee or task force who helped to draft the protocol are a valuable resource for maximizing dissemination of new information and ensuring compliance with any new procedures.

Step 6. Apply a process of continuous quality improvement.

Once a protocol has been implemented, it is important to assess compliance with the new procedures, the impact of the protocol on patient outcome, and to identify any unexpected problems. If necessary, the new protocol may need to be revised further or "fine tuned" to best fit the needs of the EMS system. Problems with the protocol may also uncover the need for further training or continuing education.

Protocol development and refinement should be an integral component of every EMS system's continuous quality improvement program. If structured properly, the process of protocol development and revision provides a unique opportunity for every member of the patient care team to participate in the pursuit of clinical care excellence.

In conclusion, protocol development and revision is a dynamic process. Existing, successful protocols used in other systems, such as those presented in this book, can serve as a model for protocol development or revision in each of our EMS systems. We believe that this compendium should be of great value to Medical Directors, Medical Control Boards, EMS administrators, EMS Council members, EMTs and paramedics. Now, for the first time with the publication of this book, we no longer have to reinvent the wheel . . . we can simply refine it!

Edward M. Racht, M.D.
Joseph P. Ornato, M.D.

Edward M. Racht, MD is Medical Director of the City of Austin/Travis County Emergency Medical Services in Austin, Texas.

Joseph P. Ornato, MD is Professor of Internal Medicine & Cardiology, and is Chief of the Internal Medicine Section of Emergency Medical Services at Virginia Commonwealth University/Medical College of Virginia in Richmond, VA. He is also Medical Co-Director of Richmond's Emergency Medical Services system.

PREFACE

Over the past 20 years, there has been a monumental evolution in prehospital *emergency medical services* (EMS) systems throughout this country and the world. The days when ambulance drivers delivered sick or dying patients to a hospital in station wagons, hearses, or trucks are behind us. Ambulance drivers in fact have been replaced by professional emergency service personnel: the Emergency Medical Technician (EMT) and the Paramedic. On-the-job training has been replaced by standardized, nation-wide, entry-level or refresher EMT courses and state or regional paramedic curricula. Initial prehospital emergency medical care is usually instituted by EMTs according to their training and experience or, in some regions, according to *basic life support* (BLS) protocols. Additional *advanced life support* (ALS) treatment is generally rendered by paramedics depending on state, county, or city protocols. These protocols are based on a particular set of practice assumptions that have been found useful or necessary for a particular area, and include standing orders, medical control (telemetry) orders, or a combination of the above. State, county, and city paramedic protocols are usually developed by an Emergency Medical Services Medical Advisory Committee, consisting of physicians, nurses, paramedics, and administrators.

Since 1974, the American Heart Association issues guidelines every 6 years on *advanced cardiac life support* (ACLS) to resuscitate and treat the critically ill patient. These guidelines are incorporated into most Paramedic Life Support protocols. In the mid-1980s, several EMS systems developed Pediatric Advanced Life Support (PALS) guidelines to resuscitate and treat the critically ill child. In addition, a myriad of acute emergencies—both traumatic and nontraumatic—have led to the development of many other paramedic ALS protocols.

Paramedic Protocols presents both the "usual" and the unique protocols culled from 60 participating state, county, and city EMS systems. They represent the best of the best or sometimes slightly different ways to approach prehospital situations. The variations disclose some substantially different treatment options or highlight a cleaner or simpler path to the same result. And there are offerings of unique protocols that may help in unusual situations for many readers as well as the use of newer medications, varied routes of drug administration, or different protocol formats or designs that may be more comprehensive or more comprehensible to the staff.

Paramedic Protocols should be useful to those who are involved with writing or revising current EMT or paramedic protocols—EMT administrators, physicians, nurses, instructors—or those who are involved with EMT or paramedic programs—residents or physician assistants. In addition, and perhaps most important, this text will be useful to the EMT or paramedic student who wants to learn the kinds of skills and procedures necessary in this new career.

In this text, the Contents outlines the chapters according to type of emergency, including subsets of diagnostic treatment protocols listed by state, county, or city EMS system. Each chapter is preceded by an alphabetized listing of diagnostic treatment protocols coupled with brief comments on *why* a particular one was chosen to be included in the book. The comments highlight a particular characteristic of the protocol that seemed to me to set it apart because it was new and different or because it seemed to be the usual way to approach a situation.

The book is basically divided into two major parts—on the adult and on the child. The first two sections of the text cover common adult and unique adult prehospital situations; the third and fourth sections contain common pediatric and unique pediatric protocols. The appendices offer a list of abbreviations, a drug formulary, procedures, and selective policies.

My hope is that *Paramedic Protocols* will facilitate the process of designing and revising protocols in any EMS or paramedic facility and will help advance the prehospital practice of paramedicine.

My personal thanks to every medical director, administrative director, and administrative assistant from the 60 EMS systems who allowed me to use their contributions in this book or helped me compile it. I particularly want to thank Marlene Picone for her administrative assistance, Peter Boyle for his supervision of editing and composition of the manuscript, and my editor, Gail Gavert, for her special gift of guidance and support throughout this entire process.

Richard E. J. Westfal

STANDARD ADULT PROTOCOLS

Nontraumatic Cardiopulmonary Arrest

VENTRICULAR FIBRILLATION/PULSELESS VENTRICULAR TACHYCARDIA

1. Denver, CO—format
2. Wichita, KS—format
3. Memphis, TN—IV procainamide option
4. Seattle, WA—IV epinephrine plus study drug

ASYSTOLE

1. Anchorage, AK—early pacing
2. San Jose, CA
3. San Francisco, CA—format; protocol notes
4. Boston, MA—format; high-dose epinephrine option

PULSELESS ELECTRICAL ACTIVITY

1. San Francisco, CA—format; protocol notes
2. Chicago, IL—slow-rate vs. fast-rate options
3. Boston, MA—format; high-dose epinephrine option
4. Pittsburgh, PA—pacing option

VENTRICULAR FIBRILLATION/ PULSELESS VENTRICULAR TACHYCARDIA
DENVER, CO

Ventricular Fibrillation/Pulseless Ventricular Tachycardia

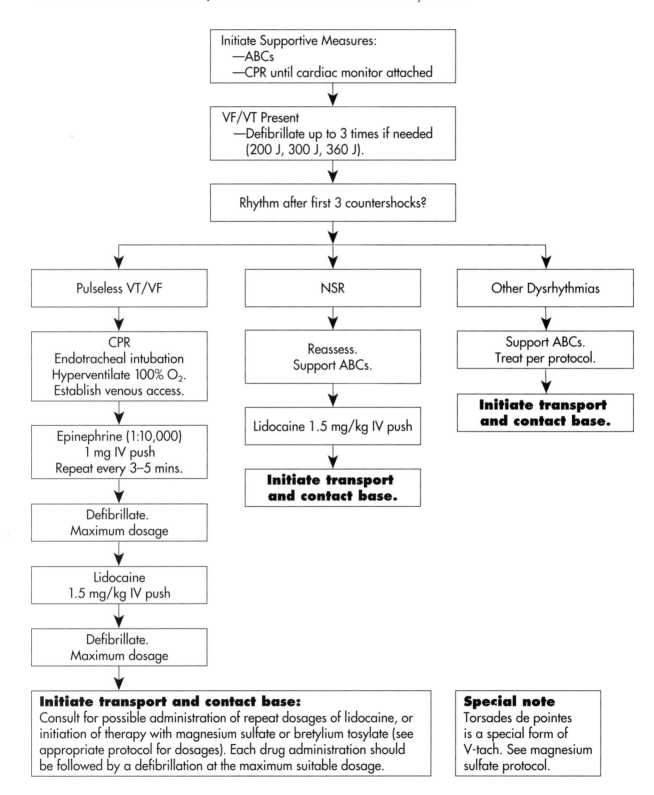

Initiate Supportive Measures:
—ABCs
—CPR until cardiac monitor attached

VF/VT Present
—Defibrillate up to 3 times if needed (200 J, 300 J, 360 J).

Rhythm after first 3 countershocks?

Pulseless VT/VF

CPR
Endotracheal intubation
Hyperventilate 100% O_2.
Establish venous access.

Epinephrine (1:10,000)
1 mg IV push
Repeat every 3–5 mins.

Defibrillate.
Maximum dosage

Lidocaine
1.5 mg/kg IV push

Defibrillate.
Maximum dosage

NSR

Reassess.
Support ABCs.

Lidocaine 1.5 mg/kg IV push

Initiate transport and contact base.

Other Dysrhythmias

Support ABCs.
Treat per protocol.

Initiate transport and contact base.

Initiate transport and contact base:
Consult for possible administration of repeat dosages of lidocaine, or initiation of therapy with magnesium sulfate or bretylium tosylate (see appropriate protocol for dosages). Each drug administration should be followed by a defibrillation at the maximum suitable dosage.

Special note
Torsades de pointes is a special form of V-tach. See magnesium sulfate protocol.

VENTRICULAR FIBRILLATION/
PULSELESS VENTRICULAR TACHYCARDIA
WICHITA, KS

Persistent or Recurrent V-Fib or Pulseless V-Tach

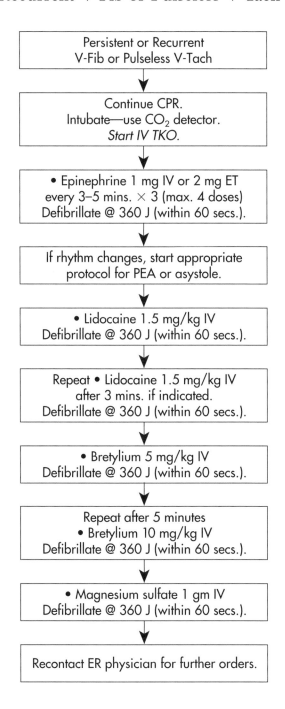

Persistent or Recurrent
V-Fib or Pulseless V-Tach

↓

Continue CPR.
Intubate—use CO_2 detector.
Start IV TKO.

↓

• Epinephrine 1 mg IV or 2 mg ET
every 3–5 mins. × 3 (max. 4 doses)
Defibrillate @ 360 J (within 60 secs.).

↓

If rhythm changes, start appropriate
protocol for PEA or asystole.

↓

• Lidocaine 1.5 mg/kg IV
Defibrillate @ 360 J (within 60 secs.).

↓

Repeat • Lidocaine 1.5 mg/kg IV
after 3 mins. if indicated.
Defibrillate @ 360 J (within 60 secs.).

↓

• Bretylium 5 mg/kg IV
Defibrillate @ 360 J (within 60 secs.).

↓

Repeat after 5 minutes
• Bretylium 10 mg/kg IV
Defibrillate @ 360 J (within 60 secs.).

↓

• Magnesium sulfate 1 gm IV
Defibrillate @ 360 J (within 60 secs.).

↓

Recontact ER physician for further orders.

VENTRICULAR FIBRILLATION/
PULSELESS VENTRICULAR TACHYCARDIA
MEMPHIS, TN

Ventricular Fibrillation

A. Assessment
- Ventricular fibrillation
- Pulseless
- Confirm cardiac rhythm with quick-lock paddles or electrodes.

B. Treatment

1. CPR with 100% oxygen (precordial thump if witnessed)
2. Check cardiac monitor and identify V-Fib or V-Tach w/o pulse.
3. Defibrillate @ 200/300/360 joules.
4. CPR if no pulse
5. Intubate and establish IV N.S.K.V.O.
6. Epinephrine 1:10,000 1 mg IVP or 2.0 mg E.T. q 3–5 mins.
7. Defibrillate @ 360 joules.*
8. Lidocaine 1.5 mg/kg IV q 3–5 mins. up to 3 mg/kg max. or 3.0 mg/kg E.T.
9. Defibrillate @ 360 joules.*
10. Bretylium 5 mg/kg IVP
11. Defibrillate @ 360 joules * (wait 1–2 mins. after bretylium).
12. Bretylium 10 mg/kg IVP q 5 mins. up to max. 30–35 mg/kg.
13. Defibrillate @ 360 joules* (wait 1–2 mins. after bretylium).
14. Repeat lidocaine 0.5 mg/kg dose q 8–10 mins. (above 3 mg/kg).
15. Defibrillate @ 360 joules.*

Contact medical control; consider:

Sodium bicarbonate 1 mEq/kg IVP
Magnesium sulfate 1 g IV
Procainamide 30 mg/min. (max. 17 mg/kg)

NOTES: *Check for pulse and rhythm after each defibrillation. Start IV infusion of antiarrhythmic agent that resolved arrythmia.

VENTRICULAR FIBRILLATION/ PULSELESS VENTRICULAR TACHYCARDIA
SEATTLE, WA

Circulatory Arrest/Standing Orders, Plans A–1, A–2, and B

I. General Policies

    A. A physician at Harborview will always be available for instructions and consultation by radio or phone. A paging device will be used to alert the Medic One or trauma doctors.

    B. Medical procedures above the level of care provided by emergency medical technicians (EMTs) will be carried out only under written orders from a responsible physician (usually the medical director) or upon radio or telephone or by personal directions from a licensed physician. Resuscitation, medications, and intravenous solutions will be administered only after orders have been received from a physician, except when treating cardiopulmonary arrest or shock requiring intravenous fluid.

II. Standing Orders for Paramedics

    A. PLAN A–1: In instances of a presumedly recent circulatory arrest, resuscitative efforts should be carried out as follows:

        1. Verify circulatory arrest by absence of consciousness, arterial pulse, and respiration and by history from witnesses.

        2. Initiate cardiopulmonary resuscitation. This will be the primary responsibility of the first emergency unit on the scene (usually aid-car or engine or ladder-company personnel).

        3. A taped recording of the resuscitation will be made in *all* cases of circulatory arrest.

      **4. The Life-300 will be used if available: place monitor/defibrillator patches appropriately.

      **5. Place the LP-300 in "MANUAL MODE" and evaluate the cardiac rhythm.

      **6. If the LP-300 is not available, determine the cardiac rhythm using quick-look paddles or cutaneous chest/extremity electrodes.

        7. IF VENTRICULAR FIBRILLATION (VF) IS THE FIRST RHYTHM IDENTIFIED AND:

            a. IF SHOCKS HAVE ALREADY BEEN DELIVERED BY OTHER RESCUERS, charge the defibrillator to MAXIMUM ENERGY and deliver shocks, assessing cardiac rhythm after each shock. Rapidly deliver up to 3 additional shocks for persistent VF regardless of the number of earlier shocks delivered by first responders.

            b. IF NO PRIOR SHOCKS HAVE BEEN DELIVERED, charge the defibrillator to 200 joules and rapidly deliver shocks, assessing the rhythm after each discharge. TWO 200-J SHOCKS may be used for persistent VF, and if unsuccessful, a THIRD using the MAXIMUM ENERGY level should be immediately given.

NOTE: *If AED (LP-300) electrode pads have been applied, they should not be removed. Continue to deliver shocks using LP-300. Be sure that the pads are adhered tightly to the skin.

8. IF VENTRICULAR TACHYCARDIA IS THE FIRST RHYTHM IDENTIFIED, FOLLOW TREATMENT FOR VENTRICULAR FIBRILLATION ABOVE.

9. IF ASYSTOLE IS THE FIRST RHYTHM IDENTIFIED:

a. If the LP-5 is being used, rotate the monitoring electrodes 90 degrees (switch paddles to left shoulder and right breast or change electrodes from lead II to lead III) and reevaluate the rhythm.

b. If either the LP-300 or LP-5 is used, deliver one 200-J shock (with paddles in the standard position) and reassess the rhythm before proceeding with drug therapy. (Delivery of a shock is not necessary when asystole develops after defibrillation.)

10. An endotracheal tube is an important adjunct, and it should be placed if it can be passed without interrupting CPR for more than 15 seconds. Ventilation is to be carried out with 100% oxygen in patients with circulatory arrest. Patients discovered in ventricular fibrillation should be SHOCKED BEFORE INTUBATION except in those rare cases with major airway obstruction/compromise.

11. An intravenous route should be established with an infusion of D5/W.

12. Five percent sodium bicarbonate should be slowly administered ("piggyback") at a rate not to exceed 180 mEq (300 ml) over 20 minutes. After return of spontaneous rhythm, pulse, and blood pressure, the sodium bicarbonate should be stopped.

In cases of cardiac arrest following arrival of SFD, the requirement for sodium bicarbonate is usually reduced. Infusion of sodium bicarbonate is not necessary when rhythm and blood pressure have been promptly restored.

13. Use maximum energy for VF persisting after the initial shocks. When ventricular fibrillation is present, a SHOCK SHOULD ALWAYS BE DELIVERED AFTER EACH PHARMACO-LOGIC INTERVENTION; e.g., after epinephrine or antiarrhythmic drugs.

14. Pharmacologic Adjuncts

a. EPINEPHRINE, 1.0 mg, should be given intravenously (not in an IV line with bicarbonate), or if necessary by endotracheal or intracardiac routes when:

i. VF is refractory to the initial 3 shocks delivered by paramedics (persistent VF), or

ii. Asystole is being treated (see No. 6 above), or

iii. QRS complexes are present but without pulse (electromechanical dissociation).

b. STUDY DRUG, 6 cc diluted in 20 cc of D5/W, should be given intravenously (give 1 mg of epinephrine first, unless epinephrine was given within 5 minutes) when:

    i. Ventricular fibrillation is refractory to the initial 3 or more shocks.

    ii. Ventricular fibrillation recurs after the initial 3 or more shocks.

c. LIDOCAINE, 100 mg, as a bolus, should be given intravenously (or, if necessary, by endotracheal tube) when:

    i. Ventricular fibrillation is refractory to both the initial 3 shocks delivered by paramedics and the administration of epinephrine and study drug as above, or

    ii. Ventricular fibrillation recurs following temporary reversion, or

    iii. Ventricular fibrillation has been successfully treated and organized rhythm, pulse, and blood pressure have returned.

*** **NOTE:** Contact Medic One doctor prior to administering lidocaine if high-degree AV block or bradycardia is present.

d. The following drugs may also be given if resuscitation has not been effective:

    i. Additional 1.0 mg EPINEPHRINE

    ii. Additional 100 mg LIDOCAINE intravenously for ventricular fibrillation

    iii. If VF persists or recurs after administration of LIDOCAINE AND EPINEPHRINE, 500 mg of PROCAINAMIDE should be administered intravenously and a shock of maximum energy delivered.

    iv. If VF persists or recurs after administration of PROCAINAMIDE, 500 mg of BRETYLIUM TOSYLATE should be given intravenously and a shock of maximum energy delivered.

15. Following the above therapy, whether effective or not, CONTACT THE MEDIC ONE DOCTOR FOR ADVICE.

16. Resuscitative efforts should not be continued indefinitely. Indications for STOPPING RESUSCITATION include:

a. Straight-line ECG (asystole) or an agonal, pulseless ventricular rhythm (electromechanical dissociation) which has not responded to treatment including epinephrine

b. If the resuscitation is prolonged because of recurrent episodes of ventricular fibrillation, resuscitation should be continued until asystole or electromechanical dissociation persists despite therapy. A PATIENT IN VENTRICULAR FIBRILLATION SHOULD NEVER BE CONSIDERED DEAD.

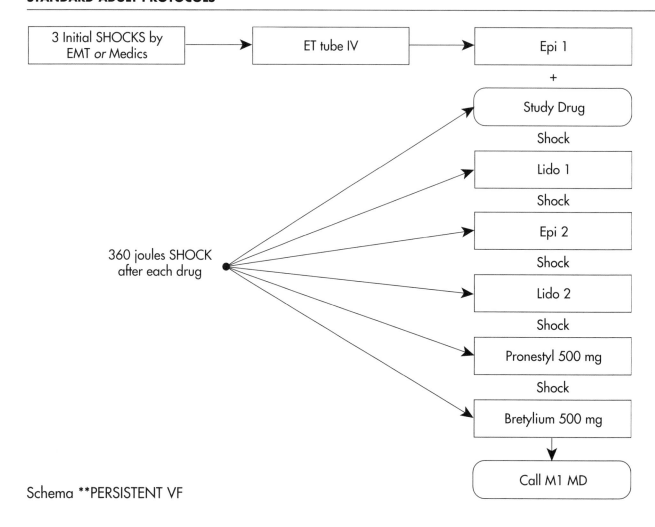

Schema **PERSISTENT VF

ACCORDINGLY, IT MAY BE NECESSARY TO TRANS-PORT A PATIENT WHO HAS REFRACTORY VEN-TRICULAR FIBRILLATION.

c. In ALL QUESTIONABLE CASES contact the Medic One doctor for advice.

17. For patients who develop CARDIAC ARREST UNDER SUR-VEILLANCE of SFD personnel, that is, patients who were conscious and/or had a pulse on arrival, PLAN A should be initiated and continued until the Medic One doctor or other responsible physician advises cessation. (In some situations it may be necessary to transport rapidly to the hospital.)

A. PLAN A-2: In instances of hypovolemic shock requiring immediate volume replacement:

1. Employ necessary first-aid measures, *e.g.*, control of hemorrhage.
2. Establish two intravenous lines with large-bore catheters. (If the IV lines cannot be rapidly established, proceed per No. 4 below.)
3. Begin rapid infusions of 2 liters of Ringer's lactate.
4. Contact HMC trauma doctor and transport the patient immediately to the appropriate medical facility per trauma doctor.

C. PLAN B: Applies to all patients not defined under Plans A–1 and A–2 above.

   1. A physician is to be contacted after briefly obtaining a history and performing a critical physical examination prior to administering any therapy beyond basic EMT-level care.

   2. Permission to infuse intravenous solutions (usually 5% dextrose in water, TKO) should be requested in virtually all potential life-threatening situations.

   3. If supplemental oxygen is indicated, conscious patients with spontaneous respirations should be given 100% oxygen, using nasal prongs at 4 liters/minute. For the patient with chronic obstructive lung disease, high concentrations of oxygen may be dangerous and further compromise respiration. Hence, oxygen in such patients should be initiated at no more than 2 liters/minute.

   4. In all questionable cases contact the Medic One doctor for advice.

ASYSTOLE
ANCHORAGE, AK

Asystole

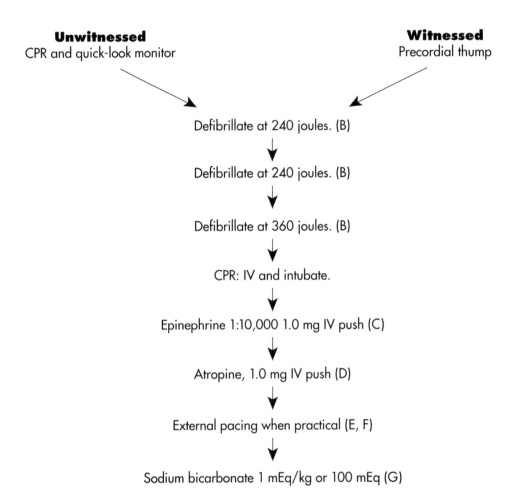

Unwitnessed
CPR and quick-look monitor

Witnessed
Precordial thump

Defibrillate at 240 joules. (B)

Defibrillate at 240 joules. (B)

Defibrillate at 360 joules. (B)

CPR: IV and intubate.

Epinephrine 1:10,000 1.0 mg IV push (C)

Atropine, 1.0 mg IV push (D)

External pacing when practical (E, F)

Sodium bicarbonate 1 mEq/kg or 100 mEq (G)

A. Asystole should be confirmed by checking amplitude calibration. Confirmation in a second lead is also desirable at such point in the flow as it becomes practical.
B. Check pulse and rhythm after each shock. Lidocaine boluses to be given on all conversions following defibrillation.
C. Use first route available (IV preferred when available). Repeat every 5 minutes.
D. Repeat in 2–5 minutes. Total dose is 2.0 mg.
E. Pacing can be initiated concurrently with epi/atropine if practical but is not to delay these two drugs.
F. When pacing does not produce mechanical capture in a short trial, the pacer can be turned off temporarily to resume CPR, then reattempted after several minutes of further resuscitative efforts. Limit CPR interruptions to 30 seconds.
G. Repeat in 10–15 minutes at ½ dose (0.5 mEq/kg or 50 mEq).

ASYSTOLE
SAN JOSE, CA

Asystole

I. STANDING ORDERS

   A. CPR
   B. Cardiac monitor
   C. Consider defibrillation if rhythm is unclear and the possibility of ventricular fibrillation exists.
   D. Appropriate airway management
   E. Establish vascular access with normal saline (macrodrip) to keep open.
   F. Epinephrine (1:10,000) 1.0 mg IVP or 2.0 mg per ET. Repeat dose every 3 minutes if no response. Starting with the third dose of epinephrine, use 10 mg of 1:1000 IVP. If ET route still being used, continue with 2.0 mg.
   G. Atropine 1.0 mg IVP or per ET. Repeat every 3–5 minutes if no response. (Maximum dose = 3 mg.)
   H. Base contact after third dose of epinephrine

II. BASE PHYSICIAN ORDER ONLY

   A. Base physician should pronounce death if it is felt that the patient is not responding to resuscitative efforts.
   B. Paramedics must have base order to transport the patient in asystole from the scene. If a patient becomes asystolic after transportation has been initiated, therapy shall continue until care of the patient has been accepted by hospital personnel.

NOTE: For administration of epinephrine per ET tube, double the IV dose listed in the protocol and dilute to 10 ml with normal saline prior to injecting down the tube.

ASYSTOLE
SAN FRANCISCO, CA

Adult Asystole

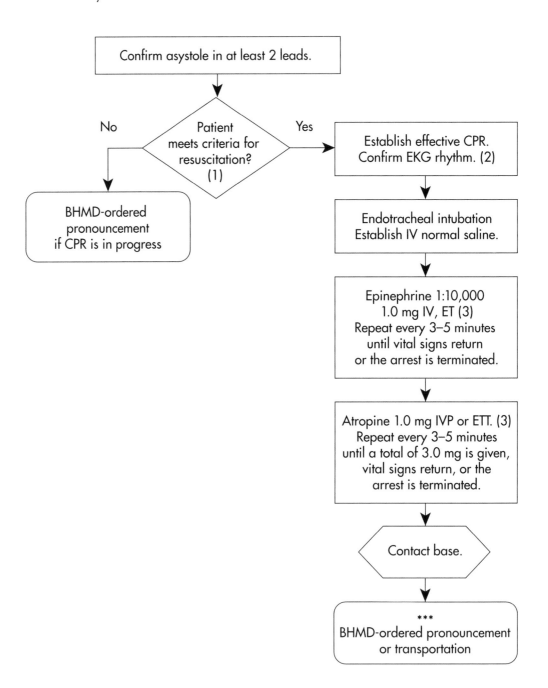

1. CPR may be withheld from patients who are apneic and pulseless when the following conditions are present:
   Patients who present with any *ONE* of the following:
   - Decapitation
   - Total incineration
   - Decomposition
   - Rigor mortis
   - Separation from the body of either the brain, liver, or heart
   - Declared multicasualty incidents where triage principles preclude initiation of CPR
   - A valid Do Not Resuscitate order

For other apneic and pulseless patients, ALS personnel shall evaluate patients for withholding CPR in the following circumstances:
   - Unwitnessed medical cardiac arrest or unwitnessed or witnessed blunt or penetrating trauma arrest who present with *ALL* of the following:
   - Unwitnessed arrest: defined as the total absence of observers or witness information pertinent to the temporal moment of patient collapse. Defined also as those situations where witness information states that collapse occurred more than fifteen minutes prior to paramedic arrival.
   - No CPR in progress
   - Absence of vital signs
   - Documented electrical asystole with documented evidence that monitor is functioning properly. (Asystolic patients with noncapturing pacemakers meet this criterion.)
   - No evidence of hypothermia, drug ingestion, or poisoning

NOTE: Vital-sign measurement and general assessment of the trauma patient should take less than one minute.

2. At any time the patient's EKG rhythm changes, switch to the appropriate protocol.
3. Medication doses administered via the endotracheal route should be double the standard amount.

ASYSTOLE
BOSTON, MA

Asystole/Agonal Idioventricular Rhythm

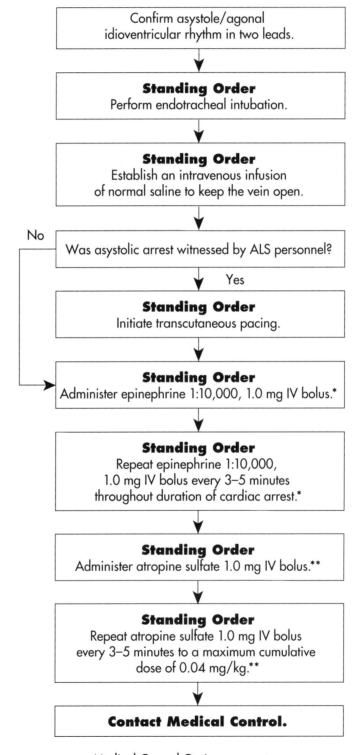

Confirm asystole/agonal
idioventricular rhythm in two leads.

Standing Order
Perform endotracheal intubation.

Standing Order
Establish an intravenous infusion
of normal saline to keep the vein open.

Was asystolic arrest witnessed by ALS personnel?

No

Yes

Standing Order
Initiate transcutaneous pacing.

Standing Order
Administer epinephrine 1:10,000, 1.0 mg IV bolus.*

Standing Order
Repeat epinephrine 1:10,000,
1.0 mg IV bolus every 3–5 minutes
throughout duration of cardiac arrest.*

Standing Order
Administer atropine sulfate 1.0 mg IV bolus.**

Standing Order
Repeat atropine sulfate 1.0 mg IV bolus
every 3–5 minutes to a maximum cumulative
dose of 0.04 mg/kg.**

Contact Medical Control.

Medical Control Options on next page

| **Medical Control Option A** |
| Transcutaneous pacing |

| **Medical Control Option B** |
| Sodium bicarbonate, 0.5–1.0 mEq/kg IV bolus |

| **Medical Control Option C** |
| Epinephrine, 1:1,000 2.0 mg– |
| 0.1 mg/kg, IV bolus every 3–5 minutes |

| **Medical Control Option D** |
| Termination of resuscitative efforts |

*Administer epinephrine 1:10,000 2.0 mg ET if IV access is not available.

**Administer atropine, 2.0 mg ET if IV access is not available. (Maximum cumulative ET dose: 0.08 mg/kg)

PULSELESS ELECTRICAL ACTIVITY/ELECTRICAL-MECHANICAL DISSOCIATION (PEA/EMD)
SAN FRANCISCO, CA

Adult Pulseless Electrical Activity

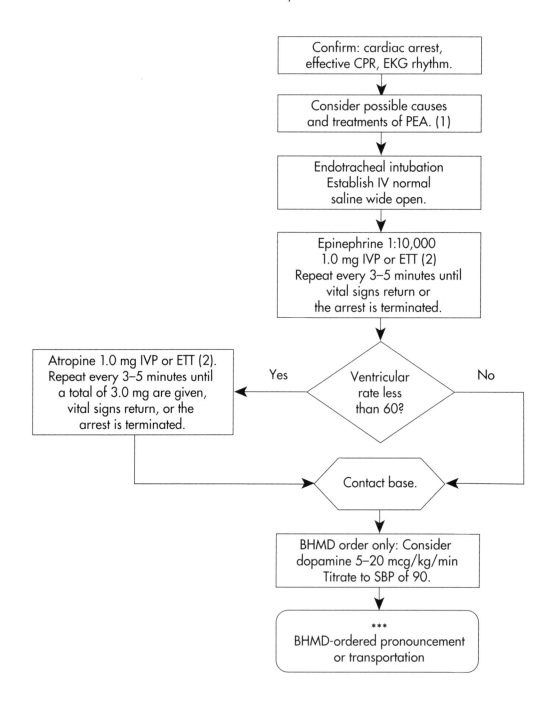

Confirm: cardiac arrest, effective CPR, EKG rhythm.

Consider possible causes and treatments of PEA. (1)

Endotracheal intubation Establish IV normal saline wide open.

Epinephrine 1:10,000 1.0 mg IVP or ETT (2) Repeat every 3–5 minutes until vital signs return or the arrest is terminated.

Ventricular rate less than 60?

Yes — Atropine 1.0 mg IVP or ETT (2). Repeat every 3–5 minutes until a total of 3.0 mg are given, vital signs return, or the arrest is terminated.

No

Contact base.

BHMD order only: Consider dopamine 5–20 mcg/kg/min Titrate to SBP of 90.

***
BHMD-ordered pronouncement or transportation

1. Pulseless Electrical Activity (PEA) can result from a variety of causes including:
   - Hypovolemia
   - Cardiac Tamponade
   - Tension Pneumothorax
   - Massive Pulmonary Embolism
   - Massive Acute Myocardial Infarction
   - Severe Hyperkalemia
   - Hypothermia
   - Hypoxia
   - Preexisting Acidosis
   - Various Drug Overdoses

2. Medication doses administered via the endotracheal route should be double the standard amount.

PULSELESS ELECTRICAL ACTIVITY/ELECTRICAL-MECHANICAL DISSOCIATION (PEA/EMD)
CHICAGO, IL

Pulseless Electrical Activity

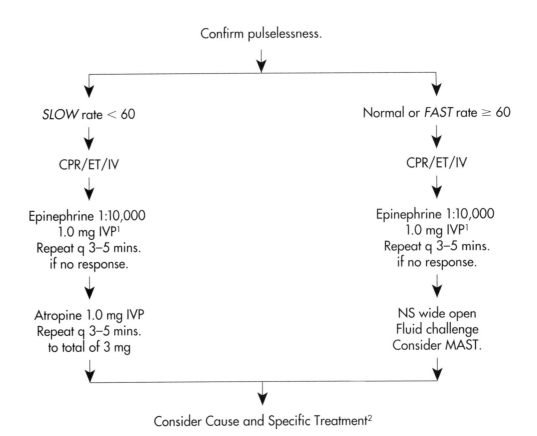

Confirm pulselessness.

SLOW rate < 60	Normal or FAST rate ≥ 60
CPR/ET/IV	CPR/ET/IV
Epinephrine 1:10,000 1.0 mg IVP[1] Repeat q 3–5 mins. if no response.	Epinephrine 1:10,000 1.0 mg IVP[1] Repeat q 3–5 mins. if no response.
Atropine 1.0 mg IVP Repeat q 3–5 mins. to total of 3 mg	NS wide open Fluid challenge Consider MAST.

Consider Cause and Specific Treatment[2]

1—At base station discretion, may request higher doses of epinephrine

2—CAUSE	SPECIFIC TREATMENT
Hypoxemia	Check ET and ventilation.
Hypovolemia	Normal saline bolus. Consider MAST.
Metabolic Acidosis	Consider bicarb 1–2 mEq/kg IVP.
Prolonged Down Time	at base station discretion.
Dialysis Patient/Renal Failure/	$CaCl_2$ 10 cc IVP/Bicarb 1–2 mEq/kg IVP/
Hyperkalemia	D50 1 amp
Tension Pneumothorax	Needle thoracentesis

PULSELESS ELECTRICAL ACTIVITY/ELECTRICAL-MECHANICAL DISSOCIATION (PEA/EMD)
BOSTON, MA

Pulseless Electrical Activity

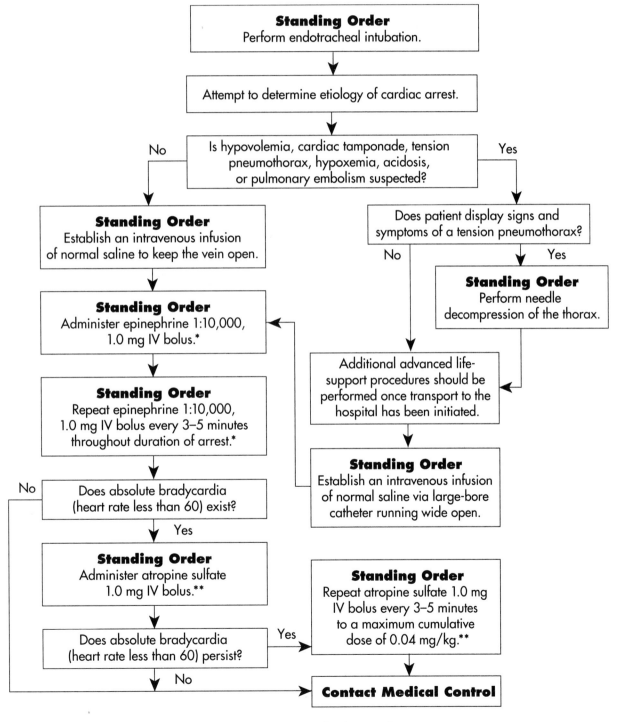

Medical Control Options on next page

Medical Control Option A
Needle decompression of the thorax

Medical Control Option B
Epinephrine, 1:10,000 1.0 IV bolus*

Medical Control Option C
Epinephrine, 1:1,000 2.0 mg–0.1 mg/kg, IV bolus every 3–5 minutes

Medical Control Option D
Atropine sulfate, 1.0 mg IV bolus (maximum cumulative dose 0.04 mg/kg)**

Medical Control Option E
Intravenous infusion of normal saline. Administer at rate specified by medical control.

Medical Control Option F
500 ml fluid bolus of normal saline

Medical Control Option G
MAST. Inflate leg compartments and abdominal compartment if indicated.

Medical Control Option H
Sodium bicarbonate, 0.5–1.0 mEq/kg IV bolus

*Administer epinephrine 1:10,000 2.0 mg ET if IV access is not available.

**Administer atropine, 2.0 mg ET if IV access is not available. (Maximum cumulative ET dose: 0.08 mg/kg.)

© *August 1993, Metropolitan Boston EMS Council*

PULSELESS ELECTRICAL ACTIVITY/ELECTRICAL-MECHANICAL DISSOCIATION (PEA/EMD)
PITTSBURGH, PA

Asystole and Pulseless Electrical Activity (PEA) [Electrical Mechanical Dissociation (EMD)]

INDICATION: All pulseless patients with any EKG rhythm other than VF or VT

PROTOCOL:

1. Follow Medical Cardiac Arrest–Initial Care Protocol

    A. Determine cardiac rhythm.
    If asystole, confirm absence of VF by checking another lead.

    B. Begin BLS.—Maintain airway patency via positioning and suctioning as necessary. Hyperventilate with 100% oxygen. Chest compressions at rate of 100/min.

    C. Contact Medical Command.—Report arrest; request MD and other help if needed.

    D. Intubate.—Follow intubation protocol.

    E. IV LR regular drip with large bore at KVO rate (preferably at/above antecubital fossa or use external jugular)

    F. Epinephrine 1:10,000 sol. 1 mg IV OR 2 mg ET via first route available
    **Repeat epinephrine every 3 mins. while in arrest.

2. Search for Potentially Treatable Causes of the Arrest, in the following order:

    A. Hypoxia:
    If primary event was respiratory, improved ventilation often leads to successful resuscitation.
    —Insure excellent ventilation.
    —Insure oxygen is flowing to patient.
    —Insure tube is in trachea. (See intubation protocol.)

    B. Rate < 50:
    —Transcutaneous pacing. (Refer to external pacing protocol.)
    —If pacer not immediately available, give atropine 2 mg ET or 1 mg IV; repeat every 3 mins. if necessary up to 3 mg.
    —If increase in rate does not result in palpable pulse, consider and treat other potential causes.

    C. Hypovolemia:
    Consider this to be present in *all* patients with clear lung sounds and not in obvious fluid-overload state.
    —LR 500 cc IV bolus; continue IVF wide open if no response and obvious case of hypovolemia.
    —Frequently reassess for pulmonary edema.
    —Command physician may order additional fluid.

23

D. Tension Pneumothorax:
Assume this to be present in all asthmatics who arrest; suspect after drug snorting and any recent chest trauma or invasive procedure involving the thorax.
—Perform needle decompression of chest (refer to needle thoracentesis protocol); both sides should be done in asthmatics unless exam reveals presence on one side.

E. Hyperkalemia/Metabolic Acidosis:
Suspect in patients with renal failure or severe infections.
—Sodium bicarbonate 1 meq/kg IV push
—Command physician may order calcium or additional bicarb.

F. Drug Overdose/Toxic Exposure:
—Attempt to determine specific substance and notify command physician for appropriate interventions.

G. Hypothermia:
—Refer to Protocol #103: Hypothermic Cardiac Arrest.

3. Refer to Protocol #104: Ceasing Resuscitative Efforts.
4. IV may be converted to saline lock prior to patient transfer.

CARDIOPULMONARY EMERGENCIES

CHEST PAIN

   1. Anchorage, AK—nitronox option
   2. Chicago, IL—BP<100 vs. BP>100 options
   3. Lexington, KY—prehospital thrombolysis questionnaire
   4. Columbus, OH—NTG spray; IV NTG drip option
   5. Milwaukee, WI—12-lead EKG required

BRADYARRHYTHMIA

   1. Scottsdale, AZ—narrow vs. wide QRS complex
   2. Rockford, IL—2nd-degree (mobitz II) or 3rd-degree AV block
   3. Columbus, OH—format
   4. Memphis, TN—IV isoproterenol; IV epinephrine drip options

VENTRICULAR TACHYCARDIA WITH PULSE

   1. Anaheim, CA
   2. San Francisco, CA—format
   3. Denver, CO—IV magnesium sulfate
   4. Austin, TX—IV procainamide; AICD discussion

CARDIOGENIC SHOCK

   1. New York, NY
   2. Charlotte, NC—IV saline fluid challenge (250 cc)
   3. Pittsburgh, PA—IV lactated Ringer's (250 cc)

SUPRAVENTRICULAR TACHYCARDIA

   1. Columbus, GA—atrial fib/flutter-treatment option
   2. Chicago, IL—BP>100; BP<100
   3. Indianapolis, IN—asymptomatic vs. urgent vs. emergent
   4. New Orleans, LA—format

PVCs

   1. Evansville, IN—procainamide option
   2. Boston, MA—atropine option
   3. Flint, MI—bretylium option

ACUTE PULMONARY EDEMA

   1. Detroit, MI
   2. New York, NY—format
   3. Columbus, OH—IV NTG drip
   4. Oklahoma City, OK—NTG One metered-dose oral puff

AIRWAY OBSTRUCTION

1. Chicago, IL—unconscious vs. conscious
2. New Orleans, LA—format
3. Boston, MA—mechanical vs. anatomic

ASTHMA

1. State of Hawaii—epi down endotracheal tube
2. Nashville, TN—format
3. Arlington, TX—IV solumedrol
4. Austin, TX—ipratroprium bromide nebulizer mixed with albuterol

COPD

1. Memphis, TN—isoproterenol IV drip
2. Nashville, TN—format
3. Arlington, TX—brethine nebulizer
4. Dallas, TX—ventolin via rotahaler inhalation device

CHEST PAIN
ANCHORAGE, AK

Cardiac Chest Pain

O$_2$, monitor, IV D5W TKO, vital signs

Nitroglycerin, 0.4 mg SL (A)

[Lidocaine only as indicated for ectopy, *etc.* (B)]

Morphine sulfate at paramedic's judgement, noting
blood pressure—*physician contact preferred* on repeat doses

Nitronox, if MS not appropriate or ineffective.
Physician contact preferred.

Proceed to various rhythms.
(Bradycardia: caution with Isuprel in this setting)

A. Can repeat q 5 minutes to a total of 1.2 mg.

B. Repeat in 10 minutes at 0.5 mg/kg to a total of 250 mg or 3 mg/kg (whichever comes first).

CHEST PAIN
CHICAGO, IL

Cardiac Chest Pain

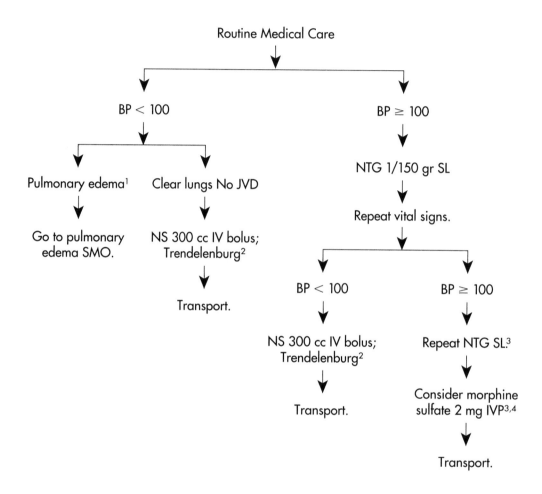

1. Patients in pulmonary edema defined as: severely short of breath, rales entire lung fields, JVD.

2. *Per base station discretion:* if no response, consider dopamine drip (400 mg/ 500 cc NS)—begin at 30 minidrops/minute.

3. If chest pain contiues and BP≥100 systolic, may repeat in 3–5 minutes.

4. If BP < 100, decreasing level of consciousness, decreased ventilatory drive, give Narcan 0.8 mg IVP.

© *August 1996, Chicago Project Medical Directors Consortium*

CHEST PAIN
LEXINGTON, KY

Adult Nontraumatic Chest Pain

Suspected MI

1.0 *Initial Medical Care*

2.0 *BCLS*

3.0 Administer *oxygen* at 6 L/minute.

4.0 *Monitor* and run 6-second rhythm strip.

5.0 Administer *nitroglycerine*, one 1/150 gr. tab sublingually or one metered-dose spray orally, *IF* BP over 100 mm Hg systolic.

6.0 May repeat one dose nitroglycerin every 5 minutes until pain relieved or total of 3 doses given. Observe carefully for hypotension.

7.0 Administer IV of *NS* at KVO rate.

8.0 If pain remains severe after 3 NTG doses as above:

    8.1 Call for possible physician's order for *morphine sulfate*.

        Dosage: *Morphine sulfate*: 2.0 mg slow IV push.
        May repeat q. 2 minutes until pain relieved or total ordered dose given (max. 8.0 mg).
        Do *NOT* give if patient bradycardic (<50 BPM) OR hypotensive (systolic <90 mm Hg OR diastolic <70 mm Hg), or has depressed respirations (<12 respirations/minute).

9.0 Transport in position of comfort ASAP.

10.0 If PVCs or other arrhythmias develop, proceed to specific applicable protocol.

11.0 If cardiogenic shock or pulmonary edema develop, proceed to the protocol.

12.0 Complete Prehospital Thrombolytic Questionnaire en route.

Prehospital Thrombolytic Questionnaire

1.0 Indications

    1.1 Chest Pain:
        Y/N   characteristic of cardiac pain
        Y/N   unrelieved by 3 doses of nitroglycerine
        Y/N   lasting more than 30 minutes but less than 6 hours

2.0 Contraindications
    Y/N   history cerebrovascular accident (stroke)?
    Y/N   active internal bleeding?
    Y/N   uncontrolled hypertension?
    Y/N   history intracranial surgery or trauma, intraspinal surgery or trauma within the preceding 2 months?
    Y/N   history of bleeding problem or problem with blood clotting, history intracranial tumor, arteriovenous malformation, or aneurysm?
    Y/N   history of previous reaction to any thrombolytic agent?
    Y/N   history of receiving a thrombolytic in the past?

3.0 Precautions

3.1. Limit the number of vascular system punctures to the absolute minimum. Thrombolytics dissolve *all* clots. Any skin puncture may bleed extensively.

CHEST PAIN
COLUMBUS, OH

Suspected Angina or Myocardial Infarction

1. ABCs.
2. If blood pressure is greater than 90 mmHg systolic, administer 1 NTG tablet $\frac{1}{150}$ (0.4 mg), sublingually or NITROGLYCERIN SPRAY.
3. Give one chewable baby ASPIRIN 81 mg.
4. Start IV of 0.9% NORMAL SALINE at keep-open rate. Consider volume infusion of 200 to 300 ml 0.9% NORMAL SALINE for hypotension.
5. If no relief in 5 minutes and systolic blood pressure is greater than 90 mmHg, repeat one NTG $\frac{1}{150}$ (0.4 mg) tablet sublingually every 5 minutes × 2 or administer NITROGLYCERIN SPRAY.

   A. If no relief after Step #5, go to the following NITROGLYCERIN DRIP protocol.

6. **NTG drip** 50 mg/250 cc D$_5$W in a glass bottle (200 mcg/cc) per IV pump

   A. Start drip at 10 mcg/minute (3 mini gtts/min=3 cc/hour).
   B. Titrate the drip as pain persists in 5–10 mcg increments, maintaining a systolic BP of 90 mmHg.
   C. If systolic BP is less than 90 mmHg, give a fluid bolus of 250 cc of 0.9% NORMAL SALINE before decreasing the drip rate. If BP does not respond, decrease the drip rate by ½ until the systolic BP is greater than 90 mmHg.

NITROGLYCERIN TABLE

MCG/MIN.	ML/HR.
10	3
15	4
20	6
25	7
30	9
35	10
40	12
45	13
50	15

*When replacing the NITROGLYCERIN drip, use only glass bottles with 50 mg NITROGLYCERIN in 250 cc of D$_5$W. Also must use VENTED IV tubing with the glass bottle.

7. In a patient with suspected MI and **PVCs present,** if the heart rate is 60 or above, and no 2d or 3d-degree block is present, institute the following:

A. LIDOCAINE* 1.5 mg/kg IV push over 1 to 2 minutes or via endotracheal tube if no IV is present and the patient is intubated.

B. After first bolus, institute a LIDOCAINE infusion, 2 g/500 of 0.9% NORMAL SALINE or D_5W, with minidrip tubing, at 30 gtts/minute (2 mg/minute).

C. If PVCs suppressed, administer one-half of the original bolus of LIDOCAINE 5–10 minutes after the initial dose.

D. If PVCs continue and the patient's hemodynamic status remains normal, rebolus with one-half the original bolus every 5–10 minutes to a maximum of 3 mg/kg. Increase LIDOCAINE infusion to 45 gtts/minute (3 mg/minute) and then to 60 gtts/minute (4 mg/minute) with each repeat bolus.

E. With patients 70 years old or older, with CHF, in shock, or with liver disease, reduce the bolus and maintenance infusion dosage by one-half.

F. If signs of LIDOCAINE toxicity develop (slurred speech, altered consciousness, muscle twitching, or seizures), discontinue infusion immediately.

*If given ETT, then 2–2.5 times the IV dose

CHEST PAIN
MILWAUKEE, WI

Cardiac Chest Pain

In cooperative, stable (defined as systolic BP 100 or greater, no second- or third-degree heart block, no ventricular tachycardia nor ventricular fibrillation) adult (defined as 16 years or older) patient with a chief complaint of nontraumatic chest pain [SOC] of suspected cardiac origin, or a symptom/sign that may indicate cardiac ischemia:

1. Begin oxygen administration if not previously established by the first responding unit. Oxygen should be delivered with a device and at a rate appropriate for the condition of the patient. [SOC][SPS]
2. Attach ECG monitoring leads and record the ECG rhythm. [SPS][PP-S.14]
3. Obtain updated vital signs. [SOC][SPS] The most recent set of vital signs prior to administration of nitroglycerin must be obtained by the paramedic.
4. The patient should be lying down or semireclining.
5. Administer up to three (3) metered spray doses—0.4 mg each—of nitroglycerin sublingually (one every five (5) minutes) provided:

   A. The systolic blood pressure is *maintained* equal to or greater than 100 mm/Hg *AND*
   B. It has been AT LEAST FIVE (5) MINUTES since the last nitroglycerin dose *AND*
   C. The patient continues to have pain/symptoms.

NOTE: The patient need not be on nitroglycerin nor have taken nitroglycerin in order to apply this protocol.

6. Start an intravenous line of normal saline with a minidrip set. [PP-M.01][SPS] In patients with delayed IV access who are not hypotensive, nitroglycerin (step 5) may be administered prior to establishing an IV line.
7. Obtain a 12-lead ECG at the earliest opportunity and transmit to base station. [SPS]
8. Contact the base station physician if the patient still has *any* pain after 3 paramedic-administered nitroglycerin, OR if the pain returns, OR if there are any single or 12-lead ECG changes (ectopy, ischemia, or injury patterns). If the patient will be transported by the paramedic unit, is pain free (with or without nitroglycerin), and the 12-lead interpretation is "normal," base physician contact is not mandatory.

NOTE: It is not necessary to complete 3 nitroglycerin administrations before contacting base. If the patient's condition appears to warrant base-station physician advice or orders, contact immediately.

9. Vital signs [SPS] are to be repeated within five (5) minutes after administration of nitroglycerin and every fifteen (15) minutes thereafter. [SOC].

These policies are under constant review and revision and may not reflect the actual practice of the Milwaukee County Paramedic Program.

BRADYARRHYTHMIA
SCOTTSDALE, AZ

Unstable Bradycardia

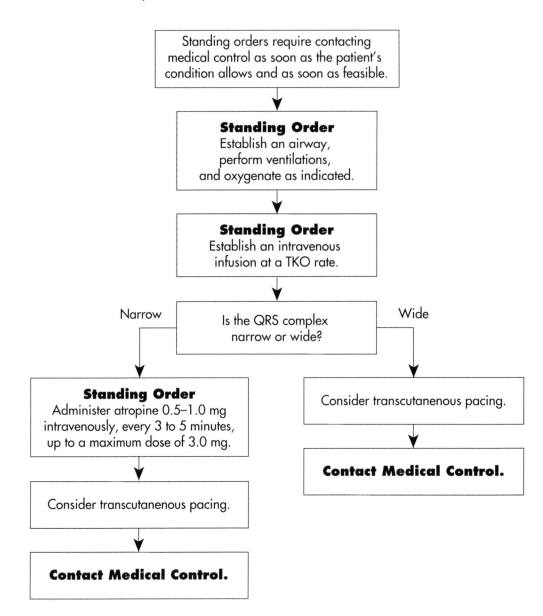

(Signs and symptoms of an unstable patient may include chest pain, shortness of breath, decreased level of consciousness, hypotension, shock, pulmonary edema, congestive heart failure, and acute myocardial infarction.)

BRADYARRHYTHMIA
ROCKFORD, IL

Bradycardia

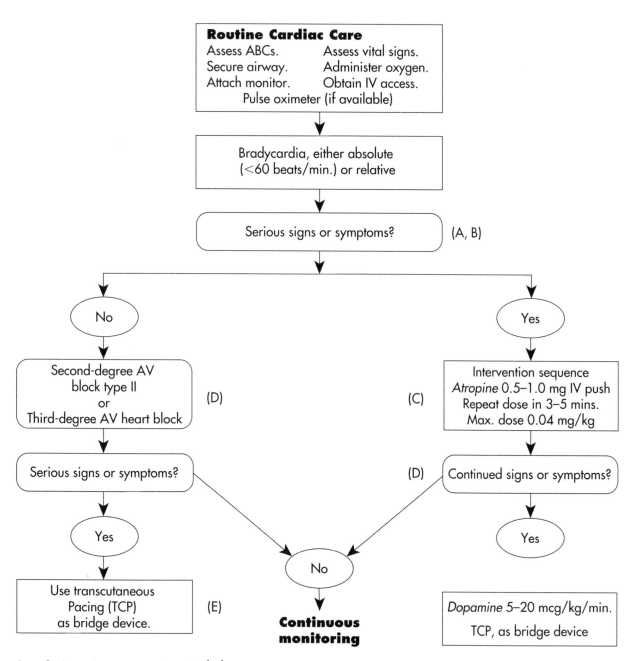

A. *Serious signs or symptoms* include
Symptoms: Chest pain, shortness of breath, decreased LOC
Signs: Hypotension, pulmonary congestion CHF < acute MI

B. Do not delay TCP while awaiting IV access or for *atropine* to take effect if patient is symptomatic.

C. Denervated transplant hearts will not respond to *atropine*. Go at once to TCP, catecholamine infusion, or both.

D. Never treat third-degree heart blocks plus ventricular escapes with *lidocaine*.

Per physician's order

E. Verify patient tolerance and mechanical capture. Use analgesia and sedation as needed.

BRADYARRHYTHMIA
COLUMBUS, OH

Bradycardia and Pacemaker Protocol

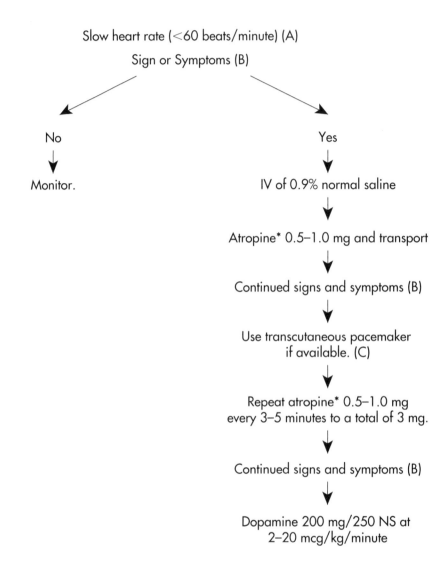

Slow heart rate (<60 beats/minute) (A)

Sign or Symptoms (B)

No → Monitor.

Yes → IV of 0.9% normal saline

Atropine* 0.5–1.0 mg and transport

Continued signs and symptoms (B)

Use transcutaneous pacemaker if available. (C)

Repeat atropine* 0.5–1.0 mg every 3–5 minutes to a total of 3 mg.

Continued signs and symptoms (B)

Dopamine 200 mg/250 NS at 2–20 mcg/kg/minute

This sequence was developed to assist in teaching how to treat a broad range of patients with bradycardia. Some patients may require care not specified herein. This algorithm should not be construed to prohibit such flexibility:

A. A solitary chest thump or cough may stimulate cardiac electrical activity and result in improved cardiac output and may be used at this point.

B. Hypotension (BP <90 mmHg), PVCs, altered mental status, or symptoms (*e.g.*, chest pain, dyspnea), ischemia, or infarction.

C. 1. If no response to atropine, attempt cardiac pacing with external pacemaker. After pacer pads are placed and connected, set rate at 70 per minute and output at 40 mA.

2. Adjust output upward in 5 mA increments to achieve cardiac capture as indicated by a QRS complex and a palpable pulse associated with electric pacing spikes. Output should be maintained at the lowest milliamps setting that achieves complete cardiac capture.

3. Should patient respond with heart rate >60 and BP< 90, assess volume status, trial of volume infusion (200–300 cc) of 0.9% normal saline. If appropriate, then initiate a dopamine infusion.

4. If patient complains of severe pain from pacer at any point during pacing, adjust the output down in increments of 10 mA as long as the paced beats have pulses. If patient continues to experience significant discomfort, give 2–5 mg valium intravenously.

BRADYARRHYTHMIA
MEMPHIS, TN

Symptomatic Bradycardia

A. Assessment
  - Heart rate less than 60 beats per min.
  - Signs of decreased perfusion
  - Rhythm may be sinus bradycardia, junctional, or heart block.

B. Treatment
  1. Oxygen 100%
  2. IV N.S.K.V.O.
  3. Transcutaneous pacing
  4. Atropine 0.5–1.0 mg IV q 3–5 mins. up to 0.04 mg/kg or 3 mg

Contact medical control, consider:

Dopamine drip 5 mcg/kg/min. to 20 mcg/kg/min. is recommended when hypotension is associated with the bradyarrhythmia.

For severe symptoms refractory to other therapy:
Isoproterenol infusion starting at 2 mcg/min. to 10 mcg/min.
Epinephrine infusion starting at 2 mcg/min. to 10 mcg/min.

VENTRICULAR TACHYCARDIA WITH PULSE
ANAHEIM, CA

Ventricular Dysrhythmias:
Ventricular Tachycardia with a Pulse

Action/Treatment:

- ABCs/monitor cardiac rhythm.
- IV access titrated to perfusion as needed
- Treatment options:
  —Lidocaine: 1 mg/kg IVP, may repeat every 5 minutes to a maximum of 3 mg/kg
    ET: 3 mg/kg once, maximum 10 cc (200 mg)
  —Cardioversion: 100 J–200 J–300 J—360 J
  —Premedication: Diazepam 5–10 mg IVP titrated to effect
  —Bretylium: 5–10 mg/kg slow IVP over 8–10 minutes, maximum total 30 mg/kg
- Following successful cardioversion to an appropriate rhythm (sinus, narrow complex), administer lidocaine 1 mg/kg/dose IVP not to exceed 3 mg/kg (if not previously administered).

Pediatric:

- Lidocaine: 1 mg/kg IVP, may repeat every 5 minutes to a maximum of 3 mg/kg ET: 3 mg/kg once
- Cardioversion 0.5 J/kg–1 J/kg–2 J/kg–4 J/kg
  —Premedication: Diazepam 0.2 mg/kg slow IVP
- Following successful cardioversion to an appropriate rhythm (sinus, narrow complex), administer lidocaine 1 mg/kg/dose IVP not to exceed 3 mg/kg (if not previously administered).

NOTES:
- May go directly to cardioversion if indicated
- Alternate synchronized cardioversion with each medication
- If "synch" mode does not work, *e.g.*, wide complex ventricular tachycardia, defibrillate at same energy levels.
- Consider adenosine before bretylium for wide complex tachycardia of an uncertain origin (see C-25).
- Shaded text indicates BH order
- Unshaded text indicates standing order

VENTRICULAR TACHYCARDIA WITH PULSE
SAN FRANCISCO, CA

Ventricular Tachycardia with a Pulse

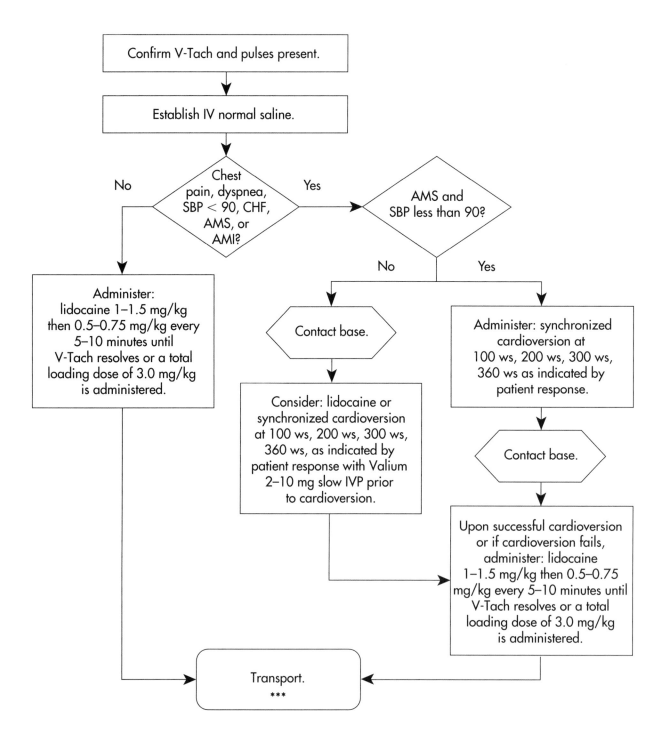

VENTRICULAR TACHYCARDIA WITH PULSE
DENVER, CO

Wide Complex Tachycardia with Pulse

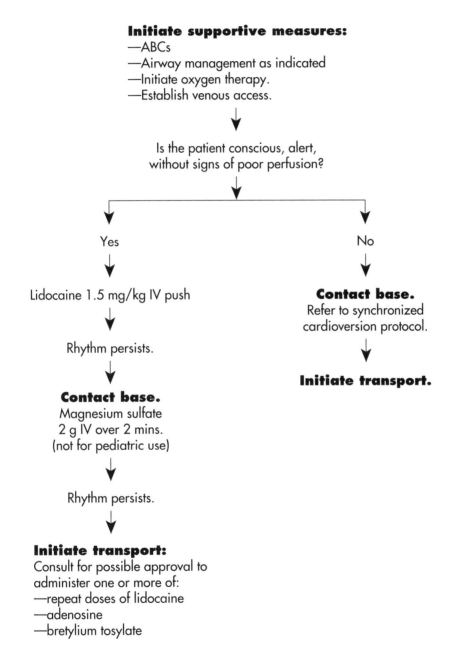

Initiate supportive measures:
—ABCs
—Airway management as indicated
—Initiate oxygen therapy.
—Establish venous access.

Is the patient conscious, alert, without signs of poor perfusion?

Yes

No

Lidocaine 1.5 mg/kg IV push

Rhythm persists.

Contact base.
Magnesium sulfate
2 g IV over 2 mins.
(not for pediatric use)

Rhythm persists.

Contact base.
Refer to synchronized
cardioversion protocol.

Initiate transport.

Initiate transport:
Consult for possible approval to
administer one or more of:
—repeat doses of lidocaine
—adenosine
—bretylium tosylate

Special notes:

A. A wide QRS complex is defined as a complex with a width greater than .12 sec.

B. A wide complex tachycardia is usually ventricular in origin but may on occasion be a supraventricular rhythm with aberrant conduction.

C. **Contact base** to consider sedation in conscious patients.

VENTRICULAR TACHYCARDIA WITH PULSE
AUSTIN, TX

Ventricular Tachycardia with Pulses

Introduction

Patients in this rhythm typically present as either stable or pulseless, although it is not impossible to see such patients deteriorating from one to the other. This rhythm can become lethal at any moment, and treatment is geared toward termination of this rhythm into a more stable one. Treatment of this rhythm is usually reserved for sustained or recurrent tachycardias.

Key Actions

ALS
1. Monitor EKG, pulse oximetry, and 12-lead EKG.
2. Initiate IV lifeline(s) PRN.
3. Lidocaine 1 mg/kg IV bolus if no effect 0.5 mg/kg IV
4. Procainamide 5–10 mg/kg over 10 minutes (max. dose 17 mg/kg total dose)
5. Bretylium tosylate 5 mg/kg IV bolus if no effect 10 mg/kg IV bolus
6. Cardioversion (indicated immediately in the unstable patient)
7. Magnesium sulfate 50% 2 gm IV, if torsades is refractory or recurs repeat dose in 3 minutes.

NOTE: For maintenance of antiarrhythmic after conversion:
Lidocaine 2–4 mg/minute
Procainamide 2–6 mg/minute
Bretylium tosylate 2–4 mg/minute

Assessment Considerations

None

Special Situations/Conditions

1. Automatic Internal Defibrillators (AICDs) present a concern for treating these patients. Since these devices are usually set to interpret either V-Tach. or V-Fib. as lethal arrhythmias, they may discharge on a stable patient with a rapid ventricular rate. In treating these patients, lidocaine is not usually considered as drug of choice; procainamide is usually indicated as first drug of choice.
2. Magnesium sulfate is primary treatment for patients in torsades de pointes.
3. Magnesium sulfate should not be used in patients on dialysis or with renal insufficiency.

CARDIOGENIC SHOCK
NEW YORK, NY

Cardiogenic Shock

1. Contact medical control for implementation of one or more of the following MEDICAL CONTROL OPTIONS:

Medical Control Options:

Option A: Administer dopamine 5.0 μg/kg/min., IV/saline lock drip. If there is insufficient improvement in hemodynamic status, the infusion rate may be increased until the desired therapeutic effects are achieved or adverse effects appear. (Maximum dosage is 20 μg/kg/min., IV/saline lock drip.)

Option B: Transportation decision

CARDIOGENIC SHOCK
CHARLOTTE, NC

Cardiogenic Shock

History

1. Complaints may include chest pain or shortness of breath.
2. No history of trauma
3. History may be significant for previously diagnosed heart disease.

Physical

1. Patients may be conscious and alert or have altered mental status/agitation.
2. Hemodynamically unstable
3. Skin may be cool, clammy, mottled, cyanotic, or pale.

Differential

Myocardial infarction
Dysrhythmias
Pulmonary embolus

Protocol

1. Maintain airway, administer oxygen via nonrebreathing mask at 15 L/min.
2. Obtain vital signs and apply cardiac monitor. Obtain rhythm strip. If particular dysrhythmia or heart rate noted, proceed to indicated protocol.
3. Initiate transport. Continue to monitor vital signs while en route.
4. If patient is experiencing chest pain, shortness of breath, seizures, or altered mental status, treat per protocol.
5. Consider and administer any or all of the following therapeutic interventions:
   IV normal saline:
   BP <80 and clear lung sounds
   250 mL bolus: reassess lung sounds.
   Clear lung sounds: repeat bolus.
   Rales/ronchi/wheezes: TKO
   BP> 80
   TKO
6. Contact medical control en route. The following intervention may be considered:
   Dopamine 2–20 μg/kg/min.

Addendum

1. Lung sounds should be reassessed after each fluid bolus. Repeat boluses may be administered if the lungs remain clear. If evidence of fluid overload occurs (manifested as rales, ronchi, or wheezes), keep fluids at TKO rate.
2. If dopamine is utilized, titrate to achieve a systolic blood pressure greater than 100 mmHg.

CARDIOGENIC SHOCK
PITTSBURGH, PA

Cardiogenic Shock

INDICATION:

Patients who meet shock criteria and have historical (chest pain, dyspnea, palpitations) or physical (rales, serious arrhythmia) evidence of cardiac dysfunction/failure

PROTOCOL:

1. Brief HISTORY, EXAM, and VITALS
2. As soon as shock identified, NOTIFY medic command and request EMS physician response.
3. ASSIST VENTILATION with 100% OXYGEN and INTUBATE if indicated; nasotracheal route may be useful for awake patients.
4. APPLY EKG MONITOR—if arrhythmia present, go immediately to appropriate protocol.
5. INITIATE TRANSPORT as soon as possible. MAXIMUM permissible on scene time is 10 minutes.
6. EN ROUTE:

    A. Reassess vitals, mental status, airway and respiratory status, and EKG rhythm frequently.
    B. Initiate IV:
    —if lungs "wet" or patient has marked dyspnea, start saline lock.
    —if no significant SOB and lungs "clear," give LR 250 cc wide open and reassess patient.

7. Consult command physician if not present.
8. If lungs clear and no significant respiratory distress, continue LR wide open until either perfusion improves, respiratory distress develops, or rales are heard on lung exam.
9. If lungs "wet," respiratory distress present or no response to fluid challenge, initiate DOPAMINE DRIP 200 mg IN 250 cc D_5W (or 400 mg in 500 cc) [this yields 800 mcg/cc] and run at rate per command physician.

    Dose range for shock is 5–20 mcg/kg/minute. (Typical starting dose of 10 mcg/kg/minute for 80 kg patient would be 60 minidrops/minute.)

SUPRAVENTRICULAR TACHYCARDIA (SVT)
COLUMBUS, GA

Supraventricular Tachycardia

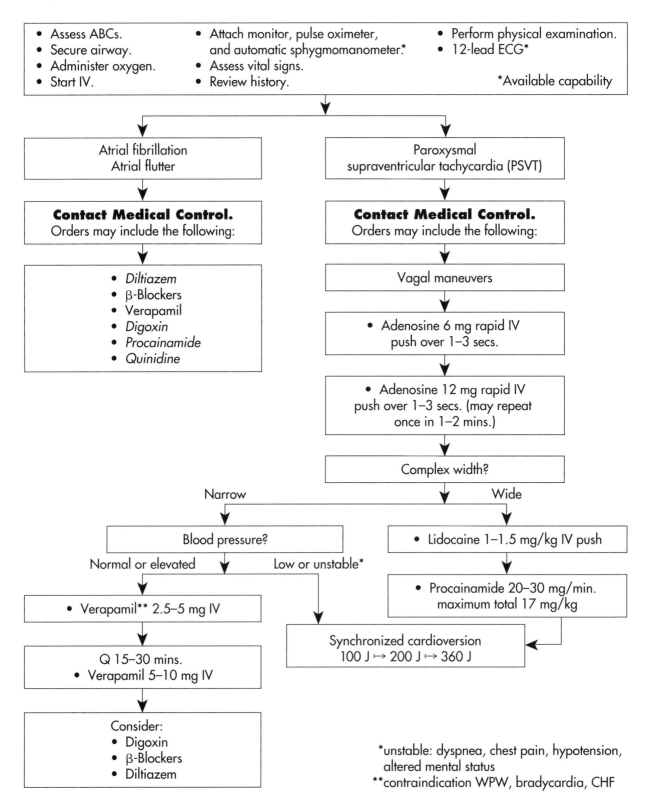

- Assess ABCs.
- Secure airway.
- Administer oxygen.
- Start IV.

- Attach monitor, pulse oximeter, and automatic sphygmomanometer.*
- Assess vital signs.
- Review history.

- Perform physical examination.
- 12-lead ECG*

*Available capability

Atrial fibrillation
Atrial flutter

Contact Medical Control.
Orders may include the following:

- *Diltiazem*
- β-Blockers
- Verapamil
- *Digoxin*
- *Procainamide*
- *Quinidine*

Paroxysmal
supraventricular tachycardia (PSVT)

Contact Medical Control.
Orders may include the following:

Vagal maneuvers

- Adenosine 6 mg rapid IV push over 1–3 secs.

- Adenosine 12 mg rapid IV push over 1–3 secs. (may repeat once in 1–2 mins.)

Complex width?

Narrow — Wide

Blood pressure?

Normal or elevated — Low or unstable*

- Verapamil** 2.5–5 mg IV

Q 15–30 mins.
- Verapamil 5–10 mg IV

Consider:
- Digoxin
- β-Blockers
- Diltiazem

- Lidocaine 1–1.5 mg/kg IV push

- Procainamide 20–30 mg/min. maximum total 17 mg/kg

Synchronized cardioversion
100 J ↦ 200 J ↦ 360 J

*unstable: dyspnea, chest pain, hypotension, altered mental status
**contraindication WPW, bradycardia, CHF

SUPRAVENTRICULAR TACHYCARDIA (SVT)
CHICAGO, IL

Narrow QRS Complex Tachycardia

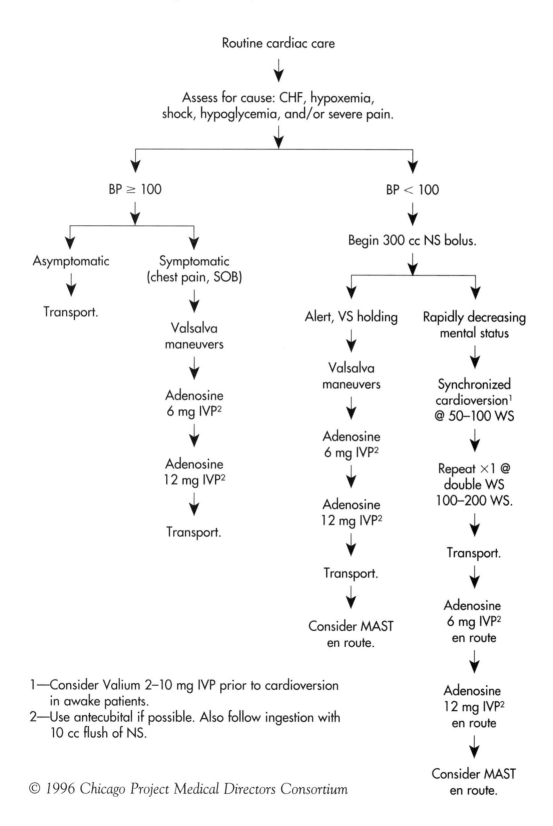

Routine cardiac care

↓

Assess for cause: CHF, hypoxemia, shock, hypoglycemia, and/or severe pain.

BP ≥ 100

Asymptomatic → Transport.

Symptomatic (chest pain, SOB) → Valsalva maneuvers → Adenosine 6 mg IVP[2] → Adenosine 12 mg IVP[2] → Transport.

BP < 100

Begin 300 cc NS bolus.

Alert, VS holding → Valsalva maneuvers → Adenosine 6 mg IVP[2] → Adenosine 12 mg IVP[2] → Transport. → Consider MAST en route.

Rapidly decreasing mental status → Synchronized cardioversion[1] @ 50–100 WS → Repeat ×1 @ double WS 100–200 WS. → Transport. → Adenosine 6 mg IVP[2] en route → Adenosine 12 mg IVP[2] en route → Consider MAST en route.

1—Consider Valium 2–10 mg IVP prior to cardioversion in awake patients.
2—Use antecubital if possible. Also follow ingestion with 10 cc flush of NS.

47

SUPRAVENTRICULAR TACHYCARDIA (SVT)
INDIANAPOLIS, IN

Narrow QRS Complex Tachycardia

A. Begin initial medical care.

    1. Administer high-flow oxygen.
    2. Establish an IV.
    3. Apply the cardiac monitor.

B. Rule out any underlying causes of tachycardia.
C. Categorize patient as below.

D. *Asymptomatic:*

1. Call medical control for further consultation.

E. *Urgent:*
    **Criteria: Anginal chest pain and/or hypotension and/or CHF.

1. Perform Valsalva.
2. If the rhythm has not converted to a sinus rhythm, and in your judgment the rhythm is PSVT, administer 6 mg of adenosine rapid IV bolus push.

    a. Immediately follow with a ten (10) ml fluid flush.
    b. Observe and anticipate AV blocks and/ or transient asystole.
    c. If after 1–2 minutes the rhythm does not convert to a sinus rhythm and no AV block or transient asystole has occurred, repeat adenosine at 12 mg IVP.

3. If unable to rapidly establish IV access or there is no response to the adenosine or a rhythm other than PSVT, contact the E.D. physician at the intended receiving facility for further consultation.

F. *Emergent:*
    **Criteria: Unconscious or no obtainable B.P.

1. Perform synchronous cardioversion @ 50 joules.
2. Perform synchronous cardioversion @ 100 joules.
3. Perform synchronous cardioversion @ 200 joules.
4. Perform synchronous cardioversion @ 300 joules.
5. Perform synchronous cardioversion @ 360 joules.
6. Contact medical control for further consultation.

SUPRAVENTRICULAR TACHYCARDIA (SVT)
NEW ORLEANS, LA

Paroxysmal Supraventricular Tachycardia

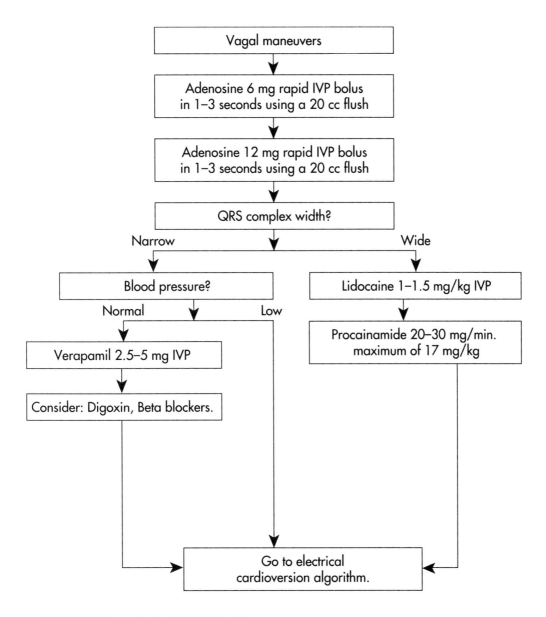

ACCEPTABLE VAGAL MANEUVERS ARE:
carotid sinus pressure, breath-holding, coughing.

PREMATURE VENTRICULAR CONTRACTIONS
EVANSVILLE, IN

Ventricular Ectopy Algorithm

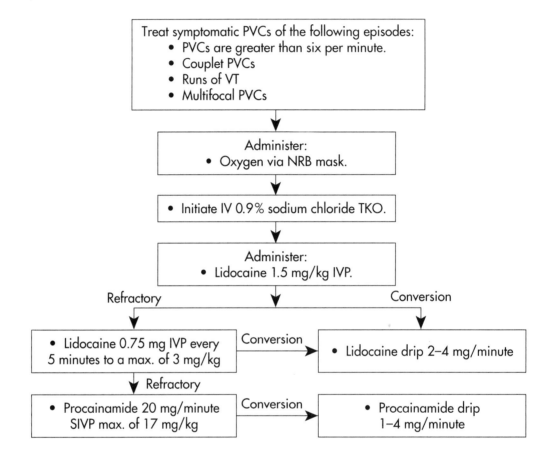

Treat symptomatic PVCs of the following episodes:
- PVCs are greater than six per minute.
- Couplet PVCs
- Runs of VT
- Multifocal PVCs

Administer:
- Oxygen via NRB mask.

- Initiate IV 0.9% sodium chloride TKO.

Administer:
- Lidocaine 1.5 mg/kg IVP.

Refractory / Conversion

- Lidocaine 0.75 mg IVP every 5 minutes to a max. of 3 mg/kg

Conversion →

- Lidocaine drip 2–4 mg/minute

Refractory

- Procainamide 20 mg/minute SIVP max. of 17 mg/kg

Conversion →

- Procainamide drip 1–4 mg/minute

PREMATURE VENTRICULAR CONTRACTIONS
BOSTON, MA

Premature Ventricular Contractions

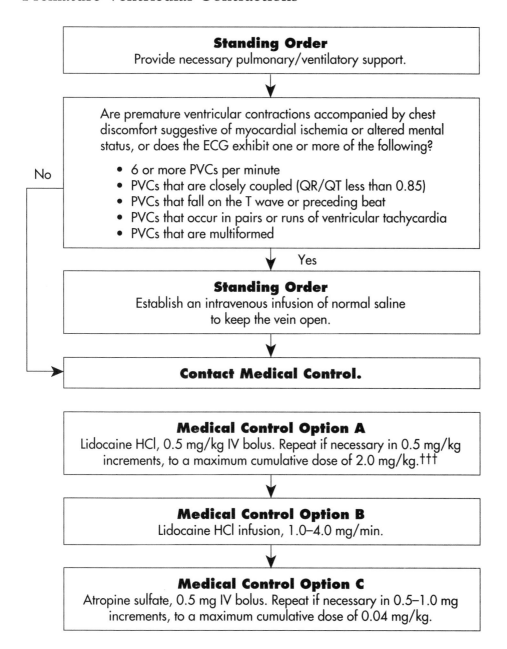

Standing Order
Provide necessary pulmonary/ventilatory support.

Are premature ventricular contractions accompanied by chest discomfort suggestive of myocardial ischemia or altered mental status, or does the ECG exhibit one or more of the following?

- 6 or more PVCs per minute
- PVCs that are closely coupled (QR/QT less than 0.85)
- PVCs that fall on the T wave or preceding beat
- PVCs that occur in pairs or runs of ventricular tachycardia
- PVCs that are multiformed

No

Yes

Standing Order
Establish an intravenous infusion of normal saline to keep the vein open.

Contact Medical Control.

Medical Control Option A
Lidocaine HCl, 0.5 mg/kg IV bolus. Repeat if necessary in 0.5 mg/kg increments, to a maximum cumulative dose of 2.0 mg/kg.†††

Medical Control Option B
Lidocaine HCl infusion, 1.0–4.0 mg/min.

Medical Control Option C
Atropine sulfate, 0.5 mg IV bolus. Repeat if necessary in 0.5–1.0 mg increments, to a maximum cumulative dose of 0.04 mg/kg.

NOTE: †††*The dose of lidocaine HCl should be reduced in patients with decreased cardiac output (e.g., in acute MI, congestive heart failure, or shock regardless of its etiology), in patients more than 70 years old, and in those with hepatic dysfunction. The aforementioned patients should receive the normal bolus dose first, followed by half the normal maintenance infusion.* The patient should be observed closely for signs of drug efficacy and toxicity.

VENTRICULAR ECTOPY
FLINT, MI

Ventricular Ectopy

Assess need for acute suppressive therapy.

↓

Rule out treatable causes.
Consider bradycardia, drugs, hypoxia, *etc.*

↓

Supplemental O_2 high flow

↓

Establish IV D_5W TKO.

↓

Contact hospital.

↓

Lidocaine 1 mg/kg IVP

↓

If not suppressed, lidocaine, 0.5 mg/kg q 2–5 minutes
until ectopy resolved or up to 3 mg/kg given

↓

If not suppressed, bretylium, 5–10 mg/kg over 8–10 minutes

Once ectopy is resolved, maintain as follows:
After Lidocaine 1 mg/kg . . . . Lidocaine Drip at 2 mg/minute
After Lidocaine 1–2 mg/kg. . . . . Lidocaine Drip at 3 mg/minute
After Lidocaine 2–3 mg/kg. . . . . Lidocaine Drip at 4 mg/minute
After Bretylium . . . . Bretylium Drip at 3 mg/minute

ACUTE PULMONARY EDEMA
DETROIT, MI

Pulmonary Edema

This is characterized by an acutely dyspneic patient with rales, wheezing, and at times frothy mouth breathing.

Prehospital contact:

1. Supplemental oxygen
2. Place patient in an upright sitting position.
3. IV line of 5% at KVO
4. ECG monitor

To expect postradio contact:

1. Nitroglycerin 0.4 mg sublingual (unless hypotension is present) and may be repeated in 3–5 minutes
2. Lasix 40 mg IVP
3. Prepare for potential intubation.

ACUTE PULMONARY EDEMA
NEW YORK, NY

Acute Pulmonary Edema

1. Begin basic life-support respiratory-distress procedures.
2. Begin cardiac monitoring; record and evaluate EKG strip.
3. Begin an IV infusion of normal saline (0.9 NS) to keep vein open, or a saline lock.
4. Monitor vital signs every 2–3 minutes.
5. Administer nitroglycerin tablet $\frac{1}{150}$ gr or spray 0.4 mg, sublingually, every 5 minutes, for a total of 3 doses. Before each administration, check the patient's pulse and blood pressure to ensure the patient is hemodynamically stable.
6. Administer nitropaste 1½ inches (if available).

NOTE: NITROGLYCERIN AND NITROPASTE MAY *NOT* BE ADMINIS-TERED TO PATIENTS WITH A *SYSTOLIC* BLOOD PRESSURE OF LESS THAN 100 mm Hg UNLESS AN IV/SALINE LOCK IS IN PLACE.

7. Administer furosemide 20–80 mg, IV/saline lock bolus. (Maximum combined total dosage is 80 mg.)
8. Contact medical control for implementation of one or more of the following:

Medical Control Options:

Option A: Administer morphine sulfate 2.0–5.0 mg, IV/saline lock bolus. Repeat doses of morphine sulfate 2.0–5.0 mg, IV/saline lock bolus, may be given as necessary. (Maximum total dosage is 15 mg.)

NOTE: IF HYPOTENSION, HYPOVENTILATION, OR STUPOR DEVELOPS DURING ADMINISTRATION OF MORPHINE SULFATE, WITHHOLD MORPHINE SULFATE, ELEVATE THE LEGS, AND ADMINISTER NALOXONE 2.0 mg, IV/SALINE LOCK BOLUS.

Option B: Repeat nitroglycerin tablet $\frac{1}{150}$ gr or spray 0.4 mg, sublingually (if transportation is delayed or extended).
Option C: Transportation decision.

COLUMBUS, OH

Acute Pulmonary Edema/Congestive Heart Failure

1. ABCs.

2. If systolic blood pressure equal to or greater than 90 mmHg, administer:

A. NITROGLYCERIN ¹⁄₁₅₀ and/or NITROGLYCERIN SPRAY sublingually.

B. FUROSEMIDE (LASIX) 40 mg, IV push (over 1 to 2 minutes). May administer 80 mg dose in 15 minutes if needed. Maximum total dose of LASIX not to exceed 120 mg.

C. NITROGLYCERIN drip 50 mg/250 cc bottle D_5W (200 mcg/cc) per IV pump and start infusion at 10 mcg/minute and titrate up 5–10 mcg/minute every 5 minutes until desired effect such as improved respirations and systolic BP 90 mmHg or above.

NITROGLYCERIN TABLE

MCG/MIN.	ML/HR.
10	3
15	4
20	6
25	7
30	9
35	10
40	12
45	13
50	15

3. If no hypotension, transport with head elevated.

4. If no response to previous therapy and/or if blood pressure less than 90 mmHg systolic, and with a heart rate greater than 60, initiate in the following order:

A. DOBUTAMINE, 250 mg/250 NS at 2–20 mcg/kg/minute. Monitor for cardiac dysrhythmia. If no response in 10 minutes, go to Step B.

B. DOPAMINE, 200 mg/250 NS at 2–20 mcg/kg/minute.

5. Intubate if patient shows signs of increasing respiratory distress, lethargy, unconsciousness, or diminished respiratory effort.

ACUTE PULMONARY EDEMA
OKLAHOMA CITY, OK

Pulmonary Edema

Indications

1. Patients presenting with dyspnea, having a history of CHF, MI, HTN, or coronary disease with three or more of the following:

    A. cyanosis
    B. rales
    C. peripheral edema
    D. frothy pink sputum
    E. respiratory rate >25 or <10
    F. neck-vein distension

2. Systolic blood pressure must be >90 mm Hg and pulse <150. (Otherwise, go to shock or arrhythmias protocol.)

    A. *Adult Care*

        I.1. General supportive care—Fowler's position, assist with ventilation, and intubate as needed.

        I.2. If normotensive or hypertensive, nitroglycerin, one metered dose, oral puff, 0.4 mg

        II.1. If normotensive or hypertensive, lasix 40 mg, IV

        II.2. If normotensive or hypertensive, morphine 2–5 mg, slow IV push

        II.3. If normotensive or hypertensive, nitroglycerin, additional dose or doses, oral puff, 0.4 mg

    B. *Pediatric Care*

        I.1. General supportive care—Fowler's position; assist with ventilation and intubate as needed.

        II.1. If normotensive or hypertensive for patient age, lasix 1 mg/kg, IV

AIRWAY OBSTRUCTION
CHICAGO, IL

Respiratory Obstruction

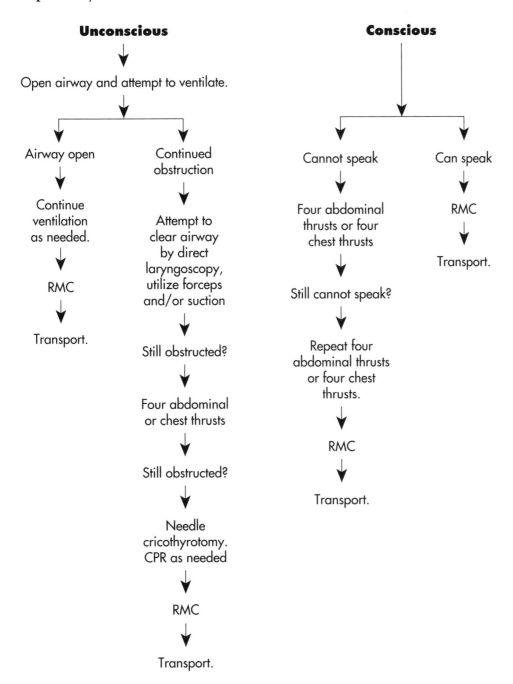

Unconscious

Open airway and attempt to ventilate.

Airway open → Continue ventilation as needed. → RMC → Transport.

Continued obstruction → Attempt to clear airway by direct laryngoscopy, utilize forceps and/or suction → Still obstructed? → Four abdominal or chest thrusts → Still obstructed? → Needle cricothyrotomy. CPR as needed → RMC → Transport.

Conscious

Cannot speak → Four abdominal thrusts or four chest thrusts → Still cannot speak? → Repeat four abdominal thrusts or four chest thrusts. → RMC → Transport.

Can speak → RMC → Transport.

NOTE: Abdominal thrusts contraindicated in children (less than 8 years old) and pregnant women.

AIRWAY OBSTRUCTION
NEW ORLEANS, LA

Airway Obstruction from Foreign Body—Nontraumatic

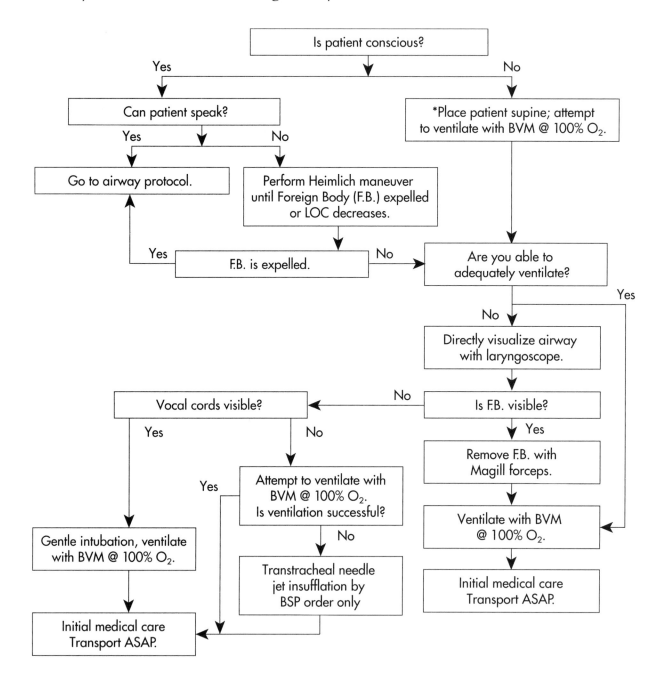

*BSP may order IVP Valium for sedation if required.

AIRWAY OBSTRUCTION
BOSTON, MA

Upper-Airway Obstruction

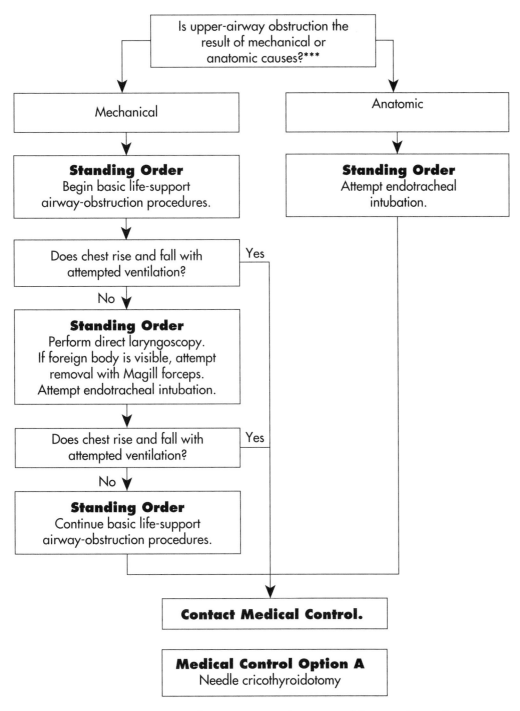

***If unable to determine cause of upper-airway obstruction, follow mechanical obstruction treatment regimen.

If upper-airway obstruction is the result of an anaphylactic reaction, refer to the anaphylaxis protocol for concurrent intervention.

© August 1993, Metropolitan Boston EMS Council

ASTHMA
STATE OF HAWAII

Bronchospasm

Standing Orders

High-flow oxygen 10–15 liters by mask or assisted bag–mask ventilation.

Inhalation treatment with *either* (a) albuterol 2.5 mg in nebulizer *or* (b) terbutaline 2 mg in nebulizer

If a patient with severe bronchospasm requires intubation and mechanical ventilation and is very hard to ventilate because of severe bronchospasm, give 10 cc of 1:10,000 epinephrine down the endotracheal tube to reduce the bronchospasm.

COMMUNICATE WITH MEDICOM PHYSICIAN FOR FURTHER ORDERS.

Extended Standing Orders

Continue 100% O_2 by mask or assisted mask ventilation.

If still in bronchospasm, administer inhalation treatment with either (a) albuterol 2.5 mg in nebulizer *or* (b) terbutaline 2 mg in nebulizer immediately following the last nebulizer treatment.

If <40 years old, no history of COPD (emphysema or bronchitis), no cardiac history (cardiac medication, angina, or MI), severe dyspnea using intercostal muscles and cyanosis unrelieved with 10–15 liters O_2 by mask, give 300 cc normal saline IV rapid infusion.

Endotracheal intubation if impending respiratory arrest

COMMUNICATE WITH MEDICOM PHYSICIAN FOR FURTHER ORDERS.

ASTHMA
NASHVILLE, TN

Respiratory Distress (Asthma/COPD)

A. *ASSESSMENT* HISTORY OF ONSET AND MEDICATIONS
   If patient takes theophylline preparation, obtain a red-top tube for a theophylline level prior to treatment or IV therapy.

B. *TREATMENT*

Assessment	Treatment Less than 45 years and NO heart disease	Treatment Greater than 45 years OR heart disease
Mild attack Slight increase in respiratory rate. Mild wheezes. Good skin color.	Oxygen and transport	Oxygen and transport
Moderate attack Marked increase in respiratory rate. Wheezes easily heard. Accessory muscle breathing.	Oxygen Identify cardiac rhythm. Epinephrine 1:1000 0.3 cc SQ IV D$_5$W TKO Transport immediately. Medical control Consider #1 below, OR Epinephrine 1:1000 0.3 cc SQ.	Oxygen Identify cardiac rhythm. IV D$_5$W TKO Transport immediately. Medical control WITH PHYSICIAN ORDER ONLY, Epinephrine 1:1000 0.3 cc SQ, OR consider #1 below.
Severe attack Respiratory rate more than twice normal. Loud wheezes or so tight no wheezes are heard. Patient anxious or with grey or ashen skin color.	Oxygen Identify cardiac rhythm. Epinephrine 1:1000 0.3 cc SQ IV D$_5$W TKO Transport immediately. Medical control Consider #1 below, OR Epinephrine 1:1000 0.3 cc SQ. Aminophylline 250 mg/50 cc D$_5$W IV. (See notes.) Run in over twenty (20) minutes.	Oxygen Identify cardiac rhythm. IV D$_5$W TKO Transport immediately. Aminophylline 250/50 cc D$_5$W IV. (See notes.) Run in over thirty (30) minutes. Medical control WITH PHYSICIAN ORDER ONLY, Epinephrine 1:1000 0.3 cc SQ, OR consider #1 below.

NOTES:

1. VENTOLIN INHALER (albuterol) two "puffs"—OR—VENTOLIN NEBULIZATION (albuterol) 2.5 mg over 5–15 minutes (0.5 cc of 0.5% solution mixed with 2.5 cc NORMAL SALINE)
2. If patient has taken any theophylline preparations (*e.g.*, theodur, theolair, *etc.*) in the past twelve (12) hours, *DO NOT* give bolus of aminophylline without contacting medical control.
3. Supplemental OXYGEN should be administered as appropriate to patient condition.
4. Monitor all patients closely for cardiac dysrhythmias. If they develop, stop the drug and treat dysrhythmia appropriately.

ASTHMA
ARLINGTON, TX

Asthma

Treatment:

1. Establish and maintain airway, as appropriate.
2. Administer high-flow oxygen.
3. Continuous cardiac monitoring
4. Establish IV access with Ringer's lactate.
5. Administer nebulized updraft as follows:
   Ventolin   2.5 mg in 2 cc normal saline
   Brethine   1.0 mg in 2 cc normal saline

NOTE: The choice between Ventolin and Brethine is left to the paramedic's discretion. If adequate response is not obtained from the initial updraft, give a second updraft with the alternate drug.

6. Contact medical control.

Physician Orders

1. Epinephrine 1:1000 0.3–0.5 mg SQ
2. Solu-Medrol 125 mg IVP
3. Aminophylline infusion 6 mg/kg in 100 cc normal saline to be given over twenty (20) minutes (55 gtts/minute with 10 gtt set up)

ASTHMA
AUSTIN, TX

Reactive Airway Diseases

Introduction

With the availability of beta-2-specific drugs given via nebulization, the paramedic can have a significant impact on the prognosis and outcome of the patient with asthma and COPD. What used to be an almost automatic inpatient stay at the hospital now has the potential to be treated and released the same day.

Key Actions

COMMUNICATIONS
1. Position/calm/reassure the patient.
2. Gather home medications.
3. N.P.O.

BLS
1. Assessment/vital signs
2. Oxygen therapy PRN

ILS
1. Assist with home medications.

ALS
1. Monitor EKG and Pulse Oximetry.
2. Albuterol nebulizer 1-unit dose q 20 minutes
3. Ipratroprium bromide nebulizer 0.5 mg mixed with albuterol 1-unit dose
4. Initiate IV lifeline(s) PRN.
5. Epinephrine 0.3 mg SQ
6. Methylprednisolone 125 mg IV

Assessment Considerations

1. Does patient have a history of asthma, COPD, or CHF? Have there been any recent surgeries? Was patient eating?
2. Able to speak without difficulty? Position of patient? Type of difficulty (noisy/hard to breathe?) Time of onset?
3. Was there activity at time of onset? Did an emotional change precipitate this episode? Was there exposure to chemicals?
4. Is there numbness in hands or around mouth? What is skin color? Is there use of accessory muscles to breathe?

Special Situations/Conditions

None

CHRONIC OBSTRUCTIVE PULMONARY DISEASE
MEMPHIS, TN

Respiratory Distress (Asthma/Chronic Obstructive Pulmonary Disease)

A. *Assessment* (History of Onset and Medications)

Mild Attack—Slight increase in respiratory rate
     Mild wheezes
     Good skin color

Moderate Attack—Marked increase in respiratory rate
     Wheezes easily heard
     Accessory muscle breathing

Severe Attack—Respiratory rate more than twice normal
     Loud wheezes or so tight no wheezes are heard, patient anxious
     Grey or ashen skin color

B. *Treatment*

Mild Attack—Oxygen appropriate to patient's condition and transport

Moderate or Severe Attack:

1. Oxygen appropriate to patient's condition
2. Evaluate cardiac rhythm
3. IV D_5W K.V.O.

Ventolin inhaler 2 puffs or nebulization 2.5 mg over 5–15 minutes (0.5 cc of 0.5% solution mixed with 2.5 cc normal saline)

Contact medical control.—Consider:

Epinephrine 1:1000 0.3 cc SQ
Isoproterenol drip for refractory, life-threatening attack

SPECIAL NOTE: Monitor all patients closely for cardiac dysrhythmias. If they develop, stop the drug and treat dysrhythmia appropriately.

CHRONIC OBSTRUCTIVE PULMONARY DISEASE
NASHVILLE, TN

Chronic Obstructive Pulmonary Disease

A. *ASSESSMENT*   HISTORY OF ONSET AND MEDICATIONS
    If patient takes theophylline preparation, obtain a red-top tube for a theophylline level prior to treatment or IV therapy.

B. *TREATMENT*

Assessment	Treatment Less than 45 years and NO heart disease	Treatment Greater than 45 years OR heart disease
Mild attack Slight increase in respiratory rate. Mild wheezes. Good skin color.	Oxygen and transport	Oxygen and transport
Moderate attack Marked increase in respiratory rate. Wheezes easily heard. Accessory muscle breathing.	Oxygen Identify cardiac rhythm. Epinephrine 1:1000 0.3 cc SQ IV D$_5$W TKO Transport immediately. Medical control Consider #1 below, OR Epinephrine 1:1000 0.3 cc SQ.	Oxygen Identify cardiac rhythm. IV D$_5$W TKO Transport immediately. Medical control WITH PHYSICIAN ORDER ONLY, Epinephrine 1:1000 0.3 cc SQ, OR consider #1 below.
Severe attack Respiratory rate more than twice normal. Loud wheezes or so tight no wheezes are heard. Patient anxious or with grey or ashen skin color.	Oxygen Identify cardiac rhythm. Epinephrine 1:1000 0.3 cc SQ IV D$_5$W TKO Transport immediately. Medical control Consider #1 below, OR Epinephrine 1:1000 0.3 cc SQ. Aminophylline 250 mg/50 cc D$_5$W IV. (See notes.) Run in over twenty (20) minutes.	Oxygen Identify cardiac rhythm. IV D$_5$W TKO Transport immediately. Aminophylline 250/50 cc D$_5$W IV. (See notes.) Run in over thirty (30) minutes. Medical control WITH PHYSICIAN ORDER ONLY, Epinephrine 1:1000 0.3 cc SQ, OR consider #1 below.

NOTES:

1. VENTOLIN INHALER (albuterol) two "puffs"—OR—VENTOLIN NEBULIZATION (albuterol) 2.5 mg over 5–15 minutes (0.5 cc of 0.5% solution mixed with 2.5 cc NORMAL SALINE)

2. If patient has taken any theophylline preparations (*e.g.*, theodur, theolair, *etc.*) in the past twelve (12) hours, *DO NOT* give bolus of aminophylline without contacting medical control.

3. Supplemental OXYGEN should be administered as appropriate to patient condition.

4. Monitor all patients closely for cardiac dysrhythmias. If they develop, stop the drug and treat dysrhythmia appropriately.

CHRONIC OBSTRUCTIVE PULMONARY DISEASE
ARLINGTON, TX

Chronic Obstructive Pulmonary Disease

NOTE: Continuously monitor the patient's respiratory rate and depth throughout transport.

Treatment:

1. Establish and maintain airway as appropriate.
2. Administer oxygen at 2 l/min. Titrate as necessary; decompensating patients need high-flow oxygen with close monitoring of respiratory status.
3. Continuous cardiac monitoring
4. Establish IV access with injection lock or Ringer's lactate
5. Administer nebulized updraft as follows:

Ventolin	2.5 mg in 2 cc normal saline
Brethine	1.0 mg in 2 cc normal saline

   (If pulse rate is 150 or greater, contact medical control.)

NOTE: The choice of Ventolin or Brethine is at the paramedic's discretion.

6. If no significant improvement after initial updraft, administer a second updraft of the alternate drug.
7. **Contact medical control.**

Physician Orders

Aminophylline infusion 6 mg/kg in 100 cc normal saline, to be given over twenty (20) minutes (55 gtts/minute with 10 gtt set up)

CHRONIC OBSTRUCTIVE PULMONARY DISEASE
DALLAS, TX

Emphysema/Bronchitis

Definition/Considerations

Patients who are complaining of shortness of breath with a history of COPD, bronchitis, or prolonged heavy cigarette use. Heart failure must be ruled out. Patients with heart failure usually have a history of PND (paroxysmal nocturnal dyspnea) but not COPD patients. Patients with COPD usually have a history of chronic shortness of breath and cough.

Continued Basic Life Support

1. 24% oxygen via **ventimask** or venturi device. The percentage of oxygen should be increased to alleviate hypoxia and/or cyanosis *as the patient tolerates*. Encourage the patient to exhale as long as possible and monitor respiratory status closely.
2. Record use of any drugs or inhaler used within the previous 24 hours.
3. Place patient in a sitting or semisitting position and transport to ambulance on stretcher.
4. Carefully monitor the patient's respirations and pulse. Assist ventilations if respirations become inadequate.

Advanced Life Support

5. IV D_5W
6. CONTACT BIOTEL.
7. Report use of any drugs or inhaler within the past 24 hours.
8. With bronchospasm or severe dyspnea, Biotel may elect to order Ventolin capsule (200 mcg) via Rotahaler inhalation device. This dosage may be repeated once for adults at Biotel's discretion.
9. Monitor ECG.

NOTE: Subcutaneous epinephrine is *NOT* an alternate drug for these patients.

MEDICAL EMERGENCIES

ANAPHYLAXIS

1. San Francisco, CA—format
2. Rockford, IL—IV Epi 1:10,000 0.5 mgm option
3. Austin, TX—IV methylprednisolone

ALTERED MENTAL STATUS

1. Anaheim, CA
2. Boston, MA—specific drug overdose antidotes
3. Philadelphia, PA

STATUS EPILEPTICUS

1. Anchorage, AK—format
2. Akron, OH—IV Versed
3. Pittsburgh, PA

HYPERTENSIVE CRISIS

1. Des Moines, IA—format
2. State of Kansas—IV Hyperstat option
3. Charlotte, NC
4. Pittsburgh, PA—IV morphine option

ANAPHYLAXIS
SAN FRANCISCO, CA

Severe Allergic Reaction

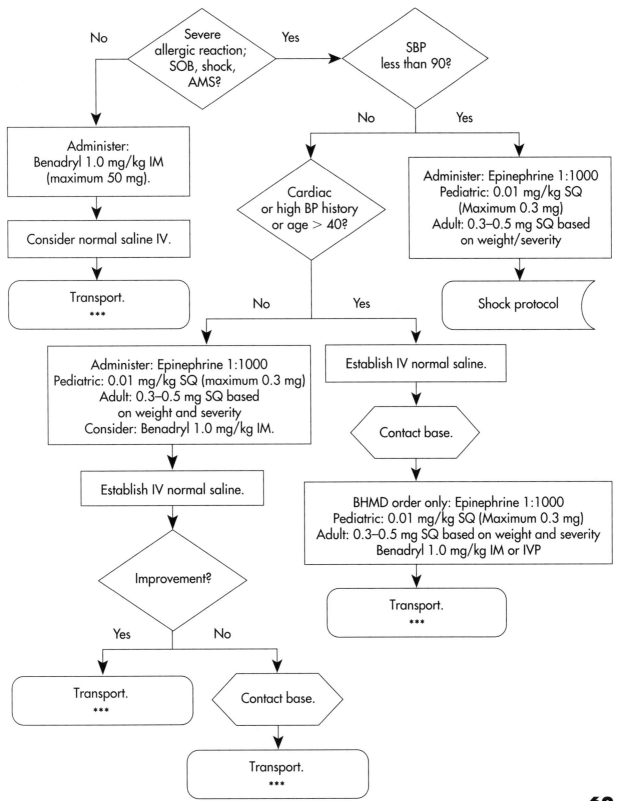

ANAPHYLAXIS
ROCKFORD, IL

Anaphylactic Shock

For life-threatening symptoms of anaphylaxis:
1. Routine trauma care
2. Monitor cardiac rhythm.
3. EPINEPHRINE 1:10,000 0.5 mg (5 ml) *slowly* IV or ET

Per physician's order:

4. DOPAMINE (Intropin) 400 mg in 500 ml of normal saline
   if B/P fails to respond to EPINEPHRINE;
   start at 5–7 mcg/kg/min., and titrate to patient's response.
   *Refer to appendix for dosage chart.

For less severe reaction or non-life-threatening symptoms of anaphylaxis:

1. Routine medical care.
2. EPINEPHRINE 1:1000 0.2–0.3 mg (0.2–0.3 ml) Sub-Q (0.01 ml/kg, max. 0.3 ml)
3. DIPHENHYDRAMINE (Benadryl) 25–50 mg IV or IM (DIPHENHY-DRAMINE (Benadryl) may be given first per physician's orders.)

ANAPHYLAXIS
AUSTIN, TX

Allergic/Anaphylactic Reaction

Introduction

This group of medical problems has a wide range of severity. At its extreme end, reactions are life-threatening with a mortality rate of approximately 3% requiring swift action. Care is focused on reducing airway obstruction and reducing or stopping the allergic reaction.

Key Actions

COMMUNICATIONS
1. Remove patient from exposure if necessary.
2. Position/calm/reassure the patient.
3. Gather home medications.
4. Assist with home Epinephrine kit PRN.
5. N.P.O.
6. Remove restrictive jewelry.

BLS
1. Assessment/vital signs
2. Oxygen therapy PRN
3. Cryotherapy to bite site

ILS
1. Assist with home medications.
2. Epinephrine Pen 0.3 mg SQ
3. Diphenhydramine 25 mg PO

ALS
1. Monitor EKG and Pulse Oximetry.
2. Initiation of IV lifeline(s). PRN.
3. Diphenhydramine 25 mg IV/IM
4. Promethazine 12.5 mg IV if nauseated
5. Epinephrine 1:1,000 0.3 mg SQ or 1:10,000 0.1 mg IV/ET if life-threatening
6. Albuterol nebulizer 1 unit dose for bronchospasms q 15 minutes PRN
7. Methylprednisolone 125 mg IV
8. Fluid therapy 10–20 ml/kg IV PRN for hypotensive patients

Assessment Considerations

1. Dyspnea present?
2. Pale cool skin with or without diaphoresis? Are there any rash or hives present? Is there any itching?

Assessment Considerations *(continued)*

3. When and what was the exposure? Has it caused a reaction before? If so, how bad was the previous reaction?

4. Common allergens include: penicillin, insect stings, shellfish, allergy treatments, and nuts or foods.

Special Situations/Conditions

1. In the ALS treatment section, it is not acceptable to administer diphenhydramine and promethazine together.

© Austin/Travis EMS Clinical Practice

ALTERED MENTAL STATUS
ANAHEIM, CA

Altered Mental Status/Coma

Action/Treatment:

- ABCs/monitor cardiac rhythm.
- IV access titrated to perfusion as needed
- Obtain venous/capillary blood sample for blood glucose analysis.
- Blood sugar < 60:
  —Oral glucose solution; administer as needed.
  —50% dextrose 50 ml IVP; repeat as needed.
  —Glucagon 1 mg IM if unable to establish IV

- Naloxone in patients with evidence of narcotic use (*i.e.,* respirations ≤ 12/min., pinpoint pupils or other signs of narcotic use present), titrated to respiratory rate ≤ 12 and awake, responsive patient without signs of withdrawal:
  —0.4–0.8 mg IVP, every 2–3 minutes PRN
  —0.8 mg IM, may repeat once
  —4 mg ET once

Pediatric:

- Oral glucose solution 30 ml PO; may repeat
- 25% dextrose 2 ml/kg if < 2 years; repeat as needed
- 50% dextrose 1 ml/kg if ≥ 2 years; repeat as needed
- Glucagon 0.5–1 mg IM if unable to establish IV
- Naloxone titrated to age-appropriate respiratory rate (see I-20) and awake, responsive patient without signs of withdrawal:
  —0.1 mg/kg IVP, every 2–3 minutes as needed to maximum of 0.4–0.8 mg per dose
  —0.1 mg/kg IM to a maximum dose of 0.4–0.8 mg; may repeat once
  —ET 0.1 mg/kg once to a maximum dose of 4 mg

NOTES:
To prepare D_{25}, discard 25 ml D_{50}, replace with NS to 50 ml total.

- Shaded text indicates BH order.
- Unshaded text indicates standing order.

ALTERED MENTAL STATUS
BOSTON, MA

Coma/Altered Mental Status/Neurologic Deficit

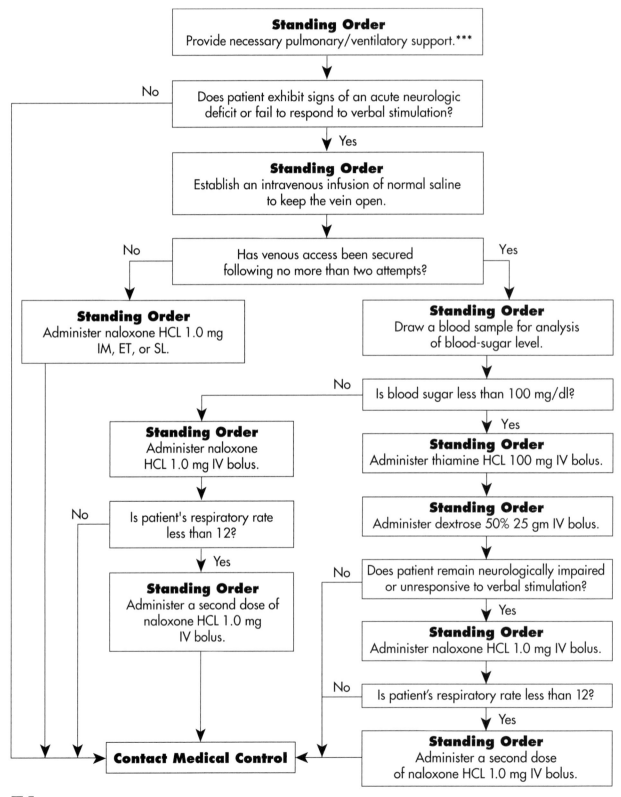

Medical Control Option A
Thiamine HCL, 100 mg IV bolus or IM

Medical Control Option B
Dextrose 50%, 25 gm IV bolus

Medical Control Option C
Naloxone HCL, 1.0 mg IV, IM, ET, or SL. Repeat if necessary in 1.0–2.0 mg
increments, to a maximum cumulative dose of 10.0 mg.

Medical Control Option D
Glucagon, 1.0 mg IM

Medical Control Option E
Intravenous infusion of normal saline. Administer at rate specified by medical control.

One of the following options may be selected by medical control to treat
a specific drug overdose:

Medical Control Option F
Glucagon, 5.0–10.0 mg IV bolus. Repeat if necessary.

Medical Control Option G
Calcium chloride 10% solution, 5.0–20.0 ml IV bolus

Medical Control Option H
Sodium bicarbonate, 0.5–1.0 mEq/kg IV bolus

Medical Control Option I
Atropine sulfate, 2.0–5.0 mg slow IV bolus.
Repeat if necessary in 2.0–5.0 mg increments

***If narcotic overdose is suspected and venous access has been secured, administer
naloxone HCL prior to endotracheal intubation.

© August 1993, Metropolitan Boston EMS Council

ALTERED MENTAL STATUS
PHILADELPHIA, PA

Unconscious/Altered Mental Status

Assess for possible causes of unconsciousness, such as:
- trauma-related central-nervous-system problems
- cardiac-related cerebrovascular problems
- medical-related metabolic problems
- toxicology-related problems, *i.e.*, drug ingestion, carbon-monoxide poisoning

Algorithm Notes

1. Start high-flow oxygen with nonrebreather mask.
2. Indicators of improved mental status include:
- orientation to time, place, and person
- increased alertness
- increased responsiveness to questions

3. Narcan can be administered IM or ETT if IV cannot be established.
4. If a patient responds to naloxone and subsequently refuses further care and transport, call medical command physician for additional IM naloxone prior to releasing patient.

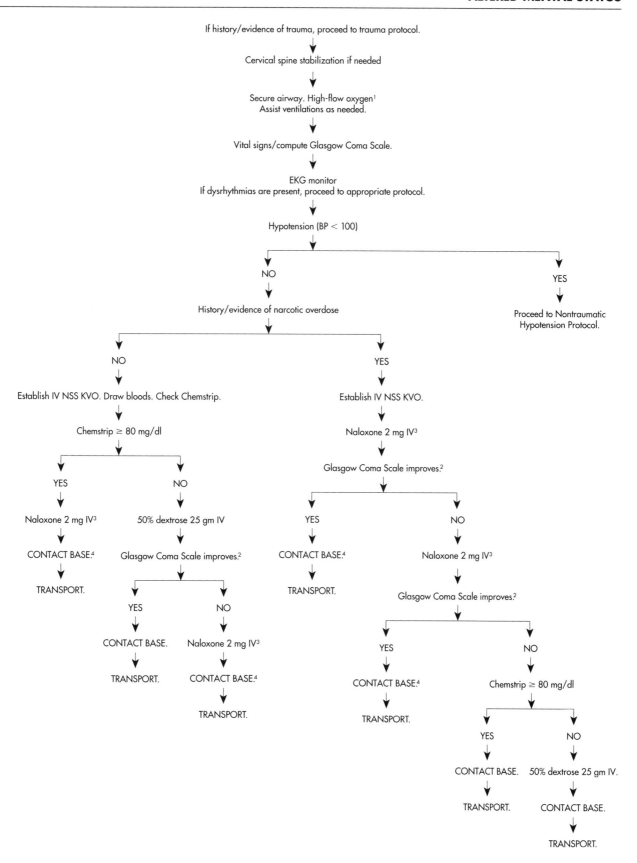

If history/evidence of trauma, proceed to trauma protocol.

Cervical spine stabilization if needed

Secure airway. High-flow oxygen[1]
Assist ventilations as needed.

Vital signs/compute Glasgow Coma Scale.

EKG monitor
If dysrhythmias are present, proceed to appropriate protocol.

Hypotension (BP < 100)

NO — History/evidence of narcotic overdose

YES — Proceed to Nontraumatic Hypotension Protocol.

History/evidence of narcotic overdose

NO — Establish IV NSS KVO. Draw bloods. Check Chemstrip.

Chemstrip ≥ 80 mg/dl

YES — Naloxone 2 mg IV[3] → CONTACT BASE.[4] → TRANSPORT.

NO — 50% dextrose 25 gm IV

Glasgow Coma Scale improves.[2]

YES — CONTACT BASE. → TRANSPORT.

NO — Naloxone 2 mg IV[3] → CONTACT BASE.[4] → TRANSPORT.

YES — Establish IV NSS KVO.

Naloxone 2 mg IV[3]

Glasgow Coma Scale improves.[2]

YES — CONTACT BASE.[4] → TRANSPORT.

NO — Naloxone 2 mg IV[3]

Glasgow Coma Scale improves.[2]

YES — CONTACT BASE.[4] → TRANSPORT.

NO — Chemstrip ≥ 80 mg/dl

YES — CONTACT BASE. → TRANSPORT.

NO — 50% dextrose 25 gm IV. → CONTACT BASE. → TRANSPORT.

STATUS EPILEPTICUS
ANCHORAGE, AK

Seizure Activity

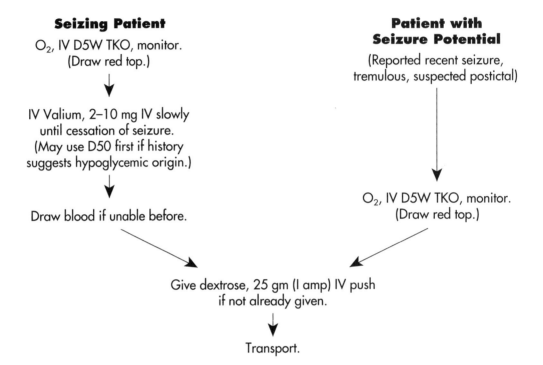

Seizing Patient

O₂, IV D5W TKO, monitor.
(Draw red top.)

↓

IV Valium, 2–10 mg IV slowly
until cessation of seizure.
(May use D50 first if history
suggests hypoglycemic origin.)

↓

Draw blood if unable before.

**Patient with
Seizure Potential**

(Reported recent seizure,
tremulous, suspected postictal)

↓

O₂, IV D5W TKO, monitor.
(Draw red top.)

Give dextrose, 25 gm (I amp) IV push
if not already given.

↓

Transport.

Control any subsequent seizure activity with Valium to 10 mg maximum.
Physician contact required if seizure not controlled with 10 mg Valium.
Consider nasopharyngeal airway.

STATUS EPILEPTICUS
AKRON, OH

Seizures

A. In a known epileptic with a single seizure who has fully regained consciousness, follow standard EMTA care.

B. In a person who is not known to have a seizure disorder, or who is in grand mal status epilepticus:

    1. **Manage airway to keep SaO_2 > 92%.**

    2. IV NS TKO

    3. Check field blood sugar. If unable or if sugar is less than 80 mg by glucometer, push 50 cc D50. If unable to start an IV, give glucagon 1 mg IM.

    4. If the patient is still seizing upon squad arrival or has a recurrent seizure, give Versed 2 to 5 mg slow IVP, titrated to desired effect. May be given IM if no IV available. Be prepared to support respirations.

STATUS EPILEPTICUS
PITTSBURGH, PA

Seizure

Indications

All patients seen with current or recent generalized seizure activity.

Protocol

1. PROTECT the patient from physical harm and embarrassment.
2. ASSESS LEVEL OF CONSCIOUSNESS and maintain AIRWAY as indicated:

   A. Place patient in lateral recumbent position to prevent aspiration.
   B. SUCTION as necessary.
   C. ASSIST VENTILATION as necessary.

3. OXYGEN 4 L NC or face mask at 10–15 L as needed to maintain pulse ox > 94%
4. SALINE LOCK IV. Attempt to draw red-top tube of blood when starting IV.
5. APPLY EKG MONITOR.
6. CHECK CHEMSTRIP READING—IF BELOW 80 mg/dl, give 50 cc of 50% DEXTROSE IV PUSH. If no IV access, give GLUCAGON 1 mg IM.
7. If seizure persists > 1 minute, administer DIAZEPAM 5 mg over 2 minutes. Repeat dose if seizure persists. Monitor need for airway and ventilatory support closely.
8. If seizure persists despite above therapies:

   A. Request EMS physician response and consult with medical command.
   B. Support airway/ventilation. Discuss need for intubation with command physician.
   C. Search for etiology:
      —head injury
      —cardiac arrhythmia
      —CNS infection
      —noncompliance with meds

9. TRANSPORT in left-lateral recumbent position if not intubated. Monitor neuro status, airway, and vitals closely en route to hospital.
10. For seizures that persist despite above therapy:

    A. DIAZEPAM 1 mg every 30 seconds until seizure stops
    B. ENDOTRACHEAL INTUBATION—nasal route preferred if breathing
11. For prolonged seizure activity upon arrival of command physician:

    A. DILANTIN 50 mg/minute up to 15 mg/kg (maximum 1 gram)
    B. VERSED 1 mg every 30 seconds.
    C. Neuromuscular blockade and direct oral intubation

HYPERTENSIVE CRISIS
DES MOINES, IOWA

Hypertensive Crisis

Any patient presenting with a systolic blood pressure of greater than 200 mm Hg, a diastolic pressure greater than 130 mm Hg and CNS dysfunction (bad headache, coma, or seizures), chest pain, or shortness of breath is a candidate to have blood pressure cautiously lowered.

A. Routine care protocol
B. Establish IV access.
C. Contact medical control for specific orders regarding:

    1. Isolated hypertension: ***Procardia** 10 mg sublingually × 1

    2. With chest pain (see also CHEST PAIN protocol):

        a. **Nitroglycerin** $\frac{1}{150}$ gr sublingually
        or
        b. ***Procardia** 10 mg sublingually

    3. With congestive failure (see also CHF protocol):

        a. **Nitroglycerin** $\frac{1}{150}$ gr sublingually
        and/or
        b. **LASIX** 40–80 mg slow IV push

D. Transport as soon as feasible to the appropriate medical facility.

*NOTE: Procardia capsule must be punctured in order to administer liquid medication to patient. Procardia is contraindicated if pulmonary edema is present or hypotension develops.

HYPERTENSIVE CRISIS
STATE OF KANSAS

Hypertensive Crisis

Rationale

Hypertension is present in varying degrees in different portions of the population, based on such variables as socioeconomic factors, race, sex, and age. From the best available data it would appear that 20 million people in the United States suffer from some degree of hypertension.

Management

1. Secure airway, breathing, and circulation. Treat the symptoms associated with hypertension—chest pain, deficits in sensory and motor function, nausea/vomiting, seizures, and coma—not just hypertension alone.
2. Oxygen 4–6 LPM/cannula or 6–10 LPM/mask
3. Obtain vital signs, LOC, physical assessment, and history.
4. A systolic pressure of 160 mm Hg or greater or a diastolic pressure greater than 95 mm Hg are considered to be hypertensive. These arbitrary levels are somewhat higher for older patients and lower for the young. A HYPERTENSIVE CRISIS IS usually signalled by a sudden, marked rise in blood pressure to levels greater than 200/130 mm Hg.
5. Maintain a calm and reassuring atmosphere; external stimuli can induce seizure activity.
6. Monitor ECG; document rhythm.
7. Establish IV D5W; TKO.
8. Establish ED contact reporting patient information; request further orders.
9. Physician's order may include:

   A. Nitroglycerine tablets or spray 0.4 mg (1/150 grain) SL
   B. Procardia 10 mg SL
   C. Hyperstat 1–3 mg/kg up to a maximum of 150 mg in a single injection. *Rapid* IV push. This dose may be repeated with intervals of 5–15 minutes until a satisfactory reduction in blood pressure (diastolic pressure below 100 mm Hg) has been achieved.

HYPERTENSIVE CRISIS
CHARLOTTE, NC

Hypertension

History

1. Complaints may include headache, nausea, vomiting, altered mental status, change in vision, chest pain, or shortness of breath.
2. No history of trauma or pregnancy
3. History may be significant for previously diagnosed heart disease or hypertension.

Physical

1. Patient may be conscious and alert or may have focal neurologic signs, altered mental status, seizures, or coma.
2. Systolic blood pressure greater than 180 mm Hg and diastolic blood pressure greater than 130 mm Hg

Differential

Myocardial infarction
Cerebrovascular accident
Anxiety/apprehension

Protocol

1. Maintain airway, administer oxygen via nonrebreathing mask at 15 l/min. if patient appears to be in severe distress. Otherwise, administer oxygen via nasal cannula 2–6 l/min.
2. Place patient in most comfortable position and reassure.
3. Obtain vital signs and apply cardiac monitor. Obtain rhythm strip. If particular dysrhythmia or heart rate noted, proceed to indicated protocol.
4. Initiate transport. Continue to monitor vital signs while en route.
5. If patient is experiencing chest pain, shortness of breath, seizures, or altered mental status, treat per protocol.
6. If patient is hypertensive as defined above and end-organ damage is suspected (chest pain, shortness of breath, seizures, visual changes, or focal neurologic signs), consider and administer any or all of the following therapeutic interventions:

    Nitroglycerin 0.4 mg SL
    Repeat dose every 5 minutes.
    Hold dose if SBP < 130 mm Hg.
    IV normal saline TKO or PRN adapter

7. Contact medical control en route. The following intervention may be considered:

Nifedipine 10 mg bite and swallow

Addendum

1. Asymptomatic hypertensive patients do not require treatment in the prehospital setting.
2. Hypertension should not be rapidly lowered in patients suspected of having transient ischemic attacks or cerebrovascular accidents. Judicious and cautious use of medication is indicated.
3. Blood-pressure monitoring should be performed before each administration of nitroglycerine and procardia. A dose should not be given if the systolic blood pressure is less than 130 mm Hg.
4. Hypertension associated with cocaine use may be difficult to control. In these patients, medical control may order valium.

HYPERTENSIVE CRISIS
PITTSBURGH, PA

Hypertensive Emergency

NOTE:

1. A hypertensive emergency is the presence of organ-system dysfunction due primarily to high blood pressure.
2. Attention in prehospital setting should be on: *CNS*—altered level of consciousness, decrease in vision, focal motor deficits
   Cardiovascular—angina, acute CHF, aortic dissection
3. Because hypertension can be a neuroprotective reflex in the setting of increased intracranial pressure, great caution must be exercised in administering antihypertensive agents.

INDICATIONS:

Adult patients with systolic B/P of 200 or above and/or diastolic of 130 or above and evidence of CNS or cardiovascular dysfunction

EXCLUSIONS:

1. Age < 16
2. Pregnancy—use eclampsia/preeclampsia protocol.
3. Trauma, especially head injury

PROTOCOL:

1. HISTORY, EXAM, and VITALS. Emphasis on neurological and cardiopulmonary systems
2. OXYGEN—4–6 L NC or 10–15 L face mask as indicated. Maintain pulse ox > 94%.
3. APPLY EKG MONITOR.
4. SALINE LOCK IV
5. CONTACT MEDICAL COMMAND and EXPEDITE TRANSPORT.
6. Command physician may elect to use:

   A. NTG 0.4 –0.8 mg SL every 3–5 minutes
   B. MORPHINE SULFATE 2–5 mg IV every 5–10 minutes

NOTE: **Blood pressure, neuro and cardiac status must be monitored closely after use of these agents.

Traumatic Emergencies

MULTIPLE TRAUMA

1. San Francisco, CA—flow-chart format
2. Kansas City, MO—complete
3. Las Vegas, NV

TRAUMATIC ARREST

1. Denver, CO—field pronouncement
2. Boston, MA—format
3. New York, NY

HEAD INJURY

1. Colorado Springs, CO—detailed
2. New Haven, CT
3. Chicago, IL—flow-chart format
4. Columbus, OH

CHEST INJURY

1. Evansville, IN—format
2. Chicago, IL—format

EXTREMITY INJURY

1. Los Angeles, CA—poor vs. good systemic perfusion
2. San Francisco, CA—format
3. Denver, CO

SPINAL INJURY

1. State of Hawaii—IV methylprednisolone
2. Philadelphia, PA—flow-chart, IV dexamethasone

NEUROGENIC SHOCK

1. Birmingham, AL
2. Nashville, TN

BURNS

1. Los Angeles, CA—format
2. Evansville, IN—flow-chart format; Haz Mat
3. Oklahoma City, OK—complete

MULTIPLE TRAUMA
SAN FRANCISCO, CA

Adult Critical Trauma

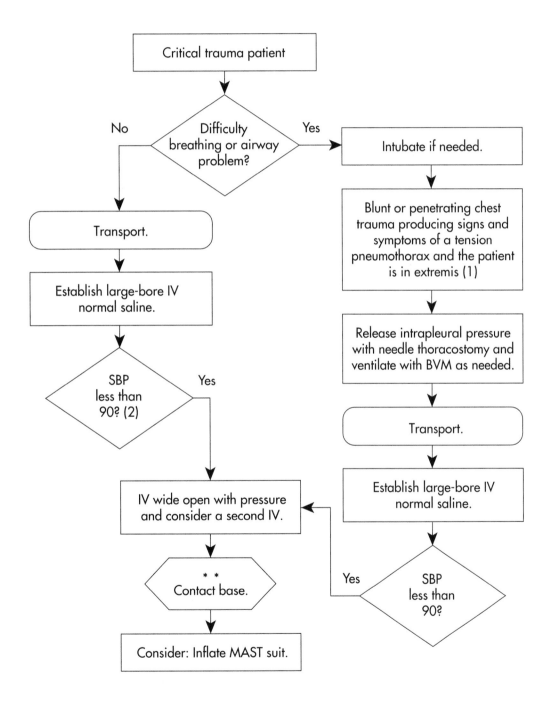

1. The clinical presentation of a tension pneumothorax may include:
   - Dyspnea
   - Chest pain referred to the arm or shoulder of the affected side
   - Decreased or absent breath sounds
   - Hyperresonance to percussion
   - Tracheal shift and mediastinal shift away from the affected side
   - Bulging of the intercostal muscles
   - Neck-vein distention
   - Shock due to diminished venous return
   - Cyanosis
   - Subcutaneous emphysema

   The above signs and symptoms may not always be present in all patients.

2. Hypotension can also be determined by the absence of radial pulses and a capillary-refill time greater than two seconds.

MULTIPLE TRAUMA
KANSAS CITY, MO

General Trauma Protocol

Assessment

1. Assess adequacy of airway and breathing with simultaneous cervical spine immobilization.
2. Assess cardiopulmonary system with attention to adequacy of perfusion (*i.e.*, mental status; presence, location, and character of pulses; skin moisture, temperature, and capillary refill).
3. Briefly assess neurologic function (*i.e.*, level of consciousness by AVPU, pupils, gross motor function).
4. Obtain brief history of incident and mechanism of injury.
5. If patient is stable, obtain vital signs and AMPLE history.

CRITERIA

PHYSIOLOGIC CRITERIA
a. B/P <90 mmHg OR absence of radial pulse.
b. RR >29 OR <10
c. GCS <13 OR AVPU scale P or U

MECHANISM OF INJURY
a. Occupant ejection
b. Fall from height more than 20 feet
c. Pedestrian hit at speed of more than 20 mph
d. Death of same-car occupant
e. Prolonged extrication >20 mins.

ANATOMIC CRITERIA
a. Penetrating injury to head, chest, abdomen, neck, or groin

Treatment

I. If patient is in no distress and meets none of the physiologic or mechanism-of-injury criteria suggestive of a potential for serious injury, then appropriately immobilize the patient and transport with frequent reassessment of vital signs and patient status.

II. If patient has sustained a mechanism of injury and/or meets anatomic criteria that suggest a potential for that severe injury but does not meet physiologic criteria (stable patient) and does not have associated symptoms (altered mental status, respiratory distress, clinical signs of shock), the EMT-P should CONTACT MEDICAL CONTROL and proceed with treatment as directed.

III. If the patient meets physiologic criteria (unstable patient) with associated symptoms (altered mental status, respiratory distress, clinical signs of shock), the EMT-P may initiate the following therapy PRIOR to contacting medical control, in accordance with the appropriate trauma protocols.

A. Secure airway and assure adequate ventilation.

1. Stabilize the cervical spine with manual in-line immobilization. DO NOT APPLY TRACTION.

2. Use chin lift or modified jaw thrust ONLY to open airway. Consider nasal airway adjunct particularly in the head-injured patient.

3. Administer oxygen 10–15 l/minute via nonrebreather mask.

4. Assist ventilation as needed using bag-valve-mask with 100% oxygen.

5. Orotracheal intubation may be attempted if unable to adequately ventilate the patient with a BVM because of severe facial trauma or excessive blood or secretions. Maintain in-line cervical spine immobilization during intubation attempts. TRANSPORT OF THE UNSTABLE TRAUMA PATIENT SHOULD NOT BE DELAYED BY ATTEMPTS AT INTUBATION UNLESS THE PATIENT CANNOT BE ADEQUATELY VENTILATED WITH BVM.

6. Needle cricothyrotomy may be attempted if unable to otherwise secure the airway in patients with severe upper-airway compromise secondary to trauma. Cervical-spine immobilization must be maintained during attempts.

B. Circulatory Support and Fluid Replacement

1. Control any external bleeding with sterile dressing and direct pressure. Place patient supine and elevate feet if possible.

2. Apply MAST suit and inflate if indicated.

3. Initiate one or two LARGE-BORE IVs with lactated Ringer's. Infuse 500 ml bolus. Repeat as indicated. TRANSPORT OF THE UNSTABLE PATIENT SHOULD NOT BE DELAYED TO INITIATE IV THERAPY. BEGIN IV EN ROUTE TO HOSPITAL!

4. Monitor cardiac rhythm.

C. Spinal Immobilization

1. In the stable patient, complete spinal immobilization as indicated by mechanism of injury, using appropriate collar, short board, and long spine board as indicated.

2. In the unstable patient, transport should not be delayed by the application of short board prior to extrication. Appropriate rapid extrication technique to long spine board with manual spinal immobilization should be used.

D. Transport

1. Monitor vital signs and continually reassess patient status.

2. Trauma *CODES* should be taken to the nearest level I/II trauma center whether the trauma center is on trauma-divert status or not. Taking a trauma patient to a "closed" trauma center applies to trauma codes (blunt or penetrating) *ONLY*.

3. Patients who meet the physiologic, mechanism-of-injury, or anatomic criteria to be considered for preferential routing to a level I/II trauma center *and* who are less than 16 years old should be considered for preferential routing to a pediatric trauma center.

REMEMBER THE GOLDEN TEN MINUTES! Rapid assessment, rapid initiation of treatment of hypoxemia and shock, and rapid transport. On-scene time should be less than TEN minutes for critically injured patients.

E. CONTACT MEDICAL CONTROL.

1. Upon beginning treatment, EMT should notify communications center of hospital destination, and if critical patient, initiate MED channel patch and inform hospital of incoming trauma patient.

MULTIPLE TRAUMA
LAS VEGAS, NV

Critical Trauma Protocol

When treating a critical trauma patient, *i.e.*, full arrest secondary to trauma, upper-airway trauma with inability to secure airway, tension pneumothorax, flail chest, open sucking chest wound, or class III shock as defined by ATLS as tachycardia, increased respiratory rate, altered mental status, and decreased blood pressure, this critical trauma protocol is to be followed.

NOTE: This protocol may always be followed prior to telemetry physician orders, except as noted below.*

The concept of "scene stabilization" has created a number of serious problems as it relates to the critical-trauma patient. There is *NO* field treatment for the *underlying* cause of such problems. The cure is surgical with time of the essence in survival.

I. Primary assessment *only*
If a full arrest secondary to trauma or upper-airway trauma with inability to secure airway:

    A. *The trauma center if transport can be accomplished within 10 minutes: OR*
    B. *The nearest hospital if transport to the trauma center cannot be accomplished within 10 minutes.*

NOTE: *THERE IS NO ON-SCENE CARE FOR A TRAUMATIC ARREST!
IMMEDIATELY—*
    Place patient on a full backboard with manual "C" spine management, if possible; load into the ambulance, and transport Code 3 to the appropriate hospital. Any care given this patient should be done in the ambulance en route to the hospital.

II. CPR
III. Airway control with "C" spine management

    A. High-flow oxygen
    B. Intubation as needed (per protocol order)
    C. Needle cricothyrotomy with transtracheal jet insufflation as needed (per physician order only)

IV. Chest-wound management

    A. Seal sucking chest wounds.
    B. Decompress tension pneumothorax as needed (per physician order only).

V. Hemorrhage control
VI. Spinal immobilization, as appropriate
VII. MAST

NOTE: *MAST ARE NOT TO BE APPLIED IF THE ESTIMATED TRANS-PORT TIME IS LESS THAN 30 MINUTES.*

VIII. Immediately load and transport per trauma patient destination protocol. The total time of transport shall in no way be added to by waiting for a second ambulance to arrive at the scene. If a single attendant needs assistance to care for a patient, an effort should be made to rendezvous en route with a second ambulance unit to obtain a second attendant.

IX. (Re)establish communication with monitoring physician for update and continuing orders.

X. *While en route*, insert two large-bore IV lines of crystalloid solution (per protocol order).

XI. Attach cardiac monitor and monitor EKG.

XII. Recheck vitals every 5–10 minutes and record findings.

NOTE: A patient treated under this critical trauma protocol is considered to be so critically injured as to have given implied consent to be treated as per this protocol. Therefore, family or patient request as to treatment facility may be disregarded by scene or emergency personnel as not being in the best interest of patient and not in keeping with the state-mandated trauma system for Clark County.

TRAUMATIC ARREST
DENVER, CO

Trauma Arrest

Trauma Treatment

SPECIFIC INFORMATION NEEDED

A. Time of arrest
B. Mechanism: blunt vs. penetrating
C. Signs of irreversible death (decapitation, dependent lividity, *etc.*)

SPECIFIC OBJECTIVE FINDINGS

A. Vital signs
B. Evidence of massive external blood loss
C. Evidence of massive blunt head, thorax, or abdominal trauma

TREATMENT

A. Blunt-trauma arrest:

   1. Initiate basic life support.
   2. Manage airway.
   3. If no vital signs or other signs of life present after above treatments, consider field pronouncement.
   4. When possible, airway and venous access should be established en route, minimizing on-scene time and any other delays in transporting patient.
   5. **Contact base.**
   6. If cardiac activity returns with above treatment, treat arrhythmias per ACLS protocols and transport rapidly to a level I or II trauma center.

B. Penetrating trauma arrest:

   1. Initiate basic life support.
   2. Manage airway.
   3. Rapid transport to a Level I or II trauma center
   4. Establish venous access, fluid bolus: IV, NS
   5. **Contact base** to report patient status.
   6. If cardiac activity returns with above treatment, treat arrhythmias per ACLS protocols.
   7. Consider field pronouncement (see resuscitation and field pronouncement guidelines protocol) for the following:

   a. Signs of irreversible death

   b. ALS has been unavailable for at least 20 minutes from the time EMS personnel initiated on-scene assessment, and there is no return of vital signs or signs of life.

SPECIFIC PRECAUTIONS

A. Victims of blunt-trauma arrest without vital signs at the scene after initiation of ALS have a mortality rate approaching 100%.

B. Trauma arrests secondary to penetrating truncal injuries can be resuscitated and saved. There is a higher rate of survival in victims of low-velocity penetrating injuries versus victims of high-velocity injuries.

TRAUMATIC ARREST
BOSTON, MA

Traumatic Cardiopulmonary Arrest

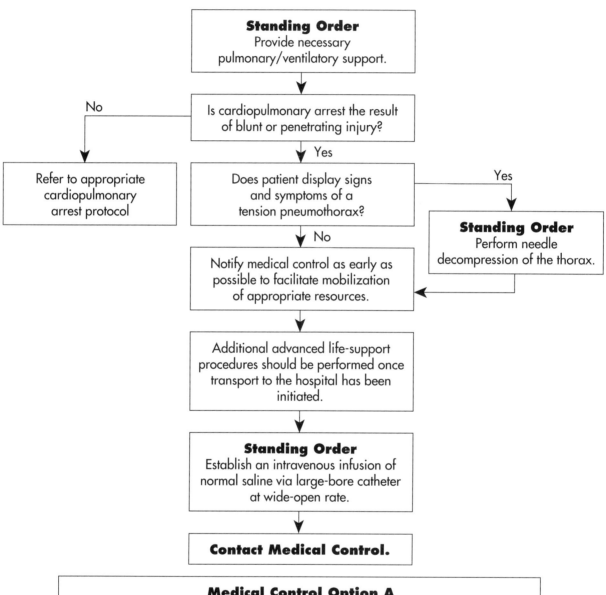

Standing Order
Provide necessary pulmonary/ventilatory support.

Is cardiopulmonary arrest the result of blunt or penetrating injury?

No → Refer to appropriate cardiopulmonary arrest protocol

Yes → Does patient display signs and symptoms of a tension pneumothorax?

Yes → **Standing Order** Perform needle decompression of the thorax.

No → Notify medical control as early as possible to facilitate mobilization of appropriate resources.

Additional advanced life-support procedures should be performed once transport to the hospital has been initiated.

Standing Order
Establish an intravenous infusion of normal saline via large-bore catheter at wide-open rate.

Contact Medical Control.

Medical Control Option A
Establish a second intravenous infusion of normal saline via large-bore catheter; infuse at rate specified by medical control.

Medical Control Option B
Normal saline; infuse at rate specified by medical control.

Medical Control Option C
MAST; inflate leg compartments and abdominal compartment if indicated.

TRAUMATIC ARREST
NEW YORK, NY

Traumatic Cardiac Arrest

NOTE: IN PATIENTS IN TRAUMATIC ARREST, RAPID TRANSPORT IS THE HIGHEST PRIORITY!

1. Begin transportation of the patient and other basic life-support traumatic cardiac arrest procedures.
2. If a tension pneumothorax is suspected, perform needle decompression.
3. Perform endotracheal intubation if other methods of airway control are not effective.
4. Begin rapid IV/saline lock infusion of normal saline (0.9 NS) or Ringer's lactate via one or two large bore (14–16 gauge) catheters, up to 3.0 liters.
5. If transportation of the patient is delayed or extended and/or the above measures fail to improve hemodynamic status, contact medical control for implementation of one or more of the following MEDICAL CONTROL OPTIONS:

Medical Control Options:

Option A: Continue rapid IV/saline lock infusion of normal saline (0.9 NS) or Ringer's lactate, up to an additional 3.0 liters (total of 6 liters).

Option B: Transportation decision

HEAD INJURY
COLORADO SPRINGS, CO

Head Trauma

Specific information needed

A. History—mechanism of injury, estimate of force involved, helmet worn with motorcycle or bicycle
B. History since injury—loss of consciousness (duration), change in level of consciousness, memory loss for events before and after trauma, movement (spontaneous or performed by bystanders)
C. Past history—medications (insulin particularly), medical problems, seizure history

Specific objective findings

A. Vital signs. (Note respiratory pattern and rate.)
B. Neurologic assessment, including pupils, response to stimuli, and Glasgow Coma Scale observations.
C. External evidence of trauma—contusions, abrasions, lacerations, bleeding from nose, ears

GLASGOW COMA SCORE

Eye opening	
None	1
To pain	2
To speech	3
Spontaneously	4
Best verbal response	
None	1
Garbled sounds	2
Inappropriate words	3
Disoriented sentences	4
Oriented	5
Best motor response	
None	1
Abnormal extension	2
Abnormal flexion	3
Withdrawal to pain	4
Localized pain	5
Obeys commands	6
Total = (15 points possible)	

Treatment

A. Assess airway and breathing. Treat life-threatening difficulties (see Trauma Overview). Use assistant to provide cervical stabilization while managing respiratory difficulty.

B. Control hemorrhage. Stop scalp bleeding with direct pressure if possible. Continued pressure may be needed.

C. Apply O_2, moderate flow (4–6 L/min.), by mask or nasal cannula (high flow by mask for seriously injured patients). Titrate to pulse oximetry >90% if possible.

D. Obtain initial vital signs, neurologic assessment, including Glasgow Coma Score.

E. If unconscious, or Glasgow Coma Score <11:

   1. Assist ventilations.
   2. Consider intubation. If time allows, administer lidocaine, 1.5 mg/kg IV, 1 minute prior to intubation.
   3. Hyperventilate at 20–30 breaths per minute.

F. Immobilize cervical spine (relieve assistant performing manual stabilization).

G. Immobilize patient on spine board (or other firm surface). Apply PASG to board prior to moving patient.

H. Secure patient to board following transfer. Be prepared to tilt for vomiting.

I. TRANSPORT RAPIDLY if patient has multiple injuries, or unstable respiratory, circulatory, or neurologic status.

J. If BP <90 mm Hg systolic and signs of hypovolemic shock are present, initiate treatment en route:

   1. Elevate legs, keep patient warm.
   2. Inflate PASG per protocol. Titrate to patient condition.
   3. IV—volume expander (NS or RL), large bore, wide open, 20 ml/kg, then TKO or as directed.
   4. Consider bleeding sources (abdomen, pelvis, chest).
   5. Stabilize and splint fractures and dress wounds if time allows.

K. If patient unconscious and showing signs of neurological deterioration (*e.g.*, dilated pupil, rising BP, slowing pulse, posturing or decreasing GCS):

   1. Hyperventilate at 20–30 breaths per minute.
   2. *Consider furosemide, 20–40 mg IV.
   3. *If transport time > 30 minutes, consider Foley catheter when diuretics have been administered.

L. If patient stable (respiratory, circulatory, neurologic):

   1. IV—volume expander (NS or RL), large bore, TKO
   2. Complete secondary survey.
   3. Splint fractures and dress wounds if time permits.

M. Monitor airway, vitals, and level of consciousness repeatedly at scene and during transport. STATUS CHANGES ARE IMPORTANT.

Specific precautions

A. When head-injury patients deteriorate, check first for airway, oxygenation, and blood pressure. These are the most common causes of "neurologic" deterioration. If the patient has tachycardia or hypotension, look for hidden hypovolemia from associated injuries and do not blame the head injury.

B. The most important information you provide for the base physician is level of consciousness and its changes. Is the patient stable, deteriorating, or improving?

C. Assume cervical-spine injury in *all patients* with head trauma.

D. Restlessness can be a sign of hypoxia. Cerebral anoxia is the most frequent cause of death in head injury.

E. If active airway ventilation is needed, intubate and hyperventilate at 20–30/minute. *Hypoventilation* aggravates cerebral edema.

F. If patient is combative from head injury or hypoxia, consider use of morphine sulfate 2 mg IV, repeated every 5 minutes, titrated to reduce combativeness. The airway and C-spine can be more appropriately managed with a relaxed patient and the effects can be reversed at the receiving facility if desired. Administer cautiously (SLOWLY) in hypovolemic patient.

G. Do not try to stop bleeding from nose and ears. Cover with clean gauze if needed to prevent further contamination.

H. Scalp lacerations can cause profuse bleeding and are difficult to define and control in the field. If direct local pressure is insufficient to control bleeding, evacuate any large clots from flaps and large lacerations with sterile gauze and use direct hand pressure to provide hemostasis. If the underlying skull is unstable, pressure should be applied to the periphery of the laceration over intact bone.

HEAD INJURY
NEW HAVEN, CT

Severe Head Trauma

I. Provide routine paramedic care.

    A. Suspect associated cervical-spine injury if sufficient mechanism of injury is involved, and treat appropriately.

    B. All unconscious patients should be considered to have an inadequate respiratory exchange and should have their airway managed aggressively.

    C. Patients with depressed or decreasing levels of consciousness should be hyperventilated to 30/min.

    D. Evaluate the patient's neurologic status based on Glasgow Coma Scale (GCS):

EYE OPENING		VERBAL RESPONSE		MOTOR RESPONSE	
Spontaneous	4	Oriented	5	Follow commands	6
Voice	3	Confused	4	Localizes pain	5
Pain	2	Inappr. words	3	Withdraws pain	4
None	1	Incom. sounds	2	Flex from pain	3
		None	1	Extend from pain	2
				None	1

ADD ONE SCORE FROM EACH CATEGORY TOGETHER TO OBTAIN GCS. (Range is 3–15.)

    E. IV fluids should be restricted unless shock is present.

    F. If shock is present, look for systemic or hidden cause of blood loss. Brain injury usually does not cause hypotension.

II. Transport without delay to an appropriate destination hospital.

NOTE: Early notification of the receiving hospital is essential to ensure immediate availability of an appropriate in-hospital response.

HEAD INJURY
CHICAGO, IL

Head Injury

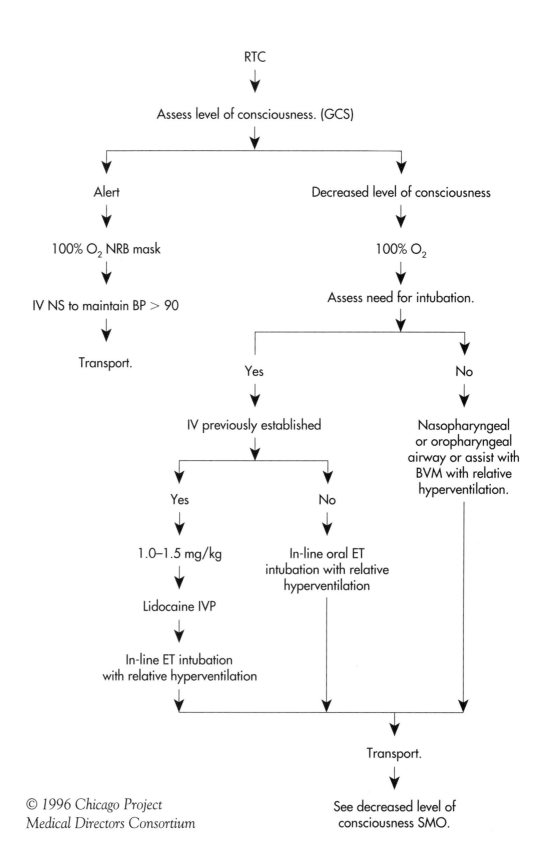

RTC

↓

Assess level of consciousness. (GCS)

Alert | Decreased level of consciousness

100% O₂ NRB mask | 100% O₂

IV NS to maintain BP > 90 | Assess need for intubation.

Transport. | Yes | No

IV previously established | Nasopharyngeal or oropharyngeal airway or assist with BVM with relative hyperventilation.

Yes | No

1.0–1.5 mg/kg | In-line oral ET intubation with relative hyperventilation

Lidocaine IVP

In-line ET intubation with relative hyperventilation

Transport.

See decreased level of consciousness SMO.

© 1996 Chicago Project
Medical Directors Consortium

HEAD INJURY
COLUMBUS, OH

Neurologic Trauma

1. See MULTIPLE TRAUMA PROTOCOL.
2. Administer high-flow OXYGEN.
3. Control severe bleeding, may apply sterile dressings.
4. Start IV 0.9% NORMAL SALINE at keep-open. If hypovolemia is present, run IV to maintain adequate perfusion.
5. Apply MAST trousers only if hypotension is unresponsive to above measures.
6. If confirmed head injury with impaired level of consciousness, hyperventilate at a rate of at least 28 per minute. Intubate severely head injured patients; administer LIDOCAINE 1.5 mg/kg IVP prior to or during intubation attempts.
7. For combative patients with head injury, administer DIAZEPAM (VALIUM) 5–10 mg IV push for sedation. May repeat in 5 minutes if the systolic BP is greater than or equal to 90 mm Hg (see TRAUMA TRANSPORT PROTOCOL).
8. Backboard with cervical spine immobilization
9. Observe spine-injured patients for neurogenic shock, *i.e.,* hypotension with bradycardia. If signs of inadequate perfusion, treat with MAST trousers and fluid administration. For obvious spinal shock with no response to the above therapy, consider administering DOPAMINE at 2–20 mcg/kg/min. Refer to table.
10. In the head-injured patient with signs of shock, look for other sources of bleeding, *i.e.,* chest, abdomen, pelvis, and femurs, and treat for hypovolemic shock.
11. Load and go in patients with either:

    A. Unilaterally dilated pupil.
    B. Deteriorating mental status.

CHEST INJURY
EVANSVILLE, IN

Respiratory Management—Traumatic

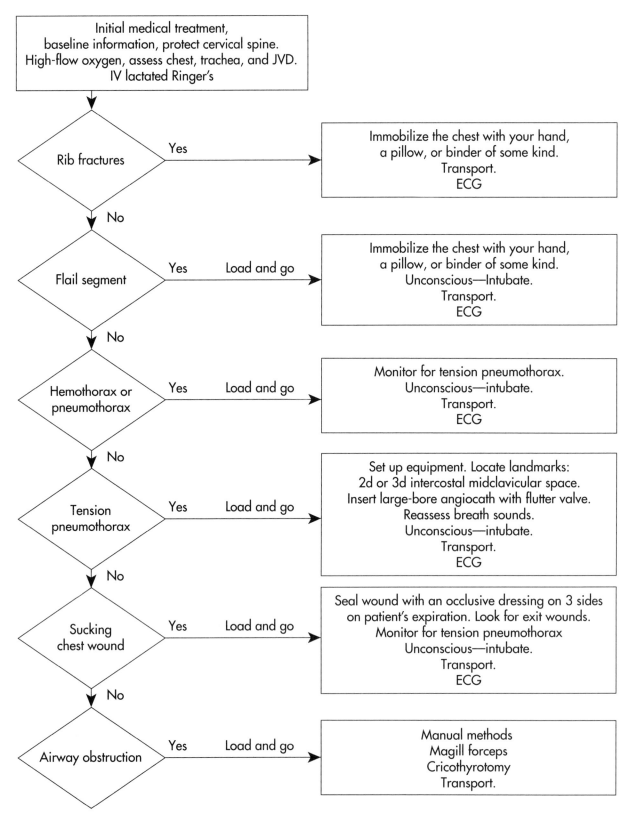

Initial medical treatment,
baseline information, protect cervical spine.
High-flow oxygen, assess chest, trachea, and JVD.
IV lactated Ringer's

Rib fractures — Yes → Immobilize the chest with your hand, a pillow, or binder of some kind. Transport. ECG

No

Flail segment — Yes — Load and go → Immobilize the chest with your hand, a pillow, or binder of some kind. Unconscious—Intubate. Transport. ECG

No

Hemothorax or pneumothorax — Yes — Load and go → Monitor for tension pneumothorax. Unconscious—intubate. Transport. ECG

No

Tension pneumothorax — Yes — Load and go → Set up equipment. Locate landmarks: 2d or 3d intercostal midclavicular space. Insert large-bore angiocath with flutter valve. Reassess breath sounds. Unconscious—intubate. Transport. ECG

No

Sucking chest wound — Yes — Load and go → Seal wound with an occlusive dressing on 3 sides on patient's expiration. Look for exit wounds. Monitor for tension pneumothorax Unconscious—intubate. Transport. ECG

No

Airway obstruction — Yes — Load and go → Manual methods Magill forceps Cricothyrotomy Transport.

CHEST INJURY
CHICAGO, IL

Chest Trauma

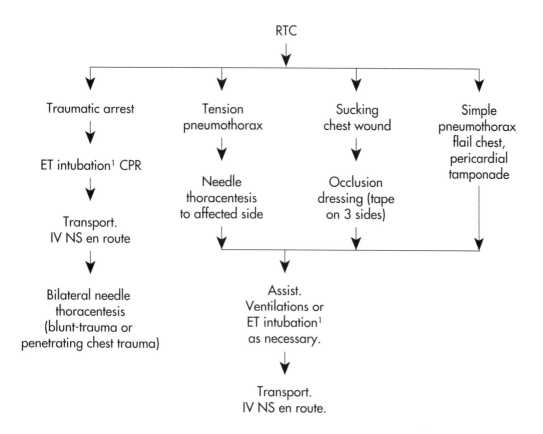

CAUTION: Aviod use of demand valve and Univent.

NOTE 1: *Attempt a maximum of two (2) times; needle cricothyrotomy if appropriate.*

EXTREMITY INJURY
LOS ANGELES, CA

Extremity Trauma

FIELD TREATMENT

1. Basic airway/spinal immobilization prn/control major bleeding
2. Oxygen prn
3. Shock-position prn

GOOD SYSTEMIC PERFUSION

4. Venous access prn
5. Traction/splints/dressings prn

Note 5

6. Consider **morphine 2–10 mg** IVP for localized trauma.

Note: 1, 2, 3, 4
☞ May Repeat prn.

7. Reassess for potential deterioration.

POOR SYSTEMIC PERFUSION

4. Antishock trousers prn.

Note: 6, 7

5. Venous access
6. Fluid resuscitate
7. Traction/splints/dressings prn

Note 5

Drug Considerations

Morphine

1. Alternate routes: 5–10 mg IM or SQ (one time only)
2. Use with caution if BP < 100 systolic or altered LOC.
3. Maximum adult dose: 20 mg
4. Pediatrics: 0.1 mg/kg IVP, IM, or SQ (one time only)

Special Considerations

5. Treatment for specific injuries:

POOR NEURO/VASCULAR STATUS—Realign and stabilize long bones.

JOINT INJURY—Splint as lies.

MIDSHAFT FEMUR—Splint with traction.
6. May be used as splinting device.
7. DO NOT delay transport for treatment.

EXTREMITY INJURY
SAN FRANCISCO, CA

Adult and Pediatric Extremity Trauma

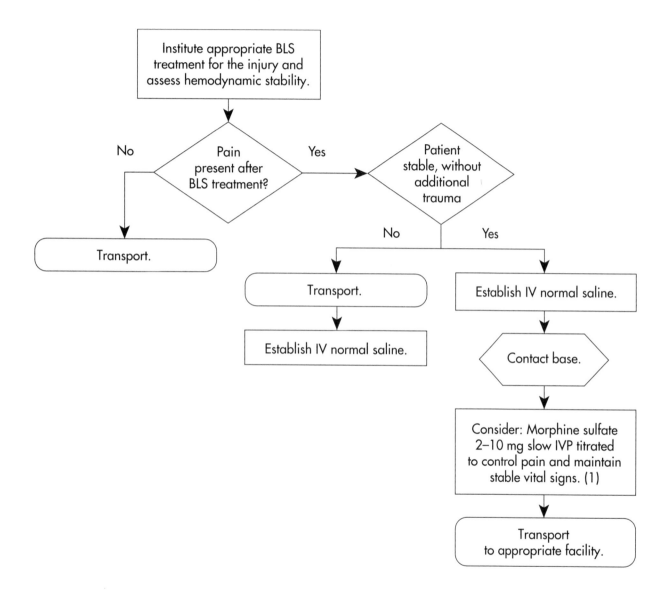

EXTREMITY INJURY
DENVER, CO

Extremity Injuries

Trauma Treatment

SPECIFIC INFORMATION NEEDED

A. Mechanism of injury: direction of forces, if known
B. Areas of pain or limited movement
C. Treatment prior to arrival: realignment of open or closed fracture, movement of patient
D. Past medical history: medications, medical illnesses

SPECIFIC OBJECTIVE FINDINGS

A. Vital signs
B. Observe: localized swelling, discoloration, angulation, lacerations, exposed bone fragments, loss of function, guarding
C. Palpate: tenderness, crepitus, instability, quality of distal pulses, sensation
D. Note estimated blood loss at scene.

TREATMENT

A. Treat airway, breathing, and hypotension as first priorities. (See Multiple Trauma Overview).
B. Immobilize cervical spine when appropriate.
C. Examine for additional injuries to head, face, chest, and abdomen; treat those problems with higher priority first.
D. If patient unstable, transport rapidly, treating life-threatening problems en route. Splint patient by securing to long board to minimize fracture movement.

   If patient stable, or isolated extremity injury exists:

   1. Check distal pulses and sensation prior to immobilization of injured extremity.
   2. Apply sterile dressing to open fractures. Note carefully wounds that appear to communicate with bone.
   3. Splint areas of tenderness or deformity: apply gentle traction throughout treatment and try to immobilize the joint above and below the injury in the splint. (See Splinting: Extremity.)
   4. Realign fractures/dislocations by applying gentle axial traction if indicated:

      a. To restore circulation distally
      b. To immobilize adequately, *i.e.*, realign femur fracture

   5. Check distal pulses and sensation after reduction and splinting.
   6. Elevate simple extremity injuries. Apply ice if time and extent of injuries allow.
   7. Monitor circulation (pulse and skin temperature), sensation, and motor function distal to site of injury during transport.

SPECIAL PRECAUTIONS

A. Patients with multiple injuries have a limited capacity to recognize areas that have been injured. A patient with a femur fracture may be unable to recognize that he has other areas of pain. Be particularly aware of missing injuries proximal to the obvious ones (*e.g.*, a hip dislocation with a femur fracture, or a humerus fracture with a forearm fracture).

B. Do not use ice or cold packs directly on skin or under air splints. Pad with towels or leave cooling for hospital setting.

C. Do not attempt to realign dislocations in the field unless circulation is compromised. Splint in the position of comfort.

D. Injuries around joints may become more painful, and circulation may be lost with attempted realignment. If this occurs, stabilize the limb in the position of most comfort with the best distal circulation.

SPINAL INJURY
STATE OF HAWAII

Adult Spinal-Cord Injury

In patients with acute spinal-cord injury with any neurologic motor-function deficits:

Provide 100% oxygen via mask at 10 l/min. or if apnea or impending respiratory arrest, via endotracheal tube.

Establish large-bore IV with normal saline or lactated Ringer's and infuse at TKO rate if not in shock.

Administer methylprednisolone 30 mg/kg IV over 15 minutes.

COMMUNICATE WITH MEDICOM PHYSICIAN FOR FURTHER ORDERS.

SPINAL INJURY
PHILADELPHIA, PA

Isolated Spinal-Cord Trauma

This protocol applies to patients with isolated spinal-cord injuries. If patients have other traumas, proceed to trauma protocol.

Algorithm Notes

1. If BP <100 and there is no evidence of other trauma, patient may be in spinal shock. Administer IV bolus of 200 ml NSS and CONTACT BASE.

2. Transport to Spinal-Cord Injury Center of Thomas Jefferson University Hospital for patients located in all sections of the city if Spinal-Cord Injury Scale 6 or less and in the absence of other traumas.

Isolated spinal-cord trauma

↓

Cervical spine control

↓

Appropriate airway maintenance
High-flow oxygen
Intubate with C-spine precautions as necessary.

↓

Assess pulse, control bleeding.
EKG monitor
Manage only lethal dysrhythmias.

↓

Control bleeding.

↓

Initiate IV NSS TKO.

↓

Vital signs
If BP <100, assess for other traumas.
If found, proceed to trauma protocol.

↓

Dexamethasone 100 mg IV

↓

BP may be volume dependent.[1]

↓

Complete spinal immobilization.

↓

Glasgow Coma Scale
Spinal-cord index
Trauma score

↓

CONTACT BASE en route.
TRANSPORT to spinal-cord center as appropriate.[2]

NEUROGENIC SHOCK
BIRMINGHAM, AL

Neurogenic Shock

1. Note warm, dry skin with hypotension and pulse less than 100.
2. Trendelenburg entire patient, not just lower extremities,
   or
   apply MAST with as little movement as possible and inflate to maintain systolic pressure of 90 mm Hg.
3. Insert large-bore IV with lactated Ringer's 100 cc/hr.
4. Apply nasal cannula O_2 at 6 l/min. If no COPD, MASK O_2 at 12–15 l/min.
5. Record neurologic and vitals frequently (every 5–10 minutes).
6. Drug therapy
   dopamine 400 mg in 500 cc D5W and begin at ½ cc/min.

NEUROGENIC SHOCK
NASHVILLE, TN

Neurogenic Shock

A. Assessment

   1. Associated with spinal-cord injuries and overdoses
   2. Signs of hypovolemic shock without peripheral vasoconstriction (warm shock)

B. Treatment

   1. Secure spine and airway.
   2. OXYGEN 100% and control ABCs.
   3. Position MAST.
   4. Primary IV access with large-bore catheter bolus 10 cc/kg of normal saline or lactated Ringer's
   5. Secondary IV access with large-bore catheter TKO of normal saline or lactated Ringer's
   6. Inflate MAST if perfusion is not restored.
   7. Consider occult bleeding and treat as hypovolemia.
   8. Neurologic assessment
   9. Contact medical/trauma control.
   10. INTROPIN (dopamine) 200 mg/250 cc D5W IV admix.
   Begin at 15 cc/hr and titrate if perfusion is not restored.

BURNS
LOS ANGELES, CA

Burns

FIELD TREATMENT

1. Basic airway/spinal-immmobilization prn
2. Oxygen prn

Note 6

3. Advanced airway prn
4. Shock-position prn

THERMAL

5. Remove jewelry and clothing
6. Cool burn area(s) and cover with dry dressings/sheet.

Note: 7, 8

7. Venous access prn
8. Elevate burned extremities if possible.
9. Consider **morphine 2–10 mg** IVP.

Note: 1, 2, 3, 4, 5
☞May repeat prn

10. Reassess for potential deterioration.

CHEMICAL

5. Remove jewelry and clothing
6. *If dry,* brush and flush with copious amount of water. *If liquid,* flush with copious amount of water.
7. Venous access prn

Note: 7, 8

8. Consider **morphine 2–10 mg** IVP.

Note: 1, 2, 3, 4, 5
☞May repeat prn

9. Reassess for potential deterioration.

ELECTRICAL

5. Cardiac monitor

Note 7, 8

6. Venous access
7. Treat dys-rhythmias by appropriate protocol.
8. Cool burn area(s) and cover with dry dressings/sheet.
9. Consider **morphine 2–10 mg** IVP.

Note: 1, 2, 3, 4, 5
☞May repeat prn

10. Reassess for potential deterioration.

Drug Considerations

Morphine

1. Alternate routes: 5–10 mg IM or SQ (one time only)
2. Maximum adult dose: 20 mg
3. Use caution if BP < 100 systolic, altered LOC or respiratory depression.
4. Not recommended if signs of major system injury
5. Pediatrics: 0.1 mg/kg IVP, IM, or SQ (one time only)

Special Considerations

6. High-flow oxygen is essential with known or potential respiratory injury.
7. DO NOT delay transport for treatment.
8. If poor perfusion, fluid resuscitate/antishock trousers and consider other injuries; however, DO NOT apply antishock trousers over burned areas.
9. If eye involvement, continuous flushing with NS during transport. Allow patient to remove contact lenses if possible.

BURNS
EVANSVILLE, IN

Burns

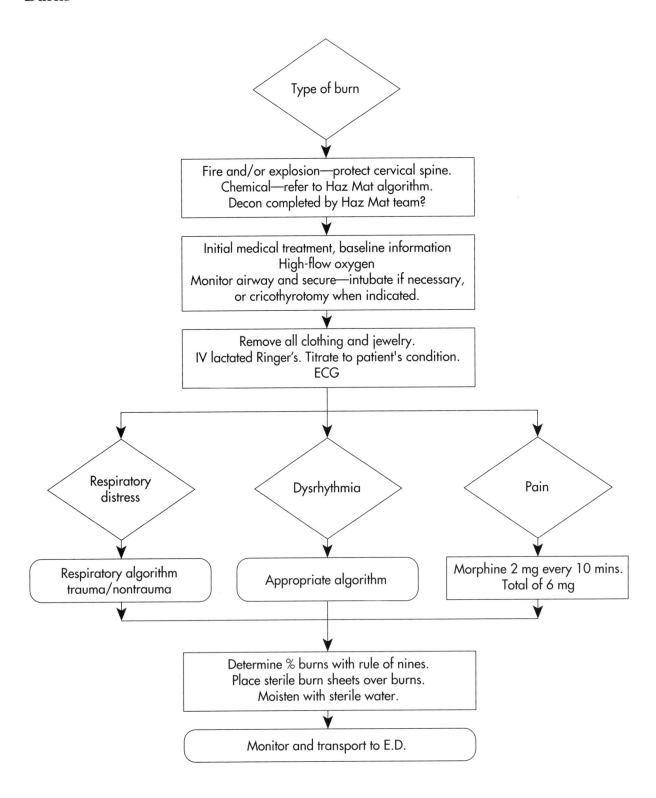

BURNS
OKLAHOMA CITY, OK

Burns

NOTE:

A. Thermal Burns

  1. Gasses, usually carbon monoxide, are given off. It is important to record if the burn occurred inside and what materials were burning.
  2. Two percent or greater burns should be seen by a physician.

B. Chemical Burns

  1. Usually more localized than thermal burns.
  2. Noxious gases often affect the lungs to produce pulmonary insult. Laryngeal and bronchial edema may cause subsequent airway obstruction.
  3. Remove dry particles, then flood the area with water.
       a. If lime is in the eyes, WASH IT OUT.

C. Electrical Burns

  1. Be sure the patient is no longer in contact with the electrical source.
  2. Evaluate airway and cardiac status.
  3. Patients often suffer from fall injuries.
  4. Even though the surface area of the burn may be small, involvement of muscle and bone are often extensive.
  5. All electrical burns should be seen by a physician.

D. Assess the burns by the following criteria:

  1. Percent of body burn:
       a. "Rule of nines" (see chart)

  2. Depth of burn:
       a. First, Second or Third Degree (see chart)

  3. Age of the patient.
  4. Site of burns:
       a. Face, extremities, etc.

E. American Burn Association criteria for transport to burn center:

  1. Second and third degree burns of 10% or more of the body surface in patients under 10 or over 50 years.
  2. Second and third degree burns of more than 20% of the body surface area in other age groups.
  3. Third degree burns of more than 5% of the body surface area in any age group.
  4. Second and third degree burns that involve the face, hands, feet, genitalia, perineum, or major joints.
  5. Electric burns, including lightning injury.

6. Chemical burns with serious threat of functional or cosmetic impairment.
7. Inhalation injury.
8. Lesser burns in patients with pre-existing medical problems that could complicate management.
9. Combined mechanical and thermal injury in which the burn injury poses the greater risk.

A. Adult Care

I.1. Trauma and hypovolemia supportive care.
I.2. Stop the burn process:

   a. Remove clothes.
   b. Flood with water only if flames not extinguished, smoldering present, or significant heat still being dissipated.

I.3. Obtain information regarding possibility of smoke/toxic fume inhalation. Treat with 100% NRB.
I.4. Advanced Burn Life Support guidelines for fluid resuscitation:
   a. Indications:

      1. Burns exceeding 20% BSA and transport time greater than 60 minutes.
      2. Potential for hypovolemic shock from associated injuries.
      3. Management of life-threatening ventricular arrhythmias.
      4. Patients requiring endotracheal intubation.

   b. IV NS fluid rates for above indications:
      1. 500 ml/hour, age >15.

I.5. Cover burned area with clean, dry sheets or appropriate burn dressing.
I.6. Notify Burn Unit and transport.
   a. Transport to nearest emergency facility if patient is in acute respiratory distress.

II.1. Morphine sulfate, 2 to 10 mg slowly.

B. Pediatric Care

I.1. Trauma and hypovolemia supportive care.
I.2. Stop the burn process:

   a. Remove clothes.
   b. Flood with water only if flames not extinguished, smoldering present, or significant heat still being dissipated.

I.3. Obtain information regarding possibility of smoke/toxic fume inhalation. Treat with 100% NRB.
I.4. Advanced Burn Life Support guidelines for fluid resuscitation:
   a. Indications:

      1. Burns exceeding 20% BSA and transport time greater than 60 minutes.

2. Potential for hypovolemic shock from associated injuries.
3. Management of life-threatening ventricular arrhythmias.
4. Patients requiring endotracheal intubation.

b. IV NS fluid rates for above indications:

1. 250 ml/hour, age 5–15
2. Do not initiate fluid resuscitation in field IV in ages <5.

I.5. Cover burned area with clean, dry sheets or appropriate burn dressing.
I.6. Notify Burn Unit and transport.
   a. Transport to nearest emergency facility if patient is in acute respiratory distress.

II.1. Morphine sulfate, 0.1 mg/kg slowly (not to exceed 5 mg).

TABLE A   PERCENTAGE OF BURNS FOR CHILDREN USE TABLE

AREA	NEWBORN	3-YEARS	6-YEARS	12-YEARS
Head and Neck	18%	15%	12%	6%
Trunk	40%	40%	40%	38%
Arms	16%	16%	16%	18%
Legs	26%	29%	32%	38%

TABLE B   CHARACTERISTIC OF BURNS

DEGREE	APPEARANCE	SENSATION	DEPTH INVOLVEMENT
First	Erythema (reddening) of the skin	Painful	Confined to epidermis
Second	Blisters	Painful	Epidermis and part of dermis lost
Third	Unblistered—May be white, leathery, with thrombosed vessels seen beneath or charred	Not painful	Epidermis and full dermal layer, and may go down to muscle or bone

Rule of nines

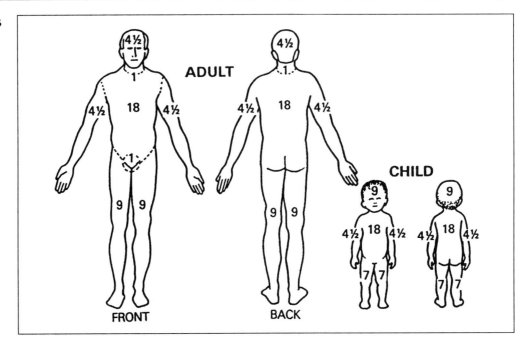

Areas in which small burns are more serious. Second or third degree burns in these areas (shaded portions) should be treated in the hospital.

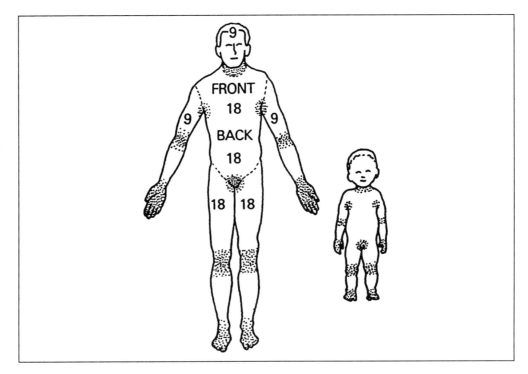

© *Tulsa/Oklahoma City Medical Control Board*

TOXICOLOGIC EMERGENCIES

TOXIC INHALATION

1. Washington, DC

TOXIC INGESTION

1. Los Angeles, CA—format
2. Sacramento, CA—complete; hydrofluoric acid
3. San Mateo, CA—flow chart format

TOXIC INHALATION
WASHINGTON, DC

Toxic Gas Inhalation

This protocol is designed to address the treatment of patients exposed to toxic gases (*i.e.*, carbon monoxide) from any source without associated significant burns and/or trauma (as defined in ADULT-PATIENT TRANSPORT CATEGORIZATION).

Cardiopulmonary arrest, major trauma, and/or burn patients are to be treated and transported in accordance with the applicable protocol.

A specialty referral protocol for toxic-gas inhalation has been developed. Exposure to these gases may be related to a fire scene with smoke inhalation or inhalation of exhaust fumes.

It is not feasible to list the absolute triage for every possible toxic-gas inhalation patient, nor to define which patients should go directly to George Washington University's Department of Hyperbaric Medicine vs. a closer facility.

The following guidelines are intended to aid in decision making, with the understanding that medical control consultation should be obtained if there is any question regarding treatment, transport, or patient destination.

Primary Assessment

A. Perform primary assessment as per medical-patient assessment protocol. Assign treatment priority.

B. Obtain relevant patient history as per medical-patient assessment protocol.

   1. Nature of the injury—toxic-gas inhalation vs. toxic-gas inhalation with burns and/or associated injuries

   2. Specifics to the exposure

      a. Type of fire and/or combustible involved if known (PVC, acrylics, styrofoam, petroleum products, wood, *etc.*)

      b. If other than fire related—type of gas involved (carbon monoxide, cyanide, hydrogen sulphide, *etc.*)

      c. Area of confinement (dwelling, vehicle)

      d. Duration of exposure

C. Relevant physical findings

   1. Level of consciousness

   2. Lung sounds

   3. Vital signs, GCS

   4. Level of respiratory distress (none, mild, moderate, severe)

   5. Cough or hoarseness

   6. Singed nasal or facial hair

   7. Soot or erythema of mouth

Resuscitation

A. Administer 100% oxygen—Assist ventilations as necessary.
B. Perform ALS interventions.

   1. Intubate and ventilate if necessary as per intubation protocol.
   2. Apply cardiac monitor and pulse oximeter. If arrythmia is noted, treat as per applicable protocol.
   3. Start largest IV possible with N/S.

      a. Toxic-gas inhalation only—KVO
      b. Toxic-gas inhalation with burns or associated trauma—flow at rate to maintain a systolic pressure of at least 90 mm Hg

Establish Medical-Control Communications

A. Ensure notification of receiving facility and establish contact with medical control.
B. Anticipate that the medical-control physician will continue with the following protocol, but expect that there may be some variation within the ACLS guidelines of the American Heart Association.
C. If unable to establish contact with medical control, refer to "Inability to establish medical-control protocol," and continue to follow these guidelines.

   1. If physical exam reveals pulmonary wheezing, administer 2.5 mg of albuterol by nebulization.
   2. Continue administration of 100% after completion of albuterol treatment.

Secondary Assessment

A. Perform secondary assessment as soon as possible as per medical patient assessment protocol.

Transport Destination

A. For patients with toxic-gas inhalation, transport to George Washington if:

   1. Toxic gas only (with pulse and blood pressure)
   2. Unconscious
   3. Incoherent, does not follow verbal commands
   4. Other neurological compromise following exposure to toxic gas

      a. headache
      b. vertigo
      c. irritability
      d. acute vision impairment

B. Category 1 burn patients should be transported to the burn center regardless of toxic-gas inhalation.

C. Prior to transporting a pediatric patient for hyperbaric therapy, a *joint* consultation with Children's and George Washington must be completed. Since Children's Hospital is primary medical control for all pediatric patients, any orders for patient care must come from them. GW will only provide on-line hyperbaric medicine consultation.

D. Due to the extreme toxicity and cumulative effects of certain by-products of combustion and/or incomplete combustion, any person suspected of toxic-gas exposure who refuses treatment shall be advised of the possible consequences. Be sure to adhere to the REFUSAL OF TREATMENT PROTOCOL.

TOXIC INGESTION
LOS ANGELES, CA

Overdose/Poisoning (Suspected)

FIELD TREATMENT

1. Basic airway
2. Oxygen

Note 6

3. Advanced airway prn
4. Cardiac monitor
5. Venous access prn/blood-glucose test prn

Note 7

6. If hypotension, use NONTRAUMATIC HYPOTENSION **M8** guidelines.

Note 8

ALERT AND ORIENTED

7. Consider **activated charcoal 25–50 gm** PO.

Note: 1, 2

8. Reassess for potential deterioration.

ALTERED LOC

7. **Narcan® 0.8–2 mg** IVP

Note: 3, 4
☞ May repeat every 5 minutes prn if strong suspicion of narcotic overdose exists or partial response is noted

8. If hypoglycemia, **dextrose 50% 50 ml** IVP

Note 5
☞ May repeat one time

Note 9

Drug Considerations

ACTIVATED CHARCOAL:
1. Contraindicated if patient cannot voluntarily swallow.
2. Pediatrics:
    0–2 years—not recommended
    Over 2 years—adult dose as tolerated

NARCAN® (NALOXONE):
3. Alternate routes: ET (double IV dose), IM or SL
4. Pediatrics: 0.02 mg/kg IVP or IM; ET (double IV dose)

DEXTROSE 50%:

5. Pediatrics: 2 ml/kg of dextrose 25% IVP

Special Considerations

6. If narcotic overdose, consider venous access and Narcan prior to advanced airway.

7. If unable to establish venous access and known diabetic, consider **glucagon 1 mg** IM or SQ. Same for pediatrics.

8. Bring substance/container to hospital for chemical analysis.

9. Drugs to consider for specific history:
   —Calcium channel blocker—**calcium chloride** 500–1000 mg IVP
   —Tricyclic with dysrhythmia or hypotension—**sodium bicarbonate 1 mEq/kg** IVP and see appropriate dysrhythmia.

© 1993 (Revised), Los Angeles County Base Hospital Treatment Guidelines

TOXIC INGESTION
SACRAMENTO, CA

Ingestions and Overdoses

Procedural Protocol:

Always use universal precautions

BASIC THERAPY
1. Ensure a patient airway.
2. Oxygen therapy—Be prepared to support ventilations with appropriate airway adjuncts.
3. Identify substance and the time of ingestion. Bring sample medication bottles to the hospital, if possible.
4. CARDIAC MONITOR
5. CONTACT BASE HOSPITAL.
6. Treat specific ingestions according to specific treatment guidelines.

MICN should contact Poison Control Center by direct 911 access number.

(916) 734-3681

7. Activated charcoal: (EMT-P ONLY) Adult 50 grams PO. Administer if the patient is awake.

Activated charcoal is CONTRAINDICATED in the following ingestions:

a. Acids and alkalis
b. Corrosives
c. Foreign-body ingestions
d. Ipecac administered previously

SPECIFIC THERAPY: INGESTIONS AND OVERDOSES
1. Iron or Vitamins with Iron

a. BASIC THERAPY
b. EMT-II AND EMT-PARAMEDIC: CONTACT BASE HOSPITAL.
c. IPECAC—30 cc PO—may be administered if patient is awake and has gag reflex.
d. SODIUM BICARBONATE—Dilute the contents of one ampule of $NaHCO_3$ with 200 cc water and have patient drink the solution following ipecac administration.

2. Tricyclic Antidepressants and Related Compounds

a. BASIC THERAPY—Be prepared to manage airway en route with intubation as these patients can deteriorate rapidly.
b. EMT-II: CONTACT BASE HOSPITAL.
c. IV ACCESS—Initiate IV of normal saline at TKO rate.
d. EMT-PARAMEDIC: CONTACT BASE HOSPITAL.

e. Sodium bicarbonate—may administer one mEq/kg IV push if patient has any of the following signs of cardiac toxicity:
   i. Heart rate > 120
   ii. Systolic blood pressure < 90 mm Hg
   iii. QRS Complex > .12 m/sec. (3 small (.04) boxes)
   iv. Seizures
f. *Examples of tricyclic antidepressants and related compounds (in alphabetical order):

ADAPIN	ENDEP	PROTRIPTYLINE
AMITRIPTYLINE	IMIPRAMINE	SINEQUAN
AMOXAPINE	LIMBITROL	SURMONTIL
ASENDIN	LUDIOMIL	TRAZODONE
AVENTYL	MAPROTILINE	TRIAVIL
BUPROPION	MERITAL	TRIMIPRAMINE
DESIPRAMINE	NOMIFENSINE	TOFRANIL
DESYREL	NORPRAMIN	VIVACTIL
DOXEPIN	NORTRIPTYLINE	WELLBUTRIN
ELAVIL	PAMELOR	

*These lists were formulated at the time of policy development. They should not be considered all-inclusive. New drugs in this class may have been introduced since.

3. Beta Blockers

a. BASIC THERAPY—Be prepared to manage airway with intubation as these patients can deteriorate rapidly.
b. EMT-II: CONTACT BASE HOSPITAL.
c. IV ACCESS—Initiate IV of normal saline with macrodrip tubing. Administer 500 cc fluid challenge if systolic blood pressure < 90 mm Hg.
d. EMT-PARAMEDIC: CONTACT BASE HOSPITAL.
e. ATROPINE—Administer 1 mg IV push if heart rate remains below 50/min. after fluid challenge. May repeat every 5 mins. to 3 mg maximum total dose.
f. GLUCAGON (EMT-P ONLY)—1 unit IV if heart rate remains below 50/min. or blood pressure remains below 90 mm Hg.
g. EPINEPHRINE—1:10,000 solution. Administer 0.1 mg increments slow (over 60 secs.) IV push if systolic blood pressure remains less than 60 mm Hg. Repeat until systolic blood pressure is > 90 mm Hg.
h. *Examples of beta blockers and combination products (in alphabetical order).

ACEBUTOLOL	INDERIDE	PENBUTOLOL
ATENOLOL	KERLONE	PINDOLOL
BETAXOLOL	LABETALOL	PROPANOLOL
BLOCADREN	LEVATOL	SECTRAL
CARTROL	LOPRESSOR	TENORETIC
CARTEOLOL	LOPRESSOR HCT	TENORMIN
CORGARD	METOPROLOL	TIMOLOL
CORZIDE	NALDOLOL	TIMOZIDE
INDERAL	NORMODYNE	TRANDATE
INDERAL LA	NORMOZIDE	VISKEN

*These lists were formulated at the time of policy development. They should not be considered all-inclusive. New drugs in this class may have been introduced since.

4. Calcium Channel Blockers

a. BASIC THERAPY—Be prepared to intubate as these patients can deteriorate rapidly.

b. EMT-II: CONTACT BASE HOSPITAL.

c. IV ACCESS—Initiate IV of normal saline via macrodrip tubing. Administer 500 cc fluid challenge if systolic blood pressure < 90 mm Hg.

d. EMT-PARAMEDIC: CONTACT BASE HOSPITAL.

e. ATROPINE—Administer 1 mg IV push if heart rate < 50 min. and systolic BP < 90. May be repeated every 5 mins. to 3 mg maximum total dose.

f. CALCIUM CHLORIDE—10% solution—Administer 10 cc slow (1 cc/min.) IV push. Administer only if systolic blood pressure < 90 mm Hg. May be repeated every 5 min for a total of 4 doses.

g. EPINEPHRINE—1:10,000 solution—Administer 0.1 mg increments slow (over 60 secs.) IV push if systolic blood pressure remains less < 60 mm Hg. Repeat until systolic blood pressure is > 90 mm Hg.

h. *Examples of calcium channel blockers (in alphabetical order.)

ADALAT	DYNACIRC	NIMOTOPP
AMLODIPINE	FELODIPINE	NORVASC
BEPRIDIL	ISOPTIN	PLENDIL
CALAN	ISRADIPINE	PROCARDIA
CARDIAZEM	NICARDIPINE	VASCOR
DILACOR XR	NIFEDIPINE	VERAPAMIL
DILTIAZEM	NIMODIPINE	

*These lists were formulated at the time of policy development. They should not be considered all-inclusive. New drugs in this class may have been introduced since.

5. Narcotics

a. BASIC THERAPY
- Intubate patient if Glasgow Coma Score is < 6.

b. EMT-II: CONTACT BASE HOSPITAL.

c. IV ACCESS—Initiate IV of normal saline at TKO rate.

    d.   IF NARCOTIC OVERDOSE IS SUSPECTED:

NALOXONE (NARCAN)—Administer up to 2 mg dose slow IV push—Titrate to respiratory response.

Narcan 2 mg may be administered IM if unable to establish IV.

Do not administer Narcan if patient is intubated.

Narcan is to be administered only for respiratory depression (not sleepiness) if respiratory rate is < 12 breaths per minute or respiratory efforts are inadequate.

EMT-PARAMEDIC: CONTACT BASE HOSPITAL.

6.   Insulin or Antidiabetic Agents

    a.   BASIC THERAPY
    b.   EMT-II: CONTACT BASE HOSPITAL.
    c.   IV ACCESS—Initiate IV of normal saline at TKO rate.
    d.   IF HYPOGLYCEMIA IS SUSPECTED:

Obtain finger-stick capillary blood sample for glucose determination and perform glucometer reading.

If glucometer reading is less than 80 mg/dl:

DEXTROSE—Administer 25 gm of 50% solution slow IV push if glucometer reading is less than 80 mg/dl.

NOTE: If the patient's history and clinical picture fits hypoglycemia yet the glucometer reading is above 80 mg/dl, contact base hospital.

GLUCAGON (EMT-P ONLY)—If IV access is NOT available, or delay in IV access is anticipated, administer glucagon 1 unit IM.

    e.   EMT-PARAMEDIC: CONTACT BASE HOSPITAL.

7.   Organophosphate or Carbamate Pesticides

Precautions must be taken to prevent direct contact with secretions of the patient who has ingested organophosphate or carbamate pesticides.

    a.   BASIC THERAPY
    b.   EMT-II: CONTACT BASE HOSPITAL.
    c.   IV ACCESS—Initiate IV of normal saline.
    d.   EMT-PARAMEDIC: CONTACT BASE HOSPITAL.
    e.   ATROPINE—2.0 mg IV push if heart rate < 60 bpm. May be repeated every 3 mins. to heart rate > 80. *No* maximum dose.

See S-SV protocol, "Hazardous Material Exposure," Reference No. E-7, if exposed to pesticides externally.

8.   Hydrofluoric Acid

Oral ingestions require immediate treatment as hydrofluoric acid can cause fatal hypocalcemia. Provide continuous cardiac monitoring to look for QT interval prolongation, which is an early sign of hypocalcemia.

    a.   BASIC THERAPY
    b.   EMT-II: CONTACT BASE HOSPITAL.
    c.   IV ACCESS—Initiate IV of normal saline at TKO rate.

   d. EMT-PARAMEDIC: CONTACT BASE HOSPITAL.

   e. Calcium chloride 10%—Administer 10 cc slow (1 cc/min.) IV push.

        If an alert patient has a clear airway and there is no respiratory distress, empty contents of one ampule of calcium chloride 10% into a cup and have patient drink the solution.

        See S-SV protocol "Hazardous Material Exposure," Reference No. E-7, if externally exposed to hydrofluoric acid.

Cross-References:

POLICY AND PROCEDURE MANUAL

Coma of questionable Etiology/Altered Level of Consciousness, Reference No. N-1

Hazardous Material Exposure, Reference No. E-7

TOXIC INGESTION
SAN MATEO, CA

Poisoning and Overdose

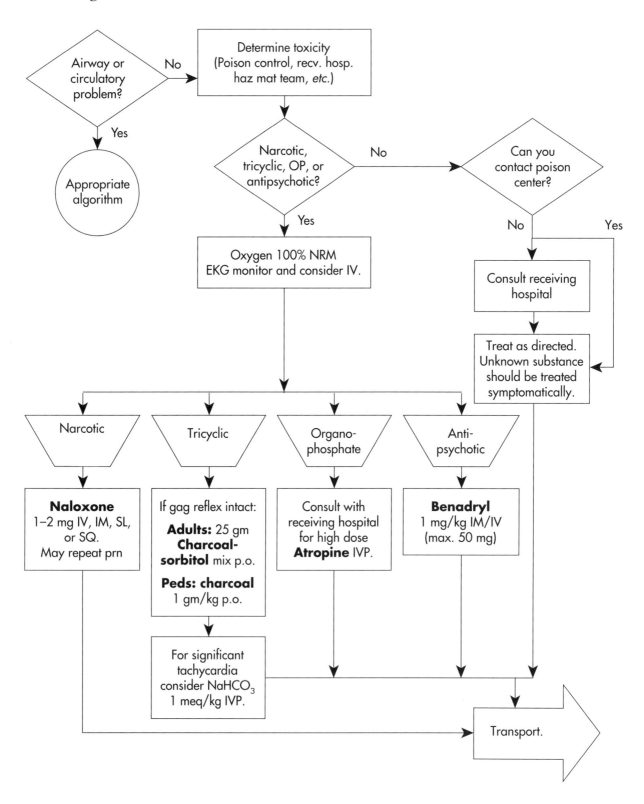

UNIQUE ADULT PROTOCOLS

DROWNING CARDIOPULMONARY ARREST
STATE OF HAWAII

Drowning Cardiopulmonary Arrest

Because drowning-cardiac-arrest patients can be considerably acidotic, if there is no pulse after 2 doses of epinephrine, they should be given sodium bicarbonate:
    (Follow standing orders for cardiopulmonary arrest.)
    Administer second epinephrine; if still pulseless:
    Administer 1 mEq/kg IV sodium bicarbonate.
    Administer third dose epinephrine.
    If still pulseless:
    Repeat 1 mEq/kg IV sodium bicarbonate.
    Continue standing orders.

CAUTION: Be aware of possible hypothermia. Cover patient with blankets and turn off the air conditioner in the ambulance patient compartment.

RENAL DIALYSIS CARDIAC ARREST
STATE OF HAWAII

Renal Dialysis Cardiac Arrest

Because *renal dialysis* patients in cardiac arrest (of any type) can have profound hyperkalemia, administer these medications as soon as the IV is established per other applicable standing orders:

    2 gm calcium chloride IV push

    Flush IV line thoroughly.*

    100 mEq sodium bicarbonate IV

    Continue standing orders.

*Calcium chloride can precipitate in the presence of sodium bicarbonate.

POSTRESUSCITATION
ARLINGTON, TX

Postresuscitation

Treatment:

1. Establish and maintain airway as appropriate.
2. Administer high-flow oxygen. Hyperventilate if possible.
3. Continuous cardiac monitoring. Refer to appropriate algorithm.
4. Assure patency of IV and infusion rates to maintain B/P >100/s.
5. Monitor vital signs every 5–10 minutes.
6. Infuse a maintenance dose of the drug that originally converted the rhythm if ventricular in nature:
   - Lidocaine **2.0–4.0 mg/min.**—not indicated for patients with bradycardia or rate-dependent PVCs.
   - Bretylium **2.0 mg/min.**
7. If bradycardic, refer to the bradycardia algorithm.
8. **Contact medical control.**

Physician Orders

- Dopamine **2–20 mcg/kg/min.,** titrated to B/P
- Further drug therapy as directed

SYMPTOMATIC TACHYCARDIAS
WICHITA, KS

Symptomatic Tachycardia

SVT, Wide-Complex, V-Tach

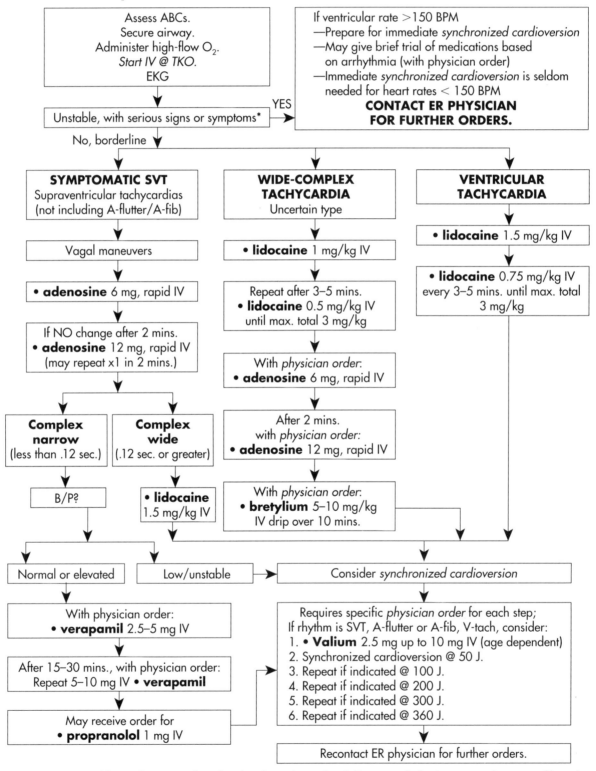

Assess ABCs.
Secure airway.
Administer high-flow O₂.
Start IV @ TKO.
EKG

If ventricular rate >150 BPM
—Prepare for immediate *synchronized cardioversion*
—May give brief trial of medications based on arrhythmia (with physician order)
—Immediate *synchronized cardioversion* is seldom needed for heart rates < 150 BPM
CONTACT ER PHYSICIAN FOR FURTHER ORDERS.

Unstable, with serious signs or symptoms* → YES

No, borderline

SYMPTOMATIC SVT
Supraventricular tachycardias (not including A-flutter/A-fib)

Vagal maneuvers

• **adenosine** 6 mg, rapid IV

If NO change after 2 mins.
• **adenosine** 12 mg, rapid IV (may repeat x1 in 2 mins.)

Complex narrow (less than .12 sec.)

Complex wide (.12 sec. or greater)

B/P?

• **lidocaine** 1.5 mg/kg IV

WIDE-COMPLEX TACHYCARDIA
Uncertain type

• **lidocaine** 1 mg/kg IV

Repeat after 3–5 mins.
• **lidocaine** 0.5 mg/kg IV until max. total 3 mg/kg

With *physician order:*
• **adenosine** 6 mg, rapid IV

After 2 mins.
with *physician order:*
• **adenosine** 12 mg, rapid IV

With *physician order:*
• **bretylium** 5–10 mg/kg IV drip over 10 mins.

VENTRICULAR TACHYCARDIA

• **lidocaine** 1.5 mg/kg IV

• **lidocaine** 0.75 mg/kg IV every 3–5 mins. until max. total 3 mg/kg

Normal or elevated

Low/unstable → Consider *synchronized cardioversion*

With physician order:
• **verapamil** 2.5–5 mg IV

After 15–30 mins., with physician order:
Repeat 5–10 mg IV • **verapamil**

May receive order for
• **propranolol** 1 mg IV

Requires specific *physician order* for each step;
If rhythm is SVT, A-flutter or A-fib, V-tach, consider:
1. • **Valium** 2.5 mg up to 10 mg IV (age dependent)
2. Synchronized cardioversion @ 50 J.
3. Repeat if indicated @ 100 J.
4. Repeat if indicated @ 200 J.
5. Repeat if indicated @ 300 J.
6. Repeat if indicated @ 360 J.

Recontact ER physician for further orders.

*Unstable condition must be related to the tachycardia. S/S may include chest pain, shortness of breath, decreased level of consciousness, low blood pressure, shock, pulmonary congestion, CHF, AMI.

ATRIAL FIBRILLATION AND ATRIAL FLUTTER
ALBUQUERQUE, NM

Atrial Fibrillation and Atrial Flutter

Designation of Condition

The patient will have a heart rate greater than 150 with atrial flutter or **new onset** atrial fibrillation on the EKG.

Field Treatment

- If the patient is SOB, has chest pain, is hypotensive, or has decreased mental status:
- **Contact MCEP.**
  - Sedate with **diazepam** (Valium, 2–5 mg increments, SIVP as appropriate up to a total dose of 0.2 mg/kg).
  - **Atrial fibrillation**—Synchronized cardioversion at 100 joules; proceed to 200, 300, 360 joules as needed for conversion.
  - **Atrial flutter**—Synchronized cardioversion at 50 joules; proceed to 100, 200, 300, 360 joules as needed for conversion.

ATRIAL FIBRILLATION AND ATRIAL FLUTTER
MEMPHIS, TN

Atrial Fibrillation and Flutter

A. Assessment
   - (Paroxysmal atrial tachycardia)
   - Atrial flutter
   - Atrial fibrillation
   - Symptomatic

B. Treatment

   1. Oxygen at flow rate appropriate to patient's condition
   2. IV access
   3. Valsalva maneuver

Contact medical control; consider:

   If blood pressure is stable, administer verapamil 2.5–5 mg IV slowly over two minutes.

   Synchronous cardioversion (Valium 5 mg IV if conscious)
   Atrial flutter @ 50 joules
   Atrial fibrillation @ 100 joules

NOTE: When treating the elderly or patients who have blood pressures in the lower range of normal, a lower dose of verapamil (2–4 mg) is given over a longer period of time (3–4 mins.).

Immediate synchronized cardioversion (100/200/300/360 joules) is recommended when there is an unstable rhythm with serious signs and symptoms (*i.e.*, chest pain, shortness of breath, decreased level of consciousness, low blood pressure).

ATRIAL FIBRILLATION/ATRIAL FLUTTER
AUSTIN, TX

Introduction

These patients present a peculiar problem in terms of treatment. Many people are able to live with atrial arrhythmias for long periods of time without showing any signs or symptoms; unfortunately, when the ventricular rate increases, these patients can become hemodynamically unstable, thus requiring intervention. Special attention needs to be given to these patients given their potential for CVAs due to the irregularity of this rhythm.

Key Actions

ALS
1. Monitor EKG, Pulse Oximetry, and 12-Lead EKG.
2. Initiate IV lifeline(s) PRN.
3. Verapamil 5 mg IV
4. Aspirin 5 gr chew/swallow
5. Cardioversion for extremely unstable patients.

Assessment Considerations

None

Special Situations/Conditions

Above treatment modality should only be considered in a patient with new onset or a patient with chronic problems associated with unstable vital signs.

© *Austin/Travis EMS Clinical Practice*

THROMBOLYTIC THERAPY STUDY
HOUSTON, TX

Thrombolytic Therapy Study

In the era of evolving early thrombolytic therapy for patients with acute myocardial ischemia in progress, it is incumbent upon EMS personnel to *rapidly* identify patients who are potential candidates for this important time-dependent intervention.

Effective immediately, the Houston Fire Department will begin a Thrombolytic Therapy Study (TTS), which will examine the feasibility of administering thrombolytic therapy in the prehospital environment. Only paramedics who have completed the training on the operation of the Marquette 1500 Responder monitor/defibrillator *and* the administration of thrombolytic agents (tissue plasminogen activator (TPA), heparin, and aspirin) shall be permitted to function under the study protocol.

The following ALS (medic) units have been equipped to participate in the Thrombolytic Therapy Study:

Medic 1	Medic 29
Medic 3	Medic 33
Medic 7	Medic 40
Medic 9	Medic 46
Medic 18	Medic 55

The cellular telephones installed on the forementioned units shall be used for sending a 12-lead ECG and obtaining ECG interpretation and verbal orders for thrombolytic therapy from the TTS physician. *Unauthorized use of these phones SHALL be dealt with in accordance with departmental policy.* The monitor/defibrillator shall be fastened securely to the monitor/defibrillator bracket or in the securing strap provided whenever it is used in the patient compartment during transport.

Paramedics (as outlined in paragraph two above) working on the specially equipped medic units shall utilize the Chest Pain Evaluation Form (*CPEF* updated 10/92) for the TTS whenever a patient meets the following criteria:

1. Nontraumatic chest pain
2. Age 40–80
3. Destination Ben Taub

Patients who meet *all* of the inclusion criteria for this study shall be eligible for thrombolytic therapy administered in accordance with the study protocol.

NOTE: The assessment, treatment, transport, and documentation of all other nontraumatic chest-pain patients shall be initiated as outlined in the HFD chest pain protocol (Order #1, March 2, 1992). When a 12-lead ECG is performed on a patient who does not meet the TTS Protocol, the ECG shall *not* be transmitted to the study center.

Thrombolytic Therapy Study Protocol:

When patients are eligible for inclusions, the paramedic shall:

1. Complete CPEF steps 1–7.
2. Transmit the 12-lead ECG obtained in step 6 via cellular or land-line telephone, to the study center.
3. Contact the base station via telephone, identify the patient as a TTS protocol patient, and request a three-way communication with the TTS physician in order to:

   A. Verify the 12-lead transmission was received
   B. Report patient-assessment findings
   C. Obtain verbal interpretation of the 12-lead ECG
   D. Obtain verbal order to administer:

   > 20 mg TPA, IV bolus
   > 5,000 units heparin, IV bolus
   > 160 mg aspirin, PO

4. Complete CPEF steps 8–11.
5. TTS patients shall be presented to the emergency department physician with a complete, concise report of assessment findings and treatment provided. The TTS yellow-top tube and the appropriately completed CPEF and the 12-lead ECG strips shall be given to the base-station personnel prior to returning to service.

NOTE: Contact with the TTS physician via the base station should be done while at the scene. However, if the patient is unstable, rapid transport should not be delayed and contact with the TTS physician should be made en route to the hospital.

If the patient's condition warrants further medical orders, the paramedic shall request them through the base-station physician at Ben Taub.

DOCUMENTATION:
For TTS patients, the paramedic shall include the following information in the HFD Form 188, 188A:
1. Study Code B box—"12"
2. Narrative section:

   A. Name of TTS physician
   B. TTS physician's 12-lead ECG interpretation
   C. Name(s) of thrombolytic agent(s), dose, route, and rate of each

SUPPLIES:
Supplies required for this study (*i.e.*, ECG recording tape, defibrillation pads, chest pain evaluation forms, TTS yellow-top tubes, and TTS drugs) will be issued by the TTS coordinator during normal business hours.

REPAIRS:

If the Marquette Responder 1500 monitor/defibrillator or the batteries become nonfunctional, the paramedic in charge shall place this piece of equipment out of service and contact the TTS coordinator at 247-3678 immediately. In such circumstances, the back-up LifePak monitor/defibrillator will be utilized until the Marquette monitor/defibrillator can be repaired and returned.

Any questions concerning this study should be directed to the TTS coordinator at EMS headquarters during business hours by calling 247-1674 or 247-3678.

RESPIRATORY ARREST OR INSUFFICIENCY
PHOENIX, AZ

Respiratory Arrest or Insufficiency

Bronchospasm, Overdose, or Anaphylaxis

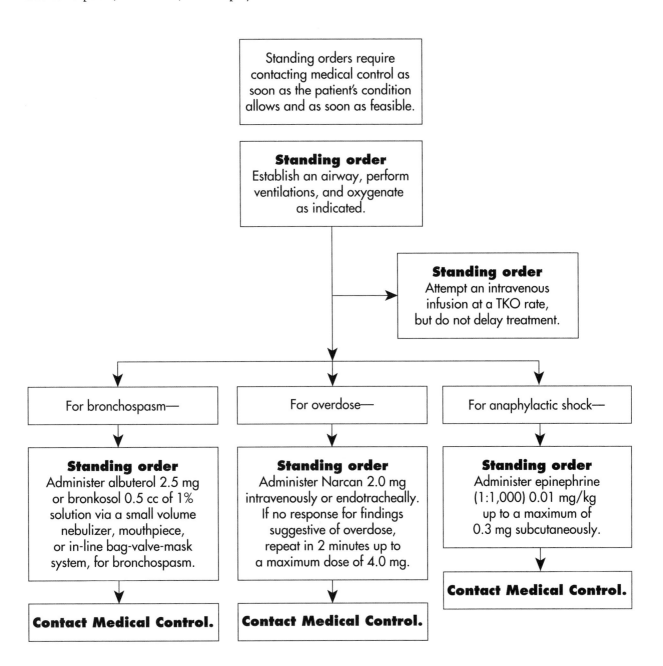

Standing orders require contacting medical control as soon as the patient's condition allows and as soon as feasible.

Standing order
Establish an airway, perform ventilations, and oxygenate as indicated.

Standing order
Attempt an intravenous infusion at a TKO rate, but do not delay treatment.

For bronchospasm—

For overdose—

For anaphylactic shock—

Standing order
Administer albuterol 2.5 mg or bronkosol 0.5 cc of 1% solution via a small volume nebulizer, mouthpiece, or in-line bag-valve-mask system, for bronchospasm.

Standing order
Administer Narcan 2.0 mg intravenously or endotracheally. If no response for findings suggestive of overdose, repeat in 2 minutes up to a maximum dose of 4.0 mg.

Standing order
Administer epinephrine (1:1,000) 0.01 mg/kg up to a maximum of 0.3 mg subcutaneously.

Contact Medical Control.

Contact Medical Control.

Contact Medical Control.

RESPIRATORY ARREST OR INSUFFICIENCY
PHILADELPHIA, PA

Apnea/Inadequate Respiration

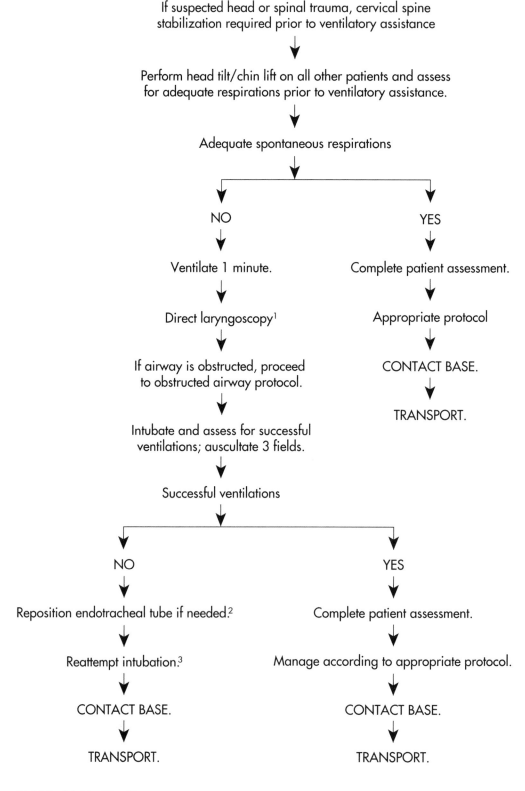

If suspected head or spinal trauma, cervical spine stabilization required prior to ventilatory assistance

↓

Perform head tilt/chin lift on all other patients and assess for adequate respirations prior to ventilatory assistance.

↓

Adequate spontaneous respirations

NO

Ventilate 1 minute.

↓

Direct laryngoscopy[1]

↓

If airway is obstructed, proceed to obstructed airway protocol.

↓

Intubate and assess for successful ventilations; auscultate 3 fields.

↓

Successful ventilations

NO

Reposition endotracheal tube if needed.[2]

↓

Reattempt intubation.[3]

↓

CONTACT BASE.

↓

TRANSPORT.

YES

Complete patient assessment.

↓

Appropriate protocol

↓

CONTACT BASE.

↓

TRANSPORT.

YES

Complete patient assessment.

↓

Manage according to appropriate protocol.

↓

CONTACT BASE.

↓

TRANSPORT.

© *Philadelphia Fire Department*

AIRWAY-MANAGEMENT PROBLEMS
SANTA ANA, CA

Airway-Management Problems

Mucus-Obstructed Tracheostomy:

ACTION/TREATMENT:
- If inner cannula in place—remove.
- Attempt to suction.
- Instill 5 ml normal saline into tracheostomy (use 10- or 12-ml syringe without needle) upon patient inspiration.
- Suction.

Expelled Tracheostomy Tube:

ACTION/TREATMENT:
- Suction if necessary.
- Insert nasopharyngeal airway into stoma to maintain patency.
- Clean tracheostomy tube using patient supplies such as soap and water and/or hydrogen peroxide.
- Remove nasopharyngeal airway.
- Reinsert tracheostomy tube.
- Secure anchor ties of tracheostomy tube around neck.

Respiratory Arrest in Stoma Patient:

ACTION/TREATMENT:
- Suction stoma to ensure patent airway.
- Select proper-size endotracheal tube.
- Test cuff inflation prior to use.
- Lubricate endotracheal tube with lubricating jelly.
- Insert tube into stoma.
- Ventilate and auscultate for bilateral breath sounds.
  —If breath sounds absent on one side, pull back on ET tube and reasses.
- Inflate cuff with minimum amount of air (3–5 ml).
- Ventilate and auscultate bilateral breath sounds.
- When bilateral breath sounds noted, ventilate using 100% oxygen.

Airway Obstruction in the Unconscious Patient:

ACTION/TREATMENT:
- If BLS methods are unsuccessful in relieving the airway obstruction, visualize airway with laryngoscope and remove visible foreign body using Magill forceps.
- Needle cricothyrotomy

LARYNGOSPASM
DURHAM, NC

Laryngospasm

Criteria

Usually occurs in the setting of inhalation injury, drowning, aspiration, or allergic reaction and is manifested by severe SOB and stridor

Standing Orders

1. Assess for foreign body in airway.
2. Appropriate airway management and oxygen. Monitor.

EMT-I
3. Consider IV LR KVO.
4. Epinephrine 1:1000 0.3–0.5 cc SC/IM

EMT-P
5. Intubate if indicated.

Contact Medical Control.

6. Medical control may order from among the following for patients in extreme distress:

   a. Epinephrine 1:1000 0.5 cc in 3 cc NS via aerosol
   b. Atropine 0.5–1.0 mg via aerosol
   c. Epinephrine 1:10,000 2–5 cc IV

ABDOMINAL PAIN
EUGENE/SPRINGFIELD, OR

Abdominal Pain

I. Specific Information Needed (subjective information):

  A. Pain: nature, duration, location, radiation; onset sudden or gradual
  B. Associated symptoms: nausea, vomiting (bloody or coffee-ground), diarrhea, constipation, melena (tarry or bloody stool), urinary difficulties, menstrual history, fever, postural hypotension, referred shoulder pain
  C. History: previous trauma, abnormal ingestion, medications, known diseases, surgery

II. Specific Physical Findings (objective information):

  A. Vital signs
  B. Abdomen: bruising, tenderness, guarding, rebound tenderness, rigidity, bowel sounds, distention, pulsating mass
  C. Emesis: type, amount
  D. Equality of peripheral pulses on suspected aneurysm

III. Treatment:

  A. Assess and support ABCs.
  B. Position of comfort. Place supine if trauma or hypotension/syncope.
  C. NPO (nothing by mouth)
  D. If vitals are unstable or pain is severe (or if mechanism of injury warrants or you suspect GI bleeding):

   1. Oxygen therapy
   2. Start IV (EMT 2, 3, 4) of normal saline with standard tubing and titrate fluid to patient needs. Use shock protocol if indicated.
   3. Consider PASG application; inflate as needed per PASG protocol (EMT 1, 2, 3, 4).

  E. Monitor vitals during transport.
  F. Consider cardiac monitor.

IV. Specific Precautions:

  A. Abdominal pain may be the first warning of catastrophic internal bleeding (ruptured aneurysm, liver, spleen, ectopic pregnancy, *etc.*). Since the bleeding is not apparent, you must think of volume depletion and monitor patient closely to recognize early shock.
  B. Analgesic administration in abdominal pain is usually contraindicated in the field since it may mask signs/symptoms of life-threatening problems.
  C. The patient's c/c of "abdominal pain" may in fact be cardiac-related. Maintain a high index of suspicion, especially if the pain is epigastric and patient is in the cardiac age group.
  D. Use caution with fluid administration in patients with suspected dissecting abdominal aneurysm. Try not to exceed systolic BP of 90–110 torr since a higher pressure may worsen the internal bleeding.

ABDOMINAL PAIN
SANTA ANA, CA

Abdominal Pain: Nontraumatic

Action/Treatment:

- ABCs/Monitor cardiac rhythm.
- IV access titrated to perfusion as needed
- Morphine sulfate: 2–20 mg IVP titrated to pain

Shaded text indicates BH order.
Unshaded text indicates standing order.

RENAL DIALYSIS
COLUMBUS, OH

Renal Dialysis Patients

1. Problems:
   A. **Pulmonary Edema:** See PULMONARY EDEMA PROTOCOL. "Load and Go."
   B. **Dysrhythmia:** See CARDIO PROTOCOLS.
   C. **Hypertensive Crisis:** 10 mg of sublingual NIFEDIPINE; may repeat NIFEDIPINE in 15 minutes
   D. **Air Embolus:** Place patient with left side down.
   E. **Aspiration:** Ventilatory support as indicated
   F. **Hypotension:** 0.9% NORMAL SALINE 300 cc, IV rapidly infused.
   G. **Hyperkalemia:** for ventricular fibrillation, asystole, or pulseless electrical activity (EMD) with suspected hyperkalemia, push 1 mEq/kg of SODIUM BICARBONATE IVP and 50 ml of 50% DEXTROSE IV push.

CAUTION: Must not give fluid bolus to patient in pulmonary edema. In these patients, look for other causes of hypotension (*i.e.*, cardiogenic shock).

2. Cautions:
   A. Do not take blood pressure on limb with shunts or fistula.
   B. Do not start IV on limb with shunts or fistula except in rapid deterioration of vital signs and no venous access.
   C. Accidental break or rupture of shunt leads to rapid blood loss. Guard shunt appropriately. Control bleeding by employing standard methods of bleeding control.

3. IV:
   A. 0.9% NORMAL SALINE at keep-open rate with minidripper.

4. Transportation:
   A. If in arrest and not responsive to resuscitative efforts, transport patient to nearest appropriate facility.

5. Personal Precautions:
   A. Serum hepatitis is common in dialysis patients.

RENAL DIALYSIS
INDIANAPOLIS, IN

Care of the Dialysis Patient

THE USE OF UNIVERSAL PRECAUTIONS IS ESPECIALLY IMPORTANT BECAUSE OF THE POSSIBILITY OF EXPOSURE TO BLOOD AND BODY FLUIDS AND THE PROBABILITY OF DIALYSIS PATIENTS BEING CARRIERS OF THE HEPATITIS-B VIRUS.

TREAT ANY PRESENTING PROBLEMS ACCORDING TO THE APPROPRIATE PROTOCOL AND NOTE THE FOLLOWING MODIFICATIONS:

A. Do not take vital signs in an extremity containing a shunt or fistula.
B. Use high-flow oxygen for any noted dyspnea.
C. Do not initiate an IV in an extremity containing a shunt or fistula unless an immediate life-threatening situation exists and there is no other IV site available.
D. If the patient is on the hemodialysis machine, have the dialysis technician disconnect the patient from the machine. If the dialysis technician is not present or is unable to disconnect the patient, turn off the machine. Clamp off the access device and disconnect the patient from the machine.
E. ACCESS DEVICE IS A SHUNT: F. ACCESS DEVICE IS A FISTULA:

E. ACCESS DEVICE IS A SHUNT:	F. ACCESS DEVICE IS A FISTULA:
1. Clamp both sides of the shunt and remove the machine tubing from the shunt.	1. Clamp the needle tubing and remove the needles from the fistula.
2. Put the shunt back together, remove the clamps, and wrap the shunt area in Kerlix.	2. Apply a pressure dressing to the site. Patients being dialyzed are receiving anticoagulant therapy.

G. If the patient is on continuous ambulatory peritoneal dialysis (CAPD), unclamp drainage tube and allow fluid in the peritoneal cavity to drain back into the bag.
H. Be alert for pathological fractures or fractures that might occur as a result of minimal trauma.
I. If a venous or arterial air embolus is suspected, immediately place the patient in Trendelenburg position on the left side.
J. Do not use Ringer's lactate for fluid replacement.
K. Lasix is of no value.
L. For refractory ventricular fibrillation, calcium may be indicated. Consult medical control.

Trauma Airway

(OBSTRUCTED AIRWAY, INADEQUATE VENTILATION)

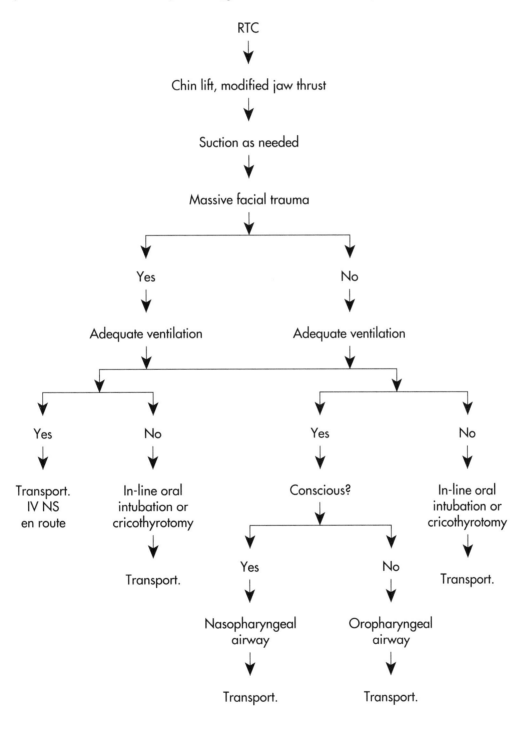

© 1996, Chicago Project Medical Directors Consortium

AMPUTATIONS
CHARLOTTE, NC

Amputations

History

1. Any traumatic insult resulting in loss of limb

Physical

1. Proximal extremity may result in severe hemorrhage, but vessels may be tamponaded upon arrival.

Differential

Amputation from accidental trauma
Amputation from self-inflicted injury

Protocol

1. Maintain airway, administer oxygen via nonrebreathing mask at 15 l/min. if patient appears to be in severe distress. Otherwise, administer oxygen via nasal cannula 2–6 l/min.
2. Protect C-spine with in-line stabilization until C-collar, head immobilization, and backboard are placed when trauma to head or spine is suspected.
3. If spinal trauma is not suspected, place patient in most comfortable position and reassure.
4. Identify and control any active-bleeding sites with manual direct pressure and/or pressure dressing.
5. Remove appropriate clothing in order to fully inspect the chest, abdomen, and extremities for any other significant injuries.
6. Attempt to locate amputated appendage or part. Gently irrigate with normal saline and wrap in sterile gauze moistened with normal saline. Place in plastic bag and put bag on ice (if available) and transport to hospital with patient.
7. Initiate transport to appropriate receiving facility as dictated in the trauma triage protocol. Continue to monitor vital signs and neurological status while en route.
8. Consider and administer the following therapeutic intervention:

   IV normal saline:
   No hemodynamic instability
   TKO

   Hemodynamic instability

Wide open

9. Contact medical control en route. The following interventions may be considered:

> Morphine sulfate 2–10 mg IV
> Nitrous oxide via patient-controlled inhalation

Addendum

1. IV lines may be started at the scene if this procedure can be performed in less than 2 minutes; otherwise, initiate IV line(s) en route.

2. Unless entrapment or rescue operations occur, total scene time should not exceed 15 minutes. Patients sustaining traumatic insults who are not entrapped should be transported to a trauma center for definitive care within 30 minutes from the time that the injury occured.

3. Isolated extremity injuries are not an indication for transporting to a trauma center.

4. Do not grossly prolong the scene time attempting to locate an amputated part. This task may be accomplished by other personnel on the scene.

5. Primary avulsed teeth (age < 5 years old) are not replaced. Secondary avulsed teeth may be replanted after irrigating with tap water or saline. Irrigation should be done gently without debriding or scrubbing the tooth. Replace the tooth in the socket if the patient will tolerate this. Otherwise, the tooth may be transported in the patient's cheek or in a container of milk.

ELECTROCUTION INJURIES
ARLINGTON, TX

Electrocution Injuries

NOTE: In addition to burns, be responsive to the high probability of associated injuries such as cardiac disturbances, musculoskeletal injuries secondary to forces involved with electrocution, blunt/penetrating trauma.

Treatment:

1. Maintain C-Spine immobilization as appropriate. Establish and maintain airway as appropriate. Intubate as needed.
2. Administer high-flow oxygen as appropriate.
3. Continuous cardiac monitoring, referring to the appropriate dysrhythmia algorithm as needed
4. Establish one (1) or two (2) large-bore IV accesses with Ringer's lactate. Fluid rate to maintain B/P > 100.
5. Strongly consider transport to Parkland Burn Center.
6. **Contact medical control.**

Physician Orders

- Morphine sulfate **2–10 mg** slow IVP
- Phenergan **12.5–25 mg** slow IVP

NOTE: Always assess severity of entrance and exit wounds and all organs in between.

Heat Cramps/Heat Exhaustion/Heat Stroke

	HEAT CRAMPS	HEAT EXHAUSTION	HEAT STROKE
Skin	Pale, excessive perspiration	Pale, cool, clammy	Hot, dry, first ruddy, later gray
Body Temperature	Normal or slightly elevated	Usually normal, subnormal, or elevated	Rapidly rising to 39° C (102.2° F)
Pulse	Rapid, strong	Rapid, weak	Rapid and full at first, then weak and thready
Blood Pressure	Normal	Decreased	Increased, then decreased
Pupils	Normal	Dilated	Dilated
Body Odor	Normal perspiration	Normal	Offensive
Muscle Cramps	Severe	None	None
Convulsions	Generalized twitching	Rare	Epileptiform in early stages
Nausea and Vomiting	Mild nausea, vomiting rare	May be prolonged	Usually does not occur
State of Consciousness	Normal	Stupor, coma in severe cases	Early loss of consciousness
Pain	Severe from muscle cramping	Headaches in mild cases	Only at onset

Heat Exhaustion

SIGNS AND SYMPTOMS:

A. Profuse sweating
B. Near-normal temperature
C. Orthostatic hypotension
D. Normal or altered consciousness
E. May be young—followed physical activity

TREATMENT:

1. ABCs
2. Vital signs, administer OXYGEN—100% by mask.
3. Monitor.
4. IV 0.9% NORMAL SALINE
5. Remove from heated environment
6. Transport.

Heat Stroke

SIGNS AND SYMPTOMS:

A. Extremely high temperature—hot to touch
B. Sweating variable
C. Flushed appearance
D. Altered consciousness
E. Usually elderly—on various medications

TREATMENT:

1. ABCs
2. Vital signs, administer OXYGEN—100% by mask.
3. Monitor.
4. IV 0.9% NORMAL SALINE
5. Support patient.
6. Cool with ice packs or water if immediately available.
7. Transport without delay.

Hypothermia/Cold Injuries

I. Specific Information Needed (Subjective Information):

    A. Length of exposure? Dry vs. immersion? Any drugs including alcohol?

II. Specific Physical Findings (Objective Information):

    A. Apnea—If suspected breathing is not obvious, put metal under nostrils for 30–45 seconds to confirm (looking for condensation to document respiratory exchange).

    B. Pulse—Palpate carotid pulse for 30–45 seconds. (Bradycardia is common.)

    C. EKG—Attach EKG leads and interpret rhythm.

    D. Mental Status—Determine verbal and motor responsiveness (GCS).

    E. Shivering

III. Treatment of Severe Generalized Hypothermia:

    A. ABCs. Start CPR if pulseless.

    B. Oxygen, warmed if possible. Assist ventilations as needed.

    C. Intubate (EMT 3, 4) if patient is unconscious with inadequate ventilations.

    D. Monitor cardiac rhythm. If in VF/VT deliver up to 3 shocks. If suspected severe hypothermia, use hypothermia algorithm (last page of this protocol). If unsure whether severe hypothermia, use regular ACLS algorithms.

    E. IV (EMT 2, 3, 4)—Use warmed solution if possible. Recommended rate: 500 ml bolus, then 200 ml/hour titrated to patient.

IV. Specific Precautions with Severe Generalized Hypothermia:

    A. Handle patient who has profound hypothermia and is in an organized cardiac rhythm gently to avoid dysrhythmias. (Remember that V Fib can occur at core temperature less than 30° C (86° F). Many physical manipulations, including intubation, external pacing, *etc.*, have been reported to precipitate VF. However, when specifically and urgently indicated, such procedures should not be withheld.

    B. Do not force oral intubation. Avoid nasotracheal intubation. Consider cricothyrotomy (needle or nutrake) only if patient deteriorates *AND* jaw is frozen.

    C. Bradycardia may be physiologic in severe hypothermia. Cardiac pacing is usually not indicated unless bradycardia persists after rewarming.

    D. The hypothermic heart may be unresponsive to cardioactive drugs, pacemaker stimulation, and defibrillation. Drug metabolism is reduced. Administered medications, including epinephrine and lidocaine, can accumulate to toxic levels if used repeatedly in the severely hypothermic patient. Active core-rewarming techniques at the hospital are the primary therapeutic modality in hypothermic patients in cardiac arrest or unconscious with a slow heart rate.

    E. Consider other protocols as appropriate (*i.e.*, altered mental status). Hypothermia may be a complication of hypoglycemia and vice versa.

F. Suspect "urban" hypothermia in situations with elderly patients or poverty and drug or alcohol use.

G. Patients are generally not pronounced dead until warmed.

H. Consult with ED about further therapies or direction of care when unclear about degree of hypothermia.

V. General Information for Severe Generalized Hypothermia:

A. Severe accidental hypothermia is currently defined in ACLS guidelines as core temperature below 30° C (86° F). Realize that most thermometers do not register below 94° F (34° C).

B. Shivering occurs between 90 and 98° F (32–37° C) but is absent or minimal below this, so it can be a useful guide to the degree of hypothermia.

C. The heart is most likely to fibrillate between 85 and 88° F (29–31° C). It may not convert readily until the patient's temperature is above 88° F (31° C) and acidosis is corrected.

VI. Treatment of Local (Frostbite) Hypothermia:

A. Protect the injured areas from pressure, trauma, friction. Remove all covering from injured parts. Do not rub. Do not break blisters.

B. Do not allow the patient to ambulate or use nicotine products.

C. Do not allow limb to thaw if there is a chance that limb may refreeze before evacuation is complete.

D. Maintain core temperature by keeping patient warm with blankets, warm fluids, *etc*.

E. Transport.

F. When severe hypothermia and frostbite coexist, treat the patient as for generalized hypothermia.

SEE ALGORITHM ON LAST PAGE OF THIS PROTOCOL FOR ACLS RECOMMENDATIONS ON TREATMENT OF GENERAL HYPOTHERMIA.

REFERENCE CHART TO COMPARE CELSIUS TO FAHRENHEIT TEMPERATURES

CENTIGRADE (CELSIUS)	FAHRENHEIT	CENTIGRADE (CELSIUS)	FAHRENHEIT	CENTIGRADE (CELSIUS)	FAHRENHEIT
0	32	36.5	97.7	39.5	103.1
30.0	86.0	37.0	98.6	40.0	104.0
32.2	90.0	37.5	99.5	40.5	104.9
34.0	93.0	38.0	100.4	41.0	105.8
35.0	95.0	38.5	101.3	41.5	106.7
36.0	96.8	39.0	102.2	42.0	107.6

ACLS Algorithm for Treatment of Severe Hypothermia

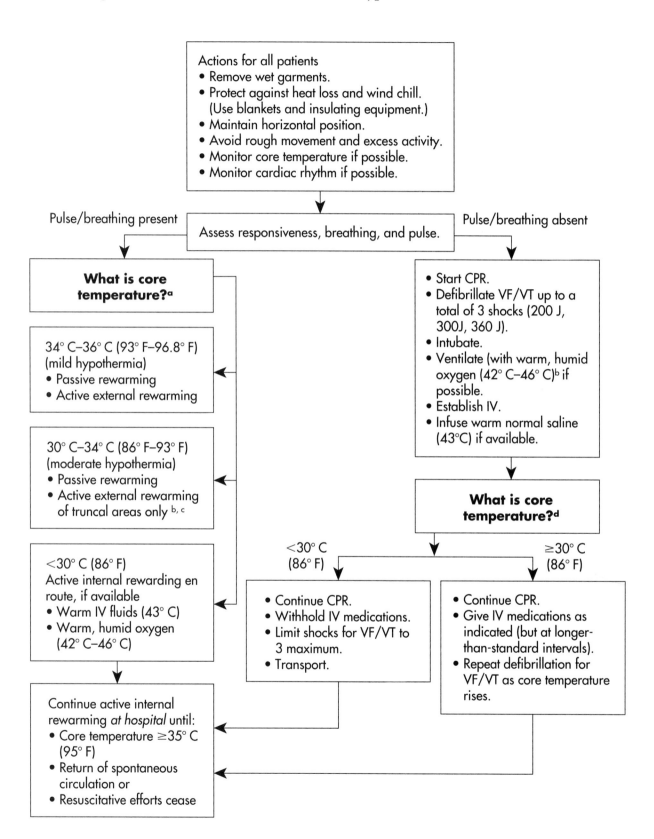

Actions for all patients
- Remove wet garments.
- Protect against heat loss and wind chill. (Use blankets and insulating equipment.)
- Maintain horizontal position.
- Avoid rough movement and excess activity.
- Monitor core temperature if possible.
- Monitor cardiac rhythm if possible.

Assess responsiveness, breathing, and pulse.

Pulse/breathing present

Pulse/breathing absent

What is core temperature?[a]

34° C–36° C (93° F–96.8° F) (mild hypothermia)
- Passive rewarming
- Active external rewarming

30° C–34° C (86° F–93° F) (moderate hypothermia)
- Passive rewarming
- Active external rewarming of truncal areas only [b, c]

<30° C (86° F) Active internal rewarding en route, if available
- Warm IV fluids (43° C)
- Warm, humid oxygen (42° C–46° C)

Continue active internal rewarming *at hospital* until:
- Core temperature ≥35° C (95° F)
- Return of spontaneous circulation or
- Resuscitative efforts cease

- Start CPR.
- Defibrillate VF/VT up to a total of 3 shocks (200 J, 300J, 360 J).
- Intubate.
- Ventilate (with warm, humid oxygen (42° C–46° C)[b] if possible.
- Establish IV.
- Infuse warm normal saline (43°C) if available.

What is core temperature?[d]

<30° C (86° F)

≥30° C (86° F)

- Continue CPR.
- Withhold IV medications.
- Limit shocks for VF/VT to 3 maximum.
- Transport.

- Continue CPR.
- Give IV medications as indicated (but at longer-than-standard intervals).
- Repeat defibrillation for VF/VT as core temperature rises.

[a]If unable to accurately assess core temperature in patient who is not in cardiac arrest, use shivering as a rough clinical guideline. If the patient is shivering, the hypothermia is mild to moderate.

[b]Many experts think these interventions should be done only in-hospital, though practices vary.

[c]Methods of active external rewarming include hot-water bottles, heating pads, radiant-heat sources. Take measures to prevent burning patient. Truncal areas include neck, armpits, and groin.

[d]If unable to accurately assess core temperature in arrested patient and unsure whether this patient is severely hypothermic, use routine ACLS guidelines.

HYPOTHERMIA
RENO, NV

Hypothermia
Priorities:

These patients appear dead but may be salvageable. The monitor often shows a slow atrial fibrillation or sinus bradycardia. In isolated hypothermia, CPR is indicated only for situations without a perfusing rhythm (*i.e.*, V-fib/asystole). CPR should be withheld for other pulseless rhythms such as atrial fibrillation or bradycardias, as these are usually adequately managed with rewarming. While no pulse may be present, these patients often have undetectable but life-sustaining cardiac function. Patients must be handled very gently to avoid producing ventricular fibrillation unresponsive to therapy.

Treatment:

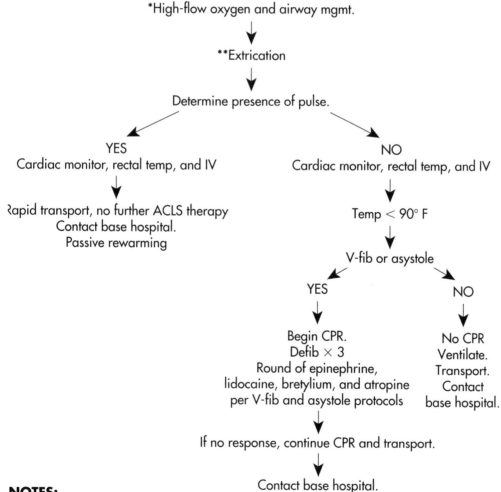

*High-flow oxygen and airway mgmt.
↓
**Extrication
↓
Determine presence of pulse.

YES
Cardiac monitor, rectal temp, and IV
↓
Rapid transport, no further ACLS therapy
Contact base hospital.
Passive rewarming

NO
Cardiac monitor, rectal temp, and IV
↓
Temp < 90° F
↓
V-fib or asystole

YES
↓
Begin CPR.
Defib × 3
Round of epinephrine,
lidocaine, bretylium, and atropine
per V-fib and asystole protocols
↓
If no response, continue CPR and transport.
↓
Contact base hospital.

NO
↓
No CPR
Ventilate.
Transport.
Contact
base hospital.

NOTES:
*1. High-flow oxygen on all patients and airway management as indicated (including intubation).

**2. Extricate to warm environment with removal of wet garments and constricting clothing. Passive rewarming with dry blankets and insulating material.

3. If altered mental status, see altered mental status protocol.

BAROTRAUMA
NORFOLK, VA

Barotrauma

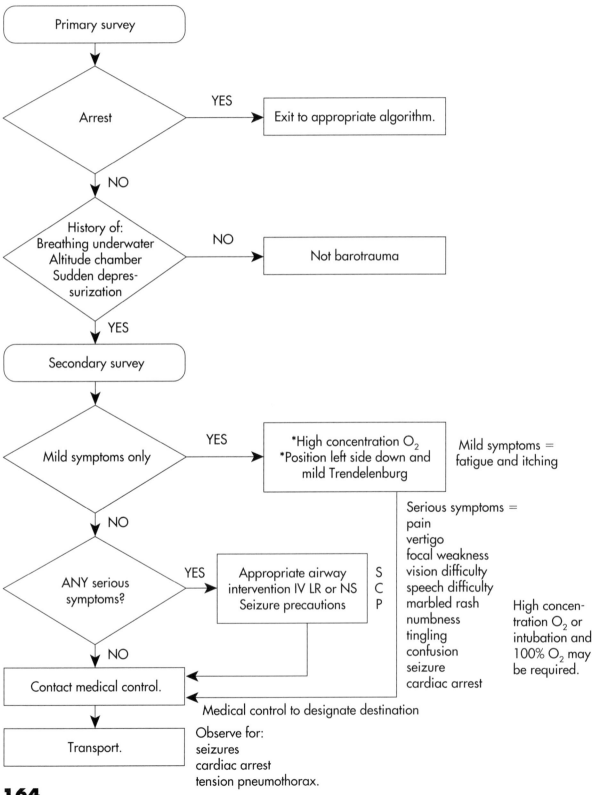

DECOMPRESSION
LOS ANGELES, CA

Decompression Emergency

FIELD TREATMENT

1. Basic airway/spinal-immobilization prn

Note 6

2. Oxygen

Note 6

3. Left lateral Trendelenburg position
4. Advanced airway prn
5. Cardiac monitor
6. Venous access prn
7. If hypotension, fluid challenge

Note 8

8. If hypotension unresponsive to fluid challenge,
   dopamine 200 mg/250 ml NS at 30 mc gtts/minute

Notes: 1, 2

9. If active grand mal seizure, **Valium® 5–10 mg** IVP
   titrated to control seizure activity

Notes: 3, 4, 5
☞ May repeat prn

Drug Considerations

Dopamine

1. Titrate to systolic BP 90–100 and signs of adequate perfusion.
2. Pediatrics: not recommended.

Valium® (diazepam):

3. Maximum adult dose: 20 mg
4. Pediatrics: 0.2 mg/kg IVP. If venous access unobtainable, administer
   0.5 mg/kg rectally.
5. Monitor airway constantly after administration.

Special Considerations

6. Consider hypothermia.
7. Oxygen-powered breathing devices should not be used in these patients.
8. Give only if breath sounds are clear bilaterally.

AIR EMBOLISM
ANAHEIM, CA

Air Embolism

1. Perform primary survey. Initiate cardiopulmonary resuscitation as indicated.

NOTE: Onset of signs and symptoms is rapid.

2. Oxygen: Administer 100%.
3. Monitor cardiac rhythm.
4. Place in 30 degrees Trendelenburg, left-lateral recumbent position.
5. Perform appropriate secondary survey and intervene appropriately. Check for tension pneumothorax and treat according to treatment guideline.
6. BASE HOSPITAL CONTACT: Required *ON PATIENT CLASSIFIED AS MODERATE, ACUTE, OR FULL ARREST.*
7. Start an IV 250 ml D_5W and run at 10–20 microdrops.

NOTE: Base hospital will arrange for transport to hyperbaric chamber.

8. Transport Code: Optional: Unless critical or full-arrest status, then Code III. Escort: Required *ON PATIENT CLASSIFIED AS MODERATE, ACUTE, OR FULL ARREST.*

SPECIAL NOTE:
- Severe loss of body heat that may cause blackout and fatigue is a common problem with divers and should be considered. These symptoms may lead to panic and near drowning.
- If intubation is required prior to transport to hyperbaric chamber, consider saline, equivalent amount, in place of air in the cuff.

HAZARDOUS MATERIALS
LOS ANGELES, CA

Hazardous Materials

FIELD TREATMENT

1. Contact HazMat resources according to departmental protocol.
2. Secure area.

Notes: 2, 3

3. Basic airway/spinal immobilization prn
4. Oxygen
5. Advanced airway prn
6. Cardiac monitor

Note 4

7. Venous access prn
8. If hypotension, consider fluid challenge.
9. If respiratory wheezing, consider **albuterol 2.5 mg/3 ml NS** via hand-held nebulizer.

Note 1
☞May repeat prn

Drug Considerations

Albuterol:

1. Pediatrics:
0–2 years—1.25 mg/1.5 ml NS
Over 2 years—adult dose

Special Considerations

2. Measures to secure area:

Wear protective equipment/gear.
Begin decontamination procedures and do not transport until fully decontaminated.

3. If eye involvement, continuous flushing with NS during transport. Allow patient to remove contact lenses if possible.

4. Dysrhythmias are common with toxic inhalation — see appropriate dysrhythmia guideline.

© 1992, Los Angeles County Base Hospital Treatment Guidelines

CYANIDE PROTOCOL
COLUMBUS, OH

Cyanide Protocol

1. Assure that the patient is decontaminated or poses no risk to those resuscitating the victim. Wear protective clothing if necessary.
2. Establish an airway; intubate if necessary; administer oxygen—100% by mask.
3. Begin IV of 0.9% NORMAL SALINE.
4. Administer 12.5 gm of SODIUM THIOSULFATE (50 ml of a 25% solution IV push) over 5 minutes. Pediatric dose is 1.65 cc/kg. This step should be omitted in victims suffering from sulfide exposure since this step occurs naturally. (Hydrogen sulfide, sulfur.)
7. This drug therapy is in addition to ventilation, respiratory support, oxygen, and rapid transport after adequate decontamination and/or protection.
8. Consider the use of SODIUM BICARBONATE 1–2 meq/kg IV push if exposure prolonged.

DYSTONIC REACTION
LOS ANGELES, CA

Dystonic Reaction

FIELD TREATMENT

1. Basic airway
2. Oxygen prn
3. Venous access
4. **Benadryl® 50–100 mg** IVP

Notes: 1, 2

Drug Considerations

Benadryl® (diphenhydramine):

1. Alternate route: deep IM
2. Pediatrics: 1 mg/kg IVP

© 1992, Los Angeles County Base Hospital Treatment Guidelines

PAIN CONTROL
COLUMBUS, OH

Pain Control

NUBAIN 5–10 mg IVP can be administered for severe pain in the following situations with adults and 0.1 mg/kg for pediatric patients.

1. Partial thickness burns without hypotension
2. Extremity trauma without hypotension
3. Avulsions or amputations without hypotension

If hypotension develops after NUBAIN is given, a fluid bolus of 200 cc should be given.

If respiratory depression occurs after NUBAIN is given, NARCAN 2 mg IVP should be administered and intubation considered.

PAIN CONTROL
PITTSBURGH, PA

Pain Control

Indication:

Patients in significant pain due to isolated injury or medical condition

Exclusions:

1. Major traumas to head, chest, abdomen, or pelvis follow appropriate protocol.
2. Patients with chest pain who meet criteria for Protocol 301 (Chest Pain)

Protocol:

1. PERFORM THOROUGH ASSESSMENT to rule out major trauma or serious medical problems. Continuously monitor vitals, pulse ox, and mental status for early signs of shock.
2. Provide patient with NITROUS OXIDE for self-administration per investigational protocol.
3. IV LR KVO. Command physician may order IVF boluses based on case specifics.
4. CONTACT MEDICAL COMMAND and request EMS physician response.
5. ANALGESIA options:

    A. MORPHINE SULFATE 2–5 mg/dose IV; repeat as tolerated until adequate relief.
    B. KETAMINE 1–2 mg/kg slow IV push or 2–3 mg/kg IM. Additional doses (one-half to full initial dose) may be repeated q 10–20 mins. as needed. It is recommended that Valium be given to prevent late dysphoric sequelae.
    C. STADOL NASAL SPRAY 1–2 mg (1–2 sprays)
    D. Procurement of FENTANYL, MEPERIDINE, or other agents from local hospital
    E. Regional or local anesthesia
    F. VALIUM 2–10 mg IV or Versed 1–10 mg IV as tolerated for amnesia and sedation

NOTE: When using narcotics and benzodiazepines, especially together, observe closely for hypotension and respiratory depression. Have Narcan available.

PAIN CONTROL
KANSAS CITY, MO

Analgesic Medication Administration Protocol

Indications:

The relief of pain in patients with:
Isolated extremity injury
Suspected shoulder/hip injury
Burns
Age 12 and older

Contraindications:

Drug/alcohol intoxication
Head injury
Altered mental status
Suspected spine injury
Multiply injured/severely injured
Hypotensive patients (systolic pressure <110 mm Hg)
Hypertensive patients (systolic pressure >180 mm Hg)
Sensitivity/allergy to Stadol (butorphanol)
Known coronary artery disease
Respiratory compromise. Asthma or COPD.

Procedure:

1. Establish that the patient meets above requirements. Patient's injuries MUST be treated PRIOR to the administration of any pain medication.
2. Contact medical control and establish need and eligibility.
3. Establish IV lactated Ringer's KVO.
4. Place on cardiac monitor.
5. Record vital signs, mental status, and neurologic exam.
6. Administer 0.5–1.0 mg butorphanol SLOWLY IV, over 1–2 minutes.
7. Closely monitor vital signs and cardiac rhythm.
8. Transport patient as indicated by primary condition, closely monitoring vital signs, respiratory effort, and level of consciousness.
9. Naloxone (Narcan) may be used to reverse respiratory depression and hypotensive effects as needed.

NAUSEA/VOMITING
ARLINGTON, TX

Nausea/Vomiting

Treatment:

1. Establish and maintain airway as appropriate.
2. Monitor for the need to suction.
3. Cardiac monitoring as appropriate
4. Establish IV access with Ringer's lactate.
5. Contact medical control.

Physician Orders

Administer phenergan 12.5–25 mg IVP or IM.

NOTE: Phenergan is contraindicated in the following conditions:
- Head injuries
- Possible acute abdomen
- Patients with allergies to any phenothiazines
- Use caution in pregnant patients.

NOTE: Phenergan may cause extrapyramidal symptoms, *i.e.*, dystonic reactions, muscle rigidity, *etc*. This is not an allergic reaction but a side effect of phenothiazines. These symptoms may be reversed with **50 mg** Benadryl IVP or IM.

NOTE: Monitor blood pressure carefully.

SNAKEBITE
SANTA ANA, CA

Snake Envenomation

Action/Treatment:

- ABCs/monitor cardiac rhythm.
- Minimize patient movement.
- Keep affected extremity below the level of the heart.
- Wound care: mark margin of extent of swelling.
- IV access titrated to perfusion as needed
- Morphine sulfate for severe pain: 2–20 mg IVP titrated to pain

Pediatric:

- Morphine sulfate for severe pain: 0.1 mg/kg slow IVP

NOTES:

- Caution: A dead snake may envenomate.
- Use of a constricting band or cold packs is not recommended.
- IV access frequently indicated due to delayed symptoms

Shaded text indicates BH order.
Unshaded text indicates standing order.

SNAKEBITE
STATE OF MARYLAND

Field Management of Snakebites

1. **INTRODUCTION**

   1.1 The Maryland Poison Information Center, located at the University of Maryland in Baltimore, serves as a specialty center for consultation for victims of snakebites. This center should always be contacted when a patient (seen in the field) has been bitten by a poisonous snake or when it is not known whether the snake in question was poisonous. The Maryland Poison Information Center may be contacted via the radio or telephone procedures established for your jurisdiction for medical consultations. It may also be contacted at the following telephone numbers: in the Baltimore metropolitan area, 301-528-7701; outside the Baltimore metropolitan area, 1-800-492-2414. The following information is provided to aid the prehospital care provider in determining the type of the snake involved and in the assessment and treatment of a snakebite patient. Section 5 of this protocol is the suggested hospital treatment for the snakebite patient and is offered for your information only.

2. **IDENTIFICATION OF SNAKES** (See diagram.)

   2.1 The copperhead (*Akistrodon contortrix mokesen*)

       2.1.1 The copperhead has a beige-to-pinkish-brown color with darker hourglass-shaped bands that are wider at the sides and narrow on the back. Its head is usually a bright copper color. A full-grown snake may reach 24 to 36 inches in length. The copperhead is found throughout Maryland, generally in remote, rocky, wooded areas.

   2.2 The timber rattlesnake (*Crotalus horridus horridus*)

       2.2.1 The timber rattlesnake has zigzag brown or black bands edged with a white or yellow background down its back. The background color may vary from bright yellow to dull gray. Entirely black specimens may also be seen. A timber rattlesnake may reach 6 feet in length, but a full-grown snake is usually 36 to 48 inches long. It commonly is seen in the remote, rocky, mountainous sections of the state, west of the Catoctin Ridge.

   2.3 Although the copperhead and timber rattlesnakes are the most common poisonous snakes found in Maryland, exposure to other snakes may occur. A very large number and variety of poisonous and nonpoisonous snakes are kept by private individuals and zoological concerns. When any question exists, consult the Maryland Poison Information Center for more information.

3. SIGNS AND SYMPTOMS (Pit Viper)

3.1 Snakebite without envenomation (should be treated as a puncture wound)

3.1.1 Slight local pain

3.1.2 Puncture wound may or may not be evident.

3.1.3 There may be slight local edema, erythema.

3.1.4 In rare instances, infection may develop.

3.2 Snakebite with envenomation

3.2.1 Immediate local pain: sharp, usually intense burning; develops within 5 minutes and is progressive

3.2.2 Local edema, erythema: present within 10 minutes to 4 hours. Untreated edema progresses rapidly and may involve entire extremity within several hours (8–12). May be progressive from 12–24 hours.

3.2.3 Puncture wound: one, two, or multiple may be visible.

3.2.4 Nausea, vomiting, diarrhea: possible

3.2.5 Numbness, tingling, paresthesias, muscle twitching sometimes seen in the bite area; metallic or rubbery taste in the mouth

3.2.6 Shock: hypotension, weakness, syncope, rapid and weak pulse; may be present within a few minutes to a few hours

3.2.7 Convulsions, coma, respiratory or motor paralysis possible. (Motor paralysis is very unlikely in copperhead or timber rattlesnake bites.)

3.2.8 Infection: common

3.2.9 Other signs and symptoms may be present; consult the Maryland Poison Center for more information.

4. FIELD TREATMENT

NOTE: (Snakebites are medical emergencies, requiring immediate attention and considerable judgement; obtain consultation as soon as possible.)

4.1 Poisonous snakebites

4.1.1 Perform an initial patient assessment and assign a treatment priority. Identify the snake as poisonous or nonpoisonous as soon as possible and if envenomation has occurred; no envenomation occurs in 20–30% of poisonous snakebites.

4.1.2 Maintain a patent airway. Administer 50–100% oxygen as needed.

4.1.3 Consult with the Maryland Poison Information Center and receiving hospital as soon as practical.

4.1.4 Mark the edge of swelling and note time.

4.1.5 Immobilize the extremity and minimize all movement.

4.1.6 Apply *AN ELASTIC* venous constricting band (not a tourniquet) several inches proximal to the bite. It should not occlude arterial circulation. *A DISTAL PULSE SHOULD BE PALPABLE.* Reevaluate every 10 to 15 minutes for tightness. It may be necessary to advance the band to keep ahead of the swelling.

4.1.7 Incision and suction and immersion in ice are not recommended. An ice pack may be applied to the site of the bite only for relief of pain.

4.1.8 Establish an IV of L.R. KVO in uninjured extremity.

4.1.9 Apply MAST if patient meets criteria as outlined in MAST protocol.

4.1.10 Administer epinephrine (1:1,000 solution) 0.3 mg to a maximum of 1.0 mg SC in cases of anaphylaxis, as outlined in anaphylaxis protocol.

4.1.11 Transport the patient to the appropriate hospital, closely monitoring vital signs and the injured area.

NOTE: Deliver the snake *(IF DEAD) WITH ITS HEAD INTACT* with the snakebite victim, if practical.

4.2 Nonpoisonous snakebites

4.2.1 Perform an initial patient assessment and assign a treatment priority.

4.2.2 Maintain a patent airway.

4.2.3 Identify the snake as nonpoisonous.

4.2.4 Clean the wound with soap and water.

4.2.5 Immobilize the extremity.

4.2.6 The patient should be transported to the hospital for further medical evaluation, tetanus prophylaxis if indicated, and antibiotic therapy because a high probability of infection exists.

5. *SUGGESTED HOSPITAL TREATMENT*

5.1 Laboratory work for established venomous snakbite

5.1.1 Type and crossmatch blood (STAT)

5.1.2 Clotting times

5.1.3 Complete blood count (CBC)

5.1.4 Hemoglobin (HgB), hematocrit (HCT)

5.1.5 Platelets

5.1.6 Urinalysis

5.1.7 Serum electrolytes, blood urea nitrogen (BUN), creatinine, and red-blood-cell fragility tests may also be helpful.

5.1.8 Other tests may be needed if envenomation is severe.

5.1.9 Tests may need to be repeated several times.

5.2 Immobilize the extremity.

5.3 Measure circumference of the extremity just proximal to the bite and at one or more points closer to the trunk every 15 to 30 minutes.

5.4 Cleanse the wound.

5.5 Administer IV fluids as needed.

5.6 Administer analgesics as needed.

5.7 Administer tetanus prophylaxis as needed.

5.8 Administer antibiotics prophylactically, except in mild cases.

5.9 Antivenin therapy:

5.9.1 Skin test for horse-serum sensitivity, as per antivenin insert recommendation.

NOTE: Beware of horse-serum sensitivity and previous administration of horse-serum products.

5.9.2 Must be given IV within 4 to 12 hours to be most effective. Watch for anaphylaxis.

5.9.3 Serum sickness may occur 5-to-24 hours later. Signs and symptoms may include malaise, fever, itching, edema, nausea, vomiting, muscle weakness, and pain. Treat with antihistamines and/or steroids.

5.9.4 Indications for antivenin therapy:

a. Grade O (no or minor envenomation): Signs and symptoms include fang marks, minimal pain, and less than 1 inch of surrounding swelling and redness. No systemic involvement. No antivenin therapy recommended.

b. Grade 1 (minimal envenomation): Signs and symptoms include fang marks, severe pain, and 1–5 inches of swelling and redness in the first 12 hours. May have systemic involvement, but normal laboratory values. No antivenin therapy is recommended unless signs of progression ensue.

c. Grade 2 (moderate envenomation): Signs and symptoms include fang marks, severe pain, and 6–12 inches of swelling and redness. May have systemic involvement and abnormal lab values. Recommended antivenin therapy depending on snake involved and clinical presentation of the patient.

d. Grade 3 (severe envenomation): Signs and symptoms include fang marks, severe pain, and more than 12 inches of swelling and redress. There are usually systemic involvement and significant alterations in lab values. Recommended antivenin therapy depending on snake involved and clinical presentation of the patient.

NOTE: IV FLUIDS SHOULD BE KEPT TO A MINIMUM, EXCEPT WHEN SHOCK OR HYPOVOLEMIA IS PRESENT.

NOTE: ANTIVENIN SHOULD NEVER BE GIVEN IM, ONLY IV. IF PATIENT IS SENSITIVE TO HORSE SERUM, FOLLOW DIRECTIONS IN THE ANTIVENIN BROCHURE.

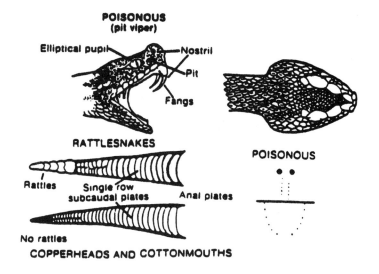

POISONOUS
(pit viper)

Elliptical pupil · Nostril · Pit · Fangs

RATTLESNAKES

Rattles · Single row subcaudal plates · Anal plates

No rattles

POISONOUS

COPPERHEADS AND COTTONMOUTHS

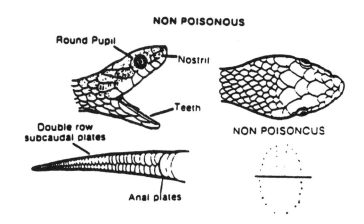

NON POISONOUS

Round Pupil · Nostril · Teeth

Double row subcaudal plates

Anal plates

NON POISONCUS

BEHAVIORAL/PSYCHIATRIC DISORDERS
DURHAM, NC

Behavioral

Criteria

A psychiatric patient who is at imminent risk of self-injury or is a threat to others.

Standing Orders

1. The patient should be prevented from self-harm or injuring others by the use of soft restraints if *verbal* techniques are unsuccessful. Be sure adequate personnel are available before attempting to restrain a violent patient. Law enforcement should always be called for assistance in difficult or potentially dangerous situations.
2. Assess possible underlying cause for behavioral changes, including substance abuse and trauma.
3. Psychiatric patients should be transported to DUMC for evaluation unless the patient has a private physician at DRH or unless the patient specifically requests treatment at DRH.
4. *Continue to reassess for medical or traumatic* causes of behavioral problems. Always consider hypoglycemia and hypoxia. The altered mental status protocol should be considered.

Contact Medical Control.

EMT-P
5. Valium 2–5 mg IV may be given in extreme situations. Additional incremental doses may be given every 5 minutes as approved by medical control. Do not exceed a total dose of 20 mg. Valium may cause apnea. Be prepared to intubate.

Behavioral Psychiatric Disorders

Assessment

1. Check vital signs.
2. Obtain brief history, noting any bizarre or abrupt changes in behavior, suicidal ideation, possible alcohol or drug ingestion, and significant past medical history (*i.e.*, diabetes, previous psychiatric disturbances).
3. Briefly evaluate neurologic system, including mental status.

Treatment

A. Probable psychiatric problem only:

1. Attempt to establish rapport with patient.
2. If patient is dangerous to himself or others, have police assist in transport. Restrain in lateral decubitus or prone position if absolutely necessary.
3. If suicidal, do not leave patient alone and if possible remove any dangerous objects (*i.e.*, guns, knives, pills, *etc.*).
4. If emergency treatment is unnecessary, do as little as possible except to reassure while transporting. Consider your own safety and limitations.

B. If lethargic, vital signs unstable, or hypoglycemia suspected:

1. Administer O_2.
2. Start an IV of LR, TKO.
3. Do a rapid bedside glucose determination.
4. Consider administration of glucose.
5. Consider administration of Narcan.
6. Transport while monitoring vital signs.

C. If agitated:

1. Consider your own safety and limitations.
2. If patient is dangerous to himself or to others, have police assist in transport. Restrain in lateral decubitus or prone position if absolutely necessary.
3. Treat as section B if safe and able.
4. Consider droperidol if the patient is violent/agitated and there is fear for patient, paramedic, police, firefighters, *etc.*, or life or limb.

BEHAVIORAL/PSYCHIATRIC DISORDERS
EUGENE/SPRINGFIELD, OR

Combative Patient/Physical and Chemical Restraints

I. Purpose: To prevent harm to patient and/or others

II. Indications:

    A. Patient restraints (physical and/or chemical) should be utilized only when necessary and only in situations where the patient is exhibiting behavior that the EMT believes will present a danger to patient or others.

    B. This procedure is not to be used on lucid patients who are refusing treatment unless they are placed under a police hold.

    C. This procedure does apply to patients treated under implied consent.

III. Procedure:

    A. Physical restraint procedure:

        1. Ensure sufficient personnel are present to control the patient while restraining him or her. USE POLICE ASSISTANCE WHENEVER AVAILABLE.

        2. Position patient for safe transport:

            a. Backboard method. (Be prepared to logroll immediately for vomiting.)

                i. Place patient face up on long backboard if at all possible.

                ii. Secure all extremities to backboard (4-point restraint).

                iii. If necessary, utilize cervical-spine precautions (tape, foam blocks, or CID, *etc.*) to control violent head or body movements.

                iv. Place padding under patient's head and wherever else needed to prevent the patient from further harming him or herself or restricting circulation.

                v. Secure the backboard onto gurney for transport, using additional straps if necessary, and be prepared at all times to logroll, suction, and maintain airway.

            b. Alternate methods without backboard. (Monitor respiratory status very closely with these alternate methods.)

                i. Prone on stretcher

        3. Monitor and document reasons for applying restraints. Monitor airway status and other vital signs and neurocirculatory status distal to restraints, and document every 15 minutes.

        4. If use of chemical restraint likely, start IV (EMT 2, 3, 4) of normal saline using standard tubing and large-bore catheter.

    B. Chemical Restraint Procedure (EMT 3, 4 only):

        1. Prepare airway equipment including suction, BVM, intubation equipment, needle cricothyrotomy equipment.

        2. Start IV (EMT 2, 3, 4) of normal saline using standard tubing with 14–16 gauge. Check blood glucose. If less than 80, give **dextrose**

50% IV push (EMT 2, 3, 4) by standing order. Usual adult dose 25 grams (50 ml). Refer to dextrose protocol, section B.

3. Administer **droperidol (Inapsine®)** IV push, or IM if unable to establish IV, by standing order (EMT 3, 4). Usual adult dose 2.5–5.0 mg. Repeat doses may be given with MD order. Refer to droperidol protocol, section B.

4. Monitor vital signs, ECG, and oxygen saturation if at all possible. Be prepared to treat hypotension with fluid and acute dystonic reactions with **diphenhydramine (Benadryl®)** 50 mg IV push (or IM if unable to establish IV) by standing order (EMT 3, 4).

5. Monitor and document reasons for using chemical restraint. Monitor airway status continuously and document ABCs and other vital signs at least every 15 minutes.

IV. Additional Information:

A. Physical-restraint guidelines:

1. Use the minimum restraint necessary to accomplish necessary patient care and ensure safe transportation. (Soft restraints may be sufficient in some cases.) If law-enforcement or additional personnel are needed, call for it prior to attempting restraint procedures. Do not endanger yourself or your crew.

2. Avoid placing restraints in such a way as to preclude evaluation of the patient's medical status (airway, breathing, circulation). Consider whether placement of restraints will interfere with necessary patient-care activities or will cause further harm.

3. Once restraints are placed, do not remove them until you arrive at hospital unless there is a complication from their use.

4. If at all possible, take extra personnel on the way in to hospital to deal with problems during transport.

B. Chemical-restraint guidelines:

1. Sedative agents may be used to provide a safe method of restraining violently combative patients who present a danger to themselves or others and to prevent violently combative patients from further injury while secured with physical restraints. These patients may include but are not limited to:
   a. Alcohol-and/or-drug-intoxicated patients
   b. Combative head-injured patients
   c. Acutely psychotic patients

PREHOSPITAL MEDICATIONS:
OUT-OF-PROTOCOL USES
FREMONT, CA

Prehospital Patient-Care Policies

Unusual circumstances may indicate special applications of medications carried in the field. *Base hospital physician order is required.*

1. *Sodium bicarbonate:*
   A. Consider with tricyclic antidepressant overdose characterized by tachycardia, hypotension, prolonged QRS intervals, and other dysrhythmias.
   B. Consider with dialysis patients (or those in severe renal failure) with fatal dysrhythmias and/or in cardiac arrest.
   C. Consider with patients in diabetic ketoacidosis in cardiac arrest or near cardiac arrest.

2. *Calcium chloride:*
   A. Consider with dialysis patients or those in severe renal failure.
   B. Consider with calcium-channel-blocker overdoses.

3. *Benadryl:*
   Consider with acute dystonic reactions secondary to phenothiazine ingestion (or other antipsychotic medications).

4. *High-dose epinephrine:*
   Consider in cardiac-arrest situations. Order and dosage per base hospital physician only.

EMERGENCY CHILDBIRTH
SAN MATEO, CA

Emergency Childbirth

XREF: Neonatal Resuscitation

Comment:

Except where indicated, the procedures described below are intended EMT-Is as well as EMT-Ps. Though fraught with anxiety, a clear majority of emergency births turn out quite well. On those rare occasions when complications develop, careful attention to the management outlined below should significantly reduce the risk to mother and child.

History:

It is important to establish the time labor began. The average length of labor for a primigravida (new mother) is 12 to 14 hours. Get history of previous deliveries. Multiparous (more than one baby) women may deliver much quicker, occasionally within a couple of hours of the onset of labor. You must also determine if there are any known complications with this or previous pregnancies, such as a breech (buttocks-first) presentation, prematurity (less than 38 weeks), twins, hemorrhage, *etc.*

Document:

1. Presentation (head, breech, *etc.*)
2. Date and time of birth of baby and placenta
3. Sex of infant
4. Position of cord at delivery and number of vessels
5. Time membranes ruptured
6. Appearance of amniotic fluid (brown, green, clear)
7. APGAR scores at 1 and 5 minutes after birth
8. Appearance of placenta
9. Any resuscitation procedures

Physical: Signs of imminent delivery are:

- Bulging perineum
- Crowning (top of baby's head visible)
- Contractions less than 2 minutes apart and strong
- Mother's insistence that baby is coming out

Ominous signs requiring immediate action (explained in detail later):

- Meconium staining of amniotic fluid
- Excessive bleeding or evidence of shock
- Prolapsed cord
- Abnormal presentation (breech, foot, arm first)
- Prematurity
- Multiple births

Subtopic: Normal Birth (No "ominous" signs)

History:

Uncomplicated pregnancy with appropriate prenatal care. No recent history of substance abuse.

Physical:

You may prepare the mother for transport unless there are signs of IMMINENT DELIVERY. (See above.) Check for "bloody show" (blood-tinged mucous plug) and clear amniotic fluid (broken "bag of water"). Check for crowning. If delivery is imminent, proceed as below:

Therapy:

- Quickly assess ABCs.
- Check for signs of imminent delivery.
- "Ominous signs" require rapid treatment and transport. Refer to appropriate algorithms such as NEONATAL RESUSCITATION.
- Assess for amniotic sac rupture (history, fluid, visualize head). If sac is intact and covering baby's head, tear it open before the head emerges.
- Oxygen @ 6 lpm via NC
- Place the mother in a comfortable "frog-leg" position at edge of bed on clean surface. Proper position may prevent shoulder impaction by baby.
- Have scissors, bulb syringe/suction, clean towels, and cord ties available. Reassure mother and significant others.
- Tell the mother to pant-breathe with each contraction and relax between.
- Apply slight pressure to perineum while head emerges. Gently ease its passage out of the birth canal. Do not allow the head to "pop" out uncontrolled; this may tear the vaginal area and/or damage the baby's brain.
- Check for umbilical cord around the neck. If present, slip it off over head. *If it is too tight to remove, quickly CLAMP IN TWO PLACES AND CUT BETWEEN CLAMPS.*
- As soon as the nose and mouth are clear, SUCTION them *immediately* to remove fluid and mucus before the baby takes a first breath or the body is delivered. *If meconium is present, refer to section on NEONATAL RESUSCITATION.*
- Ease shoulders out by gently lifting head and neck slightly.

- If the baby does not begin breathing spontaneously after delivery of the body, stimulate it by patting or slapping the feet. If normal respirations do not begin within 30 seconds, refer to section on NEONATAL RESUSCITATION.
- If pulse rate is < 100 after 30 seconds of oxygen and stimulation, refer to section on NEONATAL RESUSCITATION.
- If the baby appears healthy with a good cry and normal pulse (130–160) and respirations, dry it off, wrap it, place it on the mother's abdomen, and cover it to prevent heat loss. Some babies may want to breast-feed immediately. You do not have to cut the cord immediately but may do so at a convenient time. Place one tie or clamp at least 4 inches away from the baby. Place the next one 2 inches from the first and cut between.
- Check for bleeding from vaginal tears. You may wait up to 15 minutes for the placenta to deliver prior to transport. DO NOT PULL ON CORD. If the placenta has not delivered by this time, transport. The uterus may be massaged in the lower abdomen *after* the placenta has delivered *or* if there is excessive bleeding (more than 2 pints). Uncontrolled hemorrhage requires ALS care and rapid transport.

APGAR:

The baby's vigor should be determined by using the "APGAR" scoring method. Try to record 1 set of scores at 1 minute after birth and another set at 5 minutes. DO NOT DELAY RESUSCITATION TO SCORE THE BABY!

| | **SCORE** | | |
ITEM	0	1	2
Resp. effort	none	slow or irreg.	good cry
Heart rate	0	< 100/min.	> 100/min.
Muscle tone	limp	some flexion	active motion
Irritability on suctioning	none	grimace	sneeze or cough
Color	cyanotic	pink w/blue ext.	all pink

Subtopic: Multiple Births

History:

Known multiple fetuses demonstrated on ultrasound exam. Use of fertility medications. History of prior multiple births.

Physical:

1. Uterus remains distended after first baby.
2. Strong contractions persist after delivery.
3. First baby is smaller than expected given the size of the uterus.

Therapy:

- Quickly tie and cut first cord.
- Proceed with subsequent deliveries in same manner as first.
- Contact RECEIVING hospital.

Subtopic: Premature and/or addicted baby

History:

Substance abuse during pregnancy. No prenatal care. History of premature births. Active labor before 36 weeks gestation.

Physical:

Baby has small size at birth often associated with low APGAR scores. May see brownish/green amniotic fluid (meconium staining). Baby may be tremulous.

Therapy:

- It is very important to prevent heat loss in these infants and protect their airways.
- You may have to assist respirations (*after suctioning*) with pediatric bag mask and *gentle* ventilation.
- If infant appears distressed, refer to section on NEONATAL RESUSCITATION.

Subtopic: Prolapsed Umbilical Cord

History:

Known abnormal presentation of fetus and/or cord

Physical:

Cord drops into birth canal before baby is delivered.

Therapy

- Oxygen 100% via NRM
- DO NOT PUSH CORD BACK IN!
- Place mother in Trendelenburg *or* elevate hips with a pillow and then place in a knee-chest position.
- With gloved hand in vagina, push baby's head away from the cervix to keep pressure off of cord.
- Keep cord moist during transport with sterile saline irrigating solution or NS.
- Contact RECEIVING hospital.

Routine Medical Assessment

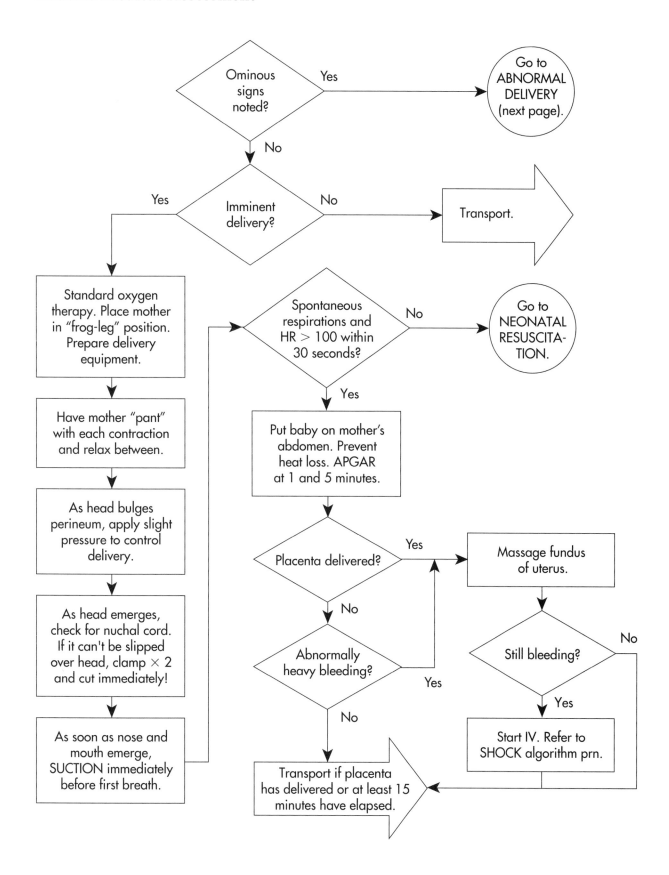

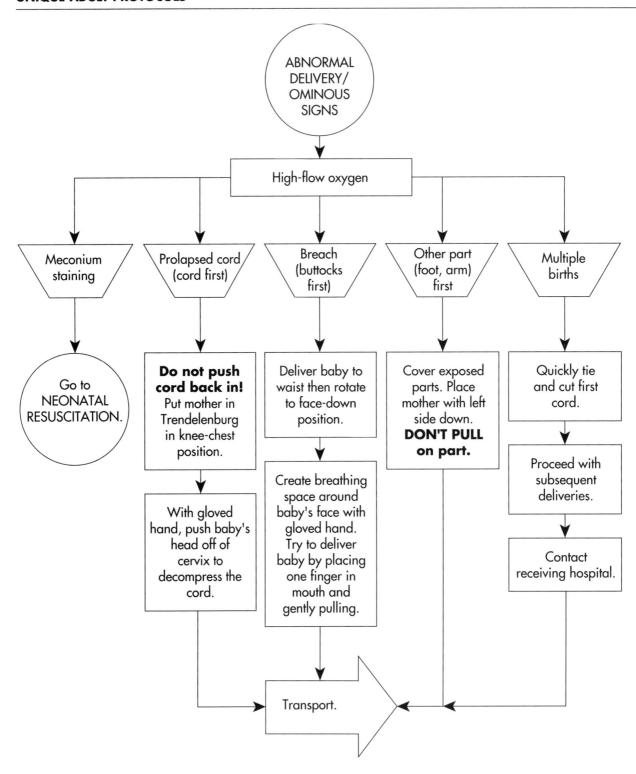

ABNORMAL DELIVERY/ OMINOUS SIGNS

High-flow oxygen

Meconium staining

Prolapsed cord (cord first)

Breach (buttocks first)

Other part (foot, arm) first

Multiple births

Go to NEONATAL RESUSCITATION.

Do not push cord back in! Put mother in Trendelenburg in knee-chest position.

With gloved hand, push baby's head off of cervix to decompress the cord.

Deliver baby to waist then rotate to face-down position.

Create breathing space around baby's face with gloved hand. Try to deliver baby by placing one finger in mouth and gently pulling.

Cover exposed parts. Place mother with left side down. **DON'T PULL on part.**

Quickly tie and cut first cord.

Proceed with subsequent deliveries.

Contact receiving hospital.

Transport.

OBSTETRIC EMERGENCIES: PRE-ECLAMPSIA AND ECLAMPSIA
PITTSBURGH, PA

Complications of Pregnancy

Indications:

Patients in third trimester of pregnancy who were normotensive prior to pregnancy and now have BP >140/90; this may be associated with edema of hands and face. This usually occurs during patient's *first* pregnancy.

NOTE: Definitive treatment is delivery of fetus. Thus, rapid transport indicated.

Protocol

1. Take OBSTETRICAL HISTORY per Protocol 601 and inquire whether patient has been diagnosed with hypertension of pregnancy or pre-eclampsia. Perform neuro exam. (Hyperreflexia and visual changes indicate imminent seizure.)
2. Place patient in comfortable position—elevate right side if supine. Administer OXYGEN and initiate IV saline lock. Check glucose level by Chemstrip.
3. If patient has generalized (grand mal) seizure:
   A. Assure adequate ventilation and oxygenation. Protect airway.
   B. Administer MAGNESIUM SULFATE 1 gram/minute IV push until seizure stops. Dilute each gram in 10 cc IVF. Maximum dose is four (4) grams.
4. Initiate transport and contact command physician. Monitor vitals, airway, and neurologic status en route.
5. Possible additional orders include:
   A. For uncontrolled seizure:
      —Valium 5 mg IV slow push (may be repeated as needed)
      —Additional magnesium sulfate
      —Intubation

   B. For BP >160/110 (not seizing):
      —Magnesium sulfate 4 gm in D_5W 250 cc IV over 10–20 minutes
      —NTG 0.4 mg sublingual or spray

CEREBROVASCULAR ACCIDENTS
COLUMBUS, OH

Transient Ischemic Attacks

1. ABCs. C-spine control for all unconscious patients with suspected trauma.
2. Hyperventilate if vital signs deteriorating:
   A. Consider the cause; transport all medications or a list to the hospital.
3. Examine the patient closely for signs of trauma. If present, refer to NEURO-LOGIC TRAUMA PROTOCOL.
4. Initiate an IV of 0.9% NORMAL SALINE at a keep-open rate.
5. Obtain blood sample for dextrostick analysis. Administer 50 cc of 50% DEXTROSE if serum glucose is less than 80.
   A. Administer GLUCAGON 1 mg subcutaneously or intramuscularly if unable to start IV.
6. In patients with decreased level of consciousness of unknown etiology, administer NALOXONE (Narcan) 2 mg, IVP. May repeat same dose in 5–10 minutes if partial response noted. May administer via ETT if unable to initiate IV.
7. If unconscious and no signs of shock, transport with head slightly elevated. If conscious, transport in position most comfortable.
8. Anyone with suspected cerebrovascular accident (CVA) or transient ischemic attack (TIA) should be transported on a cardiac monitor.

CEREBROVASCULAR ACCIDENTS
MEMPHIS, TN

Cerebrovascular Accidents (CVA)

A. *Assessment*
- Alteration in consciousness (coma, stupor, confusion, seizures, delirium)
- Intense or unusually severe headache of sudden onset or any headache associated with decreased level of consciousness or neurological deficit; unusual and severe neck or facial pain
- Aphasia (incoherent speech or difficulty understanding speech)
- Facial weakness or asymmetry (paralysis of the facial muscles, usually noted when the patient speaks or smiles); may be on the same side or opposite side from limb paralysis
- Incoordination, weakness, paralysis, or sensory loss of one or more limbs, usually involves one half of the body, particularly the hand
- Ataxia (poor balance, clumsiness, or difficulty walking)
- Visual loss (monocular or binocular); may be a partial loss of visual field
- Dysarthria (slurred or indistinct speech)
- Intense vertigo, double vision, unilateral hearing loss, nausea, vomiting, photophobia, or phonophobia

B. *Treatment*
   1. Oxygen 100% and airway maintenance appropriate to patient's condition.
   2. Evaluate cardiac rhythm and vital signs.

      Monitor airway due to decreased gag reflex and increased secretions.
      Keep head elevated if possible; monitor pupils.
      Maintain body heat; protect affected limbs from injury; anticipate seizures.

   3. IV 1/2 NS KVO
   4. Narcan 2.0 mg IVP. for respiratory depression or altered consciousness
   5. If blood sugar is less than 60 mg%: dextrose 25 gm IVP

STANDARD PEDIATRIC PROTOCOLS

PEDIATRIC RESPIRATORY EMERGENCIES

PEDIATRIC OBSTRUCTED AIRWAY

1. San Francisco, CA—upper vs. lower
2. St. Louis, MO—flow-chart format
3. Columbus, OH—croup vs. epiglottitis vs. foreign body

PEDIATRIC CROUP/EPIGLOTTITIS

1. San Mateo, CA—flow-chart format
2. Columbus, GA
3. Albuquerque, NM—surgical cricothyrotomy

PEDIATRIC ASTHMA

1. State of Hawaii—flow-chart format
2. Des Moines, IA—epi dosage chart
3. Arlington, TX—IV solumedrol option
4. Austin, TX—format

PEDIATRIC OBSTRUCTED AIRWAY
SAN FRANCISCO, CA

Pediatric Respiratory Distress

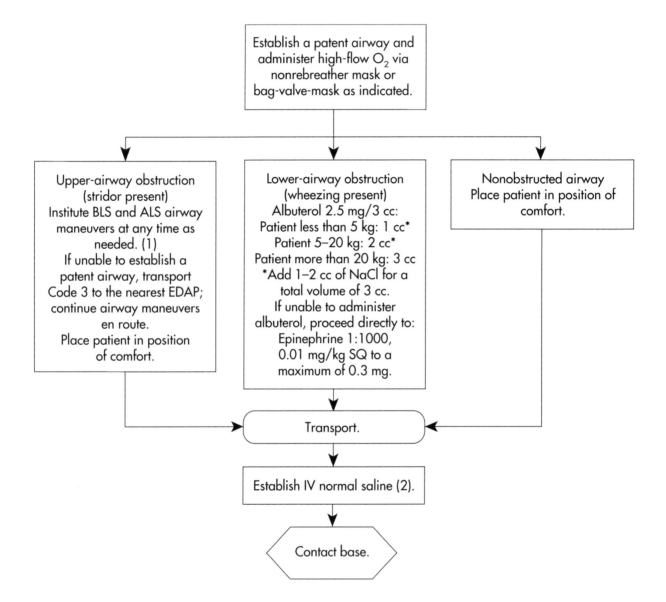

Establish a patent airway and administer high-flow O_2 via nonrebreather mask or bag-valve-mask as indicated.

Upper-airway obstruction (stridor present)
Institute BLS and ALS airway maneuvers at any time as needed. (1)
If unable to establish a patent airway, transport Code 3 to the nearest EDAP; continue airway maneuvers en route.
Place patient in position of comfort.

Lower-airway obstruction (wheezing present)
Albuterol 2.5 mg/3 cc:
Patient less than 5 kg: 1 cc*
Patient 5–20 kg: 2 cc*
Patient more than 20 kg: 3 cc
*Add 1–2 cc of NaCl for a total volume of 3 cc.
If unable to administer albuterol, proceed directly to:
Epinephrine 1:1000, 0.01 mg/kg SQ to a maximum of 0.3 mg.

Nonobstructed airway
Place patient in position of comfort.

Transport.

Establish IV normal saline (2).

Contact base.

Protocol Notes

1. Patients with suspected epiglottitis should not receive invasive airway procedures, *e.g.*, oral airways or intubation. The stimulation caused by these devices could result in a fully occluded airway. Epiglottitis is a true emergency that often requires a full surgical team to manage. Epiglottitis management in the field includes placing the patient in a position of comfort, administering high-flow oxygen, ventilating, as needed, with a bag-valve-mask device, and rapid transportation to the closest EDAP. Children with epiglottitis generally have a toxic appearance, drooling, high fever and assume a tripod position of comfort.

2. Care should be exercised to avoid overstimulating patients with suspected epiglottitis. The decision to start an IV should be based on an assessment of the patient's potential response and actual medical need. It may be safer to withhold an IV from this group of patients if the ETA is short and no further medication administration is anticipated.

PEDIATRIC OBSTRUCTED AIRWAY
ST. LOUIS, MO

Pediatric Upper-Airway Obstruction

Upper-airway obstruction (UAO) is a relatively common problem in the pediatric age group. Because of the small diameter of the upper airway, the pediatric patient is particularly vulnerable to UAO. Important causes of UAO include coma (depressed level of consciousness), infection (croup, epiglottitis), foreign-body aspiration, and anaphylaxis. Patients with UAO may decompensate very rapidly; therefore, the following principles should be adhered to when evaluating and treating these patients:

1. Allow the patient to remain in a *position of comfort* in the parent's arms if patient is conscious and ventilating adequately.
2. Assessment and management should be as brief and as noninvasive as possible. Any undue stimulation may convert a partial UAO into a complete UAO.
3. IV access should not be attempted, as it may worsen the patient's condition.
4. Definitive care of patients with UAO cannot occur in the field, so these patients should be transferred as quickly and as comfortably as possible to a pediatric facility.
5. Remember that any patient with UAO is at *high risk for sudden respiratory or cardiac arrest*; therefore, these patients should be CONTINUOUSLY VISU-ALLY INSPECTED at all times.

Assessment

A brief history should include time of onset of respiratory compromise, history of choking episode or foreign-body aspiration, history of fever, or history consistent with anaphylaxis. Physical exam should be done with great care; *do only that part of the exam that doesn't agitate the child*. Do not attempt to obtain bp or temperature on patients with UAO. The exam may include the following:

Inspection—level of consciousness
          chest rise
          respiratory rate
          retractions
          color
Ausculation—quality of aeration
          stridor
          wheezing
Palpation—pulse rate
          pulse volume
          capillary refill

Management

The rapidity with which treatment is initiated depends in part on the severity of the patient's condition after the brief assessment. Obviously a patient who is in severe respiratory distress or arrest should receive more prompt intervention (and a briefer history) than a patient in minimal distress. Always use bag-valve-mask ventilation (BVM) with 100% oxygen for patients with UAO requiring assisted ventilation. Remember that high pressures may be required to adequately ventilate these patients, but *don't use a demand-valve device*. It is also emphasized that all patients with UAO should be *visually inspected continuously* as they may decompensate within *seconds*.

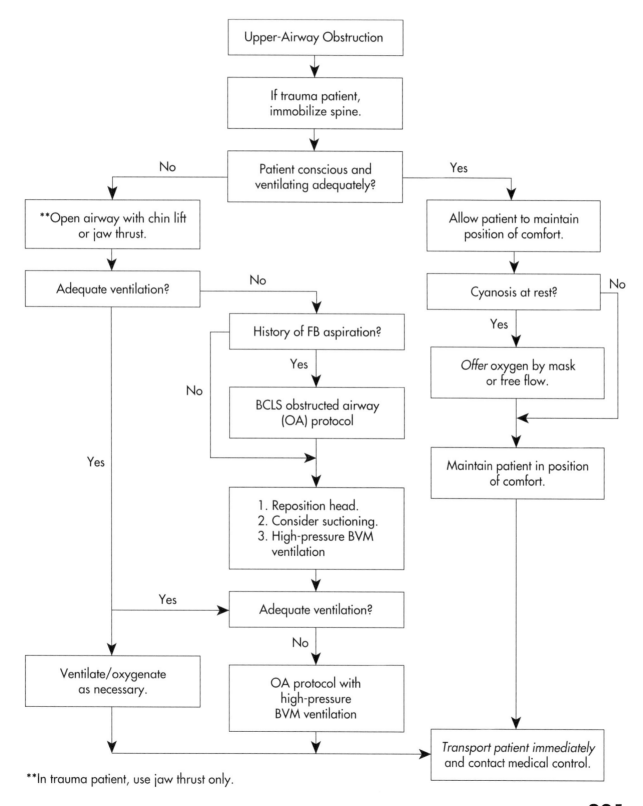

**In trauma patient, use jaw thrust only.

PEDIATRIC OBSTRUCTED AIRWAY
COLUMBUS, OH

Upper Airway Obstruction

Assess for adequate airway and ventilation. If the child is unconscious or has a decreased level of consciousness, assist with bag-valve-mask and 100% oxygen. These criteria give some broad guidelines in assessing upper-airway obstruction.

	CROUP (LTB)	EPIGLOTTITIS	FOREIGN BODY
Common age usually male	6 months– 3 years	2–6 years	6 months– 4 years
Onset of symptoms	Gradual, frequently follows course of URI	Sudden 4–12 hours	Sudden
Clinical picture	Gradual, inspiratory stridor, barky cough, hoarse voice	TOXIC-appearing, muffled voice, dysphagia, inspiratory stridor, drooling, flushed	May have: cough, drooling, stridor
Fever	Normal, low-grade temperature	High	Normal
Maximal obstruction	Subglottic	Supraglottic	Varies
Etiology	Parainfluenza	Almost always H-fluenza	Varies

Respiratory Distress

1. Relieve complete airway obstruction by using current AHA basic cardiac life support as recommended by the AHA for infants less than 1 year old. Refer to table. If more than 1 year old, follow AHA basic cardiac life support guidelines, and use the HEIMLICH MANEUVER. DO NOT attempt to remove foreign body unless clearly visualized, *i.e.*, NO BLIND FINGER SWEEPS.
2. If child is ventilating, obtain complete history prior to a medical intervention.*
3. Keep child with parent, if possible. Place child in sitting position. Keep lights and noise to an absolute minimum.
4. If child is showing signs of hypoxia (agitated, restless, *etc.*), give as high an oxygen concentration as possible—usually by placing O_2 connecting tubing directly by their face or through a disposable paper cup. Do not cause further agitation or start IV.
5. If child has a respiratory arrest, assist ventilations using the bag-valve-mask with 100% O_2 or mouth-to-mask method, and intubate if necessary. If able to adequately ventilate, continue to use bag-valve-mask or mouth-to-mask. If child arrests, follow appropriate dysrhythmia protocol.

*An accurate history is by far the most important tool for establishing a diagnosis in pediatric patients with upper-airway obstruction. Always inquire about possible foreign bodies, *i.e.*, peanuts, hot dogs, marbles, toys, *etc.*

PEDIATRIC CROUP/EPIGLOTTITIS
SAN MATEO, CA

Pediatric Upper Airway: Stridor

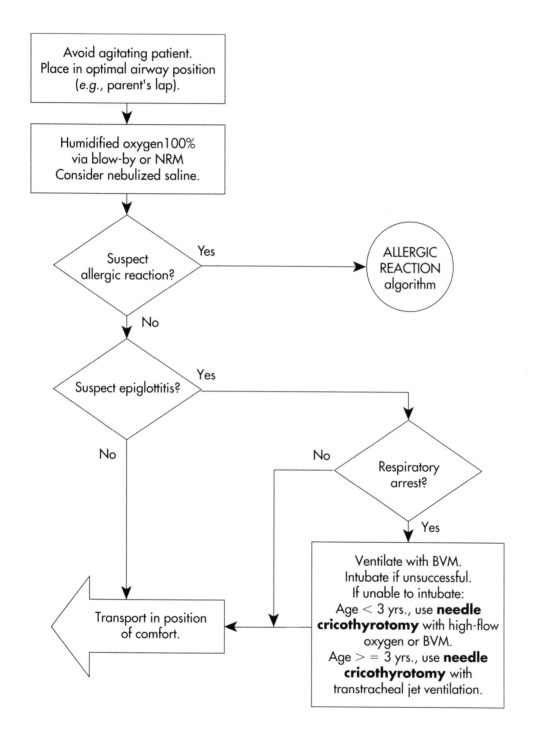

Avoid agitating patient.
Place in optimal airway position
(*e.g.*, parent's lap).

Humidified oxygen 100%
via blow-by or NRM
Consider nebulized saline.

Suspect allergic reaction? — **Yes** → ALLERGIC REACTION algorithm

No

Suspect epiglottitis? — **Yes** →

No

Respiratory arrest?

No

Yes

Ventilate with BVM.
Intubate if unsuccessful.
If unable to intubate:
Age < 3 yrs., use **needle cricothyrotomy** with high-flow oxygen or BVM.
Age > = 3 yrs., use **needle cricothyrotomy** with transtracheal jet ventilation.

Transport in position of comfort.

PEDIATRIC CROUP/EPIGLOTTITIS
COLUMBUS, GA

Pediatric Respiratory Distress—Nontraumatic

---

1. 1' Survey:
   A. Assure airway. O_2 8 to 12 l/minute by NRBM/assist PRN except known COPD, then start 2 l/minute via nasal cannula and increase as required. Be prepared to ventilate.

2. 2' Survey:

Croup < 3 yrs. (usually)/
Epiglottitis > 3 yrs. (usually)

1. Keep child calm.
2. Move to cool environment.
3. Position appropriately.
4. Offer O_2 (if tolerated).
5. If apneic, cyanotic, or gasping for air dispense with use of O_2; begin PPV.

   Contact Medical Control.
   Orders may include the following:

6. 0.03 cc/k albuterol in 2 via nebulizer
7. Needle cricothyrotomy

Asthma

1. Reassure and calm patient.
2. Allow patient to assume position of comfort.
3. Assist patient in taking their own asthma medications.
4. Provide humidified O_2 (if possible).

   Contact Medical Control.
   Orders may include the following:

5. Albuterol 0.25 cc via nebulizer
6. Epinephrine SQ (if no relief or unable to tolerate nebulizer)

Inadequate ventilatory efforts, ET tube with supplemental high flow O_2; assist PRN.

PEDIATRIC CROUP/EPIGLOTTITIS
ALBUQUERQUE, NM

Croup, Epiglottitis

Designation of Condition:

When severe, patient will be stridorous and in respiratory distress. Remember to consider foreign-body aspiration in your differential diagnosis. Watch for drooling (common in epiglottitis) and listen for a barking cough (common in croup).

Field Treatment

- Keep patient comfortable and quiet with parent. No invasive procedures.
- Allow patient to assume position of comfort.
- Administer O_2.
- Transport ASAP.
- Call ahead to receiving facility ASAP.
- Monitor HR and respirations continuously.
- In the event of respiratory arrest or extremis:
  - Provide positive pressure ventilation with BVM, using 100% oxygen.
  - If unable to adequately ventilate with BVM—intubate. An ETT one-half size smaller than usual should be used. Have suction available and use cricoid pressure.
  - **Failure to intubate requires an immediate transtracheal needle ventilation in small children. In adult, consider transtracheal needle ventilation or surgical cricothyrotomy.**

PEDIATRIC ASTHMA
STATE OF HAWAII

Bronchospasm

Respiratory distress with wheezing not involving foreign body:

Administer O_2 at 10–15 liters by mask.

Administer (a) albuterol 2.5 mg in nebulizer or (b) terbutaline 1 mg (2 mg if patient over 40 kg) in nebulizer.

If patient remains in severe bronchospasm after several minutes of nebulizer therapy, administer epinephrine 1:1000 0.01 mg/kg s.q. to maximum 0.3 mg (may be repeated every 20 minutes for a total of 3 doses).

COMMUNICATE WITH MEDICOM PHYSICIAN FOR FURTHER ORDERS.

PEDIATRIC ASTHMA
DES MOINES, IA

Asthma

Asthma is marked by recurrent attacks of dyspnea due to intermittent, reversible bronchospasms. Causes include allergic response to dust, pollen, chemicals, *etc.*, upper-respiratory infections, emotional distress, and physical exercise. There is an increased incidence in the patient 3 years of age to puberty. Treatment is aimed at providing respiratory support and includes:

A. Allow the patient to assume a position of comfort, usually sitting upright on the parent's lap

B. Administer oxygen (humidified if possible) by mask at 6–10 LPM

C. Attach cardiac monitor

D. Notify medical control and transport as soon as possible

E. If the patient's condition warrants it: initiate IV of NS run at TKO while en route to the hospital

F. Be prepared to administer **epinephrine,** 1:1,000 subQ in a dose as follows:

4 months–1 year	.1 mg (0.1 ml)
1–2 years old	0.15 mg (0.15 ml)
2–3 years old	0.2 mg (0.2 ml)
3 years and over	0.3 mg (0.3 ml)

CAUTION: The use of **epinephrine** may be hazardous if the child has already taken high doses of bronchodilator medications by inhalant. Be sure to find out what the child has taken and relay this information to medical control before administering any drugs.

PEDIATRIC ASTHMA
ARLINGTON, TX

Pediatric Asthma

Treatment:

1. Establish and maintain airway as appropriate.
2. Administer high-flow O_2.
3. Continuous cardiac monitoring
4. Establish IV/IO access with Ringer's lactate.
5. Administer nebulized updraft as follows:

Ventolin	0.1–0.3 mg in 2 cc NS	(max. 0.5 mg)
Brethine	0.25–0.5 mg in 2 cc NS	

NOTE: The choice between Ventolin and Brethine is left to the paramedic's discretion. If adequate response is not obtained from the initial updraft, give a second updraft with the alternate drug.

6. Contact medical control.

Physician Orders

1. Epinephrine 0.01 mg/kg of 1:10,000 IV/IO
2. Aminophylline infusion 5 mg/kg in 100 cc normal saline to be given over twenty (20) minutes. Drip rate—300 gtts/min. with Volutrol.
3. Solu-Medrol 1–2 mg/kg IVP

PEDIATRIC ASTHMA
AUSTIN, TX

Reactive Airway Diseases

Introduction

With the availability of beta-2-specific drugs given via nebulization, the paramedic has the capability to have a significant impact on the prognosis and outcome of the patient with asthma and COPD. What used to be an almost automatic inpatient stay at the hospital now has the potential to be treated and released the same day.

Key Actions

COMMUNICATIONS
1. ABCs
2. Position/calm/reassure the patient.
3. Gather home medications.
4. N.P.O.

BLS
1. Assessment/vital signs
2. Oxygen therapy PRN

ILS
1. Assist with home medications.
2. Saline nebulizer PRN
3. If life-threatening, use epinephrine pen per instructions.

ALS
1. Monitor EKG and pulse oximetry.
2. Albuterol nebulizer 1-unit dose q20 minutes (half dose in children <1 year old)
3. Initiate IV lifeline(s) only if absolutely necessary (to prevent aggravation).
4. Epinephrine 0.01 mg/kg SQ q20 minutes (max. dose 0.3 mg per dose/total 3 doses)
5. Methylprednisolone 2 mg/kg IV

Assessment Considerations

1. Does patient have a history of asthma or COPD? Have there been any recent surgeries? Was patient eating?
2. Able to speak without difficulty? Position of patient? Type of difficulty (noisy/hard to breathe)? Time of onset?
3. Was there activity at time of onset? Did an emotional change bring on this episode? Was there exposure to chemicals?
4. Is there numbness in hands or around mouth? What is skin color? Is there use of accessory muscles to breathe?

Special Situations/Conditons

1. In upper-airway disorders (*i.e.*, epiglottitis, croup, foreign body airway obstruction), invasive airway maneuvers should only be attempted if patient is in respiratory arrest, as aggravation of irritated tissues can cause further airway obstruction.

© *Austin/Travis EMS Clinical Practice*

PEDIATRIC NONTRAUMATIC CARDIAC ARREST

PEDIATRIC V—FIBRILLATION/PULSELESS V—TACHYCARDIA

1. San Francisco, CA—flow-chart format
2. Boston, MA—complete
3. Charlotte, NC

PEDIATRIC ASYSTOLE

1. Lexington, KY
2. Boston, MA—complete

PEDIATRIC PULSELESS ELECTRICAL ACTIVITY

1. Boston, MA—complete
2. Charlotte, NC—high-dose Epi

NEONATAL RESUSCITATION

1. Fremont, CA—format
2. Boston, MA—format
3. Portland, OR—meconium aspiration

PEDIATRIC VENTRICULAR FIBRILLATION
AND PULSELESS VENTRICULAR TACHYCARDIA
SAN FRANCISCO, CA

Pediatric V-Fib and Pulseless V-Tach

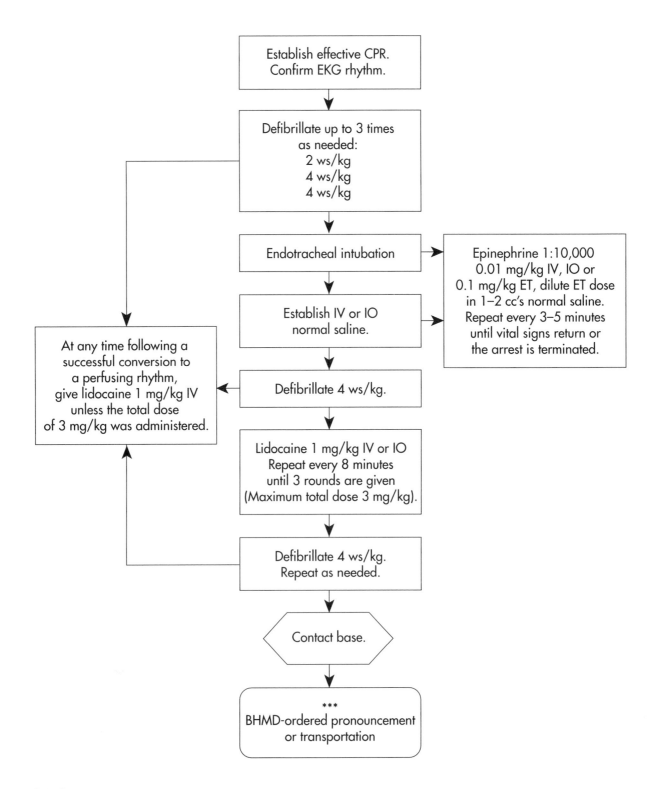

PEDIATRIC VENTRICULAR FIBRILLATION AND PULSELESS VENTRICULAR TACHYCARDIA
BOSTON, MA

Pediatric Ventricular Fibrillation/
Pulseless Ventricular Tachycardia

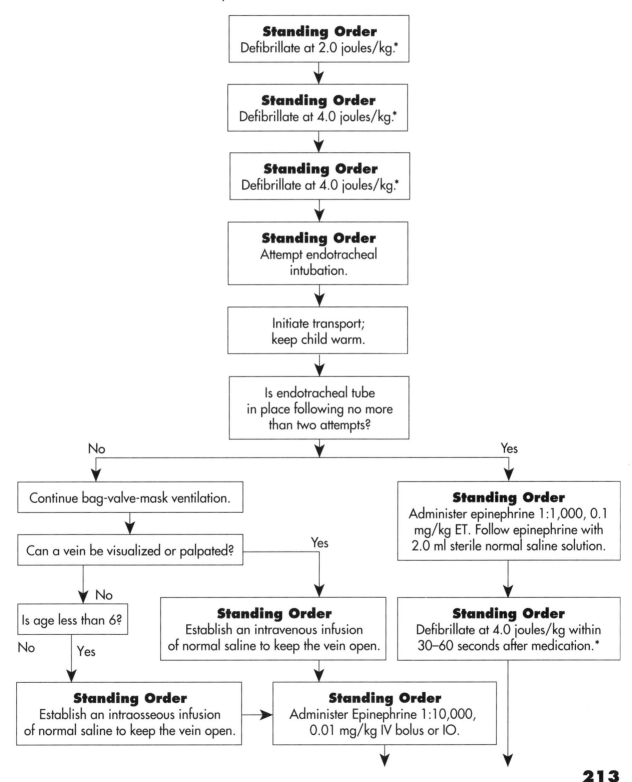

Standing Order
Defibrillate at 2.0 joules/kg.*

Standing Order
Defibrillate at 4.0 joules/kg.*

Standing Order
Defibrillate at 4.0 joules/kg.*

Standing Order
Attempt endotracheal intubation.

Initiate transport;
keep child warm.

Is endotracheal tube in place following no more than two attempts?

No — Continue bag-valve-mask ventilation.

Can a vein be visualized or palpated?

No — Is age less than 6?

No   Yes

Standing Order
Establish an intraosseous infusion of normal saline to keep the vein open.

Yes — **Standing Order**
Establish an intravenous infusion of normal saline to keep the vein open.

Standing Order
Administer Epinephrine 1:10,000, 0.01 mg/kg IV bolus or IO.

Yes — **Standing Order**
Administer epinephrine 1:1,000, 0.1 mg/kg ET. Follow epinephrine with 2.0 ml sterile normal saline solution.

Standing Order
Defibrillate at 4.0 joules/kg within 30–60 seconds after medication.*

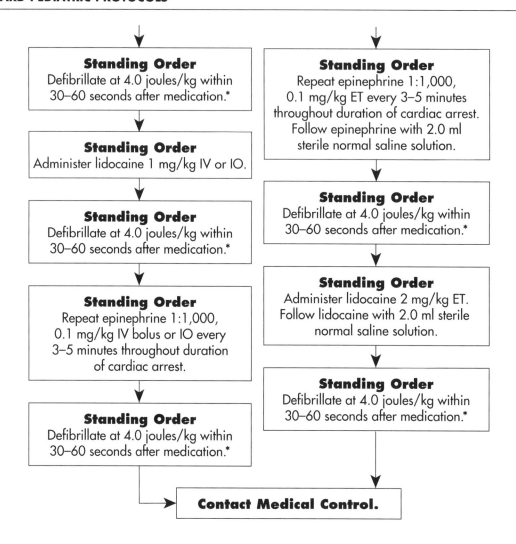

Standing Order
Defibrillate at 4.0 joules/kg within
30–60 seconds after medication.*

Standing Order
Administer lidocaine 1 mg/kg IV or IO.

Standing Order
Defibrillate at 4.0 joules/kg within
30–60 seconds after medication.*

Standing Order
Repeat epinephrine 1:1,000,
0.1 mg/kg IV bolus or IO every
3–5 minutes throughout duration
of cardiac arrest.

Standing Order
Defibrillate at 4.0 joules/kg within
30–60 seconds after medication.*

Standing Order
Repeat epinephrine 1:1,000,
0.1 mg/kg ET every 3–5 minutes
throughout duration of cardiac arrest.
Follow epinephrine with 2.0 ml
sterile normal saline solution.

Standing Order
Defibrillate at 4.0 joules/kg within
30–60 seconds after medication.*

Standing Order
Administer lidocaine 2 mg/kg ET.
Follow lidocaine with 2.0 ml sterile
normal saline solution.

Standing Order
Defibrillate at 4.0 joules/kg within
30–60 seconds after medication.*

Contact Medical Control.

Medical Control Option A
Defibrillation 4.0 joules/kg*

Medical Control Option B
Lidocaine HCL, 1.0 mg/kg IV bolus or IO. Administer 2 times selected doses if given ET.
(If administered ET, follow lidocaine with 2.0 ml sterile normal saline solution.)

Medical Control Option C
Sodium bicarbonate 4.2%, 1.0 mEq/kg IV bolus (for infants less than three months of age). (Do not repeat.)

Medical Control Option D
Sodium bicarbonate 8.4%, 1.0 mEq/kg IV bolus. (Do not repeat.)

Medical Control Option E
Dextrose 25% (if estimated body weight is less than 50 kg, 0.5 gm/kg IV bolus)

Medical Control Option F
Dextrose 50% (if estimated body weight is 50 kg or greater, 0.5 gm/kg IV bolus)

Medical Control Option G
Bretylium tosylate, 5.0 mg/kg IV bolus or IO.
If conversion does not occur, administer bretylium tosylate, 10.0 mg/kg IV bolus or IO.

Medical Control Option H
Intravenous infusion of normal saline to keep the vein open

Medical Control Option I
Intraosseous infusion of normal saline to keep the vein open (if age less than 6 years)

---

*Following conversion of a perfusing rhythm, assess and support respiration, initiate transport, keep child warm, and contact medical control.

© August 1993, Metropolitan Boston EMS Council

PEDIATRIC VENTRICULAR FIBRILLATION
AND PULSELESS VENTRICULAR TACHYCARDIA
CHARLOTTE, NC

Pulseless Ventricular Tachycardia and Ventricular Fibrillation

History

1. Patient < 14 years old
2. May have history of congenital heart disease or may be on antidysrhythmics
3. Witnesses may report a sudden collapse with or without antecedent signs and symptoms.

Physical

1. Patient is unresponsive.
2. Absent respirations
3. No palpable pulse

Electrocardiogram

1. Ventricular tachycardia or fibrillation

Differential

Myocardial infarction
Lead misplacement
Artifact

Protocol

1. Check for breathing and pulses and apply cardiac monitor or quick-look paddles. May obtain rhythm strip.
2. Maintain airway and administer assisted ventilations with bag-valve mask and 100% oxygen
3. Initiate CPR.
4. Consider and administer any or all of the following therapeutic interventions:

    Defibrillation (unsynchronized) at 2 joules/kg
       If no response:
    Defibrillation (unsynchronized) at 4 joules/kg
       If no response:
    Defibrillation (unsynchronized) at 4 joules/kg
       If no response:
    Reassess ABC's

    If no response: Continue CPR.

Perform orotracheal intubation and ventilate with 100% oxygen.

IV or IO normal saline wide open

Epinephrine 1:10,000 0.01 mg/kg (0.1 ml/kg) IV or IO

Lidocaine 1 mg/kg IV or IO

Defibrillation (unsynchronized) at 4 joules/kg

Epinephrine 1:1,000 0.2 mg/kg (0.2 ml/kg) IV
  or IO
  Dose may be repeated every 5 minutes if patient remains pulseless.

Lidocaine 1 mg/kg IV or IO

Defibrillation (unsynchronized) at 4 joules/kg

If patient converts to a rhythm associated with palpable pulses, and lidocaine has not been given, administer the following:

Lidocaine 1 mg/kg IV
  May repeat 0.5 mg/kg IV dose every 10 minutes throughout transport until total dose of 3 mg/kg has been given

If patient converts to a different rhythm but dysrhythmia (VT/VF) recurs

Defibrillate at most-recent energy level.
  If no response:
Defibrillate at next-highest energy level.

5. Initiate transport. Continue to monitor vital signs while en route.
6. Contact medical control en route. The following intervention may be considered:

Sodium bicarbonate 1 mEq/kg IV
  May repeat 0.5 mEq/kg IV dose every 10 minutes

Addendum

1. Ventricular fibrillation is rare in children. In this age group, it is mostly seen in cardiomyopathies, myocarditis, hypoxia, or intoxication.
2. Airway control and oxygenation are of paramount importance with any pediatric arrest patient.
3. The following medications may be administered by the endotracheal route after dilution 1:1 with normal saline:

Epinephrine 1:1000 0.1 mg/kg (0.1 ml/kg)
Lidocaine 2 mg/kg

4. Pulses should be checked after each defibrillation.
5. If vascular access is unsuccessful after 2 attempts, proceed with intraosseous infusion.

PEDIATRIC ASYSTOLE
LEXINGTON, KY

PEA—Asystole

1.0 Definition
Extreme bradycardia with uncertain pulse ('agonal")

2.0 *Initial Medical Care*

3.0 *BCLS*

    3.1 Ventilate with 100% oxygen.

4.0 Monitor and record 6-sec. rhythm strip. Always recheck leads and confirm PEA in two leads before proceeding.

5.0 If you suspect the child is hypothermic, transport ASAP, giving first round of drugs en route if possible.

6.0 Establish IV of *NS* at KVO. May use IO route if unable to establish IV.

7.0 *Epinephrine* IV, IO, or ET tube when available (if IV or IO not available). Repeat this dose every 3–5 minutes as long as child remains in these rhythms.

IV/IO dosage:
first dose: 10 mcg/kg 1:10,000 IV/IO
additional doses: 100 mcg/kg 1:1,000 IV/IO

ET dosage:
all doses: 100 mcg/kg 1:1,000

8.0 Airway-per-Airway Protocol

9.0 *Atropine* by IV, IO; or ET tube (when available):
Dosage: (0.02 mg/kg) (minimum dose 0.10 mg)

AGE	WEIGHT	DOSE
Newborn	approx. 3 kg =	0.10 mg
1 Yr.	approx. 10 kg =	0.20 mg
6 Yr.	approx. 20 kg =	0.40 mg
10 Yr.	approx. 30 kg =	0.60 mg

10.0 If one of these dysrhythmias persists, continue resuscitation, reassess and optimize ventilation and oxygenation. Check carefully for signs of tension pneumothorax, hypovolemia, or cardiac tamponade; if present, proceed to proper protocol.

11.0 Transport as soon as possible.

12.0 If PEA/asystole persists, attempt DC cardioversion once only at 2 J/kg, since apparent asystole may be fine VF.

PEDIATRIC ASYSTOLE
BOSTON, MA

Asystole/Agonal Idioventricular Rhythm

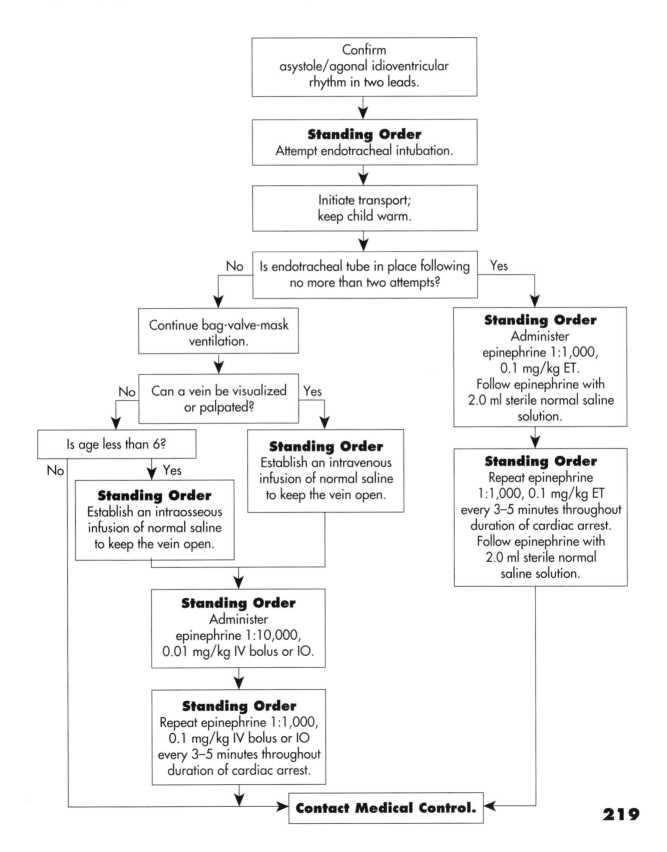

Confirm asystole/agonal idioventricular rhythm in two leads.

Standing Order
Attempt endotracheal intubation.

Initiate transport; keep child warm.

Is endotracheal tube in place following no more than two attempts?

No → Continue bag-valve-mask ventilation.

Can a vein be visualized or palpated?

No → Is age less than 6?

No / **Yes**

Standing Order
Establish an intraosseous infusion of normal saline to keep the vein open.

Yes → **Standing Order**
Establish an intravenous infusion of normal saline to keep the vein open.

Standing Order
Administer epinephrine 1:10,000, 0.01 mg/kg IV bolus or IO.

Standing Order
Repeat epinephrine 1:1,000, 0.1 mg/kg IV bolus or IO every 3–5 minutes throughout duration of cardiac arrest.

Yes → **Standing Order**
Administer epinephrine 1:1,000, 0.1 mg/kg ET. Follow epinephrine with 2.0 ml sterile normal saline solution.

Standing Order
Repeat epinephrine 1:1,000, 0.1 mg/kg ET every 3–5 minutes throughout duration of cardiac arrest. Follow epinephrine with 2.0 ml sterile normal saline solution.

Contact Medical Control.

219

Medical Control Option A

Atropine sulfate, 0.02 mg/kg IV bolus or IO (minimum single dose 0.1 mg; maximum single dose 0.5 mg for child, 1.0 mg for adolescent; maximum cumulative dose 1.0 mg for a child, 2.0 mg for an adolescent). Administer 2 times the selected dose if given ET. (If administered ET, follow atropine with 2.0 ml sterile normal saline solution.)

Medical Control Option B

Sodium bicarbonate 4.2%, 1.0 mEq/kg IV bolus (for infants less than three months of age). (Do not repeat.)

Medical Control Option C

Sodium bicarbonate 8.4%, 1.0 mEq/kg IV bolus. (Do not repeat.)

Medical Control Option D

Dextrose 25% (if estimated body weight is less than 50 kg, 0.5 gm/kg IV bolus)

Medical Control Option E

Dextrose 50% (if estimated body weight is 50 kg or greater, 0.5 gm/kg IV bolus)

Medical Control Option F

Naloxone HCL (if age less than 5 years, 0.1 mg/kg IV bolus, ET, or IO; if age 5 years or greater, 2.0 mg IV bolus, ET, or IO). If administered ET, follow naloxone with 2.0 ml sterile normal saline solution.

Medical Control Option G

Intravenous infusion of normal saline to keep the vein open

Medical Control Option H

Intraosseous infusion of normal saline to keep the vein open (if age less than 6 years)

Medical Control Option I

20 ml/kg fluid bolus of normal saline

© *August 1993, Metropolitan Boston EMS Council*

PULSELESS ELECTRICAL ACTIVITY
BOSTON, MA

Pulseless Electrical Activity

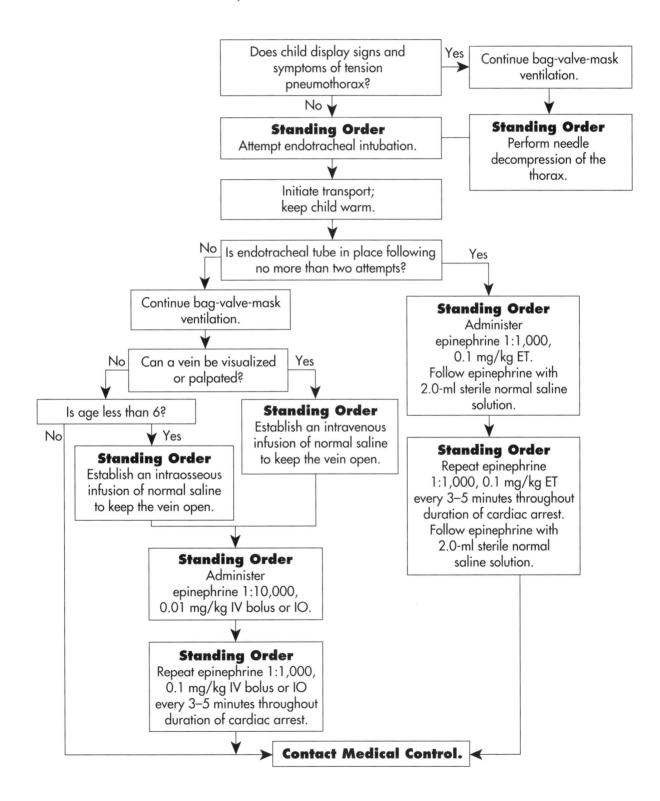

Medical Control Option A
Epinephrine, 1:1,000, 0.1 mg/kg ET. If administered ET,
follow epinephrine with 2.0 ml sterile normal saline solution.

Medical Control Option B
Atropine sulfate, 0.02 mg/kg IV bolus or IO (minimum single dose 0.1 mg; maximum single dose 0.5 mg
for child, 1.0 mg for adolescent; maximum cumulative dose 1.0 mg for a child, 2.0 mg for an adolescent).
Administer 2 times the selected dose if given ET. (If administered ET,
follow atropine with 2.0-ml sterile normal saline solution.)

Medical Control Option C
Sodium bicarbonate 4.2%, 1.0 mEq/kg IV bolus (for infants less than three months of age). (Do not repeat.)

Medical Control Option D
Sodium bicarbonate 8.4%, 1.0 mEq/kg IV bolus. (Do not repeat.)

Medical Control Option E
Dextrose 25% (if estimated body weight is less than 50 kg, 0.5 gm/kg IV bolus)

Medical Control Option F
Dextrose 50% (if estimated body weight is 50 kg or greater, 0.5 gm/kg IV bolus)

Medical Control Option G
Naloxone HCL (if age less than 5 years, 0.1 mg/kg IV bolus, ET, or IO; if age 5 years or greater,
2.0 mg IV bolus, ET, or IO). If administered ET, follow naloxone with 2.0-ml sterile normal saline solution.

Medical Control Option H
Intravenous infusion of normal saline to keep the vein open

Medical Control Option I
Intraosseous infusion of normal saline to keep the vein open (if age less than 6 years)

Medical Control Option J
20 ml/kg fluid bolus of normal saline

Medical Control Option K
Needle decompression of the thorax

PULSELESS ELECTRICAL ACTIVITY
CHARLOTTE, NC

Pulseless Electrical Activity

History

1. Patient <14 years old
2. May have history of congenital heart disease or may be on antidysrhythmics
3. Witnesses may report a sudden collapse with or without antecedent signs and symptoms.

Physical

1. Patient is unresponsive.
2. Absent respirations
3. No palpable pulse

Electrocardiogram

1. Appears as normal sinus rhythm with normal QRS complexes

Differential

Hypoxia
Tension pneumothorax
Pulmonary embolus
Myocardial infarction

Profound hypotension
Pericardial tamponade
Hypothermia

Protocol

1. Check for breathing and pulses and apply cardiac monitor or quick-look paddles. May obtain rhythm strip.
2. Maintain airway and assist ventilations with bag-valve mask and 100% oxygen.
3. Begin CPR.
4. Perform orotracheal intubation and ventilate with 100% oxygen.
5. Consider and administer any or all of the following therapeutic interventions:

   Normal saline IV or IO wide open

   Epinephrine 1:10,000 0.01 mg/kg (0.1 ml/kg) IV or IO

   Repeat epinephrine 1:1,000 0.2 mg/kg
   (0.2 ml/kg) IV or IO.
   Dose may be repeated every 5 minutes if patient remains pulseless.

If pulse less than 60 and no response from above,
Atropine 0.02 mg/kg IV or IO
minimum: 0.1 mg
maximum: 0.5 mg—child
        1.0 mg—adolescent
Dose may be repeated once in 5 minutes.

6. Initiate transport. Continue to monitor vital signs while en route.

7. Contact medical control en route. The following interventions may be considered:

   Fluid bolus 20 ml/kg IV or IO

   High-dose epinephrine 1:1000 0.5–5 mg IV or IO

   Sodium bicarbonate 1 mEq/kg IV
      May repeat 0.5 mEq/kg IV dose every 10 minutes

   Needle thoracostomy

Addendum

1. Since hypoxemia is a major cause of EMD, intubation should be considered early in the treatment protocol.

2. The following medications may be administered by the endotracheal route after dilution from 1:1 with normal saline:
   Epinephrine 1:1000 0.1 mg/kg (0.1 ml/kg)
   Atropine 0.4 mg/kg

NEONATAL RESUSCITATION
FREMONT, CA

Neonatal Resuscitation

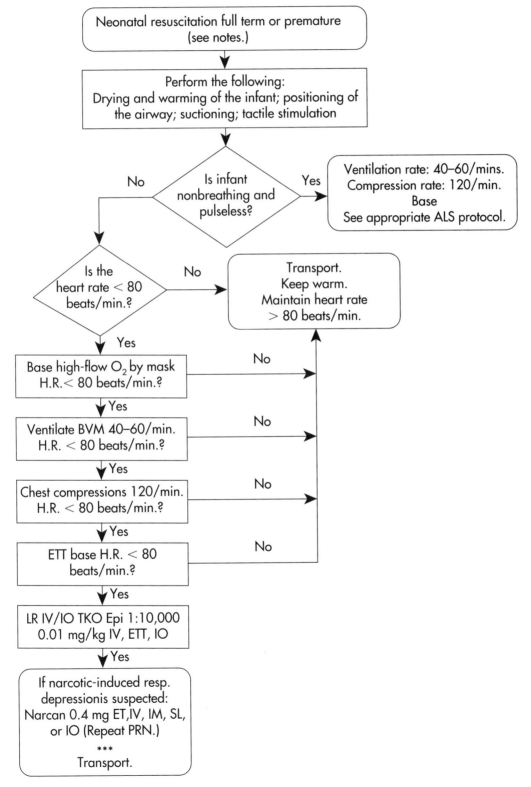

NOTE: If clinical symptoms suggest a narcotic-induced respiratory depression, Narcan may be given earlier in the algorithm.

NEONATAL RESUSCITATION
BOSTON, MA

Newborn Resuscitation

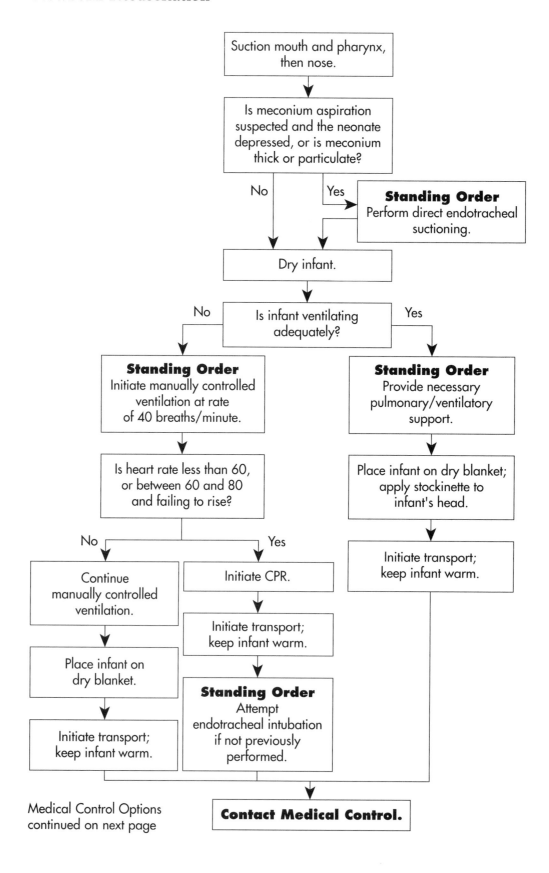

Medical Control Options
continued on next page

| **Medical Control Option A** |
| Naloxone HCL, 0.5 mg IM or ET |

| **Medical Control Option B** |
| Epinephrine, 1:10,000, 0.03 mg/kg ET |

| **Medical Control Option C** |
| Nasogastric intubation |

© *August 1993, Metropolitan Boston EMS Council*

NEONATAL RESUSCITATION
PORTLAND, OR

Neonatal Resuscitation

History:

A. Painful bleeding in mother (suggestive of abruptio placenta)
B. Prolonged rupture of membranes
C. Maternal fever
D. Maternal hypertension, hypotension, edema, seizures

Physical Findings:

A. APGAR score
B. Vital signs
C. Color
D. Meconium-stained fluid
E. Prolapsed cord

Treatment:

If time permits, contact OLMC for advice and transport to the nearest hospital.

If delivery is inevitable and imminent, prepare the mother as usual and deliver the baby, trying to prevent suffocation (*e.g.*, in breech or other abnormal presentation) by holding the vaginal wall away from the baby's face or pushing the baby back up a little if a prolapsed cord is present.

If the presentation is a normal-vertex (headfirst) presentation and the amniotic fluid is clear, briefly suction the mouth and then the nose when the head is first delivered before the chest is delivered and before the infant takes his or her first breath.

If there is no thick or particulate meconium, proceed as in the following paragraph. If there is thick or particulate meconium, go to "Meconium Aspiration."

A. GENERAL RESUSCITATION:

  1. When the newborn is delivered, clamp and cut the cord, holding the child level with the mother's perineum.
  2. Dry thoroughly, position for optimal airway, and suction mouth and then nose.
  3. Evaluate the respirations:

      a. If the newborn is apneic or gasping, provide 15–30 seconds of positive-pressure ventilation (PPV) using a bag-valve mask attached to high-flow, 100% O_2; continue 100% O_2 and evaluate heart rate.
      b. If there are adequate, spontaneous respirations, evaluate heart rate.

  4. Evaluate the heart rate:

      a. If the heart rate is >100 bpm, watch for spontaneous respirations. Discontinue PPV if spontaneous respirations are adequate and color is good. If cyanosis is present, provide supplemental O_2. Continue to observe and monitor in either case.

b. If the heart rate is < 80 bpm and is increasing with PPV, continue PPV until heart rate is > 100 bpm and proceed as above.

c. If the heart rate is < 80 bpm and is not increasing with PPV, continue PPV and begin chest compressions. Begin compressions immediately if heart rate is < 60 bpm.

5. If respirations or heart rate remain inadequate, intubate and ventilate.

6. Initiate medications if heart rate remains < 80 bpm after 30 seconds of PPV with 100% O_2 and chest compressions or immediately if the heart rate is zero.

a. Epinephrine 1:10,000: rapid infusion of 0.01 mg/kg (0.1 ml/kg) IV, IO, or ET. (May dilute 1:1 if giving by ET.) May repeat q 3 to 5 minutes if still needed.

b. Heart rate should rise to greater than 100 bpm within 30 seconds after epinephrine. If heart rate remains less than 100 bpm despite repeated epinephrine and there is evidence of acute blood loss or signs of hypovolemia, administer 10 ml/kg of BSS. After effective ventilation has been established and has failed to improve the baby's condition, administer sodium bicarbonate, 2 meq/kg, slowly over at least 2 minutes IV.

c. Obtain capillary blood glucose if neonate remains depressed. For glucose less than 40, administer 2 cc/kg D25 (single dilution of D50).

d. Atropine and calcium have not been shown to be useful in the acute phase of neonatal resuscitation.

7. Remember to *Keep the Infant Warm!!!*

B. Meconium Aspiration

Meconium in the amniotic fluid can be aspirated, resulting in a potentially fatal course or requiring high-pressure ventilation and resulting chronic lung disease. Many of these complications can at least be attenuated, if not prevented, by suctioning meconium from the airway *prior* to ventilating. This can be emotionally difficult to do when confronted with a depressed, blue, bradycardic newborn, but direct tracheal suctioning through the ET tube should be considered part of establishing a patent airway in these newborns. With all infants who have passed meconium, as soon as the baby's head is delivered (before delivery of the shoulders), using a 10 French or larger suction catheter, suction the mouth, pharynx, and nose.

After delivery, proceed with intubation for all infants who are depressed and have passed meconium or any infant passing thick, particulate meconium.

PROCEDURE

1. Suction the mouth, nose, and posterior pharynx using a 10 French or larger catheter hooked to machine suction when the head is delivered and again after the rest of the infant has been delivered.

2. Intubate the infant with the appropriately sized endotracheal tube and suction with a meconium-suction adapter or use a specially designed meconium

aspiration catheter/endotracheal tube such as Neovac.® Suction should not last more then 3–5 seconds. *DO NOT SUCTION WITH YOUR OWN MOUTH!!!* Use the portable machine suction or wall suction if available.

3. In an infant with severe asphyxia, clinical judgement should be used to determine the number of reintubations. It may not be possible to clear the trachea of all meconium before initiating other resuscitation measures.

4. Check blood glucose, and give appropriate infant dose of glucose if blood glucose is low.

PEDIATRIC CARDIAC EMERGENCIES

PEDIATRIC VENTRICULAR TACHYCARDIA WITH PULSE

1. Lexington, KY
2. Albuquerque, NM—IV bretylium option
3. Nashville, TN—IV dilantin for cocaine/crack

PEDIATRIC BRADYCARDIA

1. Phoenix, AZ—flow-chart format
2. Boston, MA—endotracheal tube atropine
3. Philadelphia, PA—Heart rate for infants, children, and adolescents triggers protocol.

PEDIATRIC TACHYARRHYTHMIAS

1. San Francisco, CA—vent. rate > 200/min.; flow-chart format
2. Charlotte, NC—vent. rate > 240/min.
3. Philadelphia, PA—vent. rate > 160/min.; flow-chart format

PEDIATRIC VENTRICULAR TACHYCARDIA WITH PULSE
LEXINGTON, KY

Ventricular Tachycardia with Pulse

1.0 *Initial Medical Care*

2.0 *BCLS*

> **2.1** Give oxygen by face mask at 6 l/min.
>
> **2.2** Assist ventilation with bag mask if cyanosis present or continues or if child is lethargic with slow breathing.

3.0 Apply *monitor* leads and record 6-second rhythm strip.

4.0 Elevate head and shoulders if child is in congestive failure (rales or jugular-venous distention present).

5.0 Establish IV of *NS* at KVO.

6.0 Administer *lidocaine* bolus 1.0 mg/kg IV push.

7.0 If ventricular tachycardia continues and child appears to be in shock (hypotensive, lethargic, poor capillary refill), radio for order to:

> *Cardiovert* (SYNCHRONIZED) at .5 J/kg. Check pulse and monitor rhythm. If different rhythm develops, proceed to appropriate protocol.

8.0 Transport ASAP with radio contact for further orders.

© Lexington Fire Department

PEDIATRIC VENTRICULAR TACHYCARDIA WITH PULSE
ALBUQUERQUE, NM

Pediatric Ventricular Tachycardia

Designation of Condition:

The patient will have a pulse and show sustained ventricular tachycardia (wide QRS) on the monitor.

Field Treatment

STABLE V-TACH
- Assess and secure airway/oxygen.
- Establish IV or IO access.
- **Lidocaine** 1 mg/kg IVP
- Transport.
- If no response to lidocaine, **contact MCEP.** Expect orders to rebolus 0.5 mg/kg every 5–8 minutes until 3 mg/kg have been given.
- Assess efficacy of ventilation/perfusion-status at regular intervals.
- If no response, contact MCEP. MCEP may order sedation for cardioversion.
- Synchronized **cardioversion** on *MCEP order only* using at 0.5–1.0 J/kg
- If unsuccessful, expect orders for **bretylium**—5 mg/kg infused slowly over 5–10 minutes and repeat **cardioversion** at 0.5–1.0 J/kg.

UNSTABLE V-TACH
- Assess and secure airway/oxygen.
- Establish IV or IO access.
- Consider sedation, **diazepam (Valium)** 0.2–.5 mg/kg.
- Synchronized **cardioversion,** 0.5–1.0 J/kg
- If response, administer **lidocaine** 1.0 mg/kg IV or IO. Rebolus in 5 mins. and start a lidocaine drip at 1 mg/min.
- If unsuccessful, administer **lidocaine** 1.0 mg/kg bolus, then repeat synchronized cardioversion at 2 J/kg up to two attempts.
- Consider **bretylium,** 5 mg/kg infused slowly over 5–10 minutes IV or IO.
- Repeat **cardioversion** at 2 J/kg.

***Defibrillate if synchronized cardioversion is delayed.

233

PEDIATRIC VENTRICULAR TACHYCARDIA WITH PULSE
NASHVILLE, TN

Ventricular Tachycardia

A. Assessment

   1. Confirm cardiac rhythm with quick-look paddles or electrodes.
   2. Check for palpable pulse (brachial for infants—carotid for adolescents).
   3. **CAUTION:** If the suspected etiology of the V-Tach is cocaine or crack ingestion or IV injection, contact medical control immediately. DILANTIN (phenytoin) is currently the drug of choice for these patients, but medical control direction is needed.

B. *TREATMENT*
   PULSELESS: Treat with ventricular fibrillation protocol.

PULSE PRESENT:	*PULSE PRESENT:*
STABLE	UNSTABLE
OXYGEN 100%	OXYGEN 100%
IV NORMAL SALINE TKO	IV NORMAL SALINE TKO
Contact medical control.	Contact medical control.
LIDOCAINE (xylocaine) 1 mg/kg	IV sedative if conscious LIDOCAINE (xylocaine) 1 mg/kg
LIDOCAINE (xylocaine) 1.0 mg/kg in 10–15 minutes	Synchronized cardioversion 0.5–1 joules/kg
Contact medical control.	Synchronized cardioversion 2 joules/kg
Cardioversion as in unstable patients	LIDOCAINE (xylocaine) 1 gm/250 cc IV admix @ 2–4 mg/min. (titrate) upon conversion

Start IV infusion of antiarrhythmic agent that resolved arrhythmia.

Unstable indicates symptoms (*e.g.*, chest pain or dyspnea), hypotension, congestive heart failure, ischemia, or infarct.

PEDIATRIC BRADYCARDIA
PHOENIX, AZ

Pediatric Bradycardia

Standing orders require contacting medical control as soon as the patient's condition allows and as soon as feasible.

↓

Standing Order
Establish an airway, perform ventilations, and administer 100% oxygen as indicated.

↓

Does cardiopulmonary compromise exist?
Signs and symptoms of cardiopulmonary compromise include poor perfusion, hypotension, respiratory difficulty, and decreased level of consciousness.

↓

Initiate chest compressions if despite oxygenation and ventilation, the heart rate is less than 60/minute in an infant or child with poor systemic perfusion.

↓

Standing Order
If unable to start an intravenous infusion and signs/symptoms of cardiopulmonary compromise exist, establish an intraosseous infusion (IO) of normal saline or lactated Ringer's at a TKO rate.

Standing Order
Establish an intravenous infusion (IV) of normal saline or lactated Ringer's at a TKO rate.

↓

Standing Order
Administer epinephrine
- IV/IO: 0.01 mg/kg (1:10,000)
- ET: 0.1 mg/kg (1:1,000).
  Repeat every 3–5 minutes.

↓

Normal Respiration Rates
- Infant   25–40 breaths/minute
- Child   20–28 breaths/minute
- Adolescent 15–20 breaths/minute

Standing Order
Administer atropine 0.02 mg/kg IV. Administer a minimum dosage of 0.1 mg and do not exceed a maximum dosage of 0.5 mg for a child or 1.0 mg for an adolescent. Repeat once.

↓

Contact Medical Control.

235

PEDIATRIC BRADYCARDIA
BOSTON, MA

Pediatric Bradydysrhythmias

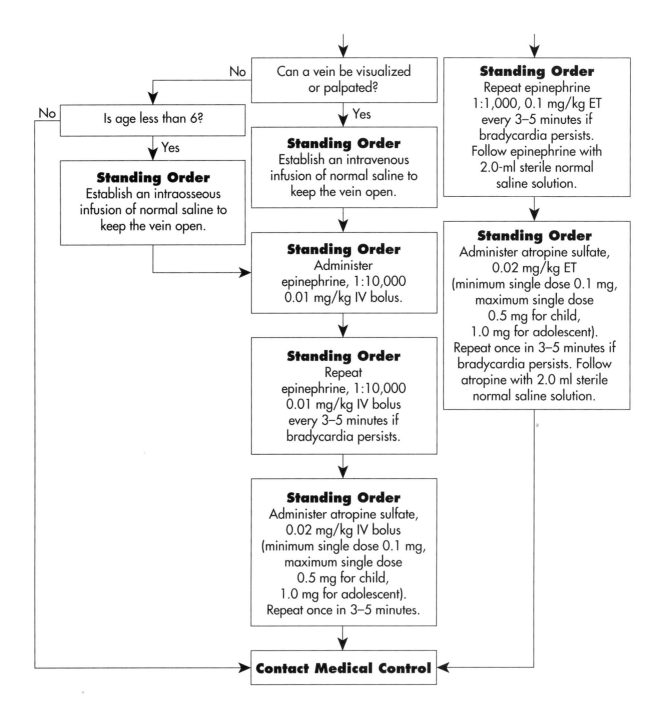

Medical Control Option A
Atropine sulfate, 0.02 mg/kg IV bolus, IO, or ET (minimum single dose 0.1 mg; maximum single dose 0.5 mg for child, 1.0 mg for adolescent; maximum cumulative dose 1.0 mg for a child, 2.0 for an adolescent). (If administered ET, follow atropine with 2.0 ml sterile normal saline solution.)

↓

Medical Control Option B
Intravenous infusion of normal saline to keep the vein open

↓

Medical Control Option C
20 ml/kg fluid bolus of normal saline

↓

Medical Control Option D
Dextrose 25% (if estimated body weight is less than 50 kg, 0.5 gm/kg IV bolus)

↓

Medical Control Option E
Dextrose 50% (if estimated body weight is 50 kg or greater, 0.5 gm/kg bolus)

↓

Medical Control Option F
Naloxone HCL (if age less than 5 years, 0.1 mg/kg IV bolus, ET, or IM; if age 5 years or greater, 2.0 mg IV bolus, ET, or IM). If administered ET, follow naloxone with 2.0 ml sterile normal saline solution.

*Primary heart block is rare in children. Bradycardia usually results from hypoxemia and hypoventilation.

© August 1993, Metropolitan Boston EMS Council

PEDIATRIC BRADYCARDIA
PHILADELPHIA, PA

Bradycardia

The rate at which a child is bradycardic depends upon age. The EKG is characterized by a slow rate, in addition to alteration of P to QRS ratio and PR interval. Bradycardia in children often responds to oxygen and ventilatory support.

Algorithm Notes

1. Serious signs or symptoms include:
   - Symptoms: chest pain, shortness of breath, decreased level of consciousness
   - Signs: low blood pressure, shock, congestive heart failure

2. Place an intraosseous (IO) line if unable to obtain intravenous (IV) access. Once established, the IO line replaces the IV line as the primary route of administration for fluid and medications.

3. When given IV or IO, epinephrine may be repeated every 3–5 minutes.

4. Atropine administration may be repeated once in five (5) minutes. Maximum dose is 2 mg.

AVERAGE PEDIATRIC VITAL SIGNS

TEMPERATURE	AGE	PULSE	BLOOD PRESSURE+	RESPIRATIONS
36–37°C	Newborn	140–160	80/50	Infant: 40
	1 year	120	82/54	Preschool: 30
	2 years	110	84/56	School age: 20
	4–6 years	100	90/60– 110/76	
	8–10 years	90	116/78	
	12 years	80	120/80	

+Hypotension implies a systolic blood pressure 10 mm Hg less than the average value for age. When in doubt, check with medical command physician.

FIFTIETH PERCENTILE (AVERAGE) WEIGHTS BY AGE [KG]
(N.B.: BROSELOW TAPE IS PREFERRED IF AVAILABLE.)

AGE (YEARS)	0.5	1	1.5	2	3	4	5	6	7
Boy	8	10	11	12	14	17	19	21	23
Girl	7	9.5	11	12	14	16	18	20	22
AGE (YEARS)	8	9	10	11	12	13	14	15	16
Boy	25	28	32	36	40	45	50	55	60
Girl	25	28	32	37	41	46	50	54	56

NOTE: If child's weight is *greater than* 50 kg enter the adult protocol.

If history/evidence of trauma, proceed to trauma protocol.

↓

Heart rate less than 80/minute in infants
Heart rate less than 70/minute in children
Heart rate less than 60/minute in adolescents

↓

Serious signs or symptoms[1]

↓

NO	YES
↓	↓
Initiative IV NSS TKO.	Initiative IV NSS TKO.[2]
↓	↓
CONTACT BASE.	Epinephrine 1:10,000 0.01 mg/kg IV[3]
↓	↓
TRANSPORT.	Continued signs and symptoms

↓

NO	YES
↓	↓
CONTACT BASE.	Atropine 0.02 mg/kg IV[4] with minimum dose of 0.1 mg
↓	↓
TRANSPORT.	CONTACT BASE.
	↓
	TRANSPORT.

PEDIATRIC TACHYARRHYTHMIAS
SAN FRANCISCO, CA

Pediatric Tachycardia > 200/Minute

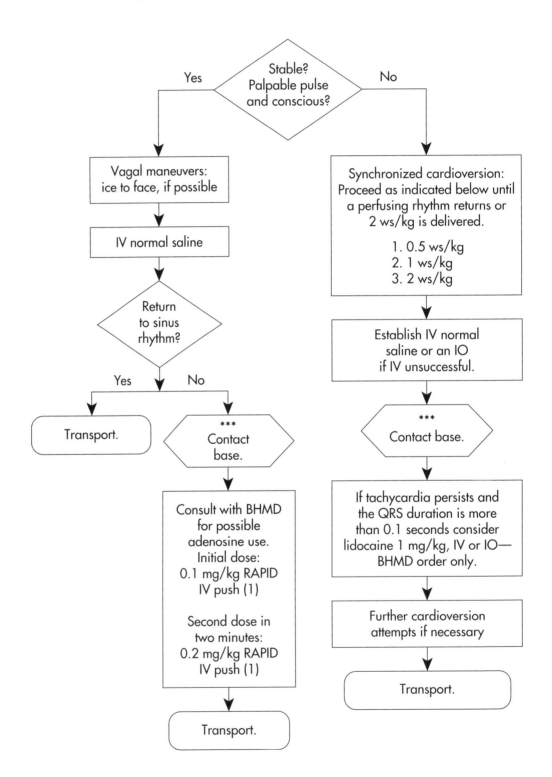

Protocol Notes

1. Due to the very short half-life of adenosine (approximately 10 seconds), a rapid normal saline flush is required immediately following the adenosine. To accomplish this, place the needle from a syringe with 10 cc of normal saline into the same IV-line medication port as the adenosine. The medication port should be the closest port to the IV catheter. The antecubital fossa vein is preferable due to the closer proximity to the central circulation. Administer the rapid adenosine push, then rapidly push the normal saline prior to removing the adenosine syringe needle.

PEDIATRIC TACHYARRHYTHMIAS
CHARLOTTE, NC

Supraventricular Tachycardia, Unstable

History

1. Patient <14 years old
2. Patient may complain of cough, congestion, shortness of breath, or dizziness/lightheadedness.
3. May have history of congenital heart disease or may be on antidysrhythmics

Physical

1. Patient may be conscious and alert or may have an altered level of consciousness.
2. Signs of uncomplicated shock may be evident, such as poor skin color, weak peripheral pulses, capillary refill > 2 seconds, or hypotension.
3. Palpable pulse

Electrocardiogram

1. Ventricular rate > 240 beats per minute
2. QRS duration < 0.12 seconds
3. P waves may be absent or difficult to see.

Differential

Sinus tachycardia
Ventricular tachycardia

Protocol

1. Maintain airway and administer oxygen via nasal cannula at 2–6 l/min. or nonrebreathing mask at 15 l/min. depending on patient's respiratory status.
2. Obtain vital signs and apply cardiac monitor or quick-look paddles. Obtain rhythm strip after monitor is attached.
3. Consider and administer any or all of the following therapeutic interventions:

   IV or IO normal saline TKO or PRN adapter
   Diazepam 0.2 mg/kg IV
   Cardioversion (synchronized) at 0.5 joules/kg
       If no response:
   Cardioversion (synchronized) at 1 joules/kg
       If no response:
   Cardioversion (synchronized) at 2 joules/kg
   Reassess ABCs and vital signs.

4. Initiate transport. Continue to monitor vital signs while en route.
5. Depending on the clinical condition of the patient and if an IV or IO line can be initiated quickly (in less than 2 minutes), contact medical control and consider the following therapeutic intervention, either at the scene or en route.

> Adenosine protocol:
> 0.1 mg/kg IV push followed by 5 ml NS flush
> > If no response after 2 minutes:
> 0.2 mg/kg IV push followed by 5 ml NS flush
> > If no response after 2 minutes:
> 0.2 mg/kg IV push followed by 5 ml NS flush
> (Maximum dose should not exceed 12 mg.)

Addendum

1. Supraventricular tachycardia is the most common dysrhythmia causing cardiovascular instability during infancy.
2. Supraventricular tachycardia with aberrant conduction that produces a wide-complex tachycardia is rare in infants and children. Therefore, all wide-complex tachycardias should be treated as ventricular in origin.
3. In older children, may consider valsalva and/or carotid sinus massage while setting up for more aggressive therapy.
4. Sedation with valium should be attempted before cardioversion unless patient is extremely unstable or unconscious.
5. Whenever cardioversion is performed, equipment for emergent intubation should be readily available (suction, bag-valve mask, laryngoscope/blades, and endotracheal tube).
6. If patient deteriorates into another abnormal or malignant dysrhythmia after therapeutic intervention, refer to appropriate protocol.

PEDIATRIC TACHYARRHYTHMIAS
PHILADELPHIA, PA

Supraventricular Tachycardia

Algorithm Notes

1. Supraventricular Tachycardia (SVT) is the most common arrhythmia-producing cardiovascular instability in pediatric patients. This rhythm is characterized by narrow QRS complexes with a rate usually greater than 200–230 beats per minute in infants, and 150–210 beats per minute in children. If entry from ventricular fibrillation/ventricular tachycardia and has not received lidocaine or bretylium, administer lidocaine 1 mg/kg IV, followed by lidocaine 0.5 mg/kg IV every 8–10 minutes according to cardiac status and medical command physician order. Lidocaine drip 1 gm in 250 ml NSS as an alternative may be ordered by medical command physician.

2. Place an intraosseous (IO) line if unable to obtain intravenous (IV) access. Once established, the IO line replaces the IV line as the primary route of administration for fluid and medications.

3. Many patients who present with SVT have evidence of cardiovascular dysfunction (low BP, chest pain, congestive heart failure, altered level of consciousness). A subset of these patients have serious signs and symptoms (such as shock, pulmonary edema, severe chest pain, decreased level of consciousness) and require immediate cardioversion. The rest, who have mild hypotension, mild shortness of breath/scattered rales, mild chest discomfort but are awake and alert, may be treated with adenosine. The following chart illustrates the continuum from borderline to critically unstable.

BORDERLINE		UNSTABLE
Low BP	←——————→	Shock
SOB, scattered rales	←——————→	Pulmonary edema
Mild chest discomfort	←——————→	Severe chest pain
Awake and alert	←——————→	Unconscious

4. Sedation should be considered if time permits. Titrate Valium 0.1 mg/kg IV as appropriate for conscious patients. If conversion occurs, followed by recurrence of SVT, repeated electrical cardioversion is *not* indicated.

5. Adenosine must be given by rapid IV push (over 1–3 seconds), followed by a rapid bolus of 5 cc NSS.

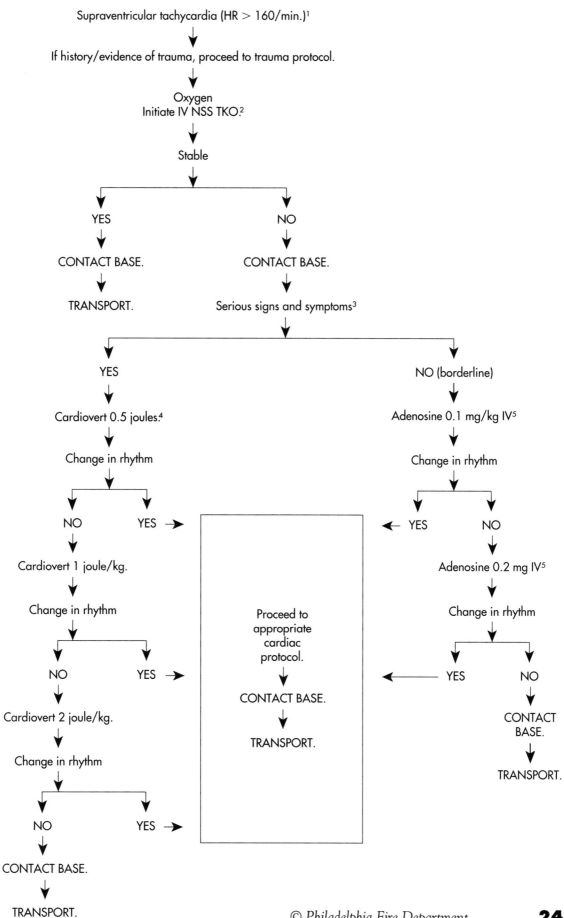

Supraventricular tachycardia (HR > 160/min.)[1]

If history/evidence of trauma, proceed to trauma protocol.

Oxygen
Initiate IV NSS TKO.[2]

Stable

YES

CONTACT BASE.

TRANSPORT.

NO

CONTACT BASE.

Serious signs and symptoms[3]

YES

Cardiovert 0.5 joules.[4]

Change in rhythm

NO   YES →

Cardiovert 1 joule/kg.

Change in rhythm

NO   YES →

Cardiovert 2 joule/kg.

Change in rhythm

NO   YES →

CONTACT BASE.

TRANSPORT.

Proceed to
appropriate
cardiac
protocol.

CONTACT BASE.

TRANSPORT.

NO (borderline)

Adenosine 0.1 mg/kg IV[5]

Change in rhythm

← YES   NO

Adenosine 0.2 mg IV[5]

Change in rhythm

← YES   NO

CONTACT
BASE.

TRANSPORT.

PEDIATRIC TRAUMATIC EMERGENCIES

PEDIATRIC TRAUMA

1. San Francisco, CA—flow-chart format
2. Kansas City, MO—complete
3. Philadelphia, PA—detailed flow chart

PEDIATRIC TRAUMATIC ARREST

1. Boston, MA—flow-chart format
2. New York, NY

PEDIATRICS BURNS

1. Sacramento, CA—albuterol option
2. Columbus, OH—sodium thiosulfate solution
3. Austin, TX—format

PEDIATRIC TRAUMA
SAN FRANCISCO, CA

Pediatric Trauma

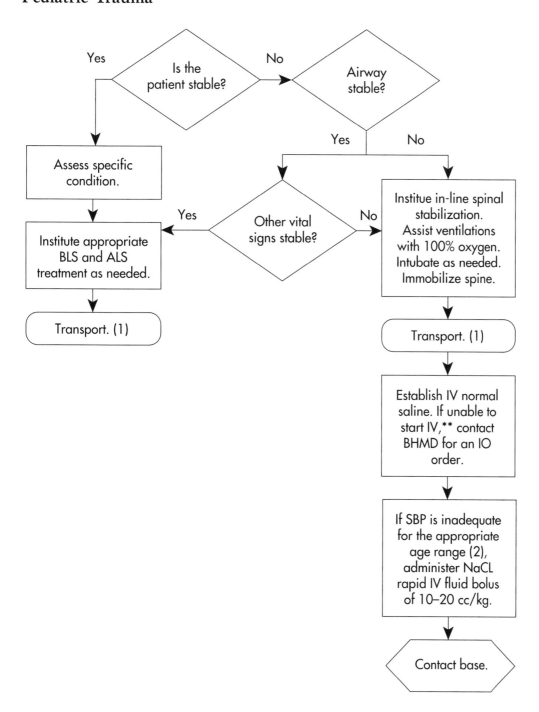

Protocol Notes

1. Transport to an EDAP or the trauma center on the basis of patient-assessment and trauma-center criteria.
2. A pediatric vital-signs chart is on another page of San Francisco, CA protocols.

PEDIATRIC TRAUMA
KANSAS CITY, MO

Pediatric Trauma

Assessment

1. Assess adequacy of airway and breathing with simultaneous cervical-spine immobilization.
2. Assess cardiopulmonary system with attention to adequacy of perfusion (*i.e.*, mental status; presence, location, and character of pulses; skin moisture, temperature, and capillary refill).
3. Briefly assess neurologic function, (*i.e.*, level of consciousness, pupils, gross motor function).
4. Obtain brief history of incident and mechanism of injury.
5. If patient is stable, obtain vital signs and AMPLE history.

Criteria

PHYSIOLOGIC CRITERIA

a. Shock (two or more of the following)

    1. Capillary refill > three (3) seconds
    2. Low blood pressure (see appendix)
    3. Rapid heart rate (see appendix)

b. Respiratory Distress (two or more of following)

    1. Decreased or absent breath sounds
    2. Accessory muscle use
    3. Increased respiratory rate (see appendix)

c. Altered Mental Status

    1. Pediatric GCS < 13 (See appendix)
    2. AVPU scale P or U

MECHANISM OF INJURY

a. Occupant ejection
b. Fall from height of more than 20 feet
c. Pedestrian hit at speed of more than 20 MPH
d. Death of same-car occupant
e. Prolonged extrication >20 minutes

ANATOMIC CRITERIA

a. Penetrating injury to head, chest, abdomen, neck, or groin

Treatment

1. If patient is in no distress and meets none of the physiologic, mechanism of injury, or anatomic criteria suggestive of potential for serious injury, then appropriately immobilize the patient and transport with frequent reassessment of vital signs and patient status.

II. If patient has sustained a mechanism of injury and/or meets anatomic criteria that suggest a potential for severe injury but does not meet physiologic criteria (stable patient) and does not have associated symptoms (altered mental status, respiratory distress, clinical signs of shock), the EMT-P should CONTACT MEDICAL CONTROL and proceed with treatment as directed.

III. If the patient meets physiological criteria (unstable patient) with associated symptoms (altered mental status, respiratory distress, clinical signs of shock), the EMT-P may initiate the following therapy PRIOR to contacting medical control, in accordance with the appropriate trauma protocols.

A. Secure airway and assure adequate ventilation.

  1. Stabilize the cervical spine with manual in-line immobilization. DO NOT APPLY TRACTION.

  2. Use chin lift or modified jaw thrust ONLY to open airway. Consider nasal airway adjunct particularly in the head-injured patient.

  3. Administer oxygen 10–15 l/minute via nonrebreather mask.

  4. Assist ventilation as needed using bag-valve mask with 100% oxygen.

  5. Orotracheal intubation may be attempted if unable to adequately ventilate the patient with a BVM because of severe facial trauma or excessive blood or secretions. Maintain in-line cervical-spine immobilization during intubation attempts. TRANSPORT OF THE UNSTABLE TRAUMA PATIENT SHOULD NOT BE DELAYED BY ATTEMPTS AT INTUBATION UNLESS PATIENT CANNOT BE ADEQUATELY VENTILATED WITH BVM.

  6. Needle cricothyrotomy may be attempted if unable to otherwise secure the airway in patients with severe upper-airway compromise secondary to trauma. Cervical-spine immobilization must be maintained during attempts.

B. Circulatory Support and Fluid Replacement

  1. Control any external bleeding with sterile dressing and direct pressure. Place patient supine and elevate feet if possible.

  2. Apply MAST suit and inflate if indicated.

  3. Initiate one or two large-bore IVs (one IO line if unable to establish IV) and give 20 cc/kg bolus of lactated Ringers. Repeat if necessary. TRANSPORT OF THE UNSTABLE PATIENT SHOULD NOT BE DELAYED TO INITIATE THERAPY. BEGIN IV EN ROUTE TO HOSPITAL!

  4. Monitor cardiac rhythm.

C. Spinal Immobilization

  1. In the stable patient, complete spinal immobilization as indicated by mechanism of injury, using appropriate collar, short board, and long spine board as indicated.

  2. In the unstable patient, transport should not be delayed by the application of short board prior to extrication. Appropriate rapid-extrication techniques to long spine board with manual spine immobilization should be used.

D. Transport.

   1. Monitor vital sings and continually reassess patient status.

   2. Trauma *CODES* should be taken to the nearest level I/II trauma center whether the trauma center is on trauma divert status or not. Taking a trauma patient to a "closed" trauma center applies to trauma codes (blunt or penetrating) *ONLY*.

   3. Patients who meet the physiologic, mechanism of injury, or anatomic criteria to be considered for preferential routing to a level I/II trauma center *and* who are less than 16 years old should be considered for preferential routing to a pediatric trauma center. REMEMBER THE GOLDEN TEN MINUTES! Rapid assessment, rapid initiation of treatment of hypoxemia and shock, and rapid transport. On-scene time should be less than TEN minutes for critically injured patients.

E. CONTACT MEDICAL CONTROL.

   1. Upon beginning treatment, EMT should notify communications center of hospital destination, and if critical patient, initiate MED channel patch and inform hospital of incoming trauma patient.

PEDIATRIC TRAUMA
PHILADELPHIA, PA

Trauma

This protocol refers to all pediatric major-trauma victims. One of the greatest causes of death and permanent morbidity in children is secondary injury to the CNS (*e.g.*, hypoxia after patient's original injury). Any child with neurologic compromise (GCS ≤ 10 or spinal deficit) should have a secured airway, adequate ventilation and spinal immobilization, and then immediate transport to an accredited pediatric trauma center.

As a goal, time on scene must not exceed ten (10) minutes for patients meeting physiologic (vital signs, GCS) or anatomy-of-injury trauma-triage criteria.

Life-threatening injuries occur less frequently in patients who meet mechanism-of-injury criteria only. Therefore, if it is necessary to complete patient immobilization and packaging, prehospital providers may extend on-scene time to twenty (20) minutes.

Circumstances such as prolonged extrication, which result in on-scene time intervals exceeding those stated above, must be documented in the narrative section of the PaEMSR.

If prolonged extrication is required, the paramedic, in consultation with the medical command physician, will recommend dispatch of a surgical response team to the PFD incident commander. If communications should fail with the medical command facility hospital, the dispatcher will relay appropriate trauma information to hospital personnel.

Refer to Appendix III.D, Determination of Receiving Hospital for Trauma Patients, for appropriate disposition of trauma patients.

AVERAGE PEDIATRIC VITAL SIGNS

TEMPERATURE	AGE	PULSE	BLOOD PRESSURE+	RESPIRATIONS
36–37°C	Newborn	140–160	80/50	Infant: 40
	1 year	120	82/54	Preschool: 30
	2 years	110	84/56	School age: 20
	4–6 years	100	90/60–110/76	
	8–10 years	90	116/78	
	12 years	80	120/80	

+Hypotension implies a systolic blood pressure 10 mm Hg less than the average value for age. When in doubt, check with medical command physician.

Algorithm Notes

1. Unresponsive patients with head injuries require hyperventilation since they are at risk for increased intracranial pressure.

2. Clinical signs of hypovolemia.
   - low systolic blood pressure+
   - tachycardia, thready pulse
   - diaphoresis, peripherally cold and clammy
   - decreased capillary nail bed filling
   - lightheadedness, vertigo
   - altered mental state
   - pallor, mottled, cyanotic
   - weakness, fatigue

3. Organized EKG activity without vital signs (PEA) indicates the need for immediate transport to an accredited trauma center. Ventricular fibrillation should be treated in accordance with the ventricular fibrillation protocol while en route.

4. For hypotensive trauma patients, an IV of NSS may be started *en route* to an accredited trauma center. Place an intraosseous (IO) line if unable to obtain intravenous (IV) access. Once established, the IO line replaces the IV line as the primary route of administration for fluid and medications.

5. Have dispatch notify the receiving trauma center by HASTE and make a hotline report.

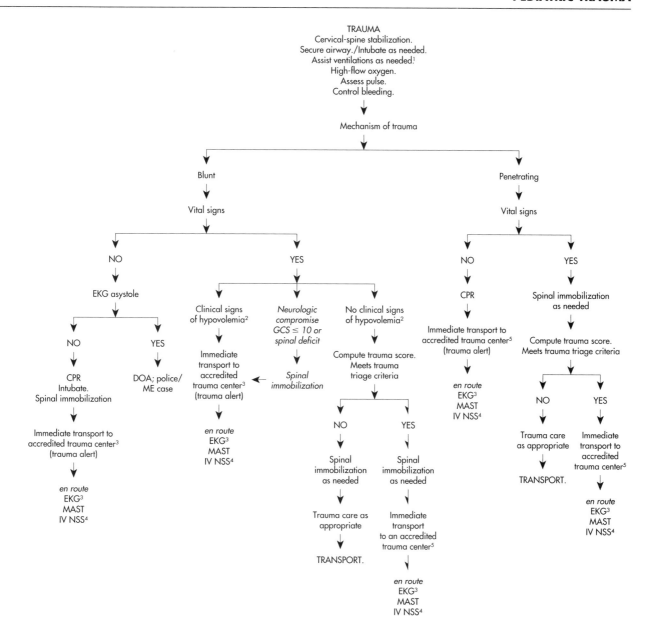

TRAUMA
Cervical-spine stabilization.
Secure airway./Intubate as needed.
Assist ventilations as needed.¹
High-flow oxygen.
Assess pulse.
Control bleeding.

↓

Mechanism of trauma

Blunt

Vital signs

NO
↓
EKG asystole

NO — YES
↓ ↓
CPR DOA; police/
Intubate. ME case
Spinal immobilization
↓
Immediate transport to
accredited trauma center³
(trauma alert)
↓
en route
EKG³
MAST
IV NSS⁴

YES

Clinical signs
of hypovolemia²
↓
Immediate
transport to
accredited
trauma center³
(trauma alert)
↓
en route
EKG³
MAST
IV NSS⁴

*Neurologic
compromise
GCS ≤ 10 or
spinal deficit*
↓
*Spinal
immobilization*

No clinical signs
of hypovolemia²
↓
Compute trauma score.
Meets trauma
triage criteria

NO — YES
↓ ↓
Spinal Spinal
immobilization immobilization
as needed as needed
↓ ↓
Trauma care as Immediate
appropriate transport
↓ to an accredited
TRANSPORT. trauma center⁵
↓
en route
EKG³
MAST
IV NSS⁴

Penetrating

Vital signs

NO
↓
CPR
Immediate transport to
accredited trauma center⁵
(trauma alert)
↓
en route
EKG³
MAST
IV NSS⁴

YES
↓
Spinal immobilization
as needed
↓
Compute trauma score.
Meets trauma triage criteria

NO — YES
↓ ↓
Trauma care Immediate
as appropriate transport to
↓ accredited
TRANSPORT. trauma center⁵
↓
en route
EKG³
MAST
IV NSS⁴

PEDIATRIC TRAUMATIC ARREST
BOSTON, MA

Pediatric Traumatic Cardiopulmonary Arrest

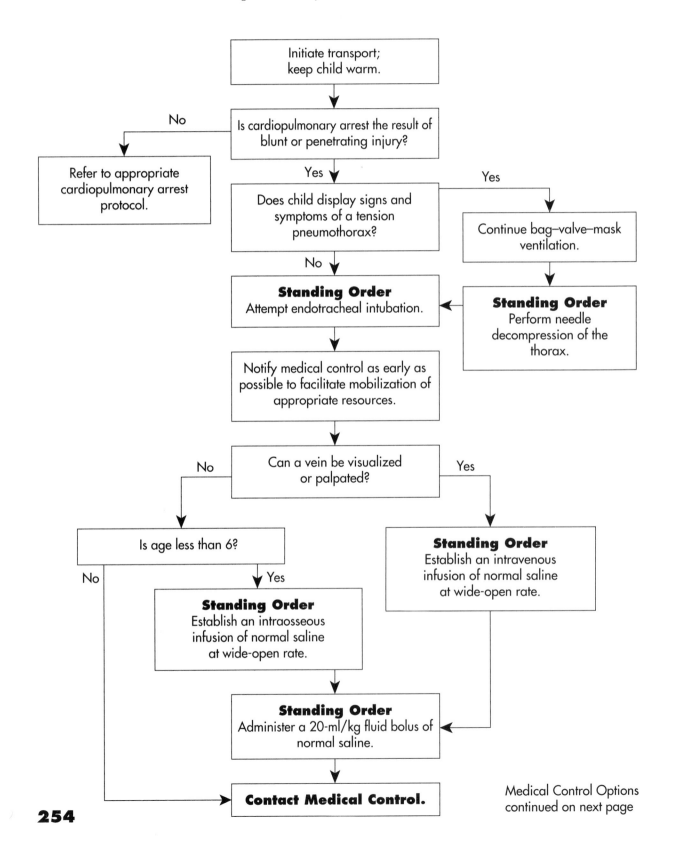

Medical Control Options continued on next page

Medical Control Option A
Needle cricothyroidotomy

Medical Control Option B
Intravenous infusion of normal saline to keep the vein open

Medical Control Option C
20 mg/kg fluid bolus of normal saline

Medical Control Option D
Needle decompression of the thorax

PEDIATRIC TRAUMATIC ARREST
NEW YORK, NY

Pediatric Traumatic Cardiac Arrest

NOTE: FOR PEDIATRIC PATIENTS IN TRAUMATIC CARDIAC ARREST, RAPID TRANSPORT IS THE HIGHEST PRIORITY!

1. Begin transportation of the patient and other basic life-support traumatic cardiac-arrest procedures.

During transport, or if the transport is delayed:

2. Perform endotracheal intubation if other methods of airway control are not effective.
3. If a tension pneumothorax is suspected, perform needle decompression. (See appendix.)
4. Begin rapid IV/saline lock or IO infusion of normal saline (0.9 NS) or Ringer's lactate, 20 ml/kg, via a large-bore IV (18–22 gauge) or IO catheter, or a saline lock. Attempt IV or IO only once each. (See Broselow Tape or appendix.)
5. If abdominal distention occurs, pass a nasogastric tube. If unsuccessful, or in patients with craniofacial trauma, pass an orogastric tube.

NOTE: DO NOT PASS A NASOGASTRIC TUBE IN PATIENTS WITH CRANIOFACIAL TRAUMA.

6. If the patient remains in traumatic cardiac arrest, repeat rapid IV/saline lock or IO infusion of normal saline (0.9 NS) or Ringer's lactate, 20 ml/kg (total of 40 ml/kg), via a second large-bore IV (18–22) catheter, or a saline lock (if necessary). Attempt second IV only once. See (Broselow Tape or appendix.)
7. If the patient still remains in traumatic cardiac arrest, contact medical control for implementation of one or more of the following MEDICAL CONTROL OPTIONS:

Medical Control Options:

Option A: Continue rapid IV or IO infusion of normal saline (0.9 NS) or Ringer's lactate up to an additional 20 ml/kg (total of 60 ml/kg). Attempt IV or IO only once each. (See appendix.)

Option B: Transportation decision

PEDIATRIC BURNS
SACRAMENTO, CA

Pediatric Burns

Procedural Protocol:

Always Use Universal Precautions
1. SAFETY FIRST—Do not expose self to hazardous materials.
2. ASSESS AIRWAY—Observe respirations; auscultate the lung fields; listen for wheezes.
3. OXYGEN—Administer 10 l/min. by mask.
4. CARDIAC MONITOR—Apply, if not already done. If dysrhythmia is noted, see appropriate pediatric protocol.
5. BURN CHART—Estimate degree of burn.
6. EMT-II: CONTACT BASE HOSPITAL.
7. APPLY DRESSINGS—moist dressing if burns <20% body surface area second or third degree, dry dressings if >20% body surface area.
8. IV ACCESS—Administer normal saline at TKO rate via volutrol with microdrip tubing. IF PATIENT SHOWS SIGNS OF SHOCK, bolus with 20 cc/kg normal saline.
9. IF WHEEZES ARE PRESENT:
   ALBUTEROL (EMT-P ONLY)—Administer 2.5 mgm diluted in 2.5 cc normal saline via hand-held nebulizer or aerosolized mask.
10. EMT-PARAMEDIC: CONTACT BASE HOSPITAL.
11. MORPHINE—if pain is severe. Administer 0.1–0.2 mg/kg slow IV push.

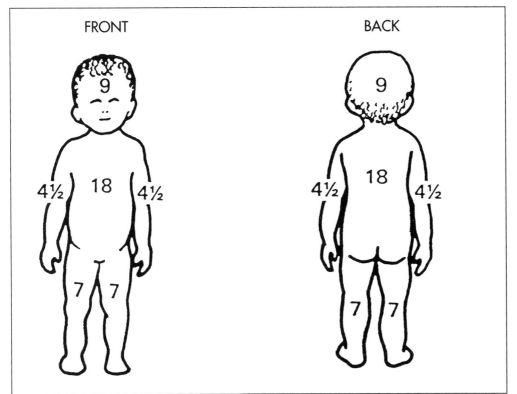

Pediatric Burn Chart

PEDIATRIC AVERAGE WEIGHTS AND
VITAL SIGNS/RECOMMENDED ET TUBE AND BLADE SIZES

AGE	(50TH %TILE) WEIGHT (KG)	PULSE/ MIN.	RESP./ MIN.	ET TUBE*	BLADE #
Premie	<1–2.5			2.5–3 (uncuffed)	0
Term NB	2.5–4	100–160	30–50	3–3.5 (uncuffed)	1
6 months	7	80–160	30–50	3.5–4 (uncuffed)	1
1 year	10	80–160	24–40	4–4.5 (uncuffed)	1
2 years	12	80–130	24–32	4.5 (uncuffed)	2
4 years	16	80–120	22–28	5.0 (uncuffed)	2
6 years	20	75–115	22–28	5.5 (uncuffed)	2
8 years	25	70–110	20–24	6.0 (either)	2
10 years	34	70–110	20–24	6.5 (either)	2
12 years	41	65–110	16–22	7.0 (cuffed)	3

Formulas for systolic BP:

50th percentile BP for over age 2 $\mapsto$ systolic BP=90 + (2 $\times$ age in yrs.)

Lower BP Limit $\mapsto$ systolic BP=70 + (2 $\times$ age in yrs.)

*ET tube selection should be based on the child's size, not age. One size larger or one size smaller should be allowed for individual variations.

PEDIATRIC BURNS
COLUMBUS, OH

Pediatric Burns

1. ABCs. Maintain a high level of suspicion for inhalation injury in patients with singed hairs or eyebrows, mucosal burns, cough. See PAIN CONTROL PROTOCOL.
   A. For patients less than age 14 with smoke inhalation who demonstrate altered level of consciousness or significant cardiac arrhythmias, administer 1.65 cc/kg of 25% SODIUM THIOSULFATE SOLUTION.

2. Establish large-bore IVs with 0.9% NORMAL SALINE and run at maintenance rate. If signs of shock are present, push 20 ml/kg or 10 ml/lb. as per MULTIPLE TRAUMA PROTOCOL.

3. Apply dry sterile dressings to all burns. May cover body part with wet dressing if burn is limited to small area (<10% BSA).

4. Transport to children's hospital if indicated as per BURN TRANSPORT PROTOCOL.

5. Consider transport for patients with burns involving the hands, face, and genitalia (critical burns).

PEDIATRIC BURNS
AUSTIN, TX

Introduction

Care of the thermal-burn patient should be guided by scene safety, cooling the burn, maintaining normal body temperature, and protecting the airway. Remember the thermal-burn patient has injured the largest organ of the body. Shock in the very early stages of a burn is not generally associated with the burn. Care should be given to rule out other life-threatening injuries. A high index of suspicion for carbon-monoxide poisoning and smoke inhalation should be maintained for any patient burned in a confined space. Care should be given to maintain normal body temperature. Use blankets as necessary. Shivering is not a normal symptom of thermal burns.

Key Actions

COMMUNICATIONS
1. Secure a safe scene.
2. Protect patient from further injury.
3. ABCs
4. If safe, stop the burning process.
5. Remove jewelry/clothing unless melted to body.

BLS
1. Assessment/Vital signs
2. Oxygen therapy
3. Dry sterile dressing (may use saline dressing for 2nd-degree burns <10% BSA)
3. Splint fractures (after applying dressing)
4. Keep patient warm. (Heat loss can occur rapidly.)

ILS
None

ALS
1. Monitor EKG and pulse oximetry.
2. Initiate IV lifeline(s) for burns involving >20% BSA.
3. Fluid therapy 20 ml/kg fast IV bolus or fast IV drip then keep vein open.
4. Morphine sulfate 0.1–0.2 mg/kg IV for pain management
5. Early intubation if airway involvement occurs

Assessment Considerations

1. Is everyone safe from further exposure? Is the patient having difficulty breathing? What caused the burn?
2. How much of the body is burned? What type of burns are they (first degree, *etc.*)?
3. Does the patient feel cold or shivering?

Special Situations/Conditions

1. Major burns: electrical and chemical burns (see adult section for considerations), inhalation injuries, burns with other injuries, burns involving the face or hands, burns involving the perineum, and burns with >10% full thickness or 20% partial thickness should be transported immediately to the nearest major burn facility for proper treatment.

© *Austin/Travis EMS Clinical Practice*

PEDIATRIC MEDICAL EMERGENCIES

PEDIATRIC ANAPHYLAXIS

1. San Mateo, CA—mild vs. moderately severe symptoms
2. Durham, NC
3. Austin, TX—IV methylprednisolone

PEDIATRIC SHOCK

1. Fremont, CA—flow-chart format
2. San Francisco, CA—septic vs. cardiogenic vs. hypovolemic vs. anaphylactic treatment options
3. Nashvile, TN—heart rate and BP shock criteria by age

PEDIATRIC STATUS EPILEPTICUS

1. San Francisco, CA—flow-chart format
2. Las Vegas, NV—algorithm
3. Akron, OH—IV Midazolam

PEDIATRIC POISONING

1. Fremont, CA—flow-chart format
2. Los Angeles, CA—calcium blocker, tricyclic OD treatments
3. Jacksonville, FL
4. Charlotte, NC

PEDIATRIC ALTERED MENTAL STATUS

1. Fremont, CA—narcan SL
2. San Mateo, CA—neonates 12.5% dextrose; infant/child 25% dextrose
3. New York, NY—<6 mos. 10% dextrose, 6 mos.–2yrs. 25% dextrose

PEDIATRIC ANAPHYLAXIS
SAN MATEO, CA

Pediatric Allergic Reaction and Anaphylaxis

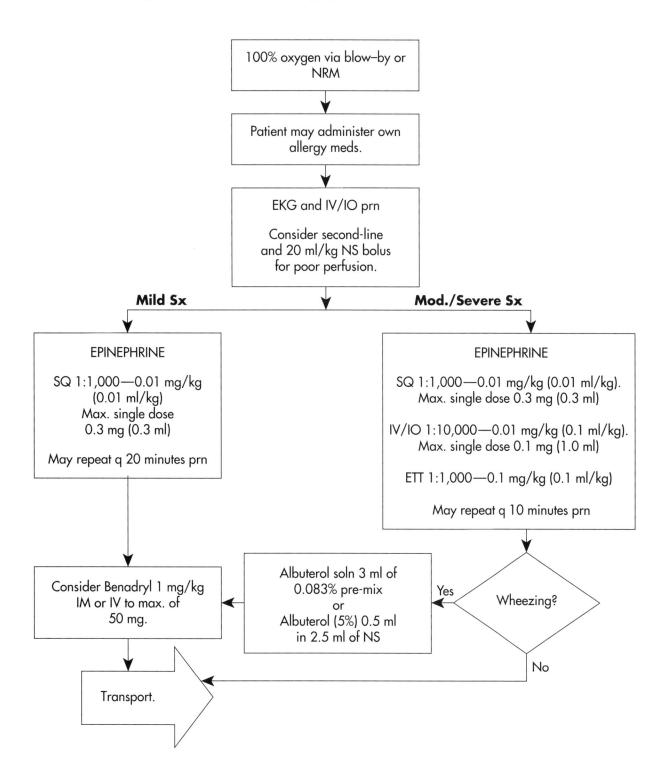

PEDIATRIC ANAPHYLAXIS
DURHAM, NC

Pediatric Anaphylaxis

Criteria

Anaphylaxis is a clinical diagnosis. There *may* be a history of an insect bite, food ingestion, new medicine, *etc*. Characteristic symptoms *may* include: dyspnea, hoarseness, pruritus, chest tightness, presyncopal feelings, *etc*. Characteristic signs *may* include: hypotension, stridor, wheezing, facial swelling, hives, *etc*. Any evidence of hypotension, airway compromise, serious systemic reaction, or history of previous serious reaction usually requires treatment.

Standing Orders

1. Appropriate airway management and oxygen. Monitor.
2. Check systolic blood pressure for evidence of hypotension:

> Newborn–1 year: Systolic BP less than 60
> 1 year or older: Systolic BP less than 70 + 2 × age in years

EMT-D
3. Epinephrine 1:1000 0.01 cc/kg SC/IM

EMT-I
4. IV fluid bolus LR 20 cc/kg

EMT-P
5. Benadryl 1–2 mg/kg IM/IV
6. Epinephrine 1:10,000 0.1 cc/kg IV/ET/IO if severe reaction not responsive to other interventions

PEDIATRIC ANAPHYLAXIS
AUSTIN, TX

Pediatric Allergy and Anaphylactic Reaction

Introduction

This group of medical problems has a wide range of severity. At this extreme end, reactions are life threatening with a mortality rate of approximately 3% requiring swift action. Care is focused on reducing airway obstruction and reducing or stopping the allergic reaction.

Key Actions Communications

1. Remove patient from exposure if necessary.
2. ABCs
3. Position/calm/reassure the patient.
4. Gather home medications.
5. Assist with home epinephrine kit PRN.
6. NPO

BLS
1. Assessment/vital signs
2. Oxygen therapy PRN
3. Cryotherapy PRN

ILS
1. Epinephrine pen per instructions on package
2. Diphenhydramine PO (dosage per instructions on package) (max. dose 25 mg)

ALS
1. Monitor EKG and pulse oximetry.
2. Initiation of IV lifeline(s). PRN
3. Epinephrine 0.01 mg/kg SQ q20 minutes (max. dose 0.3 mg)
4. Diphenhydramine 1 mg/kg IV or IM (max. dose 25 mg)
5. Albuterol nebulizer 1 unit dose q15 minutes
6. Fluid therapy 10–20 ml/kg IV PRN for hypotensive patients
7. Methylprednisolone 2 mg/kg IV (max. dose 125 mg)

Assessment Considerations

1. Dyspnea present?
2. Pale cool skin with or without diaphoresis? Is there any rash or hives present? Is there any itching?

3. When and what was the exposure? Has it caused a reaction before? If so, how bad was the previous reaction?
4. Common allergens include: penicillin, insect stings, shellfish, allergy treatments; and nuts or foods.

Special Situations/Conditions

None

© Austin/Travis EMS Clinical Practice

PEDIATRIC SHOCK
FREMONT, CA

Pediatric Shock

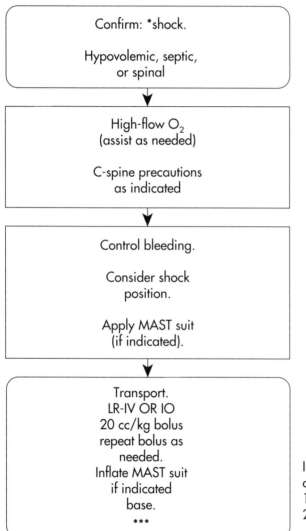

Confirm: *shock.

Hypovolemic, septic,
or spinal

High-flow O$_2$
(assist as needed)

C-spine precautions
as indicated

Control bleeding.

Consider shock
position.

Apply MAST suit
(if indicated).

Transport.
LR-IV OR IO
20 cc/kg bolus
repeat bolus as
needed.
Inflate MAST suit
if indicated
base.
***

Indications for application/inflation
of the MAST suit:
1. Suspected pelvic fracture
2. For all other reasons BHP
approval is required.

*Definition—SHOCK:
1. Shock in children is subtle and may be difficult to detect.
2. Blood pressure is difficult to determine accurately in the small child and may be of little use.
3. Important signs to watch for are:

    3.1 Pallor (secondary to decreased skin perfusion)
    3.2 Altered sensorium (secondary to decreased brain perfusion)

PEDIATRIC SHOCK
SAN FRANCISCO, CA

Pediatric Shock

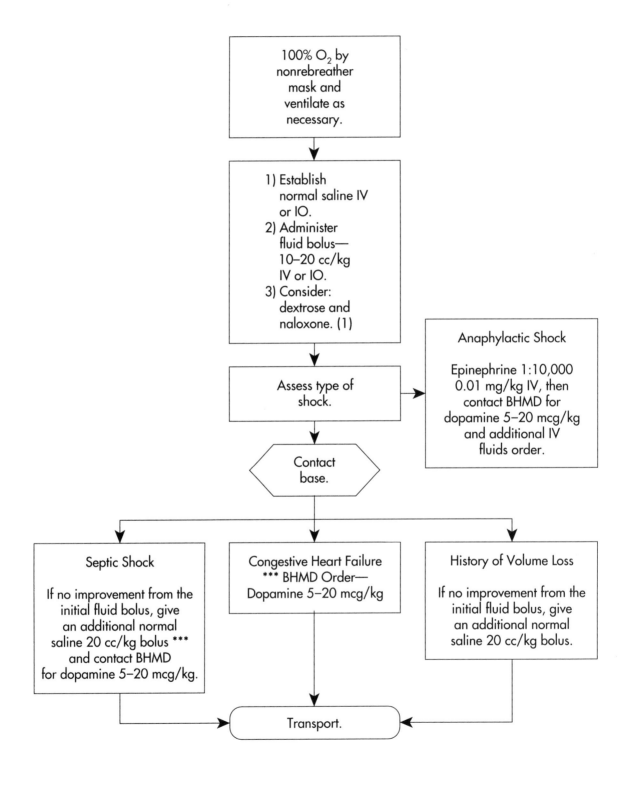

100% O$_2$ by nonrebreather mask and ventilate as necessary.

1) Establish normal saline IV or IO.
2) Administer fluid bolus—10–20 cc/kg IV or IO.
3) Consider: dextrose and naloxone. (1)

Assess type of shock.

Contact base.

Anaphylactic Shock

Epinephrine 1:10,000 0.01 mg/kg IV, then contact BHMD for dopamine 5–20 mcg/kg and additional IV fluids order.

Septic Shock

If no improvement from the initial fluid bolus, give an additional normal saline 20 cc/kg bolus *** and contact BHMD for dopamine 5–20 mcg/kg.

Congestive Heart Failure *** BHMD Order—Dopamine 5–20 mcg/kg

History of Volume Loss

If no improvement from the initial fluid bolus, give an additional normal saline 20 cc/kg bolus.

Transport.

Protocol Notes

1. Dextrose and/or naloxone are indicated in cases where hypoglycemia or opiate overdose possibly mimic shock. Appropriate assessment of the patient and history will help clarify the diagnosis.

DEXTROSE DOSAGES:
Patients less than two (2) years old—25% dextrose 2 cc/kg
Patients more than two (2) years old—50% dextrose 1 cc/kg

NALOXONE DOSAGES:
Patients less than two (2) years old—naloxone 0.4 mg IV
Patients more than two (2) years old—naloxone 2 mg IV

PEDIATRIC SHOCK
NASHVILLE, TN

Hypovolemic Shock

A. Assessment

1. Cool, clammy skin
2. Poor capillary refill (greater than 5 seconds)

TACHYCARDIA

Newborn	greater than 180/min.
Infant	greater than 160/min.
Toddler	greater than 140/min.
Preschooler	greater than 130/min.
Adolescent	greater than 120/min.

LOW SYSTOLIC BLOOD PRESSURE

Newborn	less than 60 mm Hg
Infant	less than 70 mm Hg
Toddler	less than 80 mm Hg
Preschooler	less than 90 mm Hg
Adolescent	less than 100 mm Hg

B. Treatment

1. OXYGEN 100%
2. Primary IV NORMAL SALINE 20 cc/kg over 20 minutes (large-bore catheter). Repeat once if necessary.
3. Contact medical/trauma control.
4. Secondary IV LACTATED RINGER'S (large-bore catheter)
5. Maintain temperature above 97° F; warm IV fluid.
6. IF dextrostix becomes less than 40 mg/percent, use pediatric hypoglycemia protocol.
7. Consider: MAST
INTRAOSSEOUS INFUSION

PEDIATRIC STATUS SEIZURE
SAN FRANCISCO, CA

Pediatric Status Seizure

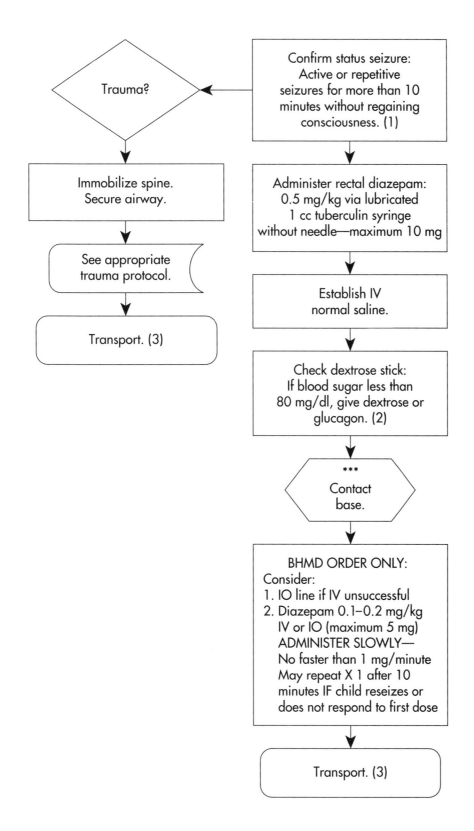

Trauma?

Confirm status seizure: Active or repetitive seizures for more than 10 minutes without regaining consciousness. (1)

Immobilize spine.
Secure airway.

Administer rectal diazepam: 0.5 mg/kg via lubricated 1 cc tuberculin syringe without needle—maximum 10 mg

See appropriate trauma protocol.

Establish IV normal saline.

Transport. (3)

Check dextrose stick: If blood sugar less than 80 mg/dl, give dextrose or glucagon. (2)

***
Contact base.

BHMD ORDER ONLY:
Consider:
1. IO line if IV unsuccessful
2. Diazepam 0.1–0.2 mg/kg IV or IO (maximum 5 mg) ADMINISTER SLOWLY— No faster than 1 mg/minute May repeat X 1 after 10 minutes IF child reseizes or does not respond to first dose

Transport. (3)

Protocol Notes

1. Paramedics should determine status seizure by either direct observation of the patient or reliable history obtained from other sources, *e.g.*, firefighters, police officers, other medical personnel, or family members. Paramedics may institute pharmacological treatment as soon as they establish this history. It is not necessary for paramedics to observe the patient seizing for prolonged time periods before beginning treatment.

2. Dextrose dosages:
   Patients less than two (2) years old—25% dextrose 2 cc/kg
   Patients more than two (2) years old—50% dextrose 1 cc/kg

3. Transport Code 3 to the closed EDAP if the patient is still seizing. If the patient is stable, the paramedic may opt to transport Code 2 to the closest EDAP.

PEDIATRIC STATUS SEIZURE
LAS VEGAS, NV

Pediatric Seizures

Objective:

To ensure that potential or actual medical causes for pediatric-seizure activity are investigated, treated, and followed/evaluated by appropriate resources.

Overview:

The etiology of seizures in children 16 years old and under includes fever, head trauma, and drug overdose, or is idiopathic in nature. The most common type of seizure for a patient under 6 years of age is a simple febrile seizure, which is usually terminated prior to EMT arrival, with the only necessary therapy being that of cooling measures and airway protection. Pharmacologic therapy of pediatric seizures in the field, which are usually the result of status epilepticus, is reserved for children who are actively seizing upon arrival of the EMT. Status epilepticus is defined as any seizure lasting more than 15 minutes or 2 or more consecutive seizures without interruption. Due to the potential for neurological sequelae and field limitations to adequately assess the etiology of pediatric seizures, the strongest recommendation for transport should be made after a complete assessment and treatment of life-threatening signs and symptoms.

Guidelines:

ASSESSMENT

I. Obtain a detailed history of the seizure activity.

    A. Previous history of seizure activity? If yes, was the seizure related to a fever, epilepsy, head injury, or other medical illness?

    B. Does the child take medication? If yes, when was the last dose taken?

    C. When did the seizure begin? How long did it last?

    D. Does the child have a fever or medical illness now? Was trauma or poisoning involved?

    E. How did the child behave when the seizure began? (Shaking of arms and legs, eye rolling, loss of consciousness, urinary incontinence?) Has the shaking of arms and legs stopped and started again?

    F. Has the child been unconscious the entire time? Has the child had any respiratory distress?

II. Perform a detailed physical exam including:

    A. Assessment of the ABCs

        1. Airway

            a. Patent

            b. Maintainable

            c. Unmaintainable

2. Breathing

   a. Respiratory rate
   b. Quality
   c. Character

B. Observe for s/s of trauma/poisoning.
C. Obtain vital signs.
D. Obtain dextrose stick.
E. Observe and record all seizure activity for duration, characteristics, and possible focality.
F. Perform frequent reassessment.

TREATMENT

I. Continuously monitor ABCs.
II. Provide airway management by positioning and suctioning when necessary.
III. Administer 100% oxygen.
IV. Use BVM if respiratory failure is present or if assistance is needed, making sure there is a tight seal.
V. Endotracheal intubation should be reserved for the patient who does not respond to BVM.
VI. Cervical-spine immobilization is indicated if there is any suspicion of trauma that may have precipitated or resulted from the seizure.
VII. Provide cooling measures if the patient has an elevated temperature.
VIII. Attempt vascular access with normal saline if:

   A. Patient is actively seizing.
   B. Respiratory failure is evident.
   C. Hypotension/shock is evident.
   D. Blood glucose is <60.

IX. Patients who are not actively seizing should NOT receive anticonvulsant therapy in the field.
X. Hypoglycemic patients (blood glucose <60) should receive D25 (children 2 years of age and under should receive D25 solution, while children over 2 years of age may receive the D50 solution), 2 cc/kg with a maximum dose of 50 ml. If an IV is not established, administer glucagon 0.5 mg IM.
XI. Actively seizing patients should receive rectal diazepam 0.5 mg/kg per rectum with the maximum dose of 10 mg. If an IV route has been established, give diazepam 0.1 to 0.3 mg/kg slow IV push until the seizure terminates or maximum dose of 10 mg is reached. These medications must be given slowly with constant reassessment of ABCs and preparedness for airway management should it become necessary.
XII. Immediate transport of all pediatric seizure patients to an appropriate facility is recommended.

Pediatric Seizure Algorithm

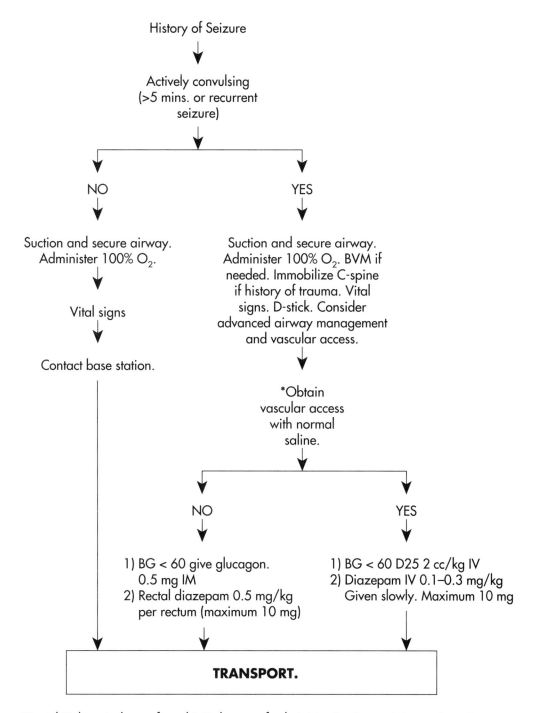

History of Seizure

↓

Actively convulsing
(>5 mins. or recurrent
seizure)

↓

NO	YES
↓	↓
Suction and secure airway. Administer 100% O_2.	Suction and secure airway. Administer 100% O_2. BVM if needed. Immobilize C-spine if history of trauma. Vital signs. D-stick. Consider advanced airway management and vascular access.
↓	↓
Vital signs	*Obtain vascular access with normal saline.
↓	
Contact base station.	

*Obtain vascular access with normal saline.

NO	YES
↓	↓
1) BG < 60 give glucagon. 0.5 mg IM 2) Rectal diazepam 0.5 mg/kg per rectum (maximum 10 mg)	1) BG < 60 D25 2 cc/kg IV 2) Diazepam IV 0.1–0.3 mg/kg Given slowly. Maximum 10 mg

TRANSPORT.

*Rectal Valium is the preferred initial route of administration in a seizing patient. Do not delay treatment in an attempt to gain IV access.

Transport with cooling measures if temperature is elevated, with frequent reassessment.

PEDIATRIC STATUS SEIZURE
AKRON, OH

Pediatric Seizures

A. in a child with a known seizure disorder and a single seizure who has fully regained consciousness, follow standard EMTA care.
B. in a child with suspected febrile seizure:

 1. Remove clothing.
 2. Do not cool with water or alcohol.

C. in a child who is in tonic-clonic grand mal status epilepticus:

 1. Establish an airway; usually a nasal airway will be best; give supplemental oxygen.
 2. IV NS TKO
 3. Midazolam 0.2 mg/kg IV push to a maximum single dose of 5 mg. May give IO or IM if no IV access.
 4. Check field blood sugar if less than 80 mg% by glucometer, push 2 cc/kg D25 if a good IV is established.

PEDIATRIC POISONING
FREMONT, CA

Poisoning/Overdose/Ingestion

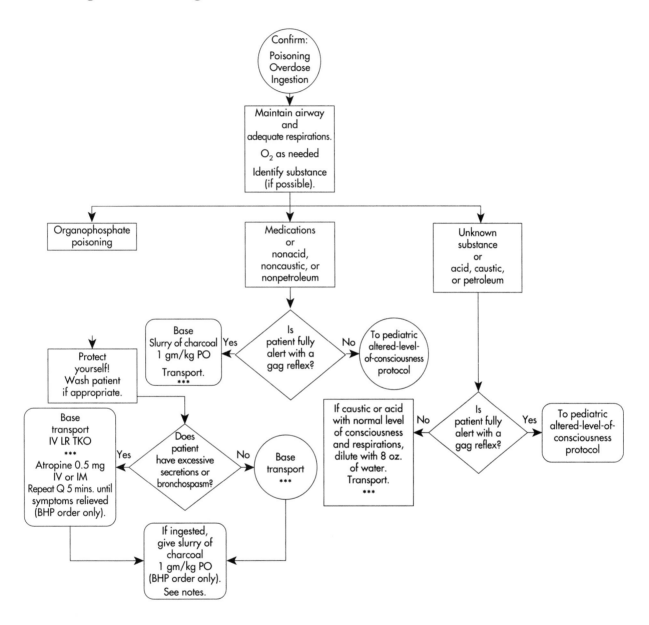

PEDIATRIC POISONING
LOS ANGELES, CA

Overdose/Poisoning—Suspected

FIELD TREATMENT

1. Basic airway
2. Oxygen

Note 6

3. Advanced airway prn
4. Cardiac monitor
5. Venous access prn/blood glucose test prn

Note 7

6. If hypotension, use NONTRAUMATIC HYPOTENSION **M8** guideline.

Note 8

ALERT AND ORIENTED

7. Consider **activated charcoal 25–50 gm** PO.

Notes 1, 2

8. Reassess for potential deterioration.

ALTERED LOC

7. **Narcan® 0.8–2 mg** IVP
☞ May repeat every 5 minutes prn if strong suspicion of narcotic overdose exists or partial response is noted

Notes 3, 4

8. If hypoglycemia, **dextrose 50% 50 ml** IVP

Note 5

☞ May repeat one time

Note 9

Drug Considerations

ACTIVATED CHARCOAL:

1. Contraindicated if patient cannot voluntarily swallow.
2. Pediatrics:
   0–2 years—not recommended
   Over 2 years—adult dose as tolerated

NARCAN® (NALOXONE):

3. Alternate routes: ET (double IV dose), IM, or SL

4. Pediatrics: 0.02 mg/kg IVP or IM; ET (double IV dose)

DEXTROSE 50%:

5. Pediatrics: 2 ml/kg of dextrose 25% IVP

Special Considerations

6. If narcotic overdose, consider venous access and Narcan prior to advanced airway.

7. If unable to establish venous access and known diabetic, consider **glucagon 1 mg** IM or SQ. Same for pediatrics.

8. Bring substance/container to hospital for chemical analysis.

9. Drugs to consider for specific history:
Calcium channel blocker—**calcium chloride 500–1000 mg** IVP
Tricyclic with dysrhythmia or hypotension—**sodium bicarbonate 1 mEq/kg** IVP and see appropriate dysrhythmia.

© 1993 (Revised), Los Angeles County Base Hospital Treatment Guidelines

PEDIATRIC POISONING
JACKSONVILLE, FL

Pediatric Poisoning

I. Patient Evaluation:
  A. History

1. Name of drug ingested or toxin exposure—obtain container if possible.
2. Time of ingestion/exposure
3. Amount ingested
4. History of other ingestion or suicide attempts
5. Current medications
6. Allergies
7. Past medical history
8. History of emesis after ingestion

  B. Physical findings

1. Breath or body odor (garlic, almond, petroleum, *etc.*)
2. Central nervous system status (level of consciousness, gag reflex, seizures, posturing, pupil size and reactivity)
3. Respiratory status.

   a. Rate and depth of respirations
   b. Secretions
   c. Breath sounds

4. Cardiovascular status

   a. Blood pressure
   b. Rate and character of pulse
   c. Capillary refill time
   d. EKG. (May have widened QRS in tricyclic overdose.)

5. Oral mucosa burns
6. SLUD (salivation, lacrimation, urination, defecation) often present in organophosphate poisoning

II. Treatment:
  A. Establish and maintain patent airway.
  B. Establish IV, normal saline, KVO.
  C. Administer oxygen as indicated.
  D. Unconscious or lethargic patient

1. Administer dextrose 25% (dilute D50W 1:1 with sterile water), 2–4 ml/kg IV push
2. Naloxone, 0.1 mg/kg IV or IM. Maximum dose 2 mg. If opiate ingestion suspected, repeat every 3–5 mins. up to maximum 10 mg.

E. In seizure patient

   1. D25W, 2–4 ml/kg
   2. Diazepam (if actively seizing) 0.3 mg/kg IV or 0.5 mg/kg rectally. Maximum dose 10 mg.

F. Dermal exposure

   1. Remove excess.
   2. Flush with water.
   3. In eye exposure, irrigate with normal saline.

G. Patients who ingest toxic substance and remain conscious, administer activated charcoal (except with caustic ingestion).

PEDIATRIC POISONING
CHARLOTTE, NC

Toxicology/Ingestions

History

1. Patient may have history of suspected, witnessed, or alleged ingestion, inhalation, or exposure.

Physical

1. Patient may appear to be intoxicated or have an altered level of consciousness.
2. Seizures may occur.
3. Vomiting may occur.
4. Skin and pupil changes may be apparent.

Differential

Electrolyte disturbance
Hypoglycemia
Psychiatric

Protocol

1. Confirm scene safety and ensure a protective environment for yourself and the patient.
2. If any evidence of contamination exists, immediately decontaminate. Protect your skin and clothes during this procedure. Methods of decontamination may include any or all of the following:

   A. remove patient from contaminated environment
   B. remove clothes
   C. wash hair and/or skin
   D. flush eyes and/or mucous membranes

3. Maintain airway, suction as appropriate, and administer oxygen via nasal cannula at 2–6 l/min. or nonrebreathing mask at 15 l/min., depending on patient's respiratory status. Consider assisted ventilations with bag-valve mask or intubate if patient is hypoventilating or airway compromise is apparent.
4. Obtain vital signs and apply cardiac monitor. Obtain rhythm strip. If particular dysrhythmia or heart rate noted, proceed to indicated protocol.
5. Attempt to locate nature of exposure or ingestion. If pill bottle(s) are found, they should be brought to the hospital with the patient.
6. Initiate transport. Continue to monitor vital signs while en route.

7. Consider any or all of the following therapeutic interventions:

IV normal saline TKO or PRN adapter
Exposure involved organophosphates and patient is symptomatic (salivation, lacrimation, urination, vomiting, or defecation)
Atropine 2 mg IV

8. Contact medical control if indicated.

Addendum

1. Carolinas Poison Center may be contacted if time permits, the patient is stable, and the scene situation allows for such. Phone: 355–4000.
2. For incidents involving industrial or chemical spills, radiation accidents, or other incidents where hazardous materials are involved, strict communication with the fire department should be established.
3. Ipecac is not to be utilized unless directed to do so by medical control.

PEDIATRIC ALTERED MENTAL STATUS
FREMONT, CA

Pediatric Altered Level of Consciousness

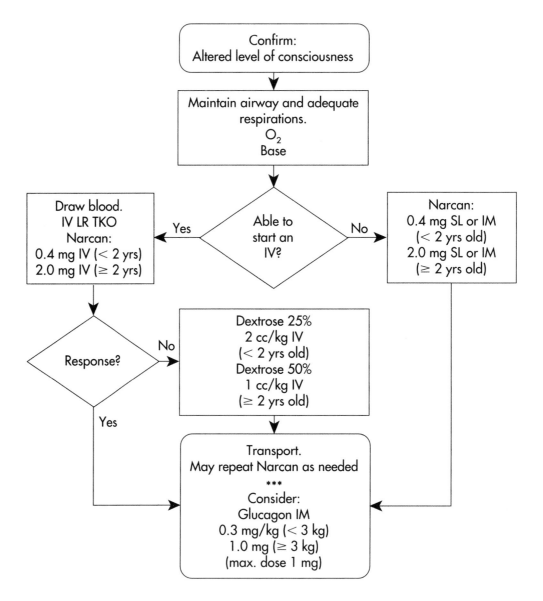

NOTES:

1. Clinical setting may dictate dextrose or Narcan as initial drug.
2. Known diabetic, able to hold head upright and gag reflex present may give glucose paste:
   - **2.1** < 5 years old, 1/2 tube (15 grams)
   - **2.2** ≥ 5 years old, 1 tube (30 grams)

PEDIATRIC ALTERED MENTAL STATUS
SAN MATEO, CA

Pediatric Altered Level of Consciousness

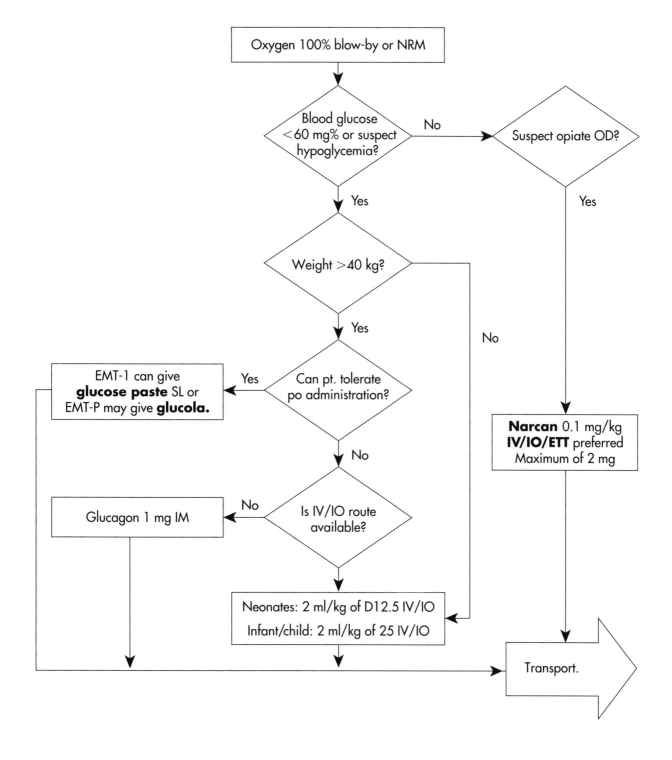

PEDIATRIC ALTERED MENTAL STATUS
NEW YORK, NY

Pediatric Altered Mental Status

For pediatric patients in coma, with evolving neurological deficit or with altered mental status of unknown etiology:

NOTE: MAINTENANCE OF NORMAL RESPIRATORY AND CIRCULATORY FUNCTION IS ALWAYS THE FIRST PRIORITY. PATIENTS WITH ALTERED MENTAL STATUS DUE TO RESPIRATORY FAILURE OR ARREST, OBSTRUCTED AIRWAY, SHOCK, TRAUMA, NEAR DROWNING, OR OTHER ANOXIC INJURY SHOULD BE TREATED UNDER OTHER PROTOCOLS.

1. Begin basic life-support altered mental status procedures.

During transport, or if transport is delayed:

2. Administer glucagon 1.0 mg, IM. (See appendix.)
3. Begin an IV or IO infusion of normal saline (0.9 NS) to keep vein open, or a saline lock. Attempt IV or IO only once each.
4. Administer dextrose 0.5 gm/kg, IV/saline lock or IO bolus. Use 10% dextrose in patients less than six (6) months of age. Use 25% dextrose in patients between six (6) months and two (2) years of age. Use 50% dextrose in patients two (2) years of age or older. Maximum dose is 25 gm. (See Broselow Tape or appendix.)
5. If there is no change in mental status, administer naloxone 2.0 mg, IV/saline lock, or IO bolus in patients two (2) years of age or older. Use half the amount (1.0 mg) of this drug in patients less than two (2) years of age. (See appendix.)
6. If there is still no change in mental status, repeat naloxone 2.0 mg, IV/saline lock or IO bolus, in patients two (2) years of age or older. Use half the amount (1.0 mg) of this drug in patients less than two (2) years of age. (See appendix.)
7. If IV/saline lock access has not been established, administer naloxone 2.0 mg, IM, in patients two (2) years of age or older. Use half the amount (1.0 mg) of this drug in patients less than (2) years of age. (See appendix.)
8. If there is still no change in mental status, contact medical control for implementation of one or more of the following MEDICAL CONTROL OPTIONS:

Medical Control Options:

OPTION A: Repeat any of the above standing orders.
OPTION B: Transportation decision

UNIQUE PEDIATRIC PROTOCOLS

PEDIATRIC RESPIRATORY ARREST
NEW YORK, NY

Pediatric Respiratory Arrest

For pediatric patients in actual or impending respiratory arrest, or who are unconscious and cannot be adequately ventilated:

1. Begin basic life-support pediatric respiratory distress/failure procedures.

NOTE: DO NOT HYPEREXTEND THE NECK. IF AN OBSTRUCTED AIRWAY IS SUSPECTED, SEE PROTOCOL.

2. Perform endotracheal intubation.
3. If a tension pneumothorax is suspected, perform needle decompression. (See appendix.)

NOTE: TENSION PNEUMOTHORAX IN A CHILD IN RESPIRATORY ARREST MAY DEVELOP AFTER RESUSCITATIVE EFFORTS HAVE BEGUN.

During transport, or if transport is delayed:

4. Administer naloxone 2.0 mg, IM, or via the endotracheal tube, in patients two (2) years of age or older. Use half the amount (1.0 mg) of this drug in patients less than two (2) years of age. (See appendix.)
5. If abdominal distention occurs, pass a nasogastric tube. If unsuccessful, pass an orogastric tube.
6. If there is insufficient improvement in respiratory status, contact medical control for implementation of one or more of the following MEDICAL CONTROL OPTIONS:

MEDICAL CONTROL OPTIONS:
OPTION A: Begin an IV or IO infusion of normal saline (0.9 NS) to keep vein open, or a saline lock. Attempt IV or IO only once each.
OPTION B: Administer naloxine 2.0 mg, IV/saline lock or IO bolus, via the endotracheal tube, or IM, in patients two (2) years of age or older. Use half the amount (1.0 mg) of this drug in patients less than two (2) years of age. (See appendix.)
OPTION C: Transportation decision

PEDIATRIC RESPIRATORY ARREST
SCOTTSDALE, AZ

Respiratory Failure/Arrest

Standing orders require contacting medical control as soon as the patient's condition allows and as soon as feasible.

↓

If the airway is obstructed, follow the AHA guidelines for foreign-body airway obstruction.

Standing Order
Establish an airway, perform ventilations, and administer 100% oxygen as indicated.

↓

Standing Order
If unable to start an intravenous infusion and signs/symptoms of cardiopulmonary compromise exist, establish an intraosseous infusion (IO) of normal saline or lactated Ringer's at a TKO rate.

Standing Order
Establish an intravenous infusion (IV) of normal saline or lactated Ringer's at a TKO rate.

↓

Standing Order
For bronchospasm: Administer albuterol 0.15 mg/kg up to a maximum of 5 mg by SVN.

↓

Standing Order
For narcotic overdose: Administer naloxone IV/IO/ET, based on the patient's age:
- *less than 5 years old*—Administer 0.1 mg/kg to a maximum dose of 2 mg.
- *5 years and older*—Administer 2.0 mg.
  The initial dose may be repeated every 3–5 minutes to a maximum of 5 doses.

↓

Standing Order
For anaphylaxis: Administer epinephrine:
- SC: 0.01 mg/kg (1:1,000)
- IV/IO: 0.01 mg/kg (1:10,000)
- ET: 0.10 mg/kg (1:1,000).

↓

Consider inserting a nasogastric or orogastric tube.

↓

Contact Medical Control.

NOTE: In patients with suspected epiglottitis or croup, rapid assessment and transportation with minimal manipulation of the airway is paramount. Keep the patient calm and quiet and attempt to provide blow-by oxygen.

NORMAL RESPIRATION RATES

• Infant	25–40 breaths/minute
• Child	20–28 breaths/minute
• Adolescent	15–20 breaths/minute

APNEA/INADEQUATE RESPIRATIONS
PHILADELPHIA, PA

Apnea/Inadequate Respirations

Inadequate respirations are indicated by anxiety, restlessness, poor or unequal chest expansion, cyanosis, extremely shallow respirations, respiratory rate as listed below, and abnormal or absent breath sounds.

The pediatric airway is very different from that of the adult, particularly in children less than two years of age. The tongue is large relative to the size of the mouth and tends to cause airway obstruction. An oral or nasal airway may be necessary in order to provide adequate ventilation.

Algorithm Notes

1. Endotracheal intubation is the preferred method of airway maintenance. Refer to table below for pediatric endotracheal tube-size guidelines. EOA is contraindicated in children less than 16 years of age.
2. Consider intubation of the right main-stem bronchus. If necessary, remove initial ET tube. Hyperventilate for one minute, then reattempt intubation.
3. If endotracheal intubation is unsuccessful after three attempts, use manual methods to maintain airway and ventilations. Immediately transport to closest appropriate hospital.

Rate of assisted ventilations for:
*   Infants: 20–25 breaths/minute
*   Children: 16–20 breaths/minute
*   Adolescents: 12–15 breaths/minute

LARYNGOSCOPE BLADE SIZE

AGE	LARYNGOSCOPE BLADE SIZE
Premature	0 straight
Term—1 year	1 straight
1–1½ years	1½ straight
1½–12 years	2 straight/curved
13+ years	3 curved

PEDIATRIC ET TUBE-SIZE GUIDELINES

AGE	NEW-BORN	SIX MOS.	ONE YR.	TWO YRS.	FOUR YRS.	SIX YRS.	EIGHT YRS.	TEN YRS.	TWELVE YRS.
ET size (mm)	3.0	3.5	4.0	4.5	5.0	5.5	6.0	6.5	7.0

ET size $= 16 +$ age (years) $\div 4$

If suspected head or spinal trauma, cervical-spine
stabilization is required prior to ventilatory assistance.

↓

Perform head tilt/chin lift on all other patients, and assess
for adequate respirations prior to ventilatory assistance.

↓

Adequate spontaneous respirations

↓

NO	YES
↓	↓
Ventilate 1 minute.	Complete patient assessment.
↓	↓
Direct laryngoscopy	Appropriate protocol
↓	↓
If airway is obstructed, proceed to obstructed airway protocol.	CONTACT BASE.
↓	↓
Intubate and assess for successful ventilations. Auscultate three fields.[1]	TRANSPORT.
↓	
Successful ventilations	

↓

NO	YES
↓	↓
Reposition endotracheal tube if needed.[2]	Complete patient assessment.
↓	↓
Reattempt intubation.[3]	Manage according to appropriate protocol.
↓	↓
CONTACT BASE. TRANSPORT.	CONTACT BASE. TRANSPORT.

PEDIATRIC RESPIRATORY DISTRESS
SAVANNAH, GA

Pediatric Respiratory Distress (Nontraumatic)

1. 1' Survey:
   A. Assure airway, O_2 8 to 12 l/minute by NRBM./Assist PRN except known COPD, then start 2 l/minute via nasal cannula and increase as required. Be prepared to ventilate.
2. 2' Survey:

Pulmonary edema
1. Reassure and calm patient.
2. Assist patient to a semisitting or sitting position.
3. Provide a high concentration of O_2 unless patient has COPD.
4. Attach cardiac monitor.
5. IV NS or RL KVO rate

CONTACT MEDICAL CONTROL. Orders may include the following:

6. Bronchodilators as per medical control.

Croup < 3 yrs. (usually)/ epiglottitis > 3 yrs. (usually)
1. Keep child calm.
2. Move to cool environment.
3. Position appropriately.
4. Offer O_2 (if tolerated).
5. If apneic, cyanotic, or gasping for air, dispense with use of O_2 and begin PPV.
6. Cardiac monitor

CONTACT MEDICAL CONTROL. Orders may include the following:

7. Epinephrine 1:1000 .2 ml in 2-ml saline via nebulizer
8. Needle cricothyrotomy

Asthma
1. Reassure and calm patient.
2. Allow patient to assume position of comfort.
3. Assist patient in taking his or her own asthma medication.
4. Provide humidified O_2 (if possible).
5. Cardiac monitor

CONTACT MEDICAL CONTROL. Orders may include the following:

6. Epinephrine 0.01 ml/kg 1:1000 solution (max. .3 ml) subq.
7. 0.03 cc/K albuterol in 2 ml/saline

Inadequate ventilatory efforts, ET tube with supplemental high-flow O_2; assist PRN.

PEDIATRIC TENSION PNEUMOTHORAX
BOSTON, MA

Pediatric Tension Pneumothorax

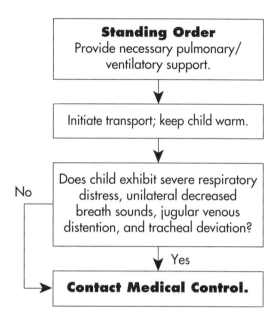

Standing Order
Provide necessary pulmonary/
ventilatory support.

↓

Initiate transport; keep child warm.

↓

Does child exhibit severe respiratory
distress, unilateral decreased
breath sounds, jugular venous
distention, and tracheal deviation?

No

Yes

Contact Medical Control.

Medical Control Option A
Needle decompression of the thorax

Medical Control Option B
Intravenous infusion of normal saline to keep the vein open

Medical Control Option C
20 ml/kg fluid bolus of normal saline

© *August 1993, Metropolitan Boston EMS Council*

PEDIATRIC DROWNING CARDIOPULMONARY ARREST
STATE OF HAWAII

Pediatric Drowning Cardiopulmonary Arrest

Because drowning cardiac arrest patients can be considerably acidotic, if there is no pulse after 2 doses of epinephrine, they should be given sodium bicarbonate.

Follow standing orders for cardiopulmonary arrest.

Administer second dose epinephrine.

If still pulseless:

Administer **0.5** mEq/kg IV sodium bicarbonate; dilute 1:1 with normal saline.

Administer third dose epinephrine.

If still pulseless:

Repeat **0.5** mEq/kg IV sodium bicarbonate; dilute 1:1 with normal saline.

Continue standing orders.

PEDIATRIC CARDIOGENIC SHOCK
NASHVILLE, TN

Pediatric Cardiogenic Shock

A. Assessment

1. Frequently associated with sepsis, carditis, or cardiomyopathy with tachy or brady dysrhythmia, or blunt chest trauma.
2. Neck-vein distention in sitting position
3. Moist-sounding lungs (rales, rhonchi)
4. Peripheral edema if chronic heart failure
5. Determine if cardiac dysrhythmia exists.
6. Consider tension pneumothorax.
7. Consider cardiac tamponade.

B. Treatment

1. Semi-Fowlers or position of comfort
2. OXYGEN 100%
3. IV NORMAL SALINE TKO with large-bore catheter
4. Treat dysrhythmia according to appropriate cardiac protocol.
5. Contact medical/trauma control.
6. INTROPIN (dopamine) 6 mg/kg in 100 cc D5W IV admix. Begin drip at 6 cc/hr. (Titrate.)
7. Consider MAST.
8. Consider INTRAOSSEOUS INFUSION.

PEDIATRIC HEAD TRAUMA
CHARLOTTE, NC

Head Trauma

History

1. Patient has history of head injury with or without loss of consciousness.
2. Patient may be found down with no evidence of trauma.

Physical

1. Patient may have visible signs of head injury, such as contusions, abrasions, or lacerations.
2. May see blood and/or cerebrospinal fluid from ears, nose, or mouth
3. Patient may show evidence of altered mental status, focal neurological deficits, or seizures.

Differential

Cerebrovascular accident   Hypoglycemia
Transient ischemic attack   Overdose
Seizure

Protocol

1. Maintain airway, suction as appropriate, and administer oxygen via nonrebreathing mask at 15 l/min. Consider assisted ventilations with bag-valve mask, or intubate if patient is hypoventilating or airway compromise is apparent. Intravenous lidocaine may be administered prior to intubating if this can be done expeditiously. If unable to intubate, consider needle cricothyrotomy. If decision made to intubate patient, ventilate at a rate of 14–16 breaths per minute.
2. Assess peripheral pulses for rate and strength. If unable to palpate, attempt to assess central pulses.
3. Protect C-spine with in-line stabilization until C-collar, head immobilization, and backboard are placed when trauma to head or spine is suspected. Maintain in-line stabilization while intubating.
4. Address any life-threatening respiratory problems, such as flail segment, sucking chest wounds, or tension pneumothorax associated with hemodynamic instability. (Refer to appropriate protocol.)
5. Identify and control any active bleeding sites with manual direct pressure and/or pressure dressing.
6. If spinal trauma suspected and if not already performed, place patient on a long backboard, maintaining C-spine control at all times. While logrolling patient, inspect the back and axillae for any additional injuries.
7. Remove appropriate clothing in order to fully inspect the chest and abdomen for any significant injuries.

8. Obtain vital signs and Glasgow Coma Score.

9. Initiate transport to appropriate receiving facility as dictated in the trauma triage protocol. Continue to monitor vital signs and neurological status and apply cardiac monitor while en route. A secondary assessment should be performed en route.

10. Consider and administer any of all of the following therapeutic interventions:

IV normal saline:
No hemodynamic instability
TKO
Hemodynamically unstable
Wide open

Suspected hypoglycemia
Obtain blood in red-top tube.

IV normal saline TKO or PRN adapter

Dextrose
Children < 8 years of age
D25 IV 1 gm/kg (4 ml/kg)
(D25 produced by diluting 1 ml/kg D50 with 1 ml/kg sterile water. Resulting solution is D25.)

Children > 8 years of age
D50 IV 1 gm/kg (2 ml/kg)

Suspected narcotic use
Naloxone 0.1 mg/kg IV or IM

11. Contact medical control en route.

Addendum

1. If a pediatric head-trauma patient is found to be in shock, other sources for hypotension should be considered. In this instance, the chest and abdomen should be thoroughly evaluated.

2. Consider intubating patients with a Glasgow Coma Score of 8 or less.

3. IV or IO lines may be started at the scene if this procedure can be performed in less than 2 minutes; otherwise, initiate IV line(s) en route.

4. Unless entrapment or rescue operations occur, total scene time should not exceed 10 minutes. To minimize morbidity and mortality, patients sustaining traumatic insults who are not entrapped should arrive at a trauma center for definitive care within 30 minutes from the time that the injury occured.

5. Agitation or restlessness may be due to hypoxia and not just the traumatic insult or mind-altering drugs.

PEDIATRIC HEAD TRAUMA
COLUMBUS, OH

Head Trauma

1. ABCs as per MULTIPLE TRAUMA PROTOCOL.
2. Do not restrict fluids in a patient who is hypotensive or has shock signs and symptoms.
3. Indications for transport include loss of consciousness, change in state of consciousness, profuse vomiting; children under 2 years of age with large hematomas; gait disturbances, seizures, and pupillary changes.
4. Patients with significant head trauma should have C-spine.
5. Patients with head trauma who need intubation or assisted ventilation should be hyperventilated at a rate 10 ventilations/minute greater than normal respiratory rate.
6. If Coma score is less than 8 or decreases by 2 points, it is generally an indication to hyperventilate the child or consider oral intubation and hyperventilation.

INFANT GLASGOW COMA SCALE

EYE OPENING	Spontaneous	4
	To voice	3
	To pain	2
	None	1
VERBAL RESPONSE	Coos, babbles	5
	Irritable cry, inconsolable	4
	Cries to pain	3
	Moans	2
	None	1
MOTOR RESPONSE	Normal movements	6
	Withdraws to touch	5
	Withdraws to pain	4
	Flexion	3
	Extension	2
	Flaccid	1

PEDIATRIC CHEST TRAUMA
COLUMBUS, OH

Chest Trauma

INJURY	SIGNS AND SYMPTOMS	TREATMENT
TENSION PNEUMO-THORAX	Severe respiratory distress, hypotension, tachycardia, decreased level of consciousness (LOC), cyanosis, absent breath sounds on affected side, distended external jugular veins	Oxygen. Needle decompression. Assist ventilation if necessary. Consider intubation.
MASSIVE HEMO-THORAX	Profound hypovolemic shock, decreased LOC, pallor, flat external jugular veins, respiratory distress	Oxygen. Treat for shock. Assist ventilation if necessary. Consider intubation.
FLAIL SEGMENT	Severe respiratory distress, unequal chest movement, cyanosis, decreased LOC	Oxygen. Assist ventilation. Consider intubation.
OPEN PNEUMO-THORAX	Respiratory distress, sucking wound	Oxygen. Nonporous dressing with pressure vent. Assist ventilation if necessary. Consider intubation.

Children presenting with significant chest trauma should, ideally, be admitted directly to a level I pediatric trauma facility.

If a tension pneumothorax is present, decompress chest on the involved side with a 16–18 gauge over-the-needle catheter. Needle decompression should be at the second intercostal space (over the top of the third rib) at the midclavicular line.

PEDIATRIC SPINAL-CORD INJURIES
ARLINGTON, TX

Spinal-Cord Injuries

Treatment:

1. Establish and maintain C-spine/T-spine/long-axis alignment.
2. Establish and maintain airway as appropriate, using in-line or nasal intubation if needed.
3. Administer high-flow oxygen.
4. Establish two (2) large-bore IV/IOs with Ringer's lactate.
5. Assess motor and sensory function/deficit:
   - Loss of sensation to extremities
   - Loss of motor function
   - Numbness/tingling of the extremities
   - Diaphragmatic breathing
6. Assess as closely as possible the patient's weight in kg.
7. If injury known to be less than eight (8) hours old: Administer high dose Solu-Medrol 30 mg/kg in 100 cc of normal saline and infuse over 15 minutes drip rate—67 gtts/min., using a standard set up.
8. Continously assess and document any neuro/motor/sensory changes.
9. **Contact medical control.**

NOTE: Do not use Solu-Medrol if injury thought to be greater than eight (8) hours old as this may cause rebound swelling of cord tissue.

PEDIATRIC ELECTROCUTION INJURIES
ARLINGTON, TX

Pediatric Electrocution Injuries

NOTE: In addition to burns, be responsive to the high probability of associated injuries such as:
- Cardiac disturbances
- Blunt or penetrating trauma
- Musculoskeletal injuries 2° to forces involved with electrocution

Treatment:

1. Maintain C-Spine immobilization as appropriate. Establish and maintain airway as appropriate. Intubate as needed.
2. Administer high-flow oxygen as appropriate.
3. Continuous cardiac monitoring, referring to the appropriate dysrhythmia algorhythm as needed
4. Establish one (1) or two (2) large-bore IV/IO accesses with Ringer's lactate. Titrate fluid rate to maintain B/P > 100.
5. Strongly consider transport to Parkland Burn Center.
6. **Contact medical control.**

NOTE: Always assess severity of entrance and exit wounds and all organs in between.

Physician Orders

Consider Analgesia:
- Morphine sulfate 0.1–0.2 mg/kg slow IVP
- Phenergan 6.25–12.5 mg slow IVP

303

PEDIATRIC AMPUTATED PARTS
ARLINGTON, TX

Pediatric Amputated Parts

Treatment:

1. Establish and maintain airway as appropriate.
2. Administer high-flow oxygen as appropriate.
3. Assure control of external hemorrhage.
4. If unable to control by means of direct pressure and bulk, use a wide tourniquet as a last resort. Do not loosen or remove after application. Document time applied.
5. Recover all amputated tissues if possible; gently, loosely dress in sterile-saline-moistened dressing; and keep in cool place. Do not apply ice or cold packs directly. Splint affected limb as an open fracture.
6. Initiate prompt transport. Consider transport without tissue if there will be a delay in recovery.
7. Establish IV/IO access with Ringer's lactate, large bore if needed.
8. **Contact medical control.**

Physician Orders

Consider analgesia as follows:
Morphine sulfate 0.1–0.2 mg/kg slow IVP
Phenergan 6.5–12.5 mg slow IVP

NOTE: Consider transport to an approved trauma center or microsurgical receiving facility.

PEDIATRIC NEUROGENIC SHOCK
NASHVILLE, TN

Neurogenic Shock

A. Assessment

    1. Associated with spinal-cord injuries and overdoses
    2. Signs of hypovolemic shock without peripheral vasoconstriction (warm shock)

B. Treatment

    1. Secure spine and airway.
    2. OXYGEN 100%
    3. Position MAST.
    4. Primary IV NORMAL SALINE 10 cc/kg bolus
    5. Contact medical/trauma control.
    6. Consider MAST if perfusion is not restored.
    7. Consider occult bleeding and treat as hypovolemia.
    8. Neurologic assessment
    9. Contact medical/trauma control
    10. Rebolus with 10 cc/kg NORMAL SALINE IV
    11. INTROPIN (dopamine) 6 mg/kg in 100 cc D5W IV admix. Begin drip at 6 cc/hr. (Titrate.)
    12. Consider INTRAOSSEOUS INFUSION.

PEDIATRIC SUBMERSION INCIDENT
PHOENIX, AZ

Submersion Incident

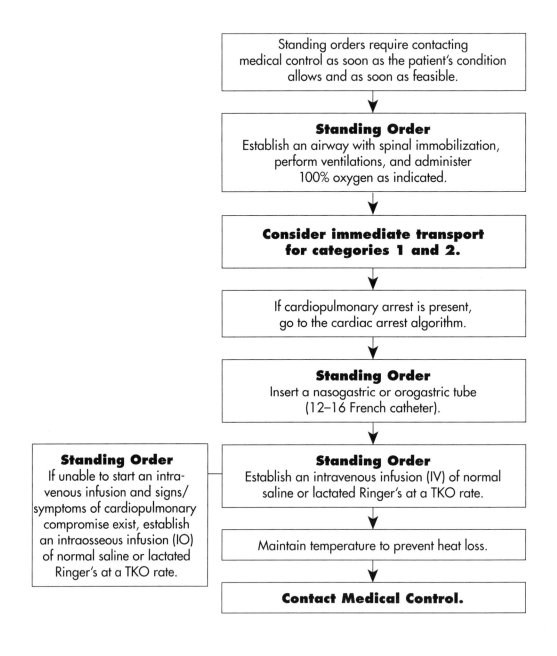

Standing orders require contacting medical control as soon as the patient's condition allows and as soon as feasible.

Standing Order
Establish an airway with spinal immobilization, perform ventilations, and administer 100% oxygen as indicated.

Consider immediate transport for categories 1 and 2.

If cardiopulmonary arrest is present, go to the cardiac arrest algorithm.

Standing Order
Insert a nasogastric or orogastric tube (12–16 French catheter).

Standing Order
If unable to start an intravenous infusion and signs/symptoms of cardiopulmonary compromise exist, establish an intraosseous infusion (IO) of normal saline or lactated Ringer's at a TKO rate.

Standing Order
Establish an intravenous infusion (IV) of normal saline or lactated Ringer's at a TKO rate.

Maintain temperature to prevent heat loss.

Contact Medical Control.

NOTE:
Categories:
- I—Cardiac arrest on arrival of EMS
- II—Flaccid, no spontaneous breathing or heart rate on arrival, but return during resuscitation
- III—Spontaneous respirations, heart rate, and an altered level of consciousness on arrival of EMS

NOTE: Rapid transport is of utmost importance and should be considered immediately after establishing an airway. If transport to the nearest pediatric critical-care facility requires extended times, consider transport to the nearest emergency facility for immediate treatment and then transfer to a pediatric facility.

NOTE:

NORMAL RESPIRATION RATES

• Infant	25–40 breaths/minute
• Child	20–28 breaths/minute
• Adolescent	15–20 breaths/minute

PEDIATRIC SNAKEBITE
SAN JOSE, CA

Snakebite

I. Standing Orders

   A. Appropriate airway management
   B. Cardiac monitor
   C. Minimize patient movement and immobilize bitten extremity. Do not elevate.
   D. Mark borders of soft tissue swelling or erythema in ink.
   E. Transport Code 3
   F. En route, establish vascular access with saline lock in an unbitten extremity.
      —If hypotensive, use 0.9% normal saline and give 20-ml/kg bolus to maintain a systolic blood pressure equal to or above 90 torr or [age × 2] + 70 torr for children under 10 years of age.

II. Base Physician Order Only

   A. Repeat fluid bolus.
   B. MAST

PEDIATRIC CARBON-MONOXIDE POISONING AND/OR SMOKE INHALATION
SAN JOSE, CA

Carbon-Monoxide Poisoning and/or Smoke Inhalation

I. Standing Orders

    A. Appropriate airway management. Supplemental high-flow O_2 by nonre-breather mask.

    B. Cardiac monitor

    C. Establish vascular access with saline lock.

    D. Transport.

    E. Consider albuterol 2.5 mg (0.5 ml in 3 ml NS) by hand-held nebulizer or by mask for bronchospasm.

PEDIATRIC SEPTIC SHOCK
NASHVILLE, TN

Septic Shock

A. Assessment

    1. Cool, clammy skin
    2. Poor capillary refill
    3. Tachycardia/hypotension
    4. Potential for underlying infection

TACHYCARDIA

Newborn	greater than 180/min.
Infant	greater than 160/min.
Toddler	greater than 140/min.
Preschooler	greater than 130/min.
Adolescent	greater than 120/min.

LOW STYSTOLIC BLOOD PRESSURE

Newborn	less than 60 mm Hg
Infant	less than 70 mm Hg
Toddler	less than 80 mm Hg
Preschooler	less than 90 mm Hg
Adolescent	less than 100 mm Hg

B. Treatment
    1. OXYGEN 100%
    2. IV NORMAL SALINE 20 cc/kg over 20 minutes
    3. Contact medical/trauma control.
    4. Consider MAST.
    5. Maintain temperature above 97° F.
    6. If dextrostix becomes less than 40 mg/percent, use pediatric hypoglycemia protocol.
    7. Consider INTRAOSSEOUS INFUSION.

PEDIATRIC ABDOMINAL PAIN/NONTRAUMATIC
ARLINGTON, TX

Pediatric Abdominal Pain/Nontraumatic

Treatment:

1. Establish and maintain airway as appropriate.
2. O$_2$ as indicated
3. Exam: history, OB, bleeding, masses
4. Establish IV/IO with Ringer's lactate, rate to maintain B/P.
5. Continuous cardiac monitoring as indicated
6. **Contact medical control.**

NOTE: Do not give analgesics or anything by mouth.

Possible causes of abdominal pain:

RUQ:	LUQ:	RLQ:	LLQ:
Liver problem	Spleen problem	Appendix	L ovary
Gallbladder	Peptic ulcer	Rt ovary	Ectopic
Pancreatitis	Perforated	Ectopic	Bowel
Peptic ulcer	esophagus	Bowel	

Physician Orders

NOTE: Consider Phenergan 0.05 mg/kg IV or IM for severe nausea and vomiting. The maximum single dose is 12.5 mg.

PEDIATRIC NAUSEA/VOMITING
ARLINGTON, TX

Pediatric Nausea/Vomiting

Treatment:

1. Establish and maintain airway as appropriate.
2. Monitor for the need to suction as needed.
3. Cardiac monitoring as appropriate
4. Establish IV access with Ringer's lactate as appropriate.
5. **Contact medical control.**

Physician Orders

Administer Phenergan .5 mg/kg IVP or IM.

NOTE: Phenergan is contraindicated in the following conditions:
- Head injuries
- Possible acute abdomen
- Patients with allergies to any phenothiazines
- Use caution in pregnant patients.

NOTE: *Phenergan may cause extrapyramidal symptoms, i.e., dystonic reactions, muscle rigidity, etc. This is not an allergic reaction but a side effect of phenothiazines. These symptoms may be reversed with 25 mg benadryl IVP or IM.*

PEDIATRIC PAIN CONTROL
COLUMBUS, OH

Pediatric Pain Control

NUBAIN 5–10 mg IVP can be administered for severe pain in the following situations with adults and 0.1 mg/kg for pediatric patients.

1. Partial thickness burns without hypotension
2. Extremity trauma without hypotension
3. Avulsions or amputations without hypotension

If hypotension develops after NUBAIN is given, a fluid bolus of 200 cc should be given.

If respiratory depression occurs after NUBAIN is given, NARCAN 2 mg IVP should be administered and intubation considered.

PEDIATRIC TEDDY BEAR DISTRIBUTION
JACKSONVILLE, FL

Pediatric Teddy Bear Distribution

The "Heart Throb" teddy bear is intended as a gift to pediatric patients in need of emotional support during crisis situations. The bear may assist rescue personnel in establishing a distraction and sense of security in the toddler or child who is frightened. The particularly appropriate age range is 18 months to 6 years.

I. Distribution of bear: The bear should be given to the toddler or child in those instances where a positive beneficial outcome is expected.
   A. The toddler or child involved in a crisis situation

   1. When the parent is sick or injured and the toddler or child must accompany the parent to the hospital, or
   2. Hostage situation, kidnapping or attempt, or other extraordinary situation that would put an emotional strain on the toddler or child, and
   3. When the toddler or child is visibly upset or disturbed and the officer in charge reasonably believes that the bear would help alleviate anxiety, reduce fear, and assist in distracting from the threatening situation

   B. The sick or injured toddler or child

   1. When a toddler or child is sick or injured and must be transported, and
   2. When the toddler or child is visibly upset or disturbed and the officer in charge reasonably believes that the bear would help alleviate anxiety, reduce fear, and assist in distracting from the threatening situation

      a. IV must be initiated.
      b. Administration of oxygen
      c. Patient must be immobilized.
      d. Patient must be separated from parent.
      e. Other extenuating circumstances

II. Conservation of resources: The bear is a limited-resource item and should be used sparingly and only when the need arises.

   A. The bear is not to be distributed unnecessarily or indiscriminately (*e.g.*, public relations).
   B. The bear is not to be given to children when it would not achieve positive results.

   1. Causes increased fear or anxiety
   2. Toddler or child needs only parental reassurance and support.
   3. Unconscious patients

   C. The ultimate decision to give the bear will rest with the officer in charge and be based on the individual circumstances.

The guidelines listed above indicate possible situations and are not all-inclusive. The best interests of the toddler or child should be the primary concern, and the distribution should be based on overall considerations.

APPENDICES

Abbreviations

COMMONLY ACCEPTED ABBREVIATIONS FOR FIELD USE
DENVER, CO

$\bar{a}$	before
AA	auto accident
AAOx_____	awake, alert, and oriented times _____
abd	abdomen
AB	abortion
ABC	airway, breathing, circulation
ACLS	Advanced Cardiac Life Support
adm	admission
ALS	Advanced Life Support
am	morning
AMA	against medical advice
amp(s)	ampule(s)
ant	anterior
AOB	odor of alcohol on breath
app	approximately
asa	aspirin
ASCVD	arteriosclerotic cardiovascular disease
ASHD	arteriosclerotic heart disease
ass't	assisted/assist
asys	asystole
ATLS	Advanced Trauma Life Support
A&P	anterior and posterior
a&p	auscultation and percussion
≈	approximately
@	at
BBB	Bundle Branch Block
BCLS	Basic Cardiac Life Support
BLS	Basic Life Support
bil	bilateral
BM	bowel movement
BP	blood pressure
BS	breath sounds
BVM	bag-valve mask
BS=& clr bil↑↓ A&P fields	breath sounds equal and clear in high and low fields both anterior and posterior chest
$\bar{c}$	with
C	centigrade
Ca	cancer
Ca++	calcium
CAB	coronary artery bypass
CAD	coronary artery disease
cath	catheter, catheterization
CBC	complete blood count
cc	cubic centimeter
CC	chief complaint

CCU	coronary care unit
CHF	congestive heart failure
CHI	closed head injury
circ	circulation
cm	centimeter
CMS	circulation, movement, sensation
CNS	central nervous system
CO	carbon monoxide
c/o	complaining of
CO_2	carbon dioxide
code 2	nonemergent
code 3	emergent
COLD	chronic obstructive lung disease
chg/Δ	change
COPD	chronic obstructive pulmonary disease
COR-O	cardiopulmonary arrest
CS	central supply
C-spine	cervical spine
C-section	Cesarean section
CSF	cerebrospinal fluid
CSM	carotid sinus massage
CVA	cerebral vascular accident
CVP	central venous pressure
CPR	cardiopulmonary resuscitation
dc/DC	discontinue
D & C	dilation and curettage
detox	detoxification
DOA	dead on arrival at hospital
DOE	dyspnea on exertion
DOS	dead on scene in field
Dr	doctor
drsg/dsg	dressing
DT	delirium tremens
Dx	diagnosis
D5W	5% dextrose in water
D50	50% dextrose in water
↓	decrease
$\bar{ea}$	each
ED	Emergency Department
ECG/EKG	electrocardiogram
EENT	eye, ear, nose, throat
ENT	ear, nose, throat
EOA	esophageal obturator airway
EOM	extraocular movement
ET	endotracheal
ETA	estimated time of arrival
etc.	and so on

ETOH	alcohol
exam	examination
=	equal
$\bar{q}$	every
F	Fahrenheit
FB	foreign body
FD	fire department
fl	fluid
Fx	fracture
♀	female
1°	first degree
GB	gallbladder
GC	gonococcus or gonorrhea
GCS	Glasgow Coma Scale
GI	gastrointestinal
gm	gram
gr	grain
GSW	gunshot wound
gtt(s)	drop(s)
GU	genitourinary
GYN	gynecology
↦	going to/leading to
>	greater than
h	hour
HA	headache
HB	heart block
Hct	hematocrit
Hg	mercury
Hgb/Hb	hemoglobin
H&P	history and physical
HR	heart rate
ht	height
Hx	history
hypo	hypodermic
H_2O	water
IC	intracardiac
ICS	Intercostal space
ICU	Intensive-care unit
I&D	incision and drainage
IM	intramuscular
inf	inferior
IV	intravenous
↑	increase
J	joules
JVD	jugular-venous distention
K+	potassium
KO	knocked out
KVO	keep vein open
l	liter
Ⓛ	left
lac	laceration
lat	lateral

LBBB	left bundle branch block
lb	pound
lg	large
liq	liquid
LLL	left lower lobe
LLQ	left lower quadrant
LMP	last menstrual period
LOC	loss of consciousness/level of consciousness
L-spine	lumbar spine
lt	left
LUL	left upper lobe
LUQ	left upper quadrant
<	less than
○⌐	lying
MAE	moves all extremities
MAST	medical antishock trousers
mcg	microgram
MCL	midclavicular line
meds	medications
mEq	milliequivalent
Mg	magnesium
mg/mgm	milligram
MI	myocardial infarction
misc.	miscellaneous
ml	milliliter
mm	millimeter
MOEx____	movement of extremities times ____
MS	multiple sclerosis
MS/MSO_4	morphine sulfate
MVA	motor vehicle accident
♂	male
NA	not applicable
NaCl/NS	normal saline
$NaHCO_3$	sodium bicarbonate
NC	nasal cannula
neg./⊖	negative
neuro	neurology
NH	nursing home
NKA	no known allergies
noc/noct	night
NPO	nothing by mouth
NSR	normal sinus rhythm
NTG	nitroglycerin
N&V&D	nausea and vomiting and diarrhea
∅	none
O_2	oxygen
OB	obstetrics
occ	occasional
OD	overdose

OJ	orange juice		sol	solution
ophth	ophthalmology		sm	small
OR	operating room		stat	at once
Orth	orthopedics		sub-q	subcutaneous
os	left eye		sup	superior
od	right eye		Sx	sign/symptom
oz/ʒ	ounce		surg	surgery
			SVT	supraventricular tachycardia
p̄	after		synch	synchronous
PAC	premature atrial contraction		2°	second degree/secondary
para	number of pregnancies		⚓	sitting
PASG	pneumatic antishock garment		⚓	standing
PAT	paroxysmal atrial tachycardia			
path	pathology		TAB	therapeutic abortion
PD	police department		TB	tuberculosis
PE	physical examination/		tbsp	tablespoon
	pulmonary edema/		temp	temperature
	pulmonary embolus		TIA	transient ischemic attack
peds	pediatrics		tid	three times a day
per	by or through		TKO	to keep open
PERL	pupils equal and react to light		TLC	tender loving care
PERLA	pupils equal and react to light		TM	tympanic membranes
	and accommodation		tol	tolerated
PG	pregnant		TPR	temperature, pulse, respirations
PID	pelvic inflammatory disease		tsp	teaspoon
PND	paroxysmal nocturnal dyspnea		Tx	treatment
po	by mouth		∴	therefore
pos/⊕	positive		3°	third degree
post	posterior			
PSVT	paroxysmal supraventricular		UA	upon arrival
	tachycardia		uncons	unconscious
psych	psychiatric		unk	unknown
pt	patient		URI	upper-respiratory infection
PTA	prior to arrival		uro	urology
PVC	premature ventricular		UTI	urinary-tract infection
	contractions		≠	not equal/unequal
pvt	private			
Px	physical		vag	vaginal
Ψ	psychiatric		VD	venereal disease
			VF	ventricular fibrillation
®	right		via	by way of
RBBB	right bundle branch block		vol	volume
RBC	red blood cell		VS	vital signs
resp	respirations		VT	ventricular tachycardia
RHD	rheumatic heart disease		WAP	wandering atrial pacemaker
RLQ	right lower quadrant		WBC	white blood cell
RO	rule out		wc	wheelchair
ROM	range of motion		WNL	within normal limits
ROS	review of systems		WPW	Wolfe Parkinson White
RSR	regular sinus rhythm			Syndrome
RUQ	right upper quadrant		wt	weight
Rx	take, treatment			
			×	times
s̄	without			
SL	sublingual		YO	year old
SOB	shortness of breath		yr	year(s)

FORMULARY

COMMON PRESCRIPTION MEDICATIONS
ARLINGTON, TX

Name	Use
Adapin/Doxepin/Sinequan	Tricyclic antidepressant
Aldomet/Methyldopa	Antihypertensive
Alprazolam/Xanax	Sedative
Amitryptyline/Elavil	Tricyclic antidepressant
Amoxil/Amoxicillin	Antibiotic
Atenolol/Tenormin	Hypertension/Asthma
Ativan/Lorazepam	Antianxiety
Augmentin/Amoxil	Antibiotic
Buproprion/Wellbutrin	Nontricyclic antidepressant
Calan/Verapamil	Slows pulse/antihypertensive
Capoten/Captopril	Antihypertensive, CHF
Captopril/Capoten	Antihypertensive, CHF
Carbamazepine/Tegretol	Anticonvulsant/mood stabilizer
Cardizem/Diltiazem	Angina
Ceclor/Cefaclor	Antibiotic
Cefaclor/Ceclor	Antibiotic
Chlordiazepoxide/Librium	Antianxiety/Benzodiazepine
Chlorpromazine/Thorazine	Antipsychotic
Chlorpropamide/Diabeta	Antidiabetic
Cimetidine/Tagamet	Ulcer treatment
Clonazepam/Klonopin	Anticonvulsant/mood stabilizer
Coumadin/Warfarin	Anticoagulant
Dalmane/Flurazepam	Sedative/hypnotic
Depekene/Valproic Acid	Anticonvulsant/mood stabilizer
Desipramine/Norpramine	Tricyclic antidepressant
Desyrel/Trazadone	Nontricyclic antidepressant
Diabeta/Chlorpropamide	Antidiabetic
Digoxin/Lanoxin	Slows/regulates heart rate
Diltiazem/Cardiazem	Angina
Doxepin/Adapin/Sinequan	Tricyclic antidepressant
Dyazide/Hydrochlorothiazide	Diuretic/antihypertensive
Elavil/Amitriptyline	Tricyclic antidrepressant
Enalapril/Vasotec	Hypertension/CHF
Feldene/Piroxicam	Anti-inflammatory
Fluoxetine/Prozac	Nontricyclic antidrepressant
Fluphenazine/Prolixin	Antipsychotic
Flurazepam/Dalmane	Sedative/hypnotic
Glipizide/Glucotrol	Antidiabetic
Glucotrol/Glipizide	Antidiabetic
Glyburide/Micronase	Diabetes
Halcion/Triazolam	Sedative
Hydrochlorothiazide/Dyazide	Diuretic/antihypertensive
Imipramine/Tofranil	Tricyclic antidepressant
Inderal/Propranolol	Angina/antihypertensive
Klonopin/Clonazepam	Anticonvulsant/mood stabilizer
Lanoxin/Digoxin	Slows/regulates heart rate
Levothyroxine/Synthroid	Thyroid hormone replacement
Librium/Chlordiazepoxide	Antianxiety/Benzodiazepine
Lithium/Lithobid	Mood stabilizer
Lithobid/Lithium	Mood stabilizer
Lopressor/Metoprolol	Antihypertensive
Lorazepam/Ativan	Antianxiety

Name	Use
Maxzide/Triamterene	Diuretic
Medroxyprogesterone/Provera	Amenorrhea
Mellaril/Thioridazine	Antipsychotic
Mesoridazine/Serentil	Antipsychotic
Methyldopa/Aldomet	Antihypertensive
Metoprolol/Lopressor	Antihypertensive
Micronase/Glyburide	Diabetes
Minipress/Prazisin	Anti-hypertensive
Naprosyn/Naproxen	Anti-inflammatory
Naproxen/Naprosyn	Anti-inflammatory
Nardil/Phenelzine	Antidepressant—MAO
Norpramine/Desipramine	Tricyclic antidepressant
Nortriptyline/Pamelor	Tricyclic antidepressant
Oxazepam/Serax	Antianxiety/benzodiazepine
Pamelor/Nortriptyline	Tricyclic antidepressant
Parnate/Tranylcypromine	Antidepressant—MAO
Perphenazine/Trilafon	Antipsychotic
Phenelzine/Nardil	Antidepressant—MAO
Piroxicam/Feldene	Anti-inflammatory
Prazisin/Minipress	Antihypertensive
Premarin/Estrogen	Hormone replacement
Prolixin/Fluphenazine	Antipsychotic
Propranolol/Inderal	Angina/antihypertensive
Protriptyline/Vivactil	Tricyclic antidepressant
Provera/Medroxyprogesterone	Amenorrhea
Prozac/Fluoxetine	Nontricyclic antidepressant
Ranitidine/Zantac	Ulcer treatment
Restoril/Temazapam	Sedative/hypnotic
Seldane/Terfenadine	Allergies
Serax/Oxazepam	Antianxiety/benzodiazepine
Serentil/Mesoridazine	Antipsychotic
Sinequan/Adapin/Doxepin	Tricyclic antidepressant
Stelazine/Trifluoperazine	Antipsychotic
Synthroid/Levothyroxine	Thyroid hormone replacement
Tagamet/Cimetidine	Ulcer treatment
Tegretol/Carbamazepine	Anticonvulsant/mood stabilizer
Temazapam/Restoril	Sedative/hypnotic
Tenormin/Atenolol	Hypertension/asthma
Terfenadine/Seldane	Allergies
Thioridazine/Mellaril	Antipsychotic
Thorazine/chlorpromazine	Antipsychotic
Tofranil/Imipramine	Tricyclic antidepressant
Tranylcypromine/Parnate	Antidepressant—MAO
Trazadone/Desyrel	Nontricyclic antidepressant
Triamterene/Maxzide	Diuretic
Triazolam/Haldol	Sedative
Trifluoperazine/Stelazine	Antipsychotic
Trilafon/Perphenazine	Antipsychotic
Valproic Acid/Depekene	Anticonvulsant/mood stabilizer
Vasotec/Enalapril	Hypertension/CHF
Verapamil/Calan	Slows pulse/antihypertensive
Vivactil/Protriptyline	Tricyclic antidepressant
Warfarin/Coumadin	Anticoagulant
Wellbutrin/Buproprion	Nontricyclic antidepressant
Xanax/Alprazolam	Sedative
Zantac/Ranitidine	Ulcer treatement

MEDICATIONS AND THERAPEUTIC MODALITIES
BIRMINGHAM, AL

DRUG	HOW SUPPLIED (IN DRUG KITS)	RECOMMENDED ADULT DOSE
1. Atropine Sulfate	1 mg/10 ml (0.1 mg/ml) (prefilled syringe)	0.5 mg IV, push or via ET tube
2. Bretylium Tosylate (Bretylol)	50 mg/ml 10-ml prefilled syringe	3–5 mg/kg IV 1–4 mg/min. infusion
3. Calcium Chloride	10% Injection, 10 ml (prefilled syringe)	5 ml IV
4. Dextrose 50% in Water	50-ml prefilled syringe	50 ml (25 gm)
5. Diazepam (Valium)	5 mg/ml (2-ml prefilled syringe)	2–10 mg slow IV
6. Diphenhydramine (Benadryl)	50 mg/ml (1-ml prefilled syringe)	50 mg IV or IM
7. Dopamine (Intropin)	80 mg/ml–5-ml prefilled syringe (800 mg/500D_5W)	Initial infusion 5 μg/kg/min.
8. Epinephrine (Adrenalin)	1:10,000–10 ml (0.1 mg/ml) prefilled syringe (1½″ needle) 1:1,000–1 ml (1 mg/ml) ampule	5 ml IV or 10 cc via ET tube 0.3 cc sub. cu.
9. Furosemide (Lasix)	10 mg/ml–4-ml prefilled syringe	0.5–1.0 mg/kg IV
10. Glucose, Oral Paste	1 Tube=25 gm	½ Tube=12.5 gm
11. Isoproterenol (Isuprel)	1-mg/5-ml prefilled syringe	2–20 μg/min., titrating to response.
12. Lidocaine HCL	0.4% 250 ml premixed (4 mg/ml) nonbreakable container 100 mg/5-ml prefilled syringe	2 mg/min. 1-mg/kg push or via ET tube
13. Naloxone (Narcan)	1.0 mg/ml (2-ml ampule)	0.4–2.0 mg IV, titrate to response.
14. Nitroglycerine Tablets	0.4 mg (sublingual tablets) 1/150 gr	1 tablet (0.4 mg) may repeat every 5 mins. x 3

DRUG	HOW SUPPLIED (IN DRUG KITS)	RECOMMENDED ADULT DOSE
15. Sodium Bicarbonate	50-mgEq/50-ml prefilled syringe	1 mgEq/kg IV push
16. Syrup of Ipecac		30 ml orally
17. Thiamine HCL	100 mg/1 ml	50 mg IM followed by 50 mg IV
18. Verapamil	5 mg/2 ml (2.5 mg/ml) prefilled syringe	5 mg slow IV, repeat 15–20 minutes 10 mg slow IV

IV FLUIDS

1. D_5W	1,000-ml, 500-ml, 250-ml plastic containers
2. $D_5\frac{1}{2}NS$	1,000-ml, 500-ml, 250-ml plastic containers
3. Lactated Ringer's	1,000-ml, 500-ml, 250-ml plastic containers
4. Normal Saline	1,000-ml, 500-ml, 250-ml plastic containers

MAST—Inflate to maintain systolic BP of 90–100mm of Hg.
Defibrillation—according to joules ordered by physician

PEDIATRIC DRUGS AND DOSAGE
BIRMINGHAM, AL

	WT (LB) WT (KG) AGE (YEARS)	22 10 1	26.4 12 2	35.2 16 4	44 20 6	57.2 26 8	70.4 32 10	88 40 12	121 55 15	154 70 18
1.	Atropine 0.1 mg/cc	3 cc	3.5 cc	4.8 cc	5 cc	5 cc	5 cc	5 cc	5 cc	5 cc
2.	Bretylium Tosylate	1 cc	1.2 cc	1.6 cc	2 cc	2.6 cc	3.2 cc	4 cc	5.5 cc	7 cc
3.	Calcium Chloride 100 mg/cc	2 cc	2.4 cc	3.2 cc	4 cc	5.0 cc	5 cc	5 cc	5 cc	5 cc
4.	Dextrose $D_{50}W$ 25 gm/50 cc dilute 1.1 with sterile water	10 cc	12 cc	16 cc	20 cc	26 cc	32 cc	40 cc	50 cc	50 cc
5.	Diazepam 5 mg/cc		0.12 cc	0.15 cc	0.2 cc	0.25 cc	0.3 cc	0.4 cc	1 cc	1 cc
6.	Diphenhydramine		0.2 cc	0.5 cc	0.6 cc	1.0 cc	1.0 cc	1.0 cc	1.0 cc	1.0 cc
7.	Dopamine*									
8.	Epinephrine 1:10,000	1 cc	1.2 cc	1.6 cc	2 cc	2.6 cc	3.2 cc	4 cc	5 cc	5 cc
9.	Furosemide	0.5–1 cc	0.6–1.25 cc	0.8–1.6 cc	1–2 cc	1.25-2.5 cc	1.6–3.25 cc	2–4 cc	2.75–5.5 cc	3.5–7 cc
10.	Glucose	paste								
11.	Isoproterenol*									
12.	Lidocaine Bolus	1 cc	1.2 cc	1.6 cc	2 cc	2.6 cc	3.2 cc	4 cc	5.5 cc	7 cc
13.	Naloxone 1 mg/cc		0.1 cc	0.1 cc	0.15 cc	0.2 cc	0.25 cc	0.3 cc	0.4 cc	0.6 cc	0.8 cc
14.	Sodium Bicarbonate $NaHCO_3$ Dilute 1:1 Sterile Water	10 cc	12 cc	16 cc	20 cc	26 cc	32 cc	40 cc	55 cc	70 cc

WT (LB)	22	26.4	35.2	44	57.2	70.4	88	121	154
WT (KG)	10	12	16	20	26	32	40	55	70
AGE (YEARS)	1	2	4	6	8	10	12	15	18
15. Ipecac	15 cc	15 cc	15 cc	15 cc	15 cc	15 cc	30 cc	30 cc	30 cc
16. Verapamil	N/A	0.5 cc	0.6 cc	0.8 cc	1.0 cc	1.3 cc	1.6 cc	2.0 cc	2.0 cc
ET Tubes	3.5 mm	4 mm	4.5 mm	5.5 mm	6.0 mm	6.5 mm	6.5–7 mm	7.0 mm	7.5–8.0 mm

*Infusion of lidocaine, dopamine, or isuprel is inappropriate in prehospital pediatric patients under most circumstances. If required, see next page.

ALTERNATE DRUG ROUTES
CHICAGO, IL

In the prehospital setting, most drugs will be administered via the intravenous route. If there is a delay or inability to establish an IV, certain drugs may be administered via alternate routes. These include in order of preference:

Intraosseous (IO)
Endotracheal (ET)
Sublingual (SL)
Intramuscular (IM)

The dosage and/or dilution of the drug may vary from the usual IV dosage and/or dilution.

Intraosseous Injection

*Refer to *Intraosseous Infusions*.

ENDOTRACHEAL INSTILLATION OR VIA CRICOTHYROTOMY

DRUG	DOSE PREPARATION	ADULT DOSE	PEDIATRIC DOSE
Lidocaine, 1%	100 mg/10 cc	1 mm/kg	1 mg/kg
Atropine	1 mg/10 ml	1 mg	0.01–0.03 mg/kg (minimum dose 0.16 mg)
Narcan	0.4 mg/1 ml	0.8–2.0 mg	0.1 mg/kg
Epinephrine 1:10,000	1 mg/10 ml	1 mg	0.1 cc/kg

NOTE: *Pneumonic LANE*

Endotracheal Installation Procedure

1. While performing CPR, after ventilation, without stopping compression, inject medication down the lumen of the endotracheal tube (or cricothyrotomy).
2. Ventilate patient briskly for 5 seconds, or resume automatic ventilator settings. (Do not use sigh setting.)
3. Resume normal CPR and evaluate response.
4. Doses are doubled for endotracheal administration.

Precautions:

1. Avoid needle punctures of the endotracheal tube.
2. If medication used is not a "preload," remove needle before instilling medication.
3. If the medication is forced out of the ET tube during compressions, continue to ventilate and consider readministration.

SUBLINGUAL INJECTION

DRUG	DOSE PREPARATION	ADULT DOSE
Epinephrine 1:1000 Solution	1 mg/1 cc	1 mg
Narcan	0.4 mg/ml	0.8–1.2 mg

NOTE: *For pediatric dose see *Pediatric Drug Dosing*.

INTRAMUSCULAR INJECTION

DRUG	DOSE PREPARATION	ADULT DOSE
Atropine	1 mg/10 ml	1 mg
Diazepam (Valium)	10 mg/2 ml	5–12 mg
Diphenhydramine (Benadryl)	50 mg/1 cc	25–50 mg
Epinephrine	1:1000	0.3 mg
Furosemide (Lasix)	10 mg/ml	20–80 mg
Glucagon	1 mg powder	1.0 mg (IU)
Lidocaine 1%	100 mg/10 ml	300 mg (3 sites 100 mg each)
Morphine Sulfate	10 mg/10 ml	5–10 mg
Narcan	0.4 mg/1 ml	0.8–1.2 mg

NOTE: *For pediatric dose see *Pediatric Drug Dosing*.

© 1996 Chicago Project Medical Directors Consortium

INTRAVENOUS DRIP MEDICATIONS
DURHAM, NC

Indications

As per specific protocols

Procedure

1. Lidocaine 2 gm in 500 cc

> 1 mg/min. = 15 drops per minute
> 2 mg/min. = 30 drops per minute
> 3 mg/min. = 45 drops per minute
> 4 mg/min. = 60 drops per minute

Start infusion at 2 mg per minute and titrate upward if persistent ectopy as discussed with medical control.

2. Isoproterenol 2 mg in 500 cc
Start infusion at 15 drops per minute and titrate to heart rate of 60 per minute.

3. Dopamine 400 mg in 500 cc
In patients without any blood pressure, start at wide open and titrate to systolic blood pressure of 90. Individualize other treatment as discussed with medical control.

4. Bretylium 2 gm in 500 cc

> 1 mg/min. = 15 drops per minute
> 2 mg/min. = 30 drops per minute
> 3 mg/min. = 45 drops per minute
> 4 mg/min. = 60 drops per minute

Start infusion at 2 mg per minute and titrate upward if persistent ectopy as discussed with medical control.

Certification Requirements

1. EMT-P
2. Attend in-service and pass skill exam.

ADENOSINE
SANTA ANA, CA

MEDICATION: ADENOSINE (Adenocard®)

CLASSIFICATION:
Antidysrhythmic agent

MECHANISM OF ACTION:
- Depresses automaticity in the sinus node and Purkinje fibers
- Slows AV conduction and interrupts reentry pathways through AV node
- Immediate onset, duration less than 10 seconds

INDICATIONS:
- PSVT in a conscious patient, with signs and/or symptoms of cardiac ischemia or poor perfusion, including associated chest pain, shortness of breath, pulmonary congestion or congestive heart failure, hypotension or shock, altered skin signs, or decreased capillary refill
- Wide-complex tachycardia as diagnostic and/or therapeutic maneuver, usually after trial of lidocaine
- May be used in critical patients if administration will be substantially faster than immediate countershock

CONTRAINDICATIONS:
- Known hypersensitivity to adenosine

DOSAGE FORM:
- 6 mg/2 ml in 2-ml vials

ADULT DOSE
- 6–12 mg rapid IVP over 1–3 seconds followed by rapid flush of 5–10 ml NS
- May repeat in 1–2 minutes
- Drug is metabolized in less than 10 seconds.
- Use port closest to patient and flush with 5–10 ml NS bolus, injecting immediately after drug administration. Opening IV to flush *not* adequate.

PEDIATRIC DOSE
- 0.1–0.2 mg/kg rapid IVP over 1–3 seconds to maximum dose of 6 mg. Follow with a rapid flush of 5–10 ml NS.
- May repeat in 1–2 minutes. Maximum dose 12 mg.
- Drug is metabolized in less than 10 seconds.
- Use port closest to patient, and flush with 5–10 ml NS bolus, injecting immediately, after drug administration. Opening IV to flush *not* adequate.

SIDE EFFECTS
- chest pain/pressure*
- hypotension
- transient PACs, PVCs
- transient bradycardia/sinus arrest
- metallic taste
- throat tightness
- facial flushing*

*More common side effects

PRECAUTIONS/COMMENTS
- History of "sick-sinus" syndrome, second-or-third-degree heart block without pacemaker
- Reactive airway disease (asthma, COPD) — may have bronchospasm
- Adenosine does not convert atrial flutter, atrial fibrillation, or ventricular tachycardia to sinus rhythm.
- Persantine (dipyridamole) and Tegretol (carbamazepine) potentiate the action of adenosine resulting in increased heart block — use lower dose.
- Due to denervation of heart use with extreme caution in cardiac transplant recipients—may have persistent asystole.
- Use in children *only* for definite/highly suspected SVT. (Children's heart rates are faster; SVT usually must be more than 200/minute to warrant treatment.)
- Theophylline preparations may render adenosine ineffective; higher dose may be required.

ADENOSINE
LAS VEGAS, NV

Adenosine (Adenocard)

Form:

6 mg/2 ml

Class:

Antiarrhythmic

Action:

Conversion of paroxysmal supraventricular tachycardia to sinus rhythm including that associated with WPW accessory bypass tracts. Adenosine slows conduction through the Av node and can interrupt reentry pathways.

INDICATIONS	PHYSICIAN'S ORDERS
PSVT not responsive to vagal maneuvers	YES

Dose:

ADULT:
6 mg

PEDIATRIC:
(0.1 mg/kg IV for use in SVT only)

Route:

By rapid IV bolus followed by a 12-mg bolus if the first is unsuccessful within 1 to 2 minutes. (To assure solution reaches systemic circulation, administer into IV line as proximally as possible over 1 to 2 seconds, follow with rapid saline flush.)

Duration of Action:

Less than 10 seconds

Side Effects:

Facial flushing, headache, sweating, palpitations, and chest pain. Due to short half-life, adverse effects are generally self-limiting.

Contraindications:

Second or third-degree AV block or sick-sinus syndrome unless patient with a functional artificial pacemaker

Adenosine is ineffective in converting atrial flutter, atrial fibrillation, or ventricular tachycardia to sinus rhythm but may slow the rhythm enough momentarily to aid in arrhythmia diagnosis.

Repeat doses of adenosine are not indicated if the dysrhythmia reoccurs after conversion. Alternate pharmacological therapy may be necessary.

ALBUTEROL NEBULIZER TREATMENT
0.5% Solution (2.5 mg albuterol diluted to 3 ml)
EUGENE/SPRINGFIELD, OR

I. Purpose:

  A. To administer aerosolized medication via a nebulizer

II. Pharmacology and Actions:

  A. Sympathomimetic drug (stimulates sympathetic nervous system) with beta effects

   1. Dilates bronchioles (beta-2)
   2. Stimulates heart (beta-1)

  B. This drug is considered beta-2-selective.

III. Indications:

  A. Used to bronchodilate a patient who has respiratory distress with bronchospasm (*e.g.*, asthma, emphysema, bronchitis, *etc.*). THIS MAY BE DONE BY STANDING ORDER IN A PATIENT WHO HAS WHEEZING OR OTHER EVIDENCE OF BRONCHOSPASM AND A HEART RATE UNDER 160.

IV. Precautions and Side Effects:

  A. Contraindicated in patient with hypersensitivity to albuterol (VENTOLIN®)
  B. Use cautiously in patients with cardiovascular disease, especially coronary insufficiency, cardiac dysrhythmias, hypertension, and congestive heart failure; in patients with convulsive disorders, diabetes mellitus, or hyperthyroidism; and in patients who are unusually responsive to sympathomimetic amines (drugs that stimulate sympathetic nervous system).
  C. IF HEART RATE OVER 160 OR PATIENT HAS EVIDENCE OF MYOCARDIAL ISCHEMIA (*e.g.*, CHEST PAIN), CONSULT WITH MD PRIOR TO USE.
  D. Adverse reactions include tachycardia, nervousness, tremors, dizziness, palpitations, nausea, vomiting, headache, nasal congestion, hypertension, and a bad taste.
  E. After use of bronchodilator medication, an increased volume of liquefied bronchial secretions may occur. Be prepared to suction if necessary to maintain a patent airway.
  F. Paroxysmal bronchoconstriction can occur in patients with repeated excessive administration.

V. Administration (EMT 3 or 4):

  A. **Adult by standing order:**

   1. Usual adult dose by nebulizer is 3-ml-unit-dose preparation of .083% albuterol sulfate (2.5 mg albuterol diluted to 3 ml with sterile normal saline solution). Oxygen flow is set at 6 liters/minute to the nebulizer.

2. If additional oxygen is needed by the patient, use a cannula at appropriate liter flow.

3. Prior to treatment, document baseline lung sounds and BP, pulse, and respiratory rate.

4. During and after treatment, assess and document lung sounds and vital signs. IF HEART RATE INCREASES BY MORE THAN 20 BEATS PER MINUTE, DISCONTINUE THE NEBULIZER TREATMENT AND CONSULT WITH MD PRIOR TO FURTHER ALBUTEROL TREATMENT.

E. **Pediatric under age 12 years by standing order:** Use premix and watch closely for side effects. Stop administration if side effects develop.

VI. Special Notes:

A. Albuterol should be kept out of direct light. Do not use if it becomes yellow.

B. Start oxygen flow-through nebulizer at 6 l/minute. This liter flow can be adjusted up or down so that the treatment takes about 10 minutes. If the oxygen flow to nebulizer is turned too high, it will nebulize the medicine too fast, and the patient will not get the full benefit.

C. Albuterol by nebulizer is an adjunct drug in allergic reaction; it is not a substitute for epinephrine in severe anaphylaxis.

D. An increase in wheezing may reflect hypersensitivity to sympathomimetic amines (rare), or it may demonstrate increase in air movement. Consult with MD if you think patient is worsening.

E. Pediatric albuterol doses are still under investigation by the FDA, but the drug is in common use for the pediatric population. Calculated pediatric dose is 0.03 ml/kg, but premix may be used if treatment is stopped immediately, if the treatment is effective, or there are side effects. Rarely given to infants.

F. Some trade names for albuterol are Proventil® and Ventolin®.

ALBUTEROL SULFATE
DENVER, CO

Pharmacology and Actions

A. Has selective B2 adrenergic-stimulating properties resulting in potent bronchodilation
B. Relatively few cardiovascular effects compared with metaproterenol HCL (Alupent)
C. Rapid onset of action (under 5 minutes) and a duration of action from 2 to 6 hours

Indications

A. For relief of bronchospasm in patient with obstructive airway disease (asthma, emphysema, COPD)

Precautions

A. Albuterol sulfate has sympathomimetic effects. Discontinue immediately if patient develops chest pain or arrhythmias.
B. Inhaled, albuterol sulfate can result in paradoxical bronchospasm, which can be life threatening. If this occurs, the preparation should be discontinued immediately.

Administration

A. For nebulizer use only
   1. For adults and children: place 2.5 mg diluted in 3 ml of normal saline into an oxygen-powered nebulizer. Deliver as much of the mist as possible by nebulizer over 5 to 15 minutes.
   2. Endotracheally intubated patients may be given albuterol sulfate by attaching the nebulizer in-line.

Side Effects and Special Notes

A. Monitor blood pressure and heart rate closely **and contact base physician** if any concerns arise.
B. If no history of airway disease or no response to therapy, **contact base physician**, as presenting symptoms may instead be manifestations of severe allergic reaction.
C. Medication such as MAO inhibitors and tricyclics may potentiate tachycardia and hypertension.

AMMONIA, AROMATIC SPIRITS
SANTA ANA, CA

MEDICATION: AMMONIA, AROMATIC SPIRITS	ADULT DOSE	PEDIATRIC DOSE	SIDE EFFECTS	PRECAUTIONS/ COMMENTS
CLASSIFICATION: Respiratory Irritant **MECHANISM OF ACTION:** • Mucous-membrane-irritant properties act as stimulus to the reticular activating system of the brain. This regulatory system is responsible for the level of consciousness. **INDICATIONS:** • Syncope • Assessing level of consciousness **DOSAGE FORMS:** • Crushable vaporoles: 0.33 ml	• Break ampule, and pass under nostrils several times until patient regains consciousness. • Repeat as needed to maintain consciousness.	• Break ampule, and pass under nostrils several times until patient regains consciousness. • Repeat as needed to maintain consciousness.		• Avoid direct contact with skin and/or nasal mucosa—may cause chemical burns. • Avoid prolonged use—may induce bronchospasm in asthmatics and other susceptible people. • Use with caution if C-spine injuries suspected.

ASPIRIN
WICHITA, KS

Aspirin (ASA)

Classification:

Nonsteroidal anti-inflammatory salicylate

Uses:

Antithromboembolic

Administration and Dose:

STANDING ORDER:
NONTRAUMATIC CHEST PAIN OR DISCOMFORT OF SUSPECTED CAR-
DIAC ORIGIN: (After nitrolycerin.) Administer ASA 5 gr PO to chew up and
swallow. May be crushed for patients who are unable to chew.

AUTHORIZED RANGE AND USE:
For the treatment of patients with nontraumatic chest pain or discomfort of sus-
pected cardiac origin, following the administration of nitroglycerin. Administer
ASA 5 gr PO. Instruct patients to chew the tablet and swallow.

PEDIATRICS:
None

Precautions:

Adverse effects are primarily gastrointestinal, including blood loss, gastritis,
esophagitis, nephropathy, and renal-function abnormalities. Hepatotoxicity, hearing loss, tinnitus, and inhibition of platelet aggregation have been reported. Caution is advised with use of the drug in children and adolescents with viral illnesses,
due to the possible association with and increased risk of Reye's syndrome.

CONTRAINDICATIONS:

RELATIVE:

See PRECAUTIONS.

ASBOLUTE:

Hypersensitivity, gastrointestinal hemorrhage

Actions:

Oral absorption occurs within 20 to 60 minutes and is dependent on dosage, gastric pH, emptying time, dissolution rate, and whether the drug is taken with ANTACIDS, meals, or during fasting. Aspirin distributes rapidly to plasma, saliva, milk, and spinal, peritoneal, and synovial fluid and is highly protein bound, 88% to 93%. Peak plasma levels of 15-to-20 mg/dl occur within 1 to 2 hours. Hepatic metabolism occurs by esterases to several inactive metabolites. Renal excretion of unchanged drug and metabolites is dose related and ranges from 5.6% to 35.6%. Half-life is dose dependent and increases with dose, range 2.4-to-19 h with doses of 0.25-to-20 g.

The exact mechanism of aspirin's effect is unknown but is thought to involve inhibition of prostaglandin synthesis and other inflammatory and immunologic processes. Diminished platelet adhesiveness may result from minimal doses of 300 to 600 mg/day. Aspirin blocks the adhesion of platelets to connective tissue and collagen fibers by several mechanisms, thus prolonging the bleeding time for several days.

Toxicity:

Normally, with doses that exceed 100 mg/kg/day

Preparation:

Unidose tablets, 5 gr per tablet

Time:

Oral absorption occurs within 20 to 60 minutes and is dependent on dosage, gastric pH, emptying time, dissolution rate, and whether the drug is taken with ANTACIDS, meals, or during fasting.

ATROPINE SULFATE
SANTA ANA, CA

	ADULT DOSE	PEDIATRIC DOSE	SIDE EFFECTS	PRECAUTIONS/ COMMENTS
MEDICATION: ATROPINE SULFATE **CLASSIFICATION:** Anticholinergic **MECHANISM OF ACTION:** • Blocks the receptors of the parasympathetic nervous system: —Increases heart rate by increasing rate of discharge of SA node —Accelerates conduction through AV node **INDICATIONS:** • Bradycardia, second-or-third-degree AV block with hypoperfusion • PEA with rate < 60 • Ventricular asystole • Organophosphate poisoning **DOSAGE FORM:** • 1 mg/10 ml, 10 ml pre-fill syringe • 1 mg/ml, 1 ml vial	• 0.5 mg IVP or SLVP every 3–5 minutes to a maximum of 0.04 mg/kg • For documented PEA HR < 60 or asystole: 1 mg IVP every 3–5 minutes to a maximum of 0.04 mg/kg • 2.0 mg ET once • 2–5 mg IVP for organophosphate poisoning • BH may order higher dose for organophosphate poisoning.	• 0.02 mg/kg IVP or SLVP every 3–5 minutes to a maximum of 0.04 mg/kg • 0.04 mg/kg ET once • 0.05 mg/kg IVP or per BH for organophosphate poisoning • BH may order higher dose for organophosphate poisoning. • Minimum dose of 0.1 mg to avoid paradoxical bradycardia	• Tachycardia • Dry mouth • Blurred vision • Dilated pupils	• May increase myocardial oxygen demands precipitating angina or extending an area of infarct • May occasionally cause ventricular tachycardia or fibrillation • Increase in heart rate may be minimal in elderly people and children.

BRETYLIUM/BRETYLOL
ARLINGTON, TX

Action:

Bretylium is an antifibrillatory, antiarrhythmic agent. It increases the V-Fib threshold. It also increases impulse formation and spontaneous firing rate of pacemaker tissue. Suppresses reentry of aberrant impulses.

Indications:

To convert life-threatening dysrhythmias such as ventricular fibrillation and ventricular tachycardia refractory to lidocaine. Also given for the prophylactic treatment of life-threatening ventricular dysrhythmias.

Contraindications:

None when used in the setting of life-threatening dysrhythmias

Potential Side Effects:

Postural hypotension, dizziness, and nausea/vomiting

Dosage:

Initial dose: **5 mg/kg** IVP. After eight minutes and no change in rhythm, a second dose may be given at 10 mg/kg IVP and repeated as necessary at eight-minute intervals to a maximum of 30 mg/kg. If rhythm is converted, initiate bretylium infusion at **2 mg/min.** as a maintenance dose.

Pediatric Usage:

5 mg/kg IV/IO for initial dose, 10 mg/kg IV/IO for second dose

CALCIUM CHLORIDE
LAS VEGAS, NV

Form:

1 gm/10 ml

Class:

Electrolyte

Action:

I. Increases myocardial contractility
II. Increases myocardial excitability
III. Decreases heart rate

	INDICATIONS	PHYSICIAN'S ORDERS
I.	Calcium channel blocker toxicity	YES
II.	Hyperkalemia with electrocardiographic symptomatology	YES

Dose:

ADULT:
5 cc or 500 mg of 10% solution (4.5 mEq) every 10 minutes, **SLOWLY**

PEDIATRIC:
20 mg/kg

Route:

IV

Side Effects:

Excessive calcium causes cell death.

Contraindications:

Patients receiving digitalis

Precautions:

IV line should be flushed between calcium-chloride and sodium-bicarbonate administration.

CHARCOAL (ACTIVATED)
WICHITA, KS

Activated Charcoal (Actidose with Sorbital)
Classification: Absorbent
Uses:

Activated charcoal is a general-purpose antidote recommended for the treatment of practically all oral poisonings except those caused by corrosive agents, cyanide, iron, mineral acids, or organic solvents. The drug may be particularly useful if it is administered during the early management of acute poisoning. It is not effective in absorbing toxins with a heavy molecular weight nor in cases of lithium ingestion.

Administration and Dose:

AUTHORIZED RANGE AND USE:
With a physician order; actidose with sorbital may be administered as follows: The single-use bottle should be shaken well prior to removing the cap. Have the patient drink the entire contents of the bottle. This treatment may be repeated with an order in the adult patient.

This solution may be administered through the NG tube with a physician order by removing the cap, clipping the end off, and inserting this into the NG tube for administration. This may be repeated one time in adult patients (50 grams total dose).

PEDIATRICS:
Over 12 years of age—same as adult
1–12 years of age—same as adult, but should not receive multiple doses
Under 1 year of age (infant)—should not receive this solution

Precautions:

Multiple doses of actidose with sorbital may cause an excessive cathartic action and thus a depletion in the electrolytes and may cause hypotension.

CONTRAINDICATIONS:
Not to be given to infants < 1 year of age, nor to patients < 16 kg in weight

Actions:

Absorbent granule or powder that is not absorbed in the GI tract nor metabolized. It is excreted in feces. Since it colors the feces black, activated charcoal may be used as a fecal marker.

Preparation:

Single-use bottles of a premixed solution. Each bottle contains 25 grams of activated charcoal in 120 ml of solution.

DEXAMETHASONE (DECADRON)
JACKSONVILLE, FL

A. Classification
   1. Anti-inflammatory steroid

B. Dosage
   1. Comes in 1-cc ampules or vials (4 mg/cc); also packaged in multidose vials of 5 and 25 cc
   2. Adult dose: 12 mg IV push. Research indicates much-larger doses being administered at this time of up to 30 mg and more IV (very controversial issue at time). Onset of action approximately 6–18 hours.
   3. Pediatric dose: 0.25–0.5 mg/kg

C. Action
   Decadron is an anti-inflammatory steroid similar to hydrocortisone but lacks the sodium-retaining property of hydrocortisone. Decadron is used for the treatment of various inflammatory diseases. It can be used in the field to prevent brain and spinal-cord edema. However, its primary use is for severe allergic or anaphylactic reactions.

D. Route of Administration
   1. IV push or intraosseous

E. Side Effects
   Decadron may cause elevation of blood pressure, increased incidence of sweating, convulsions, vertigo, glaucoma, headache, decreased resistance to infection, and increased requirements for insulin in diabetes.

REMEMBER: ADMINISTER *ONLY* with specific physician's order.

DEXTROSE INJECTION, 50% (D₅₀W)
SANTA ANA, CA

MEDICATION:	ADULT DOSE	PEDIATRIC DOSE	SIDE EFFECTS	PRECAUTIONS/COMMENTS
MEDICATION: DEXTROSE INJECTION 50% (D₅₀W) **CLASSIFICATION:** Glucose Replacement **MECHANISM OF ACTION:** • Elevates blood-glucose level **INDICATIONS:** • Blood-glucose determination < 60 **DOSAGE FORM:** • 25 gm/50 ml (50%), 50-ml prefilled syringe.	• 50 ml of 50% solution (25 gm) IVP, may repeat once	• 1 ml/kg IVP if > 2 years • 2 ml/kg 25% dextrose if < 2 years • May repeat once in 5 minutes • Do not exceed adult dose • For pediatric patients < 2 years, dilute to 25% dextrose. Discard one half the volume of the D₅₀W syringe and then draw up the same volume of NS from IV tubing. Rotate to mix prior to administration.	• Hyperglycemia • Dehydration	• Has a marked sclerosing effect on veins and can be damaging if injected into interstitial tissues • Monitor IV site for extravasation; aspirate before and during administration. • D₅₀W may exacerbate neurologic injuries in patients with CVAs, cardiopulmonary arrest, or head trauma.

DIAZEPAM (VALIUM)
SANTA ANA, CA

MEDICATION: DIAZEPAM (VALIUM)	ADULT DOSE	PEDIATRIC DOSE	SIDE EFFECTS	PRECAUTIONS/ COMMENTS
CLASSIFICATION: Anticonvulsant **MECHANISM OF ACTION:** • Decreases neural cell activity in all regions of the central nervous system **INDICATIONS:** • Prolonged and/or recurrent seizure activity • Sedation prior to synchronized cardioversion **DOSAGE FORM:** • 10 mg/2 ml, 2-ml pre-filled syringe or vial	• 5–10 mg slow IVP, titrated to effect	• 0.2 mg/kg *slow* IVP to maximum adult dose • For volume less than 1 ml, use 1-ml TB syringe; draw up 1 ml; each 0.2 ml = 1 mg. • 0.5 mg/kg rectally when an IV cannot be established • Use 1-ml TB syringe with needle removed. • Lubricate syringe and insert gently 1–2 inches into rectum or just past rectal sphincter. • Instill medication into rectum, remove syringe, and tape buttocks together to prevent loss of medication. • May repeat in 5 minutes	• Hypotension • Respiratory depression	• Diazepam is useful only in terminating seizures. • Diazepam potentiates other CNS depressants. • Diazepam should be administered via the IV injection site closest to the IV site. • Diazepam will precipitate in IV solutions.

DIAZEPAM (VALIUM), RECTAL
SAN JOSE, CA

Rectal Diazepam Administration

I. Introduction

The rectal administration of diazepam is a rapidly acting method of treatment of status epilepticus. Although the onset of action of rectally administered diazepam is slightly slower than that given per IV access, the delay and difficulty in establishing vascular access in an actively seizing patient make the use of rectal diazepam an essentially equivalent treatment modality.

II. Indications

    A. Active seizure lasting longer than 5 minutes and currently seizing

    B. Multiple seizures with no recovery of consciousness between seizures, and currently seizing

III. Contraindications

    A. Respiratory insufficiency

    B. Hypotension

IV. Equipment

    A. 5 French pediatric feeding tube

    B. Intravenous diazepam

    C. 5-ml syringe

    D. Tape

    E. Lubricant

    F. 5 ml saline

V. Procedure

    A. Carefully restrain the patient manually in the knee-chest or supine position.

    B. Assure airway patency, and administer supplemental oxygen.

    C. Draw up the calculated dose of diazepam: 0.5 mg/kg (max. 10 mg) into the syringe.

    D. Have assistant hold legs apart.

    E. Introduce lubricated 5 French pediatric feeding tube into the patient's rectum, approximately 4-to-5 cm from anus.

    F. Attach the syringe to the feeding tube, and inject the contents into the rectum.

    G. Flush the feeding tube with 5 ml of normal saline.

    H. Withdraw the tube. Facilitate drug retention with manual pressure, and tape buttocks closed.

VI. Potential Problems

    A. Respiratory depression

    B. Hypotension

    C. Administration in the anus, with inadequate absorption

    D. Forceful tube placement, with subsequent rectal injury

    E. Inadequate diazepam dose

DIAZOXIDE (HYPERSTAT)
STATE OF KANSAS

Class

Potent antihypertensive (hypotensive agent)

Pharmacologic Effects

1. Direct arterial vasodilator on smooth muscle in peripheral arterioles
2. Decreases peripheral vascular resistance
3. Accelerates heart rate, increases stroke volume and cardiac output
4. Inhibits Na and H_2O excretion by the kidney
5. Interferes with glucose metabolism creating hyperglycemia
6. Decreases arterial blood pressure rapidly

Uses

1. Hypertensive crisis characterized by hypertensive encephalopathy and extreme blood pressure elevation, especially diastolic elevations above 110–150
2. Malignant hypertension, acute heart failure with extreme hypertension, and renal impairment

Duration of Action and Excretion

1. Rapid onset acting in 3–5 minutes, lasts 3–12 hours
2. Excreted by the kidney

Preparations

1. Prefilled syringe   20 ml × 15 mg/ml = 300 mg
2. Ampules   20 ml × 15 mg/ml = 300 mg

Dosage and Administration

1. Rapid IV injection (30 seconds or less) of 1–3 mg/kg up to a maximum of 150 mg in a single injection. This dose may be repeated at intervals of 5–15 minutes until a satisfactory reduction in blood pressure (diastolic pressure below 100 mm Hg) has been achieved.
2. Or, 75-mg boluses every 5–15 minutes up to 300 mg

NOTE: The patient should be recumbent prior to and during hyperstat administration.

Antidote

1. Trendelenburg

2. If necessary, sympathomimetic agents such as dopamine or norepinephrine

Pediatric Dose

1. 1–2 mg/kg IV injection (30 seconds or less). Maximum total initial dose 5 mg/kg

DIPHENHYDRAMINE (BENADRYL)
SANTA ANA, CA

MEDICATION: DIPHENHYDRAMINE (BENADRYL) **CLASSIFICATION:** Antihistamine **MECHANISM OF ACTION:** • Antagonizes effects of histamine by blocking histamine receptors • Decreases itching, edema, broncho-constriction, and vasodilation **INDICATIONS:** • Acute allergic reaction • Anaphylaxis • Extrapyramidal side effects—dystonic reactions **DOSAGE FORM:** • 50 mg/ml, 1-ml prefilled syringe	ADULT DOSE	PEDIATRIC DOSE	SIDE EFFECTS	PRECAUTIONS/ COMMENTS
	• 25–50 mg IVP or deep IM	• 1 mg/kg IVP or deep IM	• Drowsiness • Dry mouth	• Diphenhydramine potentiates other CNS depressants.

DOPAMINE HYDROCHLORIDE (INTROPIN)
SANTA ANA, CA

MEDICATION: DOPAMINE HYDROCHLORIDE (INTROPIN)	ADULT DOSE	PEDIATRIC DOSE	SIDE EFFECTS	PRECAUTIONS/ COMMENTS
CLASSIFICATION: Sympathomimetic **MECHANISM OF ACTION:** • Stimulates alpha, beta, and dopaminergic receptors: —At lower doses, beta-adrenergic effects (increased heart rate, increased force of contraction, increased cardiac output) and dopaminergic effects (dilation of renal and mesenteric blood vessels) dominate. —At higher doses, alpha adrenergic effects (peripheral vasoconstriction) dominate, and at doses greater than 20 mcg/kg/min., constriction of renal and mesenteric vessels occurs. **INDICATIONS:** • Cardiogenic shock • Distributive shock: —Septic shock after adequate fluid administration —Neurogenic shock —Anaphylaxis with hypotension **DOSAGE FORM:** • 400 mg/10 ml, 10-ml prefilled syringe • 400 mg/250 ml D5W, prefilled bag	• 2–20 mcg/kg/ min., IV infusion. Titrate to signs of adequate perfusion. • Prepare a concentration of 1600 mcg/ml (400 mg/250 ml NS).	• 2–10 mcg/kg/min. IV infusion. Titrate to signs of adequate perfusion. • Prepare a concentration 320 mcg/ml (80 mg/250 ml NS).	• Dysrhythmias • Hypertension	• Use cautiously in patients with tachydysrhythmias. • Ventricular dysrhythmias may occur requiring a reduction in infusion rate. • Higher dosages may cause excessive vasoconstriction (10–20 mcg/kg/min.). • Do not infuse simultaneously with NaHCO₃; alkaline solutions inactivate dopamine.

351

DOPAMINE DRIP CHART
DENVER, CO

INTRAVENOUS DRIP RATES FOR DOPAMINE
CONCENTRATION: 1600 MCG/ML

	DOSE				
WEIGHT (kg)	5	10	15	20	(mcg/kg/min.)
50	10	20	30	40	microdrips/min.
60	10	25	35	45	
70	15	25	40	50	
80	15	30	45	60	
90	15	35	50	70	
100	20	35	55	75	
110	20	40	60	85	

DROPERIDOL (INAPSINE)
KANSAS CITY, MO

I. Pharmacology and Actions:

  A. A butyrophenone related to haloperidol (Haldol) but with faster onset of action and shorter half-life (onset of action 10 minutes with peak effect in 30 minutes)

  B. Acts in CNS as sedative and neuroleptic. (Neurolepsis is a state of quiescence, decreased motor activity, and indifference to surroundings.)

  C. Anticholinergic (atropine-like) and alpha-blocking agent (vasodilation)

II. Indications:

  A. Chemical restraint for the violent/agitated patient. This is a joint paramedic-base-station-physician decision that relies heavily on paramedic judgment. Most violent/agitated patients can be handled with verbal or physical restraint alone.

III. Precautions:

  A. Hypotension and tachycardia are common (20–25%) but usually self-limiting side effects.

  B. Dystonic reactions are rare.

  C. Concomitant use with other sedatives (in overdose or drug-abuse situations) may potentiate sedation.

  D. Contraindications: Allergy
                           Pediatric patients

IV. Administration:
5 mg IM (deltoid preferred for rapid absorption but gluteus or thigh acceptable)

V. Special Considerations:

  A. Always restrain patient in lateral decubitus or prone position to avoid aspiration.

  B. Onset is relatively delayed, and this drug will *not* be helpful in the *initial* restraint of the patient. By the time the patient reaches the ED, it should be taking effect.

  C. Droperidol does not replace physical restraint of the patient.

VI. Applicable Protocols:
Protocol 3: Behavioral/Psychiatric Disorders

EPINEPHRINE HYDROCHLORIDE (EPINEPHRINE)
SANTA ANA, CA

MEDICATION: EPINEPHRINE HYDROCHLORIDE (EPINEPHRINE)

CLASSIFICATION: Sympathomimetic

MECHANISM OF ACTION:
- Stimulates alpha and beta adrenergic receptors:

  Alpha
  —Peripheral vasoconstriction
  —Increases perfusion pressure during chest compressions
  —Increases diastolic pressure during hypotension

  Beta
  —Increases heart rate (increased chronotrophy)
  —Increases automaticity of heart cells (increased dromotropy)
  —Increases force of contraction (increased inotrophy)
  —Bronchodilation
  —Inhibits release of histamine during allergic reaction

INDICATIONS:
- Asystole
- Ventricular fibrillation/pulseless ventricular tachycardia
- Pulseless electrical activity (PEA)
- Anaphylaxis
- Bronchospasm
- Allergic reaction

DOSAGE FORMS:
- 1:10,000, 1-mg/10-ml prefilled syringe
- 1:1000, 1-mg/ml, 1-ml ampule
- 1:1000, 1-mg/1-ml, 30-ml vial

ADULT DOSE	PEDIATRIC DOSE	SIDE EFFECTS	PRECAUTIONS/COMMENTS
Asystole; ventricular fibrillation; pulseless ventricular tachycardia; PEA: • 1.0 mg 1:10,000 IVP every 3–5 minutes • 10 mg 1:10,000 ET once • 0.5–1.0 mg 1:1000 SLVP if unable to start IV Bronchospasm and mild allergic reactions: • 0.3–0.5 mg 1:1000 SQ • Repeat in 20 minutes if needed. Anaphylaxis in patients with absent palpable pulses or impending airway obstruction: • 0.1–0.3 mg 1:10,000 IVP, may repeat as needed	Asystole; ventricular fibrillation; pulseless ventricular tachycardia; PEA: • 0.01 mg/kg 1:10,000 IVP every 3–5 minutes • 0.1 mg/kg 1:1000 ET; repeat once in 5 minutes • 0.01 mg/kg 1:1000 SLVP; if unable to start IV, may repeat once Bronchospasm and mild allergic reactions: • 0.01 mg/kg 1:1000 SQ up to 0.3 mg maximum Anaphylaxis in patients with absent palpable pulses or impending airway obstruction: • 0.01 mg/kg 1:10,000 IVP, may repeat as needed	• Tachydysrhythmias and ventricular ectopy • Palpitations, tremor, anxiety, headache • Hypertension	• May increase myocardial oxygen demands precipitating angina or extending an area of infarct • Acidosis may render epinephrine ineffective. • Do not infuse simultaneously with sodium bicarbonate. Alkaline solutions inactive epinephrine.

354

EPINEPHRINE (PEDIATRIC)
LAS VEGAS, NEV

Form:

1:1,000	1 mg/1 ml
1:10,000	1 mg/10 ml

Class:

Sympathomimetic

Action:

I. Bronchodilation
II. Positive chronotrope
III. Positive inotrope

INDICATION				PHYSICIAN'S ORDERS
Asystole/pulseless electrical activity (PEA)				
FIRST DOSE:	IV/IO	0.01 mg/kg	1:10,000	NO
	ETT*	0.1 mg/kg	1:1,000	NO
SECOND AND SUBSEQUENT DOSES (EVERY 3 TO 5 MINS.):				
	IV/IO	0.1 mg/kg	1:1,000	NO
	ETT*	0.1 mg/kg	1:1,000	NO

INDICATION				PHYSICIAN'S ORDERS
Bradycardia				
DOSE:	IV/IO	0.01 mg/kg	1:10,000	NO
	ETT*	0.1 mg/kg	1:1,000	NO

*In neonatal resuscitation (0 to 30 days), the ETT dose remains unchanged at .01 mg/kg of the 1:10,000 solution repeated every 3 to 5 minutes, if necessary.

FUROSEMIDE (LASIX)
SANTA ANA, CA

	ADULT DOSE	PEDIATRIC DOSE	SIDE EFFECTS	PRECAUTIONS/ COMMENTS
MEDICATION: FUROSEMIDE (LASIX) **CLASSIFICATION:** Diuretic, venodilator **MECHANISM OF ACTION:** • Dilates venous vessels, reducing return of blood to heart • Stimulates diuresis **INDICATION:** • Acute pulmonary edema **DOSAGE FORM:** • 100 mg/10 ml, 10-ml prefilled syringe	• 20–100 mg	• 1 mg/kg IVP	• When given rapidly, may cause transient deafness • Hypotension	• Assess current diuretic use, including dose; patients taking furosemide may require an increased dose.

GLUCAGON
SANTA ANA, CA

MEDICATION: GLUCAGON **CLASSIFICATION:** Hyperglycemic agent **MECHANISM OF ACTION:** • Increases blood-glucose levels through release of glycogen stores from the liver **INDICATIONS:** • Blood-glucose determination < 60. **DOSAGE FORMS:** • 1-mg ampule with diluent solution, 1 ml	ADULT DOSE	PEDIATRIC DOSE	SIDE EFFECTS	PRECAUTIONS/ COMMENTS
	• 1 mg IM, may repeat once	• 0.5–1 mg IM, may repeat once • 0.5 mg IM for patients < 1 year	• Nausea, vomiting	• May exacerbate neurologic injuries in patients with CVAs, cardiopulmonary arrest, or head trauma • Only the diluent supplied by the manufacturer should be used to mix glucagon.

GLUCAGON
LAS VEGAS, NV

Form:

1 mg/1 ml

Class:

Insulin antagonist

Action:

Reverses the effects of hypoglycemia

	INDICATIONS	PHYSICIAN'S ORDERS
I.	For hypoglycemic patients in whom IV access for glucose administration cannot be achieved within 10 minutes or 3 IV attempts	NO
II.	In any suspected hypoglycemic patient who is combative	NO
III.	If in the clinical judgment of the paramedic or EMT-I, the drug indicated	NO

Dose:

ADULT:
1 mg vial reconstituted with 1 ml diluent (age 12 and up)

PEDIATRIC:
0.5 mg up to age 12 IM in the thigh

Route:

IM

Side Effects:

May cause allergic reactions in rare instances

Contraindications:

None

Special Note:

ALS ONLY—IM thiamine should be considered prior to the administration of glucagon in the suspected alcoholic patient.

Oral glucose should be given if the patient is awake and a gag reflex is present.
Response to the drug should be evident within 15 minutes.

GLUCOSE SOLUTION
SANTA ANA, CA

MEDICATION: GLUCOSE SOLUTION	ADULT DOSE	PEDIATRIC DOSE	SIDE EFFECTS	PRECAUTIONS/ COMMENTS
CLASSIFICATION: Carbohydrate **MECHANISM OF ACTION:** • Provides increase in blood-glucose level. **INDICATIONS:** • Alert hypoglycemic patient • Blood-glucose determination < 60 **DOSAGE FORM:** • 360-ml (12-oz.) bottle, 100 gm glucose	• Administer orally as needed.	• 30 ml orally, repeat as needed	• Nausea	• Administer only to alert patients. • Avoid administration to patients ≤ 6 months.

GLUTOSE
WICHITA, KS

Classification:

Oral hyperglycemic agent (concentrated sugar)

Uses:

Reverses hypoglycemia. Good for combative insulin-shock patients with good gag reflex.

Administration and Dose:

AUTHORIZED RANGE AND USE:
One entire tube PO (= 31 gm of glutose) can be given to an alert patient without physician order. (Adult and peds.). With physician order, glutose can be repeated × 1 if indicated after 10 minutes.
  Draw blood sugar first if possible.

PEDIATRICS:
Same as adult dose or as tolerated by patient

Precautions:

SIDE EFFECTS:
None

CONTRAINDICATIONS:
None

Preparation:

1.09-oz. tube of 43% solution = 31 gm of glutose

Time:

Response should occur in 10 minutes.

HALOPERIDOL
AUSTIN, TX

Haloperidol (Haldol, Halperon)

Functional class:

Antipsychotic

Chemical class:

butyrophenone

Action:

Alters the effects of dopamine in the CNS. Also has anticholinergic and alpha-adrenergic blocking activity.

Uses:

For the treatment of acute and chronic psychosis. Also used to control Tourette's syndrome and severe behavioral problems in both adults and children. Has found use recently as a calming agent in patients who have become violent due to psychotic episodes.

Dosage and routes:

Chemical restraint
Adult: IM 10 mg

Side effects/adverse reactions:

CNS:	Sedation, extrapyramidal reactions, confusion, seizures, restlessness
CV:	Hypotension, tachycardia
RESP:	Respiratory depression
EENT	Dry eyes, blurred vision
GI:	Dry mouth, anorexia, constipation, hepatitis
GU:	Urinary retention
HEMA:	Anemia, leukopenia
INTEG:	Rashes, photosensitivity, diaphoresis

Contraindications/Precautions/Drug Interactions:

Hypersensitivity to haloperidol, CNS depression, and cardiac disease
Use with caution in elderly patients, patients with cardiac disease, severely ill patients, those with respiratory insufficiency, and those with seizures.

Assessment:

Assess mental and respiratory status regularly.
Monitor vital signs.

Treatment of Overdosage:

None

© *Austin/Travis EMS Clinical Practice*

IPECAC
STATE OF MARYLAND

Classification:

Emetic

Action:

—Irritates lining of stomach
—Stimulates vomiting center in the medulla, onset within 20 to 30 minutes

Indications:

Overdose/poisoning in alert patients

Contraindications:

—Unconsciousness
—Some poisoning cases, *i.e.*, petroleum products, caustics
—Decreased level of consciousness
—For patients under 9 months

Potential Side Effects:

None for field use

Dosage/Route:

Adult—30 ml orally; repeat in 30 minutes; *must be followed by large amounts of water*
Pediatric—15 ml orally
            —For patients between 9 and 12 months, 10 ml orally are to be used.

Important Points:

—Ipecac administration must be followed by the administration of large amounts
   of water.

IPRATROPIUM BROMIDE (ATROVENT)
AUSTIN, TX

Functional Class:

Anticholinergic

Chemical Class:

Synthetic quaternary ammonium compound

Action:

Inhibits interaction of acetylcholine at receptor sites on the bronchial smooth muscle, resulting in bronchodilation

Uses:

Bronchodilation during bronchospasm in those with COPD

Dosage and Routes:

Adult: Nebulizer 0.5 mg mixed with 1-unit dose of albuterol

Side Effects/Adverse Reactions:

GI:	Nausea, vomiting, cramps
EENT:	Dry mouth, blurred vision
CNS:	Anxiety, dizziness, headache, nervousness
RESP:	Cough, worsening of symptoms, bronchospasms
INTEG:	Rash
CV:	Palpitation

Contraindications/Precautions/Drug Interactions:

Children <12 yrs., narrow-angle glaucoma, prostatic hypertrophy, and bladder-neck obstruction

Assessment:

For palpitations; if severe, drug may have to be changed.
For tolerance over long-term therapy; dose may have to be increased or changed.

Treatment of Overdosage:

None

ISOPROTERENOL (ISUPREL)
JACKSONVILLE, FL

A. Classification

    1. Sympathetic agonist

    2. Pure beta-adrenergic receptor stimulant

B. Dosage

    1. Comes in 5 cc *vial* (1 mg) or 1 cc *ampule* (0.2 mg)

    2. Adult dose: 5 cc (1mg) diluted in 250 cc of D_5W (will yield a solution containing 4 mcg/cc).

        Always to be administered with a microdrip. This dilution may be administered initially at a very slow rate of approximately 2 mcg per minute (30 microdrops) and gradually increased and titrated to the patient's needs and responses. Is no longer recommended as part of ACLS asystole protocols. Use is reserved for maintenance of adequate heart rate (after 2 mg of atropine have been used) while awaiting pacemaker insertion (for severe bradydysrhythmias, 2d and 3d-degree blocks refractory to atropine).

    3. Pediatric dose: 0.1 mcg/kg/min. Dilute 0.6 mg times weight in kilograms in D_5W to make 100 ml. 1.0 ml/hr. equals 0.1 mcg/kg/min. Titrate to patient's response.

C. Action

Isuprel is related in chemical structure to epinephrine. It is a pure beta-receptor-stimulator. It potentiates inotropic (increases contractility) and chronotropic (increases heart rate) properties, generally resulting in an increased cardiac output, even in the presence of cardiogenic shock. However, there is a great increase in myocardial oxygen requirement; therefore, there is an increasing area of necrosis in myocardial infarct patients. Venous return to the heart may be decreased with increased peripheral vascular pooling. Diastolic pressure may fall; hence, perfusion pressure may be greatly reduced. Systolic pressure is usually maintained or increased after therapeutic doses of the drug due to the increased cardiac output.

    The onset is immediate and duration of action 2–3 minutes. Isuprel is indicated in emergency cardiac care for severe bradyarrhythmias due to heart block or to sinus bradyarrhythmias refractory to atropine. (Electrical pacemaking provides better control.)

D. Route of Administration
IV or intraosseous infusion

E. Side Effects
Use of Isuprel is hazardous in patients with digitalis toxicity. Postresuscitation tachycardia may be a problem. Isuprel may cause palpitations, ventricular arrhythmias (such as V-fib) that may be refractory to defibrillation.

REMEMBER:

1. Isuprel drip is usually piggybacked into a primary IV line of D5W.
2. Patient's pulse and heart rhythm are monitored very closely.
3. Do *NOT* mix with other drugs (especially aminophylline or sodium bicarbonate), for it will precipitate.
4. ISUPREL IS AN *EXTREMELY* POTENT DRUG! Various arrhythmias may result from its administration. If undesired rhythms are generated (such as V-tach, v-fib, or *any* rapid ventricular rhythm), DISCONTINUE IMMEDIATELY!

KETOROLAC TROMETHAMINE (TORADOL)
WICHITA, KS

Classification:

Nonsteroidal anti-inflammatory drug with analgesic properties

Uses:

PRIMARY:
1. Relief of moderate-to-severe pain resulting from acute musculoskeletal injury

SECONDARY:
1. Relief of moderate-to-severe pain associated with migraine headache
2. Relief of moderate-to-severe pain secondary to rheumatologic disease
3. Relief of moderate-to-severe postoperative pain
4. Relief of moderate-to-severe prostaglandin-induced pain (including kidney-stone pain)

Administration and Dose:

AUTHORIZED RANGE AND USE:
With a physician order; 15 mg to 60 mg IM or IV
NO REPEAT
Patients less than 65 y/o: 15–30 mg IV; 30–60 mg IM
Patients 65 y/o or over, reduced renal function or < 50 kg: 15 mg IV; 30 mg IM

PEDIATRICS:
Not recommended for use in pediatrics <20 kg

Precautions:

GENERAL:
Ketorolac causes sedation and should be used cautiously in patients who are obtunded. Medications that may add additional central-nervous-system depression should be avoided, and if they are used, careful monitoring is required.

SIDE EFFECTS:
Dizziness, somnolence, nausea, dry mouth, vomiting, headache, sweating, vasodilation palpitations, dyspepsia, and GI pain

UNTOWARD EFFECTS:
Gastrointestinal ulcerations, bleeding, and perforation. Acute renal failure, hemorrhage, hypersensitivity reactions, such as anaphylaxis, bronchospasm, vascular collapse, urticaria, angioedema, and vesicular bullous rash

INTERACTIONS:
Patients in high-dose salicylate regimens, anticoagulants

CONTRAINDICATIONS:
RELATIVE:

Patients with complete or partial syndrome of nasal polyps, angioedema bronchospastic reactivity, or other allergic manifestations to ASA or other nonsteroidal anti-inflammatory drugs (NSAIDS). Patients with impaired renal or hepatic functions or a history of kidney or liver disease, renal failure, cardiac decompensation, hypertension, or peptic ulcer. Chemotherapy patients—due to decreased platelet function.

ABSOLUTE:

Patients with previously demonstrated hypersensitivity to ASA or other NSAIDS, active GI bleeding, hemophilia, acute intracerebral event, *i.e.*, CVA, aneurysm. Late pregnancy (3d trimester).

Actions:

PRIMARY:
Potent analgesic with moderate anti-inflammatory and antipyretic activities. Toradol inhibits synthesis of prostaglandins and may be considered a peripherally acting analgesic with no known effects on opiate receptors.

CVS:
Study results indicate that Toradol does not significantly affect cardiac or hemodynamic functions.

RESP:
Tests indicate that in both analgesic and supra-analgesic doses, Toradol has no effect on the ventilatory response to carbon dioxide under circumstances in which significant effects are seen with morphine.

GI:
The degree of gastric mucosal irritation is dose dependent. Nausea and vomiting may be caused by its peripheral action and would not be expected to affect the centrally mediated chemo-receptor trigger zone. Patients with long-term use of Toradol were found to have a higher cumulative occurrence of ulcers or upper-GI bleeding than with ASA use. Risks of GI ulcerations, bleeding, and perforation are most common in the elderly.

HEMATOLOGIC:
Toradol inhibits platelet aggregation and may prolong bleeding time.

RENAL:
Inhibits synthesis of prostaglandins by acting on renal function via secondary effects of reduced renal blood flow and increased sodium, potassium, and water retention

METABOLISM:
Liver

EXCRETION:
Urine and feces

Toxicity

OCCURRENCE:
Serious gastrointestinal toxicity, such as bleeding, ulceration, and perforation, can occur at any time, with or without warning symptoms, in patients treated with NSAIDS. Renal toxicity has been seen in patients with conditions leading to a reduction in blood volume and/or renal blood flow, where renal prostaglandins have a supportive role in the maintenance of renal perfusion. In these patients, administration of a NSAID may cause a dose-dependent reduction in renal prostaglandin formation and may precipitate acute renal failure.

Preparation:

60 mg: 30 mg/ml, 2-ml TUBEX syringe needle

Time:

ONSET:
Pain relief is often perceptible in about 10 minutes.

PEAKS:
30–60 minutes

DURATION:
6 hours

LIDOCAINE HYDROCHLORIDE (XYLOCAINE)
SANTA ANA, CA

MEDICATION: LIDOCAINE HYDROCHLORIDE (XYLOCAINE)	ADULT DOSE	PEDIATRIC DOSE	SIDE EFFECTS	PRECAUTIONS/COMMENTS
CLASSIFICATION: Antidysrhythmic **MECHANISM OF ACTION:** • Increases ventricular fibrillation threshold • Suppresses ventricular ectopy **INDICATIONS:** • Ventricular tachycardia and ventricular fibrillation • PVCs in patients with chest pain suggestive of an acute MI (> 6 PVCs/min, R on T, multifocal, couplets, runs of V-tach) • Following successful cardioversion or defibrillation **CONTRAINDICATIONS:** • Second and third-degree heart block • Bradycardia with ventricular escape beats **DOSAGE FORM:** • 2%, 100 mg/5 ml, 5-ml prefilled syringe	• 1 mg/kg IVP every 5 minutes to a maximum of 3 mg/kg • ET 3 mg/kg once to a maximum of 10 cc (200 mg) • Following successful cardioversion or defibrillation, 1 mg/kg not to exceed 3 mg/kg	• 1 mg/kg IVP every 5 minutes to a maximum of 3 mg/kg • ET 3 mg/kg once • Following successful cardioversion or defibrillation, 1 mg/kg	• Seizures • Hypotension • Disorientation • CNS depression	• Administer slowly over no less than 2 minutes. Rapid IV administration may cause seizures or ringing in ears. • Use cautiously in patients with liver disease, severe congestive heart failure, or other states of decreased perfusion.

LORAZEPAM
AUSTIN, TX

Lorazepam

(Activan, Alzapam, Loraz, Lorazepam, Lorazepam Intensol, Novolorazem)

Func. Class.:

Antianxiety

Chem. Class.:

Benzodiazepine

Action:

Potentiates the actions of GABA, especially in system and reticular formation

Uses:

Anxiety, irritability in psychiatric or organic disorders, preoperatively, insomnia, acute alcohol withdrawal symptoms, and as an anticonvulsant

Dosage and Routes:

ANXIETY
Adult: IV 1–2 mg
Child: IV 0.5–1.0 mg

SEIZURES
Child: IV 0.5–1.0 mg

Side Effects/Adverse Reactions:

CNS:	Dizziness, drowsiness, confusion, headache, anxiety, tremors, depression, hallucinations, and weakness
GI:	Constipation, dry mouth, nausea, vomiting, anorexia, diarrhea
INTEG:	Rashes, dermatitis, itching
CV:	Orthostatic hypotension, ECG changes, tachycardia, hypotension
EENT:	Blurred vision, tinnitus, mydriasis

Contraindications/Precautions/Drug Interactions:

Hypersensitivity to benzodiazepines, narrow-angle glaucoma, psychosis, and COPD
CNS depressants, alcohol, disulfiram, and oral contraceptives increase effects of benzodiazepines.
Incompatible with all drugs except cimetidine, and ranitidine in solution or syringe
Elderly, debilitated, hepatic disease, renal disease

Assessment:

Monitor vital signs.
Mental status: mood, sensorium, affect, sleeping pattern, drowsiness, dizziness
Suicidal tendencies

Treatment of Overdosage:

Lavage, VS, supportive care, flumazenil

© *Austin/Travis EMS Clinical Practice*

MAGNESIUM SULFATE 10%
EUGENE/SPRINGFIELD, OR

I. Pharmacology and Actions:

    A. Affects impulse formation and conduction time in myocardium and thereby reduces incidence of dysrhythmias associated with hypomagnesemia or prolonged QT interval

    B. Decreases acetylcholine in motor-end terminals, which produces anticonvulsant properties

II. Indications:

    A. Ventricular Fibrillation/Pulseless VT:

        1. Third-line antiarrhythmic (after lidocaine and bretylium) in cardiac arrests with VF/pulseless VT

        2. Give early if suspected torsades de pointes pattern.

        3. Treatment and prevention of seizures due to pregnancy (eclampsia). You may encounter a female patient on "mag drip" during an interhospital transfer.

III. Precautions and Side Effects

    A. Since magnesium sulfate affects neuromuscular transmission in body, it must be given carefully and monitored closely in the patient with a pulse.

    B. In nonarrest patient, magnesium toxicity may cause hypotension, bradycardia, and/or respiratory arrest.

    C. Early warning that magnesium toxicity is developing is decrease in reflexes measured at patella, antecubital area, or heel.

    D. Other side effects include sweating, flushing, and sensation of body warmth.

IV. Administration (EMT 3, 4):

    A. *VENTRICULAR FIBRILLATION/PULSELESS VT:*

        1. Adult by standing order: 1.0–2.0 grams IV push over 1 minute. Electrical defibrillation is then attempted again.

    B. *PREECLAMPSIA OR ECLAMPSIA:*

        1. Adult by MD order: 2.0–4.0 grams slow IV push (over at least 1 minute per gram).

    C. MAINTENANCE DRIP **by MD order:**
    15–60 gtts/min. (Add 4.0 grams to 250 ml to make concentration of 16 mg/ml. Run at 0.5–1.0 grams/hour = 30–60 gtts/min., or as directed by MD). Maintenance drips are rarely used, with the exception of interhospital transfers of the pregnant patient with preeclampsia or eclampsia. The concentration and rate of flow on OB transfers may be different than described above, but the delivered amount is generally 0.5–4.0 grams per hour by infusion.

V. Special Notes:

   A. Main prehospital indication is shockable cardiac arrest or suspected torsades.

   B. Suspect torsades in a patient in VF/pulseless, VT, or in wide complex tachycardia with classic torsades pattern (several examples below):

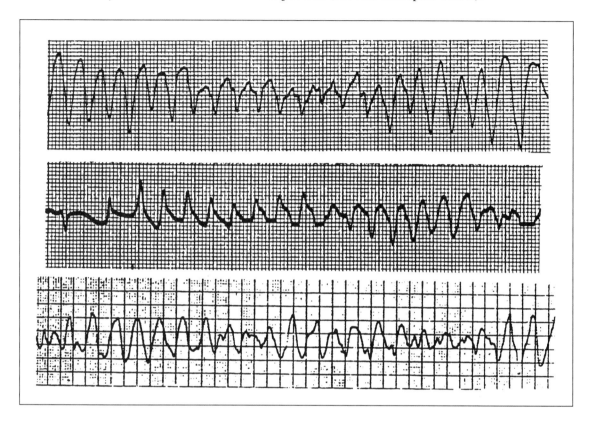

   C. Conditions of patients who are at risk to develop torsades include:

      1. Toxic level of certain antidysrhythmics including procainamide (pronestyl) and quinidine
      2. Toxic levels of certain psychotropic drugs including tricyclic antidepressants and some phenothiazines
      3. Exposure to organophosphate insecticides
      4. Cerebrovascular disease including strokes
      5. Electrolyte disorders including hypokalemia, hypomagnesemia, hypocalcemia
      6. Hypothyroidism
      7. Coronary artery disease including AMI, left ventricular failure
      8. Pacemaker malfunction

   D. Prehospital use for preeclampsia or eclampsia is usually on interhospital transfers. The drip rate and patient status must be monitored closely. Decreased reflexes, hypotension, or respiratory rate < 16/minute are reasons to stop drug.

   E. Antidote for magnesium toxicity is calcium gluconate or chloride.

MIDAZOLAM HCL (VERSED)
AUSTIN, TX

Midazolam HCL (Versed)

Functional Class:

General anesthetic

Chemical Class:

Benzodiazepine, short-acting

Action:

Depresses subcortical levels in CNS; may act on limbic system, reticular formation; may potentiate g-aminobenzoic acid (GABA) by binding to specific benzodiazepine receptors

Uses:

Preoperative sedation, general anesthesia induction, sedation for diagnostic endoscopic procedures, intubation

Dosage and Routes:

SEDATION
Adult: IV 0.02–0.08 mg/kg; IM 0.08 mg/kg
Child: IV 0.02–0.08 mg/kg

Side Effects/Adverse Reactions:

CNS: Retrograde amnesia, euphoria, confusion, anxiety, slurred speech, paresthesia, tremors, weakness, chills
RESP: Coughing, apnea, bronchospasm, laryngospasm, dyspnea
CV: Hypotension, PVCs, tachycardia, bigeminy, nodal rhythm
EENT: Blurred vision, nystagmus, diplopia, blocked ears, loss of balance
GI: Nausea, vomiting, increased salivation, hiccups
INTEG: Urticaria, pain, swelling at injection site, rash, pruritus

Contraindications/Precautions/Drug Interactions:

Hypersensitivity to benzodiazepines, shock, coma, alcohol intoxication, acute narrow-angle glaucoma.
Prolonged respiratory depression: other CNS depressants, alcohol, barbiturates

Increased hypnotic effect: fentanyl, narcotic agonists, analgesics, droperidol
COPS, CHF, chronic renal failure, chills, elderly, debilitated

Assessment:

Injection site for redness, pain, swelling
Degree of amnesia in elderly; may be increased
Anterograde amnesia

Treatment of Overdosage:

O_2, vasopressors, physostigmine, resuscitation

© *Austin/Travis EMS Clinical Practice*

MORPHINE SULFATE
ARLINGTON, TX

Action:

Morphine is an opiate derivative. It is a potent centrally acting analgesic and is a schedule II narcotic.

Indications:

Severe or acute pain, acute pulmonary edema

Contraindications:

Hypersensitivities, respiratory insufficiency, asthma, bronchospasm, intracranial or cerebrospinal pressure, head injuries or hypotension

Potential Side Effects:

Respiratory depression	Apnea
Hypotension	Nausea/vomiting
Sedation	Dizziness
Euphoria	Disorientation
Facial flushing	
Venous irritation	

Dosages:

2–10 mg IM or slow IVP. Should be diluted 1:1 with IV fluid. Closely monitor respiratory status and blood pressure. May be given concurrently with phenergan 12.5–25 mg to combat vomiting.

NOTE: Decrease dosage for patients with hepatic or renal impairment as well as for the elderly.

Pediatric Usage:

0.1–0.2 mg/kg IM, half the dose if given IV. Phenergan may also be given concurrently 6.25–12.5 mg slow IVP. Closely monitor respiratory status and blood pressure.

NALOXONE (NARCAN)
LAS VEGAS, NV

Naloxone (Narcan)

Form:

2 mg/2 ml

Class:

Narcotic antagonist

Action:

Reverses effects of narcotics

INDICATIONS	PHYSICIAN'S ORDERS
Suspected narcotic use	NO

Dose:

ADULT:
2 mg slowly IV push, titrated to effect. If no response is observed, this dose may be repeated at 2–3 minute intervals up to a maximum of 10 mg.

PEDIATRIC:
0.01 mg/kg

Route:

IV, IO, or ETT

Side Effects:

Rapid administration causes projectile vomiting.

Contraindications:

Patients with a history of hypersensitivity to the drug

Special Note:

Short-acting. May precipitate withdrawal in chronic narcotic users.

NEOSYNEPHRINE
OKLAHOMA CITY, OK

A. ACTIONS
12-hour nasal decongestant

B. INDICATIONS
May be used to facilitate nasotracheal intubation

C. WARNINGS
Do not exceed recommended dosage because symptoms may occur such as burning, stinging, sneezing, or increase of nasal discharge.

D. DOSAGE
Adults and children 8 years of age and over: With head upright, spray two or three times in each nostril.

NIFEDIPINE (PROCARDIA, ADALAT)
LAS VEGAS, NV

Form:

10-mg gelatin capsule

Classification:

Calcium channel blocker

Action:

Peripheral vasodilation

I. Highly selective for peripheral arterioles
II. Results in an increased cardiac output due to decreased afterload

INDICATIONS	PHYSICIAN'S ORDERS
For control of hypertension with a systolic BP greater than 200 mm HG and/or a diastolic BP greater than 110 mm HG **ONLY** if symptomatic with one of the following:	
I. Unstable angina	YES
II. Pulmonary edema	YES
III. Headache with mental-status changes	YES

Dose:

ADULT:
10 mg

PEDIATRIC:
Not recommended for use in children

Route:

Chew and swallow, or puncture and squirt sublingually.

Side Effects:

Excessive hypotension, tachycardia, palpitations, flushing, headache, nausea, and nervousness

Contraindications:

Known hypersensitivity to Nifedipine

NITROGLYCERINE SPRAY
SANTA ANA, CA

MEDICATION: NITROGLYCERINE SPRAY	ADULT DOSE	PEDIATRIC DOSE	SIDE EFFECTS	PRECAUTIONS/ COMMENTS
CLASSIFICATION: Vasodilator **MECHANISM OF ACTION:** The following actions decrease myocardial oxygen demand and reduce chest pain from ischemia: • Dilates coronary arteries • Dilates venous vessels reducing blood return to the heart (reduces preload) • Dilates arterial vessels reducing peripheral vascular resistance (reduces afterload) **INDICATIONS:** • Chest pain • Pulmonary edema **DOSAGE FORM:** • 0.4 mg/metered dose spray oral/lingual, 13.8 gm	• 0.4 mg/metered dose, may repeat every 5 minutes	• Not approved	• Hypotension • Reflex tachycardia • Nausea	• Use *with caution* if given with other vasodilators (*e.g.*, morphine). • BH may order administration of nitroglycerine > 3 doses.

NITRONOX
DES MOINES, IA

Indications

Are relief of pain from:

1. Musculoskeletal trauma
2. Burns
3. Chest pain secondary to suspected MI
4. Active childbirth

Contraindications

1. Head injury
2. Altered consciousness
3. Drug/alcohol intoxication
4. Dyspnea, cyanosis, suspicion of pneumothorax
5. Chronic obstructive pulmonary disease (contains 50% O_2)
6. Chest trauma (danger of pneumothorax)
7. Pulmonary edema. (Patient needs 100% O_2).
8. Abdominal pain with distention (suspicious for obstruction)
9. Abdominal trauma (danger of perforated viscus)
10. Decompression sickness, air embolism
11. Shock
12. Patient not able to understand directions for use

A. Primary survey: airway, breathing, circulation
B. Secondary survey: head-to-toe exam and history
C. Obtain physician's order for use. (Direct physician or physician-designee contact required by law to authorize use.)
D. **Nitrous oxide** is to be self-administered by the patient, using the mask or mouthpiece.
E. Keep ventilation system on to release excess gas outside of ambulance.
F. Discontinue administration upon arrival at receiving hospital; give patient 100% O_2 during last 2–3 minutes to reverse effect.
G. Report use and effect to receiving hospital upon arrival.

OXYGEN
DENVER, CO

Pharmacology and Actions

Oxygen added to the inspired air raises the amount of oxygen in the blood, and therefore the amount delivered to the tissue. Tissue hypoxia causes cell damage and death. Breathing, in most people, is regulated by small changes in the acid/base balance and CO_2 levels. It takes relatively large decreases in oxygen concentration to stimulate respiration.

Indications

A. Suspected hypoxemia or respiratory distress from any cause
B. Acute chest or abdominal pain
C. Hypotensive states from any cause
D. Major trauma
E. All acutely ill patients
F. Any suspected carbon-monoxide poisoning
G. Pregnant females in the setting of trauma

Precautions

A. If the patient is not breathing adequately on his own, the treatment of choice is ventilation, not just oxygen.
B. A small percentage of patients with chronic lung disease breathe because they are hypoxic. Administration of oxygen will inhibit their respiratory drive. ***Do not withhold oxygen because of this possibility. Be prepared to assist ventilations if needed.***
C. When pulse oximeter is available, titrate SaO_2 to 90% or greater.
D. In the COPD patient: increase oxygen in increments of 2 liters/minute every 2–3 minutes until improvement is noted (color improvement or increase in mental status).

Administration

DOSAGE		INDICATIONS
Low Flow	1–2 liters/min.	COPD patients
Moderate Flow	4–6 liters/min.	Precautionary
High Flow	10–15 liters/min.	Severe medical, trauma

Side Effects and Special Notes

A. Restlessness may be an important sign of hypoxia.
B. On the other hand, some people become more agitated when a nasal cannula is applied, particularly when it is not needed. Acquiesce to your patient if it is reasonable.
C. Nasal prongs work equally well on nose and mouth breathers, except babies.
D. Nonhumidified oxygen is drying and irritating to mucous membranes.
E. Oxygen toxicity is not a hazard of short-term use.
F. Do not use permanently mounted humidifiers. If the patient warrants humidified oxygen, use a single-patient-use device.
G. During long transports for high-altitude illness, reduce oxygen flow from high to low to conserve oxygen.

OXYGEN FLOW RATE

METHOD	FLOW RATE	OXYGEN-INSPIRED AIR (APPROX)
Room Air		21%
Nasal Cannula	1 l/min.	24%
	2 l/min.	28%
	8 l/min.	40%
Simple Face Mask	10 l/min.	50–60%
Nonrebreather Mask	10 l/min.	90%
Mouth to Mask	10 l/min.	50%
	15 l/min.	80%
Bag-Valve Mask (BVM)	Room Air	21%
	12 l/min.	40%
Bag-Valve Mask with Reservoir	10–15 l/min.	90–100%
O_2 Powered Breathing Device	Hand-Regulated	100%

NOTE: Most hypoxic patients will feel more comfortable with an increase of inspired oxygen from 21% to 24%.

OXYGEN ADMINISTRATION CHART
WASHINGTON, DC

TYPES OF OXYGEN-ADMINISTRATION DEVICES AND THEIR CHARACTERISTICS

DELIVERY DEVICE	FLOW RATE	PERCENTAGE OF OXYGEN DELIVERED
Nasal cannula	1–6 LPM	24–44%
Pocket face mask	15 LPM	50% nonbreathing pt. 80% breathing pt.
Venturi mask	Varies	24–50%
Simple face mask	6–10 LPM	35–60%
Partial rebreathing mask	6–10 LPM	35-60%
Nonrebreathing mask	8–15 LPM	80–95%

OXYTOCIN (PITOCIN®)
EUGENE/SPRINGFIELD, OR

I. Pharmacology and Actions:

    A. Hormone that increases electrical and contractile activity in uterine smooth muscle. Oxytocin can initiate or enhance rhythmic contraction at any time during pregnancy, but the uterus is most sensitive at term.

    B. Exhibits rapid onset (minutes), very short half-life, and rapid inactivation and excretion

II. Indications:
    A. Control of postpartum hemorrhage

III. Precautions and Side Effects:

    A. Prior to its administration, the presence of a second fetus must be considered. Administration with fetus in uterus can cause rupture of uterus and/or death of fetus.

    B. Administration should follow delivery of placenta whenever possible.

    C. In large amounts, oxytocin exhibits a transient but marked vasodilating effect, and reflex tachycardia.

    D. Cardiac arrhythmias, hypertension, and uterine tetany may be precipitated or aggravated by oxytocin.

IV. Administration (EMT 3 or 4) *by MD order*:

    A. Usual intravenous dose is 20 USP units added to 1000-ml-volume expander and standard tubing titrated to severity of hemorrhage and uterine response.

    B. Rarely intramuscular dose: 10 USP units (1 ml) IM only if unable to start IV

V. Side Effects and Special Notes:

    A. This is the only IV infusion we use in which it is acceptable to use standard (macro) tubing instead of a microdrip.

    B. Monitor and document blood loss and vital signs.

    C. In hospital, Pitocin® is used to induce or augment labor.

PHENERGAN (PROMETHAZINE HCL)
LAS VEGAS, NV

Form:

25-mg/1-ml tubex/ampule

Class:

Phenothiazine

Action:

Antiemetic

INDICATIONS		PHYSICIAN'S ORDERS
I.	Control of nausea and recurrent vomiting	YES
II.	Adjunct to morphine for analgesia	YES

Dose:

ADULT:
12.5 mg–25 mg slow IV push *over one minute*

PEDIATRIC
Not to be given to anyone under 16

Route:

IV

Side Effects:

Extrapyramidal reactions, excessive sedation

Contraindications:

1. Patients with a known hypersensitivity to phenothiazines
2. Patients who are allergic to sulfites
3. Altered level of consciousness

Special Note:

Subcutaneous injection or extravasation may result in tissue necrosis.

PROCAINAMIDE HCL
AUSTIN, TX

Procainamide HCl (Procan SR, Promine, Procainamide, Pronestyl, Sub-Quin, Rhythmin)

Functional Class:

Antidysrhythmic (class IA)

Chemical Class:

Procaine HCl amide analog

Action:

Depresses excitability of cardiac muscle to electric stimulation and slows conduction in atrium, bundle of His, and ventricle

Uses:

PVCs, atrial fibrillation, PAT, and ventricular tachycardia

Dosage and Routes:

ATRIAL FIBRILLATION/PAT
Adult: IV 100 mg q5 min., given 25–50 mg/min., not to exceed 500 mg; or 17 mg/kg total then IV INF 2–6 mg/min.

VENTRICULAR TACHYCARDIA
Adult: IV 100 mg q5 min., given 25–50 mg/min., not to exceed 500 mg; or 17 mg/kg total then IV INF 2–6 mg/min.

Side Effects/Adverse Reactions:

CNS:	Headache, dizziness, confusion, psychosis, restlessness, irritability, weakness
GI:	Nausea, vomiting, anorexia, diarrhea, hepatomegaly
CV:	Hypotension, heart block, cardiovascular collapse, arrest
HEMA:	SLE syndrome, agranulocytosis, thrombocytopenia, neutropenia, hemolytic anemia
INTEG:	Rash, urticaria, edema, swelling (rare), pruritus

Contraindications/Precautions/Drug Interactions:

Increases effects of neuromuscular blockers, anticholinergics, antihypertensives
Renal disease, liver disease, CHF, respiratory depression, severe heart block
Barbiturates decrease the effects of procainamide.

Assessment:

ECG continuously to determine increased PR or QRS segments; if these develop, discontinue immediately; watch for increased ventricular ectopic beats, may need to rebolus.

Cardiac rate, respiration: rate, rhythm, character
Respiratory status: rate, rhythm, lung fields; watch for respiratory depression.

Treatment of Overdosage:

None

© *Austin/Travis EMS Clinical Practice*

RACEMIC EPINEPHRINE
DENVER, CO

Racemic Epinephrine (Vaponephrine)

Pharmacology and Actions

Racemic epinephrine is an epinephrine preparation in a 1:1,000 dilution for use by **oral inhalation only**. Effects are those of epinephrine. Inhalation causes local effects on the upper airway as well as systemic effects from absorption. Vasoconstriction may reduce swelling in the upper airway, and beta effects on bronchial smooth muscle may relieve bronchospasm.

Indications

A. Life-threatening airway obstruction suspected secondary to croup or epiglottitis

Precautions

A. Mask and noise may be frightening to small children. Agitation will aggravate symptoms of respiratory obstruction. Try to enlist the support of parents and child for administration.
B. Try to differentiate croup from epiglottitis by history. Cough is usually present in croup. Do not use a tongue blade to examine the back of the throat. The diagnosis is frequently difficult in the field, but a critical patient deserves a trial of racemic epinephrine **during** transport. Although used as specific therapy for croup, it may also buy some time in patients with epiglottitis.
C. In the less-than-critical patient, saline alone via nebulizer may bring symptomatic relief from croup.
D. Racemic epinephrine is heat and light sensitive. It should be stored in a dark, cool place. Discoloration is an indication for discarding it.
E. Tachycardia and agitation are the most common side effects. Other side effects of parenteral epinephrine may also be seen. (Since these are also the hallmarks of hypoxia, watch the patient very closely!)
F. Nebulizer treatment may cause blanching of the skin in the mask area due to local epinephrine absorption. Reassure parents.
G. Clinical improvement in croup can be dramatic after administration of racemic epinephrine, and presentation in the ED may be markedly altered. Rebound worsening of airway obstruction can occur, however, in 1–4 hours. For this reason many physicians admit any patient whom they treat with racemic epinephrine. **Field administration should be limited to critical patients** during transport so as to avoid unnecessary delays.
H. If respiratory arrest occurs, it is usually due to patient fatigue or laryngeal spasm. Complete obstruction is not usually present. Ventilate the patient, administer O_2, and transport rapidly. If you can ventilate and oxygenate the patient adequately with mouth-to-mask, pocket mask, or BVM, intubation is best left to a specialist in a controlled setting.

Administration

A. **Contact base for direct physician order.**

B. 0.5 ml racemic epinephrine (acceptable dose for all ages) + 2 ml saline, via nebulizer driven by O_2 (6–8 l/minute) to create fine mist

SODIUM BICARBONATE
SANTA ANA, CA

MEDICATION: SODIUM BICARBONATE (Bicarb, NaHCO$_3$) **CLASSIFICATION:** Alkalinizing agent **MECHANISM OF ACTION:** • Chemically neutralizes acids with carbon dioxide produced as a byproduct **INDICATIONS:** • Metabolic acidosis, prolonged arrest, or known renal failure • Ventricular dysrhythmias as a result of tricyclic overdose **DOSAGE FORM:** • 50 mEq in 50-ml prefilled syringe	**ADULT DOSE** • 1 mEq/kg IVP, then 0.5 mEq/kg every 10 minutes	**PEDIATRIC DOSE** • 1 mEq/kg IVP then 0.5 mEq/kg every 10 minutes • Dilute 1:1 with NS prior to administration to neonates (0–1 month).	**SIDE EFFECTS** • Alkalosis • Volume overload	**PRECAUTIONS/ COMMENTS** • Estravasation may cause tissue necrosis. • Avoid injecting simultaneously with epinephrine or any other catecholamines. Alkaline solutions inactivate catecholamines.

SODIUM CHLORIDE
SANTA ANA, CA

MEDICATION:	ADULT DOSE	PEDIATRIC DOSE	SIDE EFFECTS	PRECAUTIONS/ COMMENTS
SODIUM CHLORIDE 0.9% (NORMAL SALINE) **CLASSIFICATION:** Parenteral-water and sodium-chloride supplement **MECHANISM OF ACTION:** Isotonic solution of sodium chloride in water **INDICATIONS:** • Volume expansion • Diluting/dissolving drugs • Flushing IV catheters **DOSAGE FORMS:** • 250-ml bags for IV infusion • 1000-ml bags for IV infusion • 10-ml prefilled syringe or vial	• Titrate to perfusion, maximum 2 liters prior to BH contact.	• Titrate to perfusion, maximum 20 ml/kg, repeated once prior to BH contact.	• Hypernatremia • Volume overload	• Use with caution in patients with renal impairment to avoid volume overload. • Use with caution in patients with congestive heart failure or liver disease. • Bacteriostatic sodium chloride injection should be avoided in neonates.

SOLU-MEDROL/METHYLPREDNISOLONE
ARLINGTON, TX

Action:

Solu-Medrol is a potent, synthetic anti-inflammatory steroid.

Indications:

Allergic reactions, asthma, spinal-cord injuries, and other edematous conditions

Contraindications:

Premature infants, spinal-cord injuries more than eight (8) hours old

Potential Side Effects:

Fluid retention, nausea/vomiting

Dosage:

Asthma/anaphylaxis 125 mg IVP. Spinal-cord injuries: 30 mg/kg added to 100 ml normal saline infused over 15–20 minutes.

NOTE: *Do not administer if spinal injury possibly greater than eight (8) hours old as rebound swelling of cord tissue may occur.*

Pediatric Usage:

Asthma/anaphylaxis: 1–2 mg/kg IVP. Spinal injuries: 30 mg/kg added to 100 ml normal saline and infused over 15–20 minutes.

SUCCINYLCHOLINE
PORTLAND, OR

Pharmacology and Actions:

Succinylcholine is a short-acting, motor-nerve-depolarizing, skeletal-muscle relaxant. Like acetylcholine, it combines with cholinergic receptors in the motor nerves to cause depolarization. Neuromuscular transmission is thus inhibited and remains so for 8–10 minutes. Following IV injection, complete paralysis is obtained within one (1) minute and persists for approximately two (2) minutes. Effects then start to fade and a return to normal is seen within six (6) minutes. Muscle relaxation begins in the eyelids and jaw, then progresses to the limbs, the abdomen, and finally the diaphragm and intercostal muscles. It has no effect on consciousness at all.

Metabolism:

Succinylcholine is excreted by the kidneys (10%) and is hydrolyzed by plasma pseudocholinesterase.

Indications:

To achieve temporary paralysis where endotracheal intubation is indicated, and where muscle tone or seizure activity prevent it

Contraindications:

Succinylcholine is contraindicated in patients with a history of hypersensitivity to the drug.

Precautions:

A. Succinylcholine should not be administered unless personnel skilled in endotracheal intubation are present and ready to perform the procedure.
B. Oxygen-therapy equipment and resuscitation drugs should be available.
C. Succinylcholine produces paralysis, but does not alter a person's level of consciousness. Paralysis in the conscious patient is very frightening; therefore, sedation should be provided in any conscious or responsive patient; also verbal explanation should be provided to the patient during the procedure—even if you do not think the patient can hear you.

Administration:

ADULTS:
1.5 mg/kg IV push

CHILDREN:
< 6 years: 2 mg/kg IV push

SUCCINYLCHOLINE (ANECTINE®, QUELICIN®)
EUGENE/SPRINGFIELD, OR

I. Pharmacology and Actions:

   A. Succinylcholine is a short-acting, depolarizing, skeletal-muscle relaxant.
   B. Like acetylcholine, it binds to cholinergic receptors in the motor neuron end plate to cause muscle depolarization (fasciculations) followed by paralysis.
   C. Following IV injection, complete paralysis is obtained within one (1) minute and persists for approximately two (2) minutes. Effects then start to fade, and a recovery is usually seen within four to six (4–6) minutes.
   D. Muscle relaxation begins in the eyelids and jaws, then progresses to the limbs, the abdomen, and finally the diaphragm and intercostal muscles.
   E. Succinylcholine has no effect on consciousness, pain threshold, or cerebration.
   F. Succinylcholine is excreted by the kidneys (10%) and is hydrolyzed by plasma cholinesterases (pseudocholinesterase and acetylcholinesterase).

II. Indications:

   A. To achieve temporary paralysis where endotracheal intubation is indicated, and where muscle tone or seizure activity prevent it

III. Contraindications:

   A. Succinylcholine is contraindicated in patients with a history of hypersensitivity to the drug.

IV. Precautions and Side Effects:

   A. May cause bradycardia especially with repeat dose of succinylcholine and in pediatric patients under age 5 years. This will usually respond to oxygenation and atropine.
   B. May cause ventricular dysrhythmias. These can usually be treated with oxygenation and lidocaine.
   C. Other cardiovascular effects include tachycardia, hypotension, hypertension and cardiac arrest.
   D. Hyperkalemia may worsen after administration of succinylcholine and may precipitate ventricular dysrhythmias or even cardiac arrest, especially in patients with crush or burn injury, kidney failure, or undiagnosed neuromuscular disease or skeletal muscle myopathy (*e.g.,* Duchenne's muscular dystrophy). The problem is not an issue in the acute burn or crush injury, since the hyperkalemia develops days after the injury.
   E. Malignant hyperthermia is a rare but life-threatening complication that can occur with administration of paralytic agents. It is a hypermetabolic state of skeletal muscles and may initially present as an intractable spasm of the jaw muscles (masseter spasm) that shows up after use of Sux and is not to be confused with more commonly seen trismus that occurs in the head-injured patient.

F.   Increased intracranial, intraocular, and intragastric pressure, especially during fasciculation phase of paralysis

G.   May cause prolonged apnea and paralysis in patient with enzyme deficiency of pseudocholinesterase

H.   Histamine release may occur.

V.   Administration (EMT 4 only):

A.   *INDUCTION OF PARALYSIS TO FACILITATE INTUBATION:*

1.   **Adult by standing order:** 1.0–1.5 mg/kg IV push
2.   **Pediatric by standing order:** 1.0–1.5 mg/kg IV push. Consult prior to use on pediatric patient if possible.
3.   A second IV dose may be given if incomplete relaxation is achieved within 60–120 seconds of initial administration and the endotracheal tube has not been placed.
4.   Can be given IM in both age groups at 2–4 mg/kg. Usual adult dose is 2X. IV dose not to exceed 150 mg. May give 150 mg IM in average-size adult. IV route is preferred. (Use IM only if absolutely necessary.)

B.   *TO MAINTAIN PARALYSIS OF INTUBATED PATIENT:*

1.   **Adult *by MD order*:** generally reduced from initial dose
2.   **Pediatric *by MD order*:** generally reduced from initial dose

VI.   Special Notes:

A.   Preoxygenation prior to the procedure is absolutely essential.
B.   Have all equipment and alternate airways prepared prior to giving succinylcholine.
C.   Perform Sellick maneuver once paralytic is administered and until patient is intubated and cuff inflated.
D.   Report masseter (jaw) spasm that occurs after administration of succinylcholine (and was not present prior to the drug). It may be an early indication of malignant hyperthermia. A second dose of succinylcholine should not be administered to the patient.
E.   Succinylcholine loses its potency in liquid form unless it is refrigerated. Therefore, when taken out of the refrigerator, it must be wrapped in foil and replaced on rotation schedule per department guidelines.
F.   A form on use of succinylcholine must be filled out by paramedic and turned in to EMS office with each use of the drug.

TERBUTALINE SULFATE
STATE OF MARYLAND

Classification:

Bronchodilator, adrenergic-agonist

Action:

Terbutaline sulfate (marketed under such names as Bricanyl and Brethine) exhibits beta-adrenergic receptor-stimulating effects. Studies have shown its relative preference for beta$_2$-receptors, which are located in the smooth muscle of the bronchioles. Terbutaline works by relieving bronchospasm in acute and chronic airway disease, while exerting minimal effect on the cardiovascular system. Patients with asthma or COPD may have the tablet form of terbutaline on hand for home use. Terbutaline has proven to be effective when administered to patients over 44 years of age who exhibit severe respiratory impairment or distress due to asthma or COPD. In such patients, it does not exert the cardiovascular side effects commonly seen with epinephrine administration.

Indications:

—Bronchial asthma
—Reversible airway obstruction associated with bronchitis and emphysema

Contraindications:

—Hypertension
—Tachycardia due to digitalis intoxication
—Children under 12 years of age

Potential Side Effects:

—Increased heart rate
—Palpitations
—Nervousness
—Dizziness
—Tremors
—Nausea, vomiting

Dosage/Route:

Adult—0.25 mg SC
　　　　Route of administration—SC
Pediatric—Contraindicated

Important Points:

—Caution should be exercised when administering to patients with a history of diabetes or seizures.

—It should be administered cautiously to patients with a cardiac history, especially if there are associated dysrhythmias.

—Because this medication is very light sensitive, it should be protected from light as much as possible.

—Terbutaline is not recommended for use with children. Instead, the recommended medication for children is epinephrine.

—Monitor the patient's ECG.

THIAMINE HYDROCHLORIDE (VITAMIN B₁)
JACKSONSONVILLE, FL

A. Classification

  1. Water-soluble vitamin
  2. Essential coenzyme for carbohydrate metabolism

B. Dosage

  1. Comes in 1-cc ampule containing 100 mg (100 mg/ml)
  2. Adult dose: 100 mg slow IV push or deep IM
  3. Pediatric dosage by physician request only

C. Action
Thiamine is an essential vitamin for glucose metabolism and is intended for use in thiamine deficiency commonly seen in the chronic alcoholic. The vitamin must be processed by the liver before it can be available for use by the body. The purpose is to prevent Wernicke's encephalopathy, which may be exacerbated by the administration of D50W in the alcoholic patient with thiamine deficiency. Thiamine should be administered within 30 minutes to all alcoholics who receive D50W.

D. Route of Administration
Preferable route is slow IV push or deep IM if IV access is not available.

E. Side Effects
None

F. Contraindication
Known allergy (rare)

REMEMBER: Adult unconscious patients of alcoholism or unknown etiology should receive thiamine.

VERAPAMIL HCL
INDIANAPOLIS, IN

Verapamil HCL (Calan)

Classification:

Slow channel inhibitor, calcium antagonist

Uses:

PRIMARY:
Supraventricular tachyarrhythmia. Temporary control of ventricular rates in A-flutter/A-fib

SECONDARY:
Angina

Administration and Dose:

AUTHORIZATION RANGE AND USE:
With Physician order
SYMPTOMATIC PSVT: following Adenocard; for narrow-complex tachycardia with normal or elevated B/P:

ADULTS:

Initial:
2.5–5 mg IV bolus over 2 minutes

Repeat:
5–10 mg, 15–30 minutes after initial dose if response is inadequate

NOTE: In older patients, should be administered over 3 minutes

PEDIATRICS:

Initial:
8–15 yrs. 0.1–0.3 mg/kg IV bolus over 2 minutes up to 5 mg

Repeat:
8–15 yrs. 0.1 mg–0.2 mg/kg, 30 minutes after first dose if response is inadequate. DO NOT EXCEED 10 MG AS A SINGLE DOSE.

NOTE: Not recommended for children under 8 yrs. of age

Precautions:

GENERAL:
Use in setting with EKG monitoring of patient and resuscitation equipment available.

Verapamil should be given as a slow IV injection over at least a 2-minute period of time.

SIDE EFFECTS:
Hypotension, rapid ventricular response in A-flutter/fib, bradycardia, heart failure, PVCs, AV block, dizziness, headache, and nausea

UNTOWARD EFFECTS:
Beta blockers and verapamil used concomittantly may result in severe adverse reactions.

CONTRAINDICATIONS:

Relative:
Sick-sinus syndrome, severe congestive heart failure, patients receiving beta blockers IV

Absolute:
Severe hypotension, cardiogenic shock, 2° or 3° heart block

Actions:

PRIMARY:
Inhibits Ca^+ ion influx through the slow channels into conductive and contractile myocardial cells and vascular smooth-muscle cells

HEART:
Reduces rapid ventricular rates due to A-flutter/A-fib, can restore RSR in patients with PAT, reduces percentage of afterload and contractility, depressed amplitude, velocity of depolarization, and conduction in depressed atrial fibers.

SERUM:
Does not alter total serum calcium levels

METABOLISM:
Liver

EXCRETION:
Kidney, intestines

NOTE: *Significant hepatic or renal failure may prolong duration; repeated injections may lead to accumulation and overdose.*

CHEMICAL INFORMATION:
Not chemically related to other antiarrhythmics

Toxicity:

SYMPTOMS:
Severe hypotension, high degrees of AV block, asystole

TREATMENT:
Beta stimulators and calcium solutions as appropriate

Preparation:

10 mg/4 ml

Time:

PEAK:
3–5 minutes

HALF LIFE:
2–5 hours

Procedures

ADMINISTRATION OF ENDOTRACHEAL MEDICATIONS
SANTA ANA, CA

Indications

The following medications may be instilled directly into an endotracheal tube prior to or when unable to establish IV access:
- Atropine
- Epinephrine
- Lidocaine
- Naloxone

Procedure

- Hyperventilate.
- Stop CPR.
- Administer drug by inserting needle of prefilled syringe into ET opening and injecting appropriate amount into tube.
  - Utilize doses in Treatment Guidelines/Pharmacology Handbook.
  - Total volume of all endotracheal medications should not exceed 30 ml, or for patients under 30 kg, a maximum of 1 ml per kg.
  - BH may consider 1 ml per kg maximum volume for adults.
  - Adult: Use a volume of approximately 10 ml for each drug administration.
  - Pediatric: Each medication should be administered in a minimum volume of 2 ml.
  - Mix volume of medication with additional normal saline to reach suggested volumes.

  NOTE: If not permanently attached to syringe, needle must be removed from the syringe prior to instilling any medication into the ET tube.

- Momentarily occlude ET tube with finger while reattaching O_2 source to prevent medication from being expelled by residual air in lungs.
- Reattach bag and ventilate forcefully 5 times to disperse drug.
- Resume CPR. (Entire process should take less than 10 seconds.)

ADMINISTRATION OF MEDICATION VIA A PREEXISTING VASCULAR ACCESS DEVICE (PVAD)
SANTA ANA, CA

Indications:

- Acute status patients
- Cardiopulmonary arrest
- For hemodialysis fistula—life-threatening condition requiring immediate vascular access

APPROVED FOR INFUSION:
- Locally approved intravenous fluids
- Medications — all medications approved for venous administration
- Administration of diazepam should always be followed by a flush of 10-ml normal saline to prevent catheter damage.

Procedure

A preexisting vascular-access device (PVAD) is an indwelling catheter/device placed into one of the central veins, to provide vascular access for patients requiring long-term intravenous therapy or hemodialysis.

Type of Catheters:

- **External silastic indwelling catheter/device**
  —**Broviac, Hickman, and others:** A silicone tube that is inserted into the distal superior vena cava or the right atrium usually via the cephalic vein. The catheter enters the skin through an incision in the chest. The line is kept heparinized and protected by an injectable cap.
  —**PICC line:** Peripherally inserted central catheter usually inserted into the right atrium via the antecubital vein
  —**Hemodialysis shunt:** A tube that diverts blood flow from an artery to a vein
- **Internal subcutaneous infusion ports: NOT** approved for access by prehospital personnel

HEMODIALYSIS FISTULA:
A surgically created arteriovenous connection used for hemodialysis. A subcutaneous fistula may be accessed in critical patients requiring immediate medication administration in life-threatening situations only.

ESTABLISH PATENCY:
- Discontinue any current IV solution.
- Use extreme caution when discontinuing a continuous IV infusion containing chemotherapy to minimize exposure.
- Apply clean gloves.
- Prepare 10-ml syringe, IV administration set, and IV solution.
- Prepare injection port with alcohol swab.
- If clamped, unclamp catheter.
- Slowly inject 5 ml normal saline into the injection port. If resistance is met when trying to inject, reclamp catheter, and do not use.
- Aspirate.
    - If no resistance is met, inject remaining 5 ml of normal saline into catheter.
    - If resistance is met, reclamp catheter, and do not use.

ADMINISTRATION OF IV FLUIDS/MEDICATIONS:
- Prepare IV solution, IV administration set, and 18 ga one (1)-inch needle.
- Prepare injection port with alcohol swab.
- Puncture injectable cap with needle.
- Adjust IV flow.
- Tape needle to catheter.
- Administer medications IVP via main line.
- Flush well following each medication administered.

ACCESSING HEMODIALYSIS FISTULA:
- Prior to access, check site for bruits and thrills.
- Access fistula on venous side (side with weaker thrill in patient with a pulse).
- Inflate BP cuff around IV bag to just above patient's systolic BP to maintain flow of IV.
- If unsuccessful in accessing site, hold direct pressure over site for 10 minutes.

COMPLICATIONS:
- **Infection**—Due to the location of the catheter, strict adherence to aseptic technique is crucial when handling a PVAD.
    —Use clean gloves at all times.
    —Prepare injection port with alcohol swab prior to attaching IV tubing.
    —Obtain new supplies if equipment becomes contaminated.
- **Air embolism**—The PVAD provides a direct line into the circulation; therefore, the introduction of air into these devices can be hazardous.
    —Do not remove injection cap from catheter.
    —Do not allow IV fluids to run dry.
    —Always expel air from preload/syringe prior to administration.

- **Thrombosis**—A blood clot within the vascular system can be caused by improper handling and maintenance of the PVAD; dislodging a clot can cause a pulmonary embolus or vascular damage.
  —Follow medications with 5 ml normal saline.
  —Do not inject medications or fluids if resistance is met when establishing patency.
- **Catheter damage**—Should damage occur to the external catheter, clamp immediately between the skin exit site and the damaged area to prevent air embolism or blood loss.
  —Use patient's clamp or padded hemostats if available, or fold and tape tubing to clamp.
  —Always use a minimum of a 10-ml syringe to prevent catheter damage from excess-infusion pressure.

AUTOMATIC EXTERNAL DEFIBRILLATOR (AED) PROTOCOL
NORFOLK, VA

I. Indications for use of the AED
   A. A patient who is unresponsive, apneic, and pulseless

II. Contraindications
   A. Under 12 years of age
   B. Weight less than 80 pounds (35 kg)
   C. Hypothermia. (Relative—contact medical control.)
   D. Rigor/livor mortis
   E. "No Code" situations

III. Protocol
   1. Establish that the patient is unresponsive, apneic, and pulseless.
   2. Move patient to the floor and bare the chest.
   3. If witnessed arrest, give precordial thump.
   4. If *two* rescuers present, one rescuer should begin CPR while the second rescuer turns on the AED and applies the defibrillator pads.

   The single rescuer with an AED should verify unresponsiveness, open the airway, give two respirations, and check the pulse. If a full cardiac arrest is confirmed, the rescuer should attach the AED and proceed with the algorithm.

Pad Placement

White lead to the right upper chest
Red lead to the precordium

   5. Begin verbal report.
   a. Give name and affiliation.
   b. Give patient's age and sex.
   c. Give brief history as known.
   d. Continue to verbalize all actions.

   6. Follow AED commands.

Special Considerations

A. If necessary to analyze the patient during transport, bring the ambulance to a *complete stop*, then allow the machine to analyze and shock.
B. Patients with implanted defibrillators and pacemakers should be treated like any other patient. The defibrillator may just go into monitor mode on patients with pacemakers.
C. Do not use the AED in the rain or if standing in water.
D. Electrical appliances such as fluorescent lights, electric blankets, TVs, clocks, and radios may interfere with rhythm analysis. Unplug appliances or remove patient as necessary.
E. Check patient for nitro-paste.

AUTOMATIC TRANSPORT VENTILATORS (ATV)
SACRAMENTO, CA

I. INDICATIONS:

    A. Adult patients who are apneic or exhibiting agonal respirations requiring ventilatory support, **after** a paramedic has established and secured the airway with either a nasal or oral tracheal tube. ATVs may be used on patients in full arrest. **NOT TO BE USED ON PEDIATRIC PATIENTS.**

II. CONTRAINDICATIONS:

    A. Patients weighing less than 40 kg (80 lbs.)
    B. Patients with suspected pneumothorax/tension pneumothorax
    C. Overpressurization syndrome (water ascent injury)

III. EQUIPMENT

    A. Approved automatic transport ventilator (type I)
    B. Oxygen source
    C. Bag-valve device
    D. Intubation equipment (all-inclusive)
    E. End-tidal CO_2 detector (if patient has pulses)

IV. PROCEDURE:

    A. Determine need for ventilations or assisted ventilations.
    B. Establish airway and employ conventional BLS airway adjuncts and ventilatory support according to protocol.
    C. Paramedic shall perform oral or nasal intubation according to appropriate protocol. Tube shall be secured and proper placement shall be confirmed using a bag-valve device and conventional assessment methods. *End-tidal CO_2 detector shall be used if patient has pulses.
    D. Assemble components of automated ventilator, and insure proper working order, including pressure-limit alarm.
    E. Determine proper tidal volume for patient. Use the following equation: 10 ml $\times$ weight in kilograms = tidal volume (10 ml/kg). Set the tidal volume on the ventilator's control module accordingly.
    F. Set desired breaths per minute on the ventilator's control module (12–15 per minute, adult).
    G. Remove bag-valve device, and attach the outlet port of the ventilator assembly to the endotracheal tube.
    H. Observe chest rise during the ventilation cycles. Chest rise should appear normal and symmetrical. **Personnel shall continue to monitor chest rise throughout the remainder of patient care, as is done normally using a bag-valve device.**
    I. Personnel shall monitor PSI level in oxygen cylinder.

V. PRECAUTIONS:

    A.   Paramedic is responsible for all airway management and must frequently reassess endotracheal tube placement. Bilateral breath sounds are to be checked after each patient movement (*e.g.*, placing patient on gurney, moving patient to ambulance, loading patient into ambulance, *etc.*)

        *Automatic-transport ventilators are not intended nor shall they be used to reduce current personnel-staffing levels.

VI. SPECIAL INFORMATION:

    A.   Agencies using this equipment must be certain to follow the manufacturer's instructions to the letter regarding the use, maintenance, cleaning, and regular testing of the devices.

        1.   The units must be disinfected, inspected, and tested after every patient use.

        2.   The units shall undergo preventive testing and maintenance by qualified personnel annually.

        3.   Agencies shall arrange for (at least) annual inspections and testing of the equipment by a manufacturer's representative (or designee). Documentation of this service shall be maintained in a service log. This record shall be kept by each agency using ATVs.

    B.   Agency personnel must be thoroughly trained and regularly retrained in the device's use. Such training shall occur semiannually (every 6 months) and shall be thoroughly documented.

    C.   Agency personnel shall continually observe the patient and document patient response to any changes while the device is operational. Personnel shall chart the initial settings (rate/tidal volume) and any subsequent changes when the device is utilized. Such documentation shall appear on the patient-care report (PCR).

VII. "CLASS I" AUTOMATIC TRANSPORT VENTILATORS:
Only "Class I" automatic transport ventilators shall be authorized for use and shall have the following minimum features: (from JAMA Supplement, October 28, 1992–Vol. 268, No. 16)

    A.   A lightweight connector with a standard 15-mm/22-mm coupling for mask, endotracheal tube, or other airway adjunct

    B.   A lightweight (2-to-5 kg), compact, rugged design

    C.   Capability of operating under all common environmental conditions and extremes of temperature

    D.   A peak inspiratory pressure-limiting valve set at 60 cm H_2O with the option of an 80 cm H_2O pressure (available for use at the discretion of the medical director) that is easily accessible to the user

    E.   An audible alarm that sounds when the peak respiratory-limiting pressure is generated to alert the rescuer that low compliance or high-airway resistance is resulting in a diminished tidal-volume delivery

F. Minimal gas consumption (*e.g.*, at a tidal volume of 1 liter and a rate of 10 breaths per minute [10-l/min. ventilation]). The device should run for a minimum of 45 minutes on an "E" cylinder.

G. Minimal gas-compression volume in the breathing circuit

H. Ability to deliver of FiO_2 of 1.0

I. An inspiratory time of 2 secs. in adults and a maximal inspiratory flow rate of approximately 30 l/min. in adults (15 l/min. children)

J. At least 2 rates, 10 breaths/min. for adults. If a demand-flow valve is incorporated into the ATV, it should deliver a peak inspiratory-flow rate on demand of at least 100/min. at 2 cm H_2O, triggering pressure to minimize the work of breathing.

AUTOVENT 3000 PORTABLE VENTILATOR
KANSAS CITY, MO

I. Indications:

    A. General: Anytime the patient's ventilations would need to be assisted with a bag-valve mask or bag-to-ET tube

    B. Specific: The following protocols allow use of the Autovent 3000 without prior approval of a base-station physician when indicated.

        1. Protocol 1 General Medical
        2. Protocol 5 Cardiopulmonary Arrest
        3. Protocol 12 Near-Drowning
        4. Protocol 13 Respiratory Distress
        5. Protocol 15 Shock (Cardiogenic)

II. Contraindications:

    A. Pediatrics: This device should not be used on patients under the age of 12.

    B. Do not use on patients who weigh less than 90 pounds or 40 kilograms ideal body weight.

    C. Patients with a suspected pneumothorax or tension pneumothorax

    D. Patients with an elevated-pulmonary-pressure syndrome (*e.g.*, blast lung, diving barotrauma)

III. Technique

    A. Secure the airway as indicated.

    B. Assist ventilations in the usual fashion until ventilator settings can be determined. Use the following table to determine ventilator volumes. All volumes are based on *ideal* body weights as judged by the patient's height and frame, *not* on gross weight.

    C. Observe patient's chest rise. Rise should be normal and equal bilaterally. If the chest does not rise, recheck airway, evaluate patient for other injuries, and recheck tidal-volume setting. If the patient's chest appears to overexpand, then decrease the tidal-volume setting.

    D. The rate of ventilation is determined by the patient's clinical condition. The minimum rate setting should not be less than 12 breaths/minute for adult patients. The maximum adult rate setting is 20 breaths per minute.

IV. Precautions:

    A. Initial airway management and ventilation cannot and must not be compromised while setting up the ventilator.

    B. If problems arise during ventilator use *or* if you are not sure about the adequacy of oxygenation and ventilations with the portable ventilator, then *STOP* and ensure oxygenation and ventilations with the usual methods.

VENTILATOR SETTINGS

IDEAL BODY WEIGHT

Weight Lbs.	Weight Kg	Initial Volume 10 cc/kg	Approx. Initial Volume	Maximum Volume 15 cc/kg
90	40	400 cc	400 cc	600 cc
100	45	450 cc	500 cc	675 cc
125	57	570 cc	600 cc	855 cc
150	68	680 cc	700 cc	1020 cc
175	80	800 cc	800 cc	1200 cc
200	90	900 cc	900 cc	1350 cc
225	102	1020 cc	1000 cc	1530 cc
250	114	1140 cc	1100 cc	1710 cc
275	125	1250 cc	1200 cc	1875 cc

C. Using a mechanical ventilation device will remove the ability to determine early changes in pulmonary compliance, such as may be detected using a bag-ventilation technique.

D. The incidence of a pneumothorax is increased in the presence of penetrating chest trauma.

E. If the rate of ventilation is set at "0" (zero), no mechanical ventilation will occur.

CARDIOPULMONARY RESUSCITATION
DURHAM, NC

Indications

A pulseless and apneic patient

Basic cardiopulmonary resuscitation techniques are essential skills for all EMTs. The procedural guidelines of the American Heart Association (AHA) and the National Conference on CPR will be followed as published. The basic approach is as follows:

1. Establish that respiratory and cardiac arrest have occurred.
2. Establish an airway, and initiate ventilation.
3. Initiate cardiac compressions.

Procedure

ADULT
1-person CPR, 2 breaths/15 compressions, 80–100 compressions/minute
2-person CPR, 1 breath/5 compressions, 80–100 compressions/minute

CHILD
1-person CPR, 1 breath/5 compressions, 100 compressions/minute
2-person CPR, 1 breath/5 compressions, 100 compressions/minute

INFANT
1-person CPR, 1 breath/5 compressions, at least 100 compressions/minute
2-person CPR, 1 breath/5 compressions, at least 100 compressions/minute

Certification Requirements

Annual recertification in BLS according to AHA guidelines

CARDIOVERSION (SYNCHRONIZED)
WICHITA, KS

Synchronized Cardioversion

Introduction:

Electrical cardioversion is the therapy of choice for symptomatic ventricular or supraventricular tachycardias. Ventricular tachycardia often precedes ventricular fibrillation, and therefore effective therapy of this arrhythmia may prevent potentially lethal ventricular fibrillation.

Indications:

1. Symptomatic V-tach
2. Symptomatic supraventricular-tach

Applications:

The use of synchronized cardioversion requires:

1. Direct physician contact for EACH attempt on patients who display signs of shock and/or serious changes in mental state, *e.g.*, verbal or less on the AVPU scale
2. That the patient has received adequate BLS, including high-flow, high concentration of O_2
3. That the patient has an IV established
4. That a physician order has been obtained for *EACH* attempt at synchronized cardioversion

Procedure:

1. Select a lead that will be sensed by the monitor (usually the most positive "R"-wave deflection).
2. Ensure the monitor is capturing the "R"-wave deflection and the synchronizer is "ON" and functioning.
3. Select the energy level that is ordered (usually 50 w/s for SVT and V-tach on the first attempt).
4. If V-fib should occur as a result of, or while attempting synchronized cardioversion, turn the synchronizer "OFF," and proceed with defibrillation as indicated.

NOTE: *THE PATIENT MAY REQUIRE SEDATION PRIOR TO ATTEMPTING THIS PROCEDURE. WITH A PHYSICIAN ORDER, VALIUM MAY BE ADMINISTERED AT THE FOLLOWING DOSE AND RATE:*

Valium, if ordered, may be administered in 2.5-mg increments or less in a large vein, not to exceed 5 mg per minute or to the onset of drowsiness. The maximum dosage of Valium may not exceed 10 mg in patients < 65 years of age and a maximum of 7.5 mg in patient > 65 years of age.

(NOTE: Valium may cause apnea, especially in older patients.)

CARDIOVERSION (SYNCHRONIZED)
LAS VEGAS, NV

Synchronized Cardioversion

INDICATIONS	PHYSICIAN'S ORDER
I. Patients in ventricular tachycardia who have adequate perfusion refractory to drug therapy	YES
II. Patients with supraventricular tachycardias with inadequate perfusion	YES
III. Ventricular tachycardia with inadequate perfusion	NO

Contraindications:

patients with digitalis toxicity

Equipment and Procedure:

as per ACLS and PALS standards

Dose for PSVT and Atrial Flutter:

ADULT:
Initial cardioversion—50 joules
If unsuccessful, cardiovert at 100, 200, and 360 respectively.

PEDIATRIC:
Initial cardioversion—0.5 to 1.0 joules per kg
If unsuccessful, cardiovert at 2 joules per kg.

Dose for V-Tach and Atrial Fibrillation:

ADULT:
Initial cardioversion—100 joules
If unsuccessful, cardiovert at 200, 300, and 360 respectively.

PEDIATRIC:
Initial cardioversion—.25 to 0.5 joules per kg
If unsuccessful, 0.5 to 1.0 joules per kg and 2.0 joules per kg respectively

Potential Complications:

I.   Ventricular fibrillation or asystole
II. Burns to patient's chest
III. Operator injury

Special Notes:

I. Consider sedation.
II. Patients should have IV access prior to elective cardioversion.

COMBITUBE™ AIRWAY
LAS VEGAS, NEV

NOTE: This protocol may always be followed prior to telemetry physician orders.*

Indications:

I. Unsuccessful endotracheal intubation
II. An apneic patient with a need to isolate the respiratory system
III. A patient with inadequate respirations with a need to isolate the respiratory system

Contraindications:

I. Patient with a gag reflex
II. Patient with a history of esophageal trauma, the recent ingestion of a caustic substance, or known esophageal disease
III. Patient 15 years of age or under, and/or under 5 feet tall
IV. Patient with a tracheostomy or laryngectomy
V. Patient with a foreign body in the trachea
VI. Patient suspected of a narcotic overdose/hypoglycemia prior to administration of Narcan/glucose 50%

Equipment and Procedure:

As per manufacturer's directions

Potential Complications:

I. Broken teeth or dentures may result in damage to the proximal cuff.
II. Edema as a result of facial trauma or respiratory burns may obstruct the airway.

Special Notes:

I. Do NOT remove the Combitube™ airway in the field unless the patient's gag reflex returns or the patient has been endotracheally intubated first.
II. Use ET CO_2 detector (ALS ONLY) to confirm ventilation of proper tube, except in cardiopulmonary arrest.

CRICOTHYROIDOTOMY
COLOMBUS, OH

NOTE: In most situations, cricothyroidotomy should be used only after other methods of airway management have failed.

1. Indications include:

    A. Suspected cervical-spine fracture with inability to control the airway by other methods
    B. Impacted foreign body
    C. Severe facial trauma
    D. Severe laryngeal trauma or oropharyngeal hemorrhage
    E. Laryngeal spasms (epiglottitis)
    F. Obstructing tumors
    G. Burns of the face and/or upper airway precluding intubation
    H. Inability to establish a patient airway by other means (*i.e.*, oral or nasal airways, EOA or EGTA, bag-valve mask)

2. Procedure: **Needle Cricothyroidotomy**

NOTE: Only needle cricothyroidotomy should be performed on a patient less than the age of 10 years who requires a surgical airway. Also consider weight of patient.

    A. Palpate cricothyroid membrane anteriorly between thyroid cartilage and cricoid cartilage.
    B. Prepare area with Betadine swabs.
    C. Use 14-gauge catheter over needle device with syringe and puncture skin midline and directly over the cricothyroid membrane.
    D. Direct needle at 45-degree angle towards the feet.
    E. Insert needle through lower half of cricothyroid membrane. Aspiration of air signifies entry into the tracheal lumen.
    F. Withdraw stylet while advancing catheter downward.
    G. Attach the catheter needle hub to IV extension tubing and then to a 3.0-mm pediatric ET tube adaptor or may use jet insufflation device. (Ventilate by allowing 4 seconds expiration for each ventilation).
    H. Auscultate chest for adequate ventilation. An end-tidal CO_2 detector placed on the end of the 3-mm pediatric endotracheal tube adapter during ventilation to assure proper tube placement.

3. Procedure: **Surgical Cricothyroidotomy**

    A. Palpate cricothyroid membrane anteriorly between thyroid cartilage and cricoid cartilage.
    B. Prepare area with Betadine.
    C. Stabilize thyroid cartilage, and make vertical skin incision approximately 2.5 cm (1 inch) over cricothyroid membrane. Carefully incise through the membrane transversely.

D. Insert scalpel handle into incision, and rotate 90 degrees to open the airway.

E. Insert an approximately sized cuffed ET tube through incision. A 6.0-mm tube is generally sufficient.

F. Inflate cuff and ventilate patient.

G. Auscultate chest. An end-tidal CO_2 detector placed on the end of the endotracheal tube during ventilation to assure proper tube placement.

H. Stabilize the endotracheal tube securely.

CRICOTHYROID PUNCTURE/TRANS-TRACHEAL VENTILATION (CTP/TTV)
OKLAHOMA CITY, OK

Advanced Airway Management: Cricothyroid Puncture/Trans-Tracheal Ventilation (CTP/TTV)

Description

CTP/TTV is an emergency procedure involving puncturing the cricothyroid membrane to access the trachea for ventilation purposes (only performed with on-line medical control authorization).

Indications

CTP/TTV is indicated for relief of life-threatening partial upper airway obstruction in situations in which manual maneuvers to establish an airway and attempts at ventilation have failed, and endotracheal intubation is not feasible. Such circumstances might include the patient with severe laryngeal edema, or facial and upper-laryngeal trauma. This procedure may also be useful in the patient whose upper airway is partially obstructed by a foreign body that cannot be extricated with direct laryngoscopy techniques.

Contraindications

CTP/TTV should not be performed on infants and children.

Precautions

This procedure is not without considerable hazards. The cricothyroid membrane must be correctly identified to prevent uncontrollable bleeding and possible damage to surrounding structures when the puncture is made.

Side Effects

The only side effect when this procedure is performed properly might be a high PCO_2 level in the blood due to passive exhalation.

Adverse Reactions

Should air escape out of the trachea through the hole created by the catheter, subcutaneous or mediastinal emphysema could develop. Also, if bleeding is severe, this could hamper proper gas diffusion in the lungs, as with pulmonary edema.

Technique

A. The laryngeal framework is made up of the thyroid cartilage and cricoid cartilage. The shield-like thyroid cartilage is the prominent "Adam's apple" that is often seen in men. At the superior aspect of the shield is a prominent notch that is easily palpable through the skin. This notch is the only reliable landmark in the neck. Attempting to find the thyroid cartilage in women or in people with short, fat necks is difficult if this notch is not sought, because the hyoid bone or the cricoid cartilage may easily be misidentified as the thyroid cartilage with disastrous surgical results. Once the thyroid cartilage is identified, the airway is followed caudally by palpation until the first complete ring is found. This is the cricoid ring, the only circumferential ring in the airway. This cartilage is shaped like a high school class ring with the shield located posteriorly. The membrane connecting the cartilages is the cricothyroid membrane.

B. With continued attempts at ventilation and oxygenation, the cricothyroid membrane is punctured by the cannula firmly attached to a 5-cc syringe filled with 1-2 cc of saline. 2 ml of 2% lidocaine can be used instead of saline, to produce local anesthesia of the mucosa in the area of the distal port of the cannula.

C. The cannula is directed downward, with continual aspiration to demonstrate entry into the larynx, identified when bubbles of air are readily aspirated. At this point, if lidocaine is contained in the syringe, it can be injected to provide some anesthesia and prevent the coughing that sometimes occurs in those patients who are somewhat responsive.

D. On entry into the larynx, the cannula is slid off the needle trocar and is held in place while the TTV device is connected to the proximal port of the cannula.

E. The patient is immediately ventilated using 1-second bursts of oxygen from the 50-psi manual source. The rate used is at least 20 per minute (i.e., an inspiratory/expiratory ratio of 1:2).

F. If a tie is available, the cannula is fixed in place. Tape can also be used, but it must be fastened firmly to the cannula and then around the patient's neck. Firm pressure at the site of insertion can reduce the small amount of subcutaneous emphysema that usually occurs with this technique.

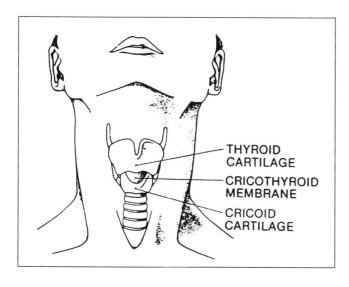

THYROID CARTILAGE

CRICOTHYROID MEMBRANE

CRICOID CARTILAGE

Basic anatomy. Note that the notch of the thyroid cartilage is the most consistently identifiable structure in the neck.

DEFIBRILLATION
LAS VEGAS, NV

INDICATIONS	PHYSICIAN'S ORDER
I. Patient who is in ventricular fibrillation	NO
II. Patient who is in ventricular tachycardia and who is pulseless and nonbreathing	NO
III. Patient who is in ventricular tachycardia and who has inadequate perfusion and for whom effective and rapid synchronized cardioversion is impossible	YES

Contraindications:

None

Equipment and Procedure:

As per ACLS standards

Dose for Ventricular Fibrillation or Pulseless Ventricular Tachycardia:

ADULT:
Initial—200 joules
If unsuccessful, 300 joules
If unsuccessful, 360 joules and continue at 360 until conversion occurs.

PEDIATRIC:
(for patients weighing less than 10 kg)
Initial—2 joules per kg
If unsuccessful, 4 joules per kg and continue at 4 joules/kg until conversion occurs.

Dose for Ventricular Tachycardia or Supraventricular Tachycardia with Inadequate Perfusion:

See cardioversion protocol.

Potential Complications:

I.   Burns to chest
II. Operator injury

Special Notes:

I. Delays in performing defibrillation will result in greater myocardial deterioration, and success will then be less likely.

II. Patient with automatic implantable cardioverter-defibrillators (AICD) will need external defibrillation if the AICD is ineffective.

III. If defibrillation is needed on a patient with a permanent implanted pacemaker, the defibrillator paddles or self-adhesive electrodes should be placed at least 5 inches from the pulse generator of the pacemaker.

IV. If conversion occurs and then the patient refibrillates, patient should be defibrillated at the same joule setting as the last shock.

END-TIDAL CO$_2$ DETECTOR
LAS VEGAS, NV

NOTE: This protocol may always be followed prior to telemetry physician order.

Indication:

To assist verification of endotracheal tube and Combitube placement after intubation and during transport

Contraindications:

I.   This device is not to be used for the detection of hypercarbia.
II. This device is not to be used for right-main-stem bronchial intubation.
III. This device is not to be used during mouth-to-tube ventilation.
IV. Not for use in patients having body weight less than 15 kg
V.   This device cannot be used to detect oropharyngeal tube placement. Standard clinical assessment should be used.

Potential Complications:

I.   INTERPRETING RESULTS BEFORE ADMINISTERING SIX BREATHS CAN YIELD FALSE RESULTS.
II. END-TIDAL-CO$_2$-DETECTOR RESULTS ARE NOT CONCLUSIVE. THE ENDOTRACHEAL TUBE SHOULD BE IMMEDIATELY REMOVED UNLESS CORRECT ANATOMIC LOCATION CAN BE CONFIRMED WITH CERTAINTY BY OTHER MEANS.
III. IN CARDIAC STANDSTILL, REESTABLISHMENT OF CARDIAC OUTPUT AND PULMONARY PERFUSION BY ADEQUATE CARDIOPULMONARY RESUSCITATION (CPR) IS NECESSARY TO INCREASE END-TIDAL CO$_2$ LEVELS THAT ARE DETECTABLE.
IV. REFLUX OF GASTRIC CONTENTS, MUCUS, EDEMA FLUID, OR INTRATRACHEAL EPINEPHRINE INTO THE DETECTOR CAN RESULT IN PERSISTENT PATCHY YELLOW OR WHITE DISCOLORATION, WHICH DOES NOT VARY WITH THE RESPIRATORY CYCLE. DISCARD DEVICE IF THIS CONDITION OCCURS.
V.   NOT TO EXCEED TWO HOURS OF USAGE.

Equipment and Procedure:

I.   Remove detector from package. Do not remove end caps until ready to use device.
II. Match initial color of the indicator to the purple color labeled CHECK on the product dome. If the purple color is not the same or darker, DO NOT USE.
III. Insert endotracheal tube. Inflate cuff.
IV. Remove end caps, and firmly attach detector between the endotracheal tube and the breathing device.

COLOR RANGE "A"   End-Tidal CO$_2$ level < 4 mm Hg
          "B"   End-Tidal CO$_2$ level < 15 mm Hg
          "C"   End-Tidal CO$_2$ level 15 to 38 mm Hg

Adequate Perfusion/Ventilation

Example: Respiratory Distress

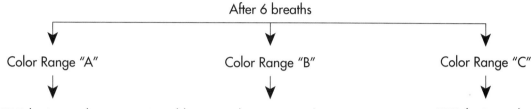

After 6 breaths

Color Range "A"	Color Range "B"	Color Range "C"
• ET Tube in esophagus • Remove ET tube • Support ventilation • Re-intubate • Re-check with *EASY CAP* detector	• Possible retained CO$_2$ in esophagus. • Possible low pulmonary perfusion, possible hypocarbia • Deliver additional 6 breaths • If color shifts to Color Range "A" remove tube • If color remains in "B" Range confirm placement by another method	• ET Tube in trachea • Auscultate breath sounds bilaterally • Secure tube • Continue to observe color change

Compromised Perfusion/Ventilation

Example: Cardiac arrest with CPR
End-Tidal CO$_2$ levels should be equal to or greater than 0.5%. ("B" or "C" range)

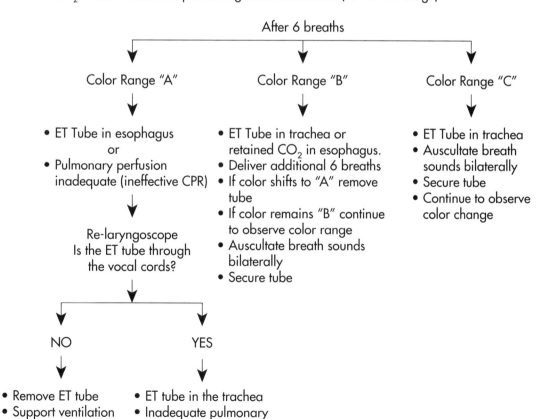

After 6 breaths

Color Range "A"	Color Range "B"	Color Range "C"
• ET Tube in esophagus or • Pulmonary perfusion inadequate (ineffective CPR)	• ET Tube in trachea or retained CO$_2$ in esophagus. • Deliver additional 6 breaths • If color shifts to "A" remove tube • If color remains "B" continue to observe color range • Auscultate breath sounds bilaterally • Secure tube	• ET Tube in trachea • Auscultate breath sounds bilaterally • Secure tube • Continue to observe color change

Re-laryngoscope
Is the ET tube through the vocal cords?

NO
• Remove ET tube
• Support ventilation
• Re-intubate
• Re-check with *EASY CAP* detector

YES
• ET tube in the trachea
• Inadequate pulmonary ventilation or perfusion
• Take appropriate clinical action

ADULT AND PEDIATRIC END-TIDAL CO₂ DETECTOR
SAN FRANCISCO, CA

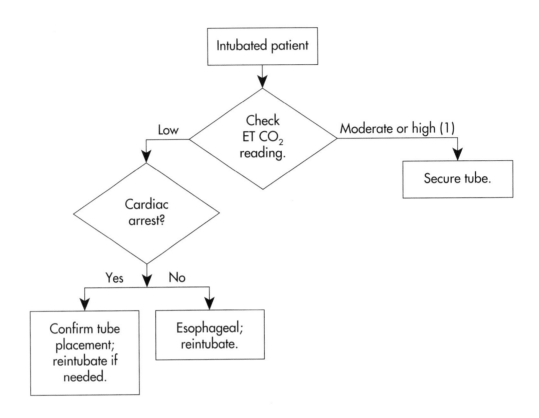

I. Readings on the colormetric end-tidal CO_2 detector devices are as follows:

LOW	MODERATE	HIGH
Color range A	Color range B	Color range C
Et CO_2 level	Et CO_2 level	Et CO_2 level
0.03% to less than 0.50%	0.50% to less than 2%	2% to 5%
0-to-4 mm Hg	4-to-less-than-15 mm Hg	15-to-38 mm Hg

ESOPHAGEAL OBTURATOR AIRWAY (EOA)
SANTA ANA, CA

Indications:

Unconscious apneic adult (age greater than 16 years or weight greater than 50 kg) without gag reflex, *e.g.*:
  —Cardiac arrest
  —Respiratory arrest
  —Severe respiratory depression with an absent gag reflex
  —Traumatic arrest

Equipment:

- EOA tube and MASK
- 35-ml syringe
- Lubricant (water soluble)
- Bag-valve mask or resuscitator
- Laryngoscope blade and handle

Preparation of Equipment:

- Assemble all equipment.
- Inflate cuffs on the mask and tube, test for leaks.
- Attach the mask to the tube.
- Lubricate the tube.

Procedure:

- Hyperventilate the patient with 100% oxygen prior to EOA insertion.
- Perform laryngoscopy prior to insertion. If foreign body present, remove with Magill forceps.
- Suction the oropharynx until clear.
- Place the head in a neutral position.
- Grasp the lower jaw with the thumb and index finger, and lift. Hold the EOA in the other hand (with its curvature in the same direction as the natural curvature of the pharynx).
- Blindly insert the tube into the mouth and advance into the throat until the mask is seated on the face.
  —Insert an oropharyngeal airway (optional).
- Open the airway, using the head tilt or jaw thrust maneuver.
- Maintain airtight face-mask seal.
- Attach the ventilation device to the mask; assess adequacy of ventilations.
- Inflate the cuff with 35 ml air.
- Maintain open airway.
- Continue ventilations.

- Ausculate the lungs bilaterally and the epigastric area for breath sounds.
  —If the chest does not rise or lung sounds are not heard, the EOA should be removed immediately and the patient ventilated by other means.
  —Extubate the patient in the following manner:
    - Have suction equipment ready.
    - Turn the patient as a unit on his side.
    - Detach the mask.
    - With suction applied, deflate cuff, and withdraw the tube.
    - Ventilate the patient by other means.
- Repeat suction as necessary.
  —The EOA is in the esophagus; secretions in the mouth may enter the trachea. Suction under the mask and into the mouth, not down the EOA.
- Documentation should include the presence of bilateral breath sounds and the absence of abdominal sounds; reassess each time patient is moved.

Contraindications:

—Caustic ingestion
—Known esophageal disease
—Age younger than 16 years

EXTERNAL CARDIAC PACING
WICHITA, KS

Introduction:

The external transcutaneous pacemaker may be rapidly applied and is a noninvasive, temporary pacing device for the emergency treatment of specific persistent cardiac dysrhythmias in the field situations.

Indications:

A. *PACING*
   1. Symptomatic bradycardias that *DO NOT* respond to atropine.

B. *CARDIAC ARREST*
   1. Asystole
   2. PEA

External cardiac pacing should not be utilized as first-line treatment. BLS should be instituted with good oxygenation of the myocardium before considering external cardiac pacing (breathing for nonbreathing patients during pacing sequence).
   If pacing is unsuccessful (after approx. 30 seconds), return to conventional therapy.

Precautions:

A. Pacing stimulus may cause pain or discomfort to conscious patients.
B. Contact with electrodes or gel during pacing may result in accidental electrical shock to the rescuer.
C. Conductive defibrillation gel applied too close to the pacing electrodes will result in the electrical energy being shunted away from the patient.
D. External pacing should not be done in a flammable atmosphere.

Considerations:

A. Extreme environmental conditions, such as moisture or conductive materials, should be avoided.
B. Explosive or combustible materials that are present may present a hazard to the rescue personnel, and pacing should not be done in their presence.

Application:

A. Electrodes are placed on the patient in an anterior-posterior position. Place the negative (−) pacing electrode on the left anterior chest halfway between the xiphoid process and the left nipple, with the upper edge of the electrode just below the nipple line.
B. Place the red positive (+) pacing electrode on the posterior left chest below the scapula and lateral to the spine.

NOTE: Pacing electrodes adhere best on a relatively flat surface. It may be necessary to shift the anterior electrode slightly to avoid placement over breast tissue. *DO NOT* place pacing electrodes directly over large bony areas, such as the spine or sternum. This placement of pacing electrodes will affect current threshold and may affect patient comfort.

C. Begin to increase the energy output in 20 ma. increments until capture has been obtained.
D. After capture of the impulse has been obtained, decrease the energy level in 5 ma. increments until capture has been lost.
E. Increase the energy level 10 ma. from the last setting. This should be the lowest setting that will obtain capture. If the capture is lost, the energy output can be increased.

Rate Selection:

SUGGESTED BEGINNING RATE:

Bradycardic rhythms . . . . 60 BPM
Asystolic rhythms . . . . 60 BPM

Contraindications:

Pacing should **NOT** be started on the following patients:

1. Traumatic-cardiac-arrest patients (except electrocutions)
2. Hypothermic patients in cardiac arrest
3. Pediatric patients on whom the patches cannot be applied due to anatomical constraints

EXTERNAL PACEMAKER USE
TAMPA, FL

A. Assess need for external pacing.

B. Place pacer pads over anterior and posterior chest walls just left of the sternum and spine, respectively.

C. Hook pacer in line with defibrillator/monitor unit (if not built into unit).

D. Set pacer rate:

   1. In patients with electrocardiographic evidence of organized cardiac activity, set pacer rate at 20–30 BPM above patient's intrinsic rate.

   2. In patients without evidence of organized activity, set pacer at rate of 70–90 BPM.

E. Set alarms and arm pacer appropriately.

F. Turn on pacing element and set amperage:

   1. In patients with intrinsic cardiac function (pulses and blood pressure present), turn on pacing element with amperage at lowest setting; gradually increase until patient demonstrates electrical capture on EKG and mechanical capture as evidenced by pulses simultaneous with paced beat. Set amperage approximately 5 milliamps above capture point.

   2. In patients with no intrinsic cardiac function, set pacer at highest amperage and maintain.

G. When mechanical capture is obtained, adjust heart rate to maintain systolic BP > 100 mm Hg. Do not exceed paced rate of 90 BPM.

H. Awake patients requiring pacing may be given diazepam 2 mg slow IV push. Titrate to patient comfort to a maximum dose of 10 mg or a systolic blood pressure of < 100 mm Hg.

EXTERNAL JUGULAR-VEIN CANNULATION
CHARLOTTE, NC

I. Indication

I. A. This route is selected only after other peripheral IV attempts have been unsuccessful and an IV line is essential to patient management.
   B. Permission is secured from medical control even in full arrests.

II. Anatomy

   A. Runs superficially along the side of the neck between the ear and the midclavicular line. (See Figure 1.)

III. Procedure

   A. Secure permission to perform procedure from medical control.
   B. Gather equipment.
   C. Place patient in supine position, with head lowered slightly and turned at a 45–60-degree angle from the midline. Locate external jugular vein.
   D. Distend vein by

   1. Tamponading just above clavicle.
   2. Lowering patient's head.
   3. Elevating lower extremities.

   E. Cleanse skin thoroughly with antiseptic swabs.
   F. Stabilize the skin above proposed puncture site by using gentle countertraction.
   G. Align the cannula in the direction of the vein with the point aimed toward the ipsilateral shoulder.
   H. Using aseptic technique, make venipuncture midway between the angle of the jaw and the midclavicular line. (See Figure 2.)
   I. Proceed as you would when starting an IV in the arm, and tape in place. BE CAREFUL NOT TO LET AIR ENTER THE CATHETER ONCE IT IS INSERTED. Quickly attach your infusion set as soon as blood return is established.
   J. Check IV site frequently.
   K. Ausculate lung sounds to rule out pneumothorax.
   L. If first attempt is not successful, *do not attempt another cannulation* on the other external jugular vein.

IV. Complications

   A. Air embolism—may be avoided by placing the patient in a Trendelenberg position, clearing the IV tubing of air, and firmly tamponading the vein while connecting the tubing to the cannula
   B. Pneumothorax—may be avoided by puncturing the vein as closely as possible to the angle of the jaw
   C. Hematoma—Monitor IV site closely.
   D. Infiltration—Monitor IV site frequently.

V. Documentation

    A. Should be the same as for starting other peripheral lines.

    B. Should include:

        1. Site location

        2. Size angiocath

        3. Time

        4. Who attempted it

        5. Results (successful or not successful)

        6. Complications

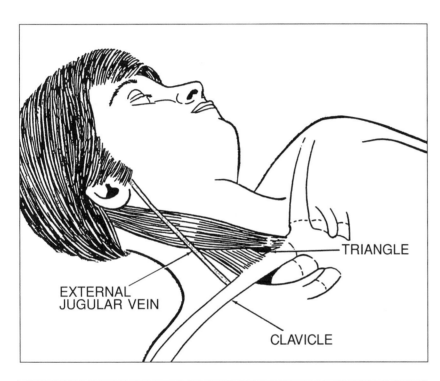

FIGURE 1.
External jugular
vein

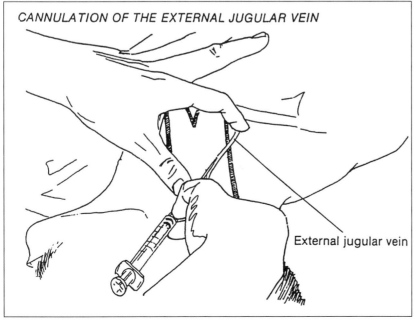

FIGURE 2.

CANNULATION OF THE EXTERNAL JUGULAR VEIN

External jugular vein

EXTUBATION PROCEDURE
STATE OF MARYLAND

1. Ensure that extubation is indicated.

   1.1 Patient must be conscious.

   1.2 Patient must be able to maintain his or her own airway.

   1.3 Patient must be able to breathe without continuous positive-pressure ventilation.

   1.4 Patient must be fighting the endotracheal tube or attempting to extubate himself or herself.

2. Make the necessary preparations for reintubation prior to removal of the endotracheal tube just in case reintubation becomes necessary.

   2.1 Have suction ready; in case of vomiting, be prepared to roll the patient to the left side.

3. Untape the tube and oropharyngeal airway.

4. The tube is removed at end-inspiration because the glottis is widest at this point.

5. Elevate the mandible.

6. Remove the endotracheal tube.

   6.1 If laryngospasm occurs, it usually resolves in less than 30 seconds with oxygenation.

   6.2 Suction prior to removal of the endotracheal tube may decrease the likelihood of laryngospasm.

7. Maintain the patient's airway, continue oxygenation, and closely monitor vital signs.

HELMET-REMOVAL PROTOCOL
STATE OF MARYLAND

1. INTRODUCTION
   1.1 Patients who become ill or injured while wearing protective helmets (*e.g.*, motorcycle, football) pose a special problem to emergency-care providers. Assessment and airway-and-injury management may prove difficult or impossible due to the limited accessibility helmets permit to the head, face, and cervical spine. Helmet removal shall be accomplished with two rescuers properly trained in the procedure.

   The following policy outlines the helmet-removal procedure to be utilized by prehospital-care providers in Maryland.

2. INDICATIONS FOR HELMET REMOVAL IN THE FIELD
   2.1 Patients with suspected head, brain, and face injuries
   2.2 Patients with suspected cervical-spine injuries requiring spinal immobilization
   2.3 Unconscious patients
   2.4 Patients requiring airway management
   2.5 Any patient requiring assessment of the head, face, and/or neck

3. CONTRAINDICATIONS FOR HELMET REMOVAL IN THE FIELD
   3.1 A patient who is obviously dead
   3.2 A patient with an impaled object involving the helmet or the removal of the impaled object to facilitate helmet removal
   3.3 A patient whose helmet is entangled with associated head injuries (*e.g.*, crush injury)

4. HELMET-REMOVAL PROCEDURE
   4.1 Initiate patient assessment, and determine level of consciousness.
   4.2 Assess airway, breathing, and circulation as one would with a patient with a suspected cervical-spine injury.

NOTE: If cervical-spine injury is not suspected (*e.g.*, uninjured patient) and the patient is conscious, assist the patient with the removal of his or her helmet, and continue assessment and/or treatment as appropriate.

   4.3 One rescuer applies in-line stabilization by placing his or her hands on each side of the helmet, with fingers on the victim's mandible. This position prevents slippage if the helmet strap and/or helmet is loose.
   4.4 The second rescuer places one hand on the patient's mandible at an angle, with the thumb on one side and the middle and index fingers on the other. With his or her other hand, he or she applies pressure from the occipital region. This transfers the in-line stabilization responsibility to the second rescuer.
   4.5 As the first rescuer removes the helmet, 3 factors should be kept in mind:
      4.5.1 The helmet is egg shaped and therefore must be expanded laterally to clear the ears.

4.5.2   If the helmet provides full facial coverage, glasses must be removed first.

4.5.3   If the helmet provides full facial coverage, the nose may impede removal. To clear the nose, the helmet must be tilted backward and raised over the nose.

4.6   Following helmet removal, the first rescuer regains in-line traction by replacing his or her hands on either side of the patient's head, as one would maintain in-line stabilization on a supine patient.

4.6   Apply a cervical collar and immobilize the spine as appropriate.

IMPLANTABLE CARDIOVERTER DEFIBRILLATOR
COLORADO SPRINGS, CO

ICD Magnet (Implantable Cardioverter Defibrillator)

Indications

ICD device that is generating inappropriate shocks (usually shocking sinus tachy-cardia or PSVT rather than ventricular tachycardia or ventricular fibrillation).

Precautions

A. Patient may be understandably quite anxious and difficult to evaluate. The call will usually be for a defibrillator that "keeps going off." The majority of the time this will be because the patient is having frequent episodes of unstable ventricular tachycardia. Occasionally, however, the device will be abnormally sensing a sinus or supra-ventricular tachycardia. Careful moni-toring will allow the paramedic to differentiate these scenarios.

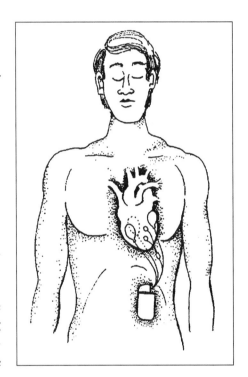

It is inappropriate to "turn off" an ICD that is properly sensing and treat-ing dysrhythmias.

B. In a patient who is determined to have an ICD that is sensing and shocking inappropriately, full resuscitation equip-ment must be available before using the magnet to "turn off" the ICD.

Technique

A. Obtain full history including brand or name of device that has been implanted.
B. Apply O_2, moderate flow (4–6 l/min.).
C. IV, D5W, TKO
D. Attach cardiac monitor.
E. Record rhythm and any defibrillations if possible.
F. If rhythm is inappropriate for internal defibrillation, assure external defibrilla-tion and intubation equipment are readily available. Use ICD magnet to turn device off. Magnet response is device-specific.

   1. CPI (1500, 1550, 1660) — Placing the magnet over the device will cause the device to beep with each R wave it senses. If it is left in place

for 30 seconds, an audible continuous tone means the device is off. Remove magnet to keep the device off.

2. CPI (PRX)—has a programmable magnet function that will allow a magnet to suspend detection of rhythm if programmed *on* and have no effect if programmed *off.*

3. Ventritex (cadence)—Magnet will suspend detection of rhythms (no therapies/shocks will be delivered) while magnet is over either end of the device. Detections will resume when magnet is removed. There is no audible tone with magnet placement. V-100 series may be programmed to ignore the application of a magnet.

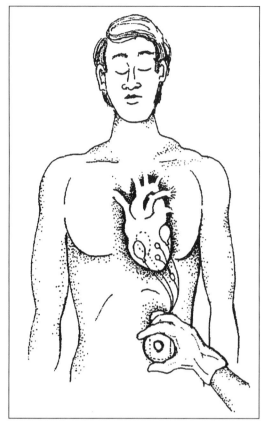

4. Intermedics (ResQ)—Magnet will suspend detection of rhythm while in place. Detection will resume (with programmed therapies) if magnet is removed.

5. Ventak PRx (1700/1705)—has a programmable magnet function that will allow a magnet to suspend detection of rhythm if programmed *on* and have no effect if programmed *off.* If magnet use is programmed *on* place the magnet over the pulse generator, and listen for tones from the device. The pulse generator is *off* or *monitor only* if a continuous tone is heard. The pulse generator is in monitor + therapy if it emits tones synchronously with each R-wave. (It will suspend therapy while magnet is in place and resume when magnet is removed.) An absence of tones indicates the device is not sensing.

G. Continue to monitor closely and transport to appropriate facility (preferably where the patient had the device implanted).

H. Be prepared to defibrillate if ICD has been turned off. If necessary to defibrillate, *anterior-posterior patch placement is preferred.* Sternum-apex paddle or patch placement may damage lead wires from ICD.

Complications

A. Since some devices react differently to the magnet, it is important to be sure which device has been implanted. The device may still be functioning though you think you have turned it off. Most of these patients will have histories of documented ventricular fibrillation or tachycardia associated with sudden death or symptomatic sustained ventricular tachycardia. The patient and his or her family will usually be quite well educated about the device. They should have written material and may even have a magnet in the home.

B. Once you have used the magnet to turn the device off, the patient is at your mercy for further care. Assure all ACLS equipment is available before turning the device off.

Special Notes

A. Patients will frequently be quite frantic if the device has fired several times. They will be most anxious for the paramedic to turn off the device. Use caution! If the device is firing appropriately you will be replacing a 5–10-joule internal shock for a 200–360-joule external shock. The patient will not be pleased with the change.

B. The magnet will also affect pacemakers but is not recommended for field use on pacemakers.

C. Touching the patient will not be deleterious to field personnel. CPR should continue normally if so indicated. ACLS protocols should also be followed as usual. Shocks can be delivered from ICD and external devices if so indicated without effect on the ICD. (The *wires*, however, may still be damaged by the shock — try to avoid.) *Monitor the patient and watch the rhythm — treat per dysrhythmia protocols.*

INTRAOSSEOUS INFUSION
LAS VEGAS, NV

NOTE: This protocol may be implemented prior to obtaining telemetry physician orders, if, in the attending paramedic's opinion, the patient's survival may be compromised by any delay caused by attempting to contact a telemetry physician.*

Indications: ALL THREE (3) MUST BE PRESENT.

I. Need for drug or fluid resuscitation of an infant or child who is unconscious, unresponsive, and in need of immediate life-saving intervention
II. The patient is less than 5 years of age.
III. The inability to establish a peripheral line within 90 seconds

Contraindications:

I. Placement of an intraosseous line in a fractured bone
II. Placement of an intraosseous line distal to a fractured bone

Relative Contraindication:

Infection or burns at the intended site — the telemetry physician should advise.

Equipment and Procedure:

As per AHA pediatric advanced life-support standards

Potential Complications:

I. Compartment syndrome
II. Fracture
III. Osteomyelitis, especially in septic patients
IV. Infusion rate is not adequate for resuscitation of ongoing hemorrhage or severe shock.

Special Notes:

I. Only **ONE** attempt per leg should be used in the field.
II. Administer drugs or fluids:
    A. Drugs should be pushed through a stopcock.
    B. Place the IV solution in pressure bag inflated to 300 torr or "push" the fluid bolus with a large-bore syringe for more-rapid infusion.
III. **All IV and IO attempts are to be documented on the prehospital record to include site and patency.**
IV. Attempts to establish an IO or IV line should not unnecessarily delay the transport of the patient.

INTRAOSSEOUS INFUSION
MILWAUKEE, WI

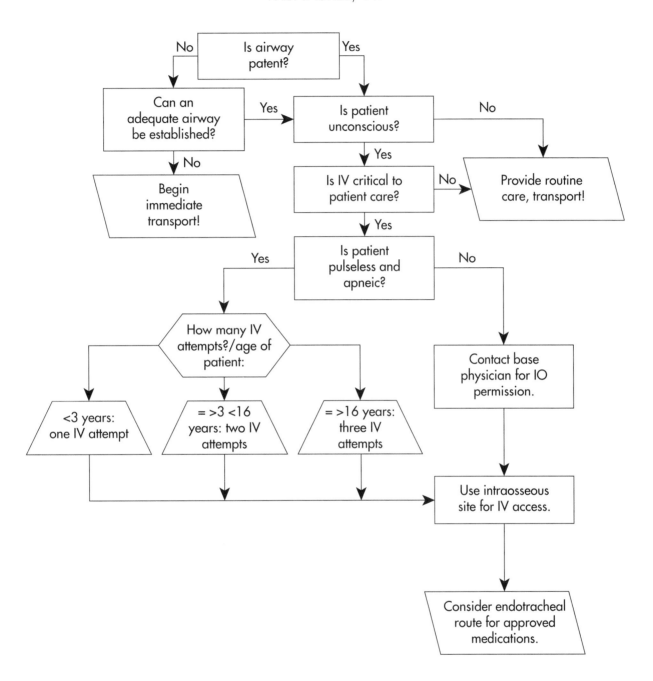

Because of the difficulty in establishing peripheral intravenous lines in critically ill patients, the intraosseous [SPS] route may be used under the following guidelines:

- Airway [SPS] is the number-one priority. Begin transport if an adequate airway cannot be maintained.
- The patient must be unconscious.
- An intravenous line [SPS] must be critical to the care of the patient (*e.g.*, hypovolemia, cardiac arrest, hypoglycemia, hypotension).
- The procedure should not significantly delay standard of care or transport.

The protocol will be as follows:

1. If the patient is not pulseless and nonbreathing, contact the base physician for permission to establish the intraosseous infusion.[SPS]
2. If the patient is pulseless and nonbreathing:

   A. If the patient is less than 3 years of age, an attempt should be made to establish the intravenous line [SPS] [PP M.01] in a peripheral vein. No more than one (1) attempt lasting one (1) minute should be made before proceeding to the intraosseous route.

   B. If the patient is 3–16 years old, a second attempt at a peripheral line should be made before intraosseous route is used. Attempts to establish a peripheral IV site should not exceed 90 seconds.

   C. If the patient is over age 16, peripheral IV attempts should not exceed 3 minutes.

   D. Consider using the endotracheal tube for those medications approved for that route of administration.

NOTE: *Inability to locate an appropriate vein site is equivalent to an attempt. It is not necessary to actually penetrate the skin with a needle.*

3. Contraindications to the use of the intraosseous route are:
   - Major-extremity trauma (fractured femur/tibia or evidence of internal/external thigh hemorrhage). Fluid will only infiltrate.
   - Area of infection over the proposed insertion site (infected skin, abscess, *etc.*).

These policies are under constant review and revision and may not reflect the actual practice of the Milwaukee County Paramedic Program.

INTUBATION, ENDOTRACHEAL (NASOTRACHEAL)
LAS VEGAS, NV

Endotracheal Intubation (Nasotracheal)

NOTE: This protocol may always be followed prior to telemetry physician orders.*

Indications:

I. A patient with a need to secure a functioning respiratory system.

II. A patient with inadequate respirations and in whom basic airway mainte-nance and ventilatory assistance techniques have not provided air exchange to manage the patient's hypoxia

Contraindications:

I. Patient suspected of a narcotic overdose/hypoglycemia prior to administra-tion of narcan/glucose 50%

II. Suspected basilar skull fracture

III. Nasal and midface fractures

IV. Coumadin anticoagulation therapy or hemostatic disorders

Relative Contraindications:

I. Respiratory arrest

II. Age of patient under 12 years

Equipment and Procedure:

Per DOT standards

Potential Complications:

I. Esophageal intubation

II. Right main-stem intubation

III. Vomiting

IV. Pneumothorax/tension pneumothorax from high-pressure ventilation

V. Inadvertent tube displacement during movement/transport

VI. Increased intracranial pressure as a result of increased vagal stimulation

VII. Epistaxis

VIII. Nasal trauma

Precautions:

I. Great caution must be taken in any patient with transtracheal-type injury.

II. Never use intubation as the initial treatment for respiratory arrest in the field.

Special Notes:

I. Since epistaxis is common, neosynephrine should be used, except in closed-head-injury patients with altered mental status.

II. Topical lidocaine ointment should be used to reduce the discomfort for the patient.

III. All intubation attempts MUST be documented on the prehospital record.

INTUBATION, ENDOTRACHEAL (OROTRACHEAL)
LAS VEGAS, NV

Endotracheal Intubation (Orotracheal)

NOTE: This protocol may always be followed prior to telemetry physician orders.

Indications:

I. A patient with a need to secure a functioning respiratory system
II. A patient with inadequate respirations and in whom basic airway maintenance and ventilatory assistance techniques have not provided sufficient air exchange

Contraindications:

Patient suspected of a narcotic overdose/hypoglycemia prior to administration of narcan/glucose 50%.

Relative Contraindications:

A patient with a gag reflex. Nasotracheal intubation should be considered.

Equipment and Procedure:

per DOT standards

Potential Complications:

I. Esophageal intubation
II. Right main-stem intubation
III. Vomiting
IV. Pneumothorax/tension pneumothorax from high-pressure ventilation
V. Inadvertent tube displacement during movement/transport
VI. Increased intracranial pressure as a result of increased vagal stimulation
VII. Fractured teeth
VIII. Pharyngeal/tracheal trauma

Precautions:

I. Great caution must be taken in any patient with transtracheal type injury.
II. Never use intubation as the initial treatment for respiratory arrest in the field.

Special Notes:

I. Nasotracheal intubation should be considered if the patient has a suspected cervical-spine injury.
II. All intubation attempts MUST be documented on the prehospital record.

449

INTUBATION, RAPID SEQUENCE
EUGENE/SPRINGFIELD, OR

Rapid Sequence Intubation (RSI)

I. Indications:

    A. Need for immediate intubation has been determined and the patient cannot be intubated without a paralytic. These patients include:

        1. Head-injured patients with trismus (clenched jaw) or posturing

        2. Those with status epilepticus not responding to anticonvulsants

        3. Those with respiratory insufficiency with altered level of consciousness

        4. Those with respiratory burns with impending respiratory failure

        5. Patients unable to protect airway (trauma, obstruction, overdose)

II. Procedure (EMT 4) by standing order:

    A. Preparation:

        1. Hyperventilate/preoxygenate; check effectiveness of ventilation with BVM.

        2. Suction available

        3. Large-bore IV secured

        4. Cardiac monitor on patient

        5. Pulse oximetry if possible

        6. ET equipment checked and ready

        7. Alternate airways prepared:

            a. Combitube if over 16 years

            b. Cricothyrotomy device (no nutrake under 5 years)

        8. Medications to treat complications prepared

            a. Atropine for bradycardia

            b. Lidocaine for ventricular dysrhythmias

    B. Premedication prn:

        1. Consider **Droperidol (Inapsine)** IV push if indicated by patient's level of awareness and/or combativeness. Usual adult dose 2.5–5.0 mg. Refer to Droperidol protocol, section B.

    C. Administer **succinylcholine** 1–1.5 mg/kg IV push. (Give rapidly.)

    D. If unable to start IV, may give succinylcholine 2–4 mg/kg IM. Usual adult dose is 2 × IV dose not to exceed 150 mg. (May give 150 in average mg - size adult.)

    E. Continue to ventilate/oxygenate patient while using Sellick manuever. Maintain Sellick maneuver until ET tube in place and cuff inflated.

    F. Intubate, and check placement of ET tube.

    G. Hyperventilate, and secure ET tube.

    H. If side effects develop from use of succinylcholine, oxygenate and:

1. Bradycardia—Give *atropine* IV push.

   a. Adult—0.5 mg MR every 3–5 minutes up to 3 mg (if needed).
   b. Pediatric—0.02 mg/kg, not to exceed 0.5 mg per single dose. Do not give less than 0.1 mg per dose. (MR every 3–5 minutes up to child max. of 1.0 mg and adolescent max of 2.0 mg).

2. Hypotension—Give fluid bolus, 20 ml/kg IV.
3. Ventricular dysrhythmias—Give **lidocaine** 1–1.5 mg/kg IV push and follow ACLS algorithms.

I. If unable to intubate the paralyzed patient, continue bagging with BVM while using Sellick maneuver.

J. If relaxation was inadequate 60–120 seconds after administration of succinylcholine, and the paramedic was unable to place the ET tube because of inadequate relaxation, the paramedic may repeat initial dose of succinylcholine and reattempt intubation.

K. If still unable to intubate, continue BVM ventilations, and consider placement of combitube in patient over age 16 years (if no contraindications to use of combitube).

L. If unable to ventilate the apneic patient, perform cricothyrotomy:

   1. Nutrake over age 10 years
   2. Needle cricothyrotomy or nutrake if age 5–10 years. (Use your judgment.)
   3. Needle cricothyrotomy (no nutrake) if under age 5 years.

III. Additional Notes:

A. This should be a two-paramedic procedure when possible.

B. Have restraints available, and use them if indicated. It is a good idea to restrain hands so that patient does not reach up and pull out ET when paralytic wears off.

C. While recognizing that this is a procedure with multiple risks and there are many opinions regarding the use of additional drugs as "premedications" to optimize the procedure under ideal conditions, your supervising physicians want you to approach the use of succinylcholine in the following manner:

> When using a paralytic, the decision to use it is not taken lightly. The paramedics who use it are well educated, take the responsibility seriously, and have good judgment. Therefore, once the decision is made to use the paralytic, go forth with a rapid and aggressive approach. Do not waste time with premedications and defasciculating doses of paralytics. Make the decision, use the drug, and get your tube in (and then make sure the tube stays in the right place at all times). Know your airway equipment well, and problem-solve any difficulties that develop. Know succinylcholine well, and be prepared to treat side effects if they become a problem.

D. If the patient is combative before or after the procedure, you may use Droperidol (Inapsine) as a sedative. However, in some situations, e.g., respiratory failure due to CHF/pulmonary edema and severe burn cases, morphine sulfate would be a preferable sedative agent because of its additional analgesic and venodilation effects. Diazepam (Valium) is the preferred agent if the patient is in status epilepticus.

E. Always consider hypoxia as a possible cause of combativeness.

F. When possible, note and document neuro status/GCS prior to use of sux.

G. Always consider ED physician as a resource if you would like a consultation or direction.

H. A form on use of succinylcholine must be filled out by paramedic and turned in to EMS office with each use of the drug.

I. Succinylcholine must be wrapped in foil and replaced per department policy due to its short shelf life.

INTUBATION, STOMAL
SACRAMENTO, CA

Stomal Intubation

I. INDICATIONS:
Indications in patients with preexisting tracheostomy:
- A. Respiratory arrest
- B. Hypoventilation
- C. Loss of gag reflex
- D. Head injury requiring hyperventilation

II. EQUIPMENT:
- A. Endotracheal tube (5.5 mm and smaller to be cuffless)
  Premie to 12 years: appropriate size according to pediatric protocols
  Adults: 7.0 mm–8.5 mm
- B. Securing device (tape, twill, or endo-lock)
- C. Syringe 10 ml
- D. Suction apparatus
- E. Bag-valve mask with oxygen source
- F. End-tidal CO_2 detector

III. PROCEDURE:
- A. Assemble the equipment while continuing ventilation.

  1. Choose the tube size.

(NOTE: You may need to use a smaller size tube [6 mm or 7 mm] if the stoma is constricted.)

  2. Introduce the stylette, and be sure it stops ½″ short of the tube's end.
  3. Connect and check suction.

- B. Position patient.
- C. Insert the tube through the stoma.
- D. Advance the tube until the cuff is just inside the stoma. Remove the stylette if used, and insert air into the cuff to prevent an air leak.
- E. Ventilate and watch for chest rise. Listen for breath sounds over stomach (should not be heard) and bilateral lung sounds.
- F. Apply an end-tidal CO_2 detector on all patients with pulses, and observe for color change to beige after four (4) breaths through the detector.
- G. Note proper tube placement, and secure tube.
- H. Reevaluate the position of the tube after each move of the patient.

IV. SPECIAL NOTE:
- A. The ET tube does not need to be cut or modified in any way. Doing so may damage the tube and result in a cuff leak.

MORGAN THERAPEUTIC LENS
EUGENE/SPRINGFIELD, OR

I. Purpose:
Continuous irrigation of eye(s) with IV solution

II. Indications:
Removal of chemical splash from the eye, especially when the agent is caustic (*e.g.*, alkalis)

III. Precautions:

    A. Use only on an intact globe.

    B. Morgan lens can cause corneal abrasions, especially if irrigation solution runs dry and lens is left in eye.

    C. Check for allergies before use of proparacaine (Alcaine®).

IV. Procedure by standing order (EMT 3, 4):

    A. Insertion:

        1. Lie patient down on stretcher with the patient's head on towels and blue pad.

        2. Instill two drops of proparacaine in affected eye(s).

        3. Attach standard IV tubing (connected to 1000-cc bag of normal saline) to Morgan lens; flush tubing and wet lens.

        4. Have your patient look down; insert lens under upper lid.

        5. Now have patient look up; retract lower lid; drop lens in place.

        6. Maintain irrigation at steady flow.

        7. Monitor patient comfort, solution flow.

    B. Removal:

        1. Have patient look up; retract lower lid behind inferior border of the lens.

        2. Have patient look down; retract upper lid and remove lens.

V. Special Notes:

    A. Change IV solution bag or DC lens as soon as bag runs dry.

    B. Coach patient to avoid blinking with lens in place.

    C. If only one eye is being irrigated, tilt head to keep runoff from contaminated eye away from other eye.

    D. Do not use a discolored proparacaine solution.

NASOGASTRIC TUBE INSERTION
ANAHEIM, CA

Indications:

Decompression of gastric distention in adult and pediatric patients

Procedure:

- Prepare equipment:
    Premature infant—size 3½–5 fr
    Infant to child—size 8–10 fr
    Adolescents to adult—size 12–16 fr

    —NG tube
    —Water-soluble lubricant
    —12-ml syringe and cath-tip syringe
    —Tape

- Prepare patient:
    —Maintain patient supine with head in neutral or slightly flexed position.

- Determine length of tube for insertion:
    —Measure and mark from earlobe to tip of nose to bottom of sternum.

- Insertion:
    —Lubricate tip of NG tube.
    —Insert tube through nose as far as marked length.
    —May insert NG tube through the mouth as alternate method.

- Assess for placement:
    —Visualize mouth and hypopharynx for inappropriately coiled tube—remove if necessary.
    —Inject 6–10 ml air into stomach while auscultating over area.
    —Aspirate stomach contents with syringe.

- Tape tube to nose.
- Allow NG tube to drain via gravity:
    —If there is excessive gastric drainage, you may place end of tube in empty IV bag for collection.
    —Consider connecting NG to suction for prompt gastric decompression.
    —If NG interferes with ability to provide adequate BVM ventilations in pediatric patients, complete gastric decompression, and remove NG tube.

PNEUMATIC ANTISHOCK GARMENT
LAS VEGAS, NV

NOTE: This protocol may always be followed prior to telemetry physician orders.

INDICATIONS		PHYSICIAN'S ORDERS
I.	Shock—hypotension (systolic blood pressure of less than 90 mm Hg) **ONLY when the estimated transport time is in excess of 30 minutes**	NO
II.	Fractures of pelvis, hip, or femur	NO
III.	Tamponade of external or internal hemorrhage of the legs and/or abdomen	NO

Absolute Contraindications:

I. Pulmonary edema/cardiopulmonary insufficiency
II. Major intrathoracic trauma or bleeding—blunt or penetrating

Relative Contraindications:

I. Evisceration of abdominal organs
II. Third-trimester pregnancy
III. Impaled objects
IV. Application over open fractures with exposed bone ends

Equipment and Procedure:

As per PHTLS standards

Potential Complications:

I. Abdominal section inflation may:

    A.   Increase the risk of emesis and thus airway compromise.
    B.   Increase work of ventilation.

II. Overwork the heart, causing dysrhythmias or enlarging area of infarction.
III. Aggravate pulmonary edema (CHF or chest trauma).
IV. Increase intracranial pressure (CVA or head trauma).
V. Increase bleeding above the level of the garment.

Special Notes:

I. Record time the garment was inflated.
II. Deflation should not be attempted in the field unless inflation has clearly aggravated ventilatory difficulty or appearance of rales.

PASG CRITERIA
WICHITA, KS

Uses:

BLUNT-TRAUMA PATIENTS WHO:
1. Are in shock secondary to blood loss
2. Present in neurogenic shock
3. Require stabilization of pelvic and lower-extremity fractures
4. Are in cardiac arrest

Application Procedures:

1. Pants style
2. Open-Face tug style
3. Log-Roll style

NOTE: Do not apply in any manner that may compromise the spinal alignment in the trauma patient. The top of the abdominal portion should be just below the lower rib margin of the patient.

Pressurization Criteria:

Inflate for *ANY* of the following:
1. B/P below 90 mm Hg systolic
2. Signs of decreased tissue perfusion (*i.e.*, clammy, cool, cyanotic skin)
3. Signs of decreased cerebral perfusion (*i.e.*, restlessness, decreased LOC, dilated pupils)

NOTE: These criteria are *NOT* required for fracture stabilization.

Pressurization Procedure:

1. Inflate leg compartments simultaneously until velcro starts to slip, garment indents slightly, and release of safety valves or B/P reaches 100 mm HG systolic.
2. Reevaluate patient status.
3. Inflate abdominal compartment if systolic pressure remains below 100 mm Hg systolic.

Contraindications:

RELATIVE:
Head injury
Chest injury
Abdominal eviscerations
Pregnancy

ABSOLUTE:
Ruptured diaphragm
Pulmonary edema
Cardiogenic shock
Penetrating trauma

NOTE: ALWAYS KEEP THE PUMP WITH THE PANTS!! NEVER ALLOW ANYONE TO CUT THE PANTS!!

NOTE: PASGs are no longer used for medical-emergency hypotensive patients.

PERICARDIOCENTESIS
ST. PAUL, MN

I. Indications

For use on adult patients with suspected cardiac tamponade or pericardial effusion, causing life-threatening decrease in cardiac output.

II. Precautions

Pneumothorax or hemopneumopericardium may result from leaving needle open to air.

III. Technique
   A. Identify landmarks on patient (costal margin, xiphoid process).
   B. Prepare site. (Attempt to maintain sterility as much as possible.)
   C. Cleanse site with provodine iodine (Betadine).
   D. Use an 18-gauge cardiac needle attached to a 3-way stopcock and 50-cc syringe.
   E. Insert the needle at the xiphocostal angle approximately 45° to the chest.
   F. Advance the needle toward the left shoulder while applying a slight negative pressure on the syringe.
   G. As you advance the needle into the pericardial sac, you should feel a slight give. Begin to withdraw 50–100 cc of blood or fluid.
   H. Monitor patient for cardiac ectopy; watch to see if there is any improvement in the patient's hemodynamic status.
   I. The needle should be stabilized on the chest as you would stabilize any foreign body.

IV. Special Notes

Physician's order required for this procedure

PULSE OXIMETRY
SACRAMENTO, CA

I. Indications:
   A. Patients with suspected hypoxemia, *i.e.*, shortness-of-breath patients, patients with decreased sensorium, and trauma patients with injury to chest or upper airway

II. Precautions:
   A. Patients with fingernail polish or artificial fingernails disturb color discrimination.

   B. Low-flow status, hypothermia, or hypovolemia do not allow adequate pulsation to provide contrast with other tissue.
   C. CO-poisoning patients, smokers, and patients on certain drugs—notably, nitroglycerin–can produce inaccurate readings.
   D. Temperature should be between 60–105 degrees Fahrenheit and humidity between 15–90%.

III. EQUIPMENT:
   A. Approved service-provider specific-pulse oximeter

IV. PROCEDURE:
   A. BLS:

   1. ABCs/vital signs
   2. Oxygen
   3. Reassurance
   4. A.M.P.L.E.

   a. Including current history of smoking
   b. Specific medication history
   c. Possible history of CO_2 poisoning

   B. ALS:

   1. Confirm BLS findings; note changes.
   2. Application of pulse oximetry

   a. Turn on machine.
   b. Allow machine to calibrate self.
   c. Apply probe to finger.
   d. Allow machine to register saturation level.
   e. Record saturation percent and pulse rate.
   f. Verify pulse rate on machine with actual pulse.
   g. Monitor patients for a period of time, as percent of saturation can vary somewhat. Trending is important, and you would like to demonstrate decreased hypoxemia with patient interventions.
   h. Document percent of oxygen saturation every time vital signs are recorded.

V. INTERPRETATION:

A. Use pulse oximetry as an added tool for patient evaluation. TREAT THE PATIENT, not the data provided by this device. Contact the base hospital with any questions about pulse oximetry or percent of oxygen saturation.

B. Percent of oxygen saturation is only one aspect of your patient evaluation and must be combined with a total patient assessment to include history and physical exam.

C. In general normal saturation is 97–99%. Below 94%—suspect a respiratory compromise. 90% and below normally requires aggressive oxygen administration, ventilation via bag-valve mask, and possibly intubation. With interventions (*e.g.*, oxygen administration, intubation, chest decompression), you would hope to demonstrate an increase in oxygen saturation.

REVERT TO THE PROTOCOL FOR THE APPROPRIATE RESPIRATORY ASSESSMENTS AND CARE.

RECTAL DIAZEPAM ADMINISTRATION
PORTLAND, OR

Definition:

The placement of a soft, flexible catheter into the rectum for the purpose of administering diazepam (Valium).

Indication:

Treatment of status seizures in pediatric patients where IV access is unobtainable.

Procedure:

Diazepam solution (.5 mg/kg) can be deposited into the rectal lumen by using a male heparin-adapter plug attached to an IV catheter that is 4–6 cm (2″) in length.

A. Remove the flexible catheter from an IV needle that is the appropriate length.
B. Attach the flexible catheter to a male heparin-adapter plug.
C. Insert the diazepam syringe into the heparin-adapter plug.
D. Ensure that the needle attached to the diazepam syringe cannot advance through the flexible catheter and subsequently perforate the rectum.
E. Advance the flexible catheter 4–6 cm into the rectum, and administer the ordered dose.
F. Flush the plug and catheter with 2–3 cc of AIR after administering the diazepam. Flushing with fluid will dilute the medication.
G. Hold the buttocks together for 1–2 minutes to prevent any leakage of medication.

Precautions:

A. Do not force the catheter in. Catheter should advance with the little or no resistance.
B. There is a risk of respiratory depression with the administration of diazepam. The patient's airway should be observed closely for signs of respiratory depression.
C. This procedure may be performed en route to the hospital. It should not delay transport.

NOTE: IV administration of diazepam is the recommended route. Diazepam administration is by MRH order only. The condition of the rectal mucosa, the presence of fecal mass, and the metabolic status of the patient may affect absorption. It is recommended that you prepare all of your equipment in advance of the procedure.

SALINE INTRAVENOUS ACCESS LOCKS
NEW HAVEN, CT

Saline Intravenous Access Locks (Intermittent Infusion Device)

I. Purpose

    A. Paramedics establish intravenous access as part of routine paramedic care. Saline lock devices can maintain intravenous access while avoiding the risk of inadvertent rapid-fluid administration and the inconvenience of manipulating IV tubing and fluid bags while moving and handling patients.

II. Equipment

    A. Infusion adaptor device
    B. Vial of normal saline for injection
    C. Syringe with needle
    D. Alcohol wipe

III. Policy

    A. Candidates for saline locks:

        1. Patients who would have an intravenous placed to establish venous access prophylactically
        2. Patients who would have an intravenous placed to administer medication

    B. Candidates for conventional IV therapy with appropriate solutions and administration sets:

        1. Patients requiring volume resuscitation
        2. Patients requiring continuous drip infusion of medication
        3. Patients requiring cardiac or other resuscitation with frequent medications in sequence

    C. If, at any time, the patient's condition deteriorates and the paramedic feels a conventional IV is necessary or desirable, it may be established by disconnecting the infusion adaptor and attaching a conventional IV set, or if low fluid volume is adequate, by piggybacking a set into the injection port. If piggybacking is performed, the needle should not be larger than 18 g due to possible injection port coring with larger sizes.

IV. Procedure

    A. Establish intravenous access via over-the-needle catheter. Draw bloods per Sponsor Hospital guidelines.
    B. Draw up at least 2.5 cc of sterile saline for injection, and fill the injection port.
    C. Remove the injection adaptor cap if present, and attach adaptor (saline lock) to catheter hub. Rotate luer hub to lock.

D. Draw back on syringe to insure patency; then if patent, inject saline. WHILE MAINTAINING POSITIVE PRESSURE TO SYRINGE PLUNGER, WITHDRAW NEEDLE FROM PORT.

E. Secure intravenous device and port if not already done. Label IV site with needle size, initials of technician, and date and time of start.

F. To give medications, either in volume or via bolus, follow established procedure for medication delivery. Inject bolus medication via needle through the lock. Upon completion, flush the lock with at least 1 (one) cc of normal saline for injection.

G. Take special care to notify receiving facility staff of saline-lock start.

H. Document saline-lock start on EMSIRS run form.

SUBLINGUAL VENOUS PLEXUS MEDICATION ADMINISTRATION
SANTA ANA, CA

Indications:

- Administration of medications when no other route is available in critical adult and pediatric patients requiring the immediate administration of medications.
- Use limited to administration of:
  —Atropine
  —Epinephrine
  —Naloxone

Procedure:

- Prepare medication by aspirating the desired amount into a 3-ml syringe with a 25-gauge, ⅝-inch needle.
- Gently elevate tip of tongue:
  —Using 4 × 4 gauze pad, place index and middle fingers on top and thumb under tip of tongue.
  —Gently lift tongue upwards.

- Identify the soft plexus of veins lying just anterior to the base of tongue.
- Inject medication rapidly without aspirating.

NOTE: 3-ml maximum amount to be instilled into sublingual venous plexus (SLVP).

- Watch for complications such as bleeding or swelling.

TENSION PNEUMOTHORAX DECOMPRESSION PROCEDURE
LAS VEGAS, NV

NOTE: This protocol may be implemented prior to obtaining telemetry physician orders, if, in the attending paramedic's opinion, the patient's survival may be compromised by any delay caused by attempting to contact a telemetry physician.*

Indications:

Signs of a tension pneumothorax, which may include any or all of the following. Item #1 and one other must be present:

I. Progressive respiratory distress and/or *increased resistance to bagging*
II. Tracheal deviation
III. Jugular-vein distention
IV. Signs of shock, low BP with chest trauma present

Equipment and Procedure:

As per PHTLS standards

Site Location for Needle Decompression:

Second intercostal space at the midclavicular line on the affected side

Potential Complications:

I. Creation of a pneumothorax if not already present
II. Laceration of blood vessels and nerves
III. Laceration of the lung
IV. Infection from poor aseptic technique

Special Notes:

I. Individuals who have chronic pulmonary disease may have a spontaneous pneumothorax progress to a "tension" state.
II. Tension pneumothorax can be precipitated by occlusion of an open chest wound with a dressing.

VAGAL MANEUVERS
LAS VEGAS, NV

INDICATIONS	PHYSICIAN'S ORDER
Patients with symptomatic supraventricular tachycardia with adequate perfusion	NO

Contraindications:

I. If cardiac monitor is not available

II. If IV access has not been established

Equipment and Procedure:

As per ACLS standards

Approved Vagal Methods:

I. Valsalva maneuver

II. Head-down tilt with deep inspiration

III. Activation of the "diving reflex" by ice water facial immersion (unless ischemic heart disease is suspected)

IV. Carotid massage (only on patients under 40 years of age)

Potential Complications:

I. Possible ventricular asystole

II. Possible bradydysrhythmias

Policies

ABUSE OF CHILDREN AND THE ELDERLY
JACKSONVILLE, FL

The City of Jacksonville has established a child and elderly adult abuse and neglect policy as a condition of employment. This policy requires reporting of all known or suspected cases of abuse or neglect where such knowledge is the result of employment with the City of Jacksonville. Any employee who fails to report or prevents another employee from reporting any such case of abuse or who discloses confidential information relating to abuse cases or who makes a false report may be charged with a second-degree misdemeanor as provided by Florida state statutes. In addition, disciplinary action, including possible termination of employment, will be taken for nonadherence to this policy.

I. Suspicion of abuse:

    A. Treat related injuries.
    B. Transport all suspected cases.
    C. If transport is refused:

        1. Request police at scene.
        2. Stay with patient until police arrival.

II. Reporting abuse:

    A. Confirm suspicion with emergency department physician.
    B. Emergency department has protocols for disposition of suspected abuse cases.

CHILD/ADULT-ABUSE MANAGEMENT AND REPORTING
TAMPA, FL

EMS providers are required to report immediately to HRS Protective Services any child or elder whom you have reasonable cause to suspect has been abused or will be abused. Failure to do so is punishable as a civil violation. It is not enough to tell someone else of your suspicions. If a child is abused and unreported, there is a 50% chance that the child will be abused again and a 10% chance that the child will die from future abuse. Statistics on elder abuse are not readily available; this unfortunate phenomenon has more recently become reportable, and these data are just beginning to be collected.

Possible indicators of abuse include:

1. Injured child under two years of age, especially hot-water burns and fractures
2. Facial, mouth, or genital injuries
3. Multiplanar injuries (front and back, right and left), especially when not over bony prominences
4. Injuries of different age (new and old)
5. Poor nutrition, poor care
6. Delay in seeking treatment
7. Vague, inconsistent, or changing history
8. The comatose child, the child in shock, the child in arrest
9. An abandoned elder or child, unable to care for self

Treatment of Suspected Abuse in the Field

1. Suspect abuse. Keep your suspicions to yourself. Do not question or accuse the caretaker.
2. Protect the child/elder. Call the police if necessary.
3. Treat the injuries according to standard protocol.
4. Convey your impressions to the hospital staff.
5. Write a detailed descriptive report. This report will likely become a legal document. Do NOT make a diagnosis of abuse. Simply describe your findings in the chart, in detail.
6. Make a report. Call HRS Abuse Hotline (phone number **1-800-96ABUSE**), 24 hours a day. You will be protected by law from civil liability for making such a report.

AIR MEDICAL SERVICES
CHARLOTTE, NC

The flight service at Carolinas Medical Center (MedCenter Air) provides the use of two rotorcraft air ambulances—a Bell 206 Long Ranger and a larger Bell 222. Two registered nurses staff each flight. Additional personnel include the pilot and possibly a "third" person (physician, paramedic, respiratory therapist, *etc.*). Both helicopters are based at Carolinas Medical Center and operated by *Air Methods*.

The following protocol should be utilized when the flight service is requested:

Criteria for Activation

1. Priority-1 patient with the potential for > 20-minute transport time
2. Entrapped patients with the potential for > 10-minute extrication time
3. Multiple-casualty incident, only if priority-1-and/or-2 patients are triaged
4. Any patient whose mechanism of injury or primary assessment imparts the potential for sustaining multisystem organ damage such that early operative intervention may be lifesaving
5. Any medical or surgical patient whose condition has the potential for rapid deterioration
6. Any potentially unstable spinal injury
7. Any case where the location, time of day, traffic conditions, *etc.*, may cause a delay in transport time from the scene to the hospital

Personnel Requirements for Activation

1. Any first responder physically present on the scene of an accident or injury, after an initial patient assessment, may request the helicopter if he or she feels that the appropriate criteria have been met as stated above.
2. Any member of the responding MEDIC crew, either en route to the scene or after arrival
3. The operations supervisor or any administrative staff personnel

Personnel Requirements for Deactivation

1. After patient evaluation, the MEDIC crew chief, operations supervisor, or administrative staff personnel may cancel the helicopter response at any time.

Activation Procedure

1. After determining that the helicopter is needed, notify CMED. The flight-service dispatcher will be notified, as well as the most appropriate fire department, depending on location and availability. No other information is necessary at this time. You will soon be notified as to the status of the

helicopter, such as available and responding, available in ? time period, or unavailable (weather, mechanical, *etc.*).

2. Continue to provide patient care until such time as the helicopter arrives. Landing-zone designation, preparation, and notification are the responsibility of the responding fire department. If patient care activities are stable and time permits, evaluating the landing zone yourself is advisable. If the designated landing zone appears to be a dangerous threat to anyone on the ground or the flight team, express those concerns to the fire-incident commander. If resistance is met, contact CMED, explain the situation, and have CMED instruct the pilot not to land the helicopter. Continue to treat and transport the patient.

Proper Landing-Zone Criteria

GENERAL:

All landing zones should be on a solid and flat surface, clear of potentially loose debris, and located approximately 200 yards from the scene of the accident. There should be no obstacles or obstructions within the zone, such as trees, telephone/power poles, light poles, vehicles, landing zone personnel, *etc.*

DIMENSIONS:
Daytime hours: 60 × 60 foot area.
Nighttime hours: 100 × 100 foot area

Patient Preparation

1. The patient should be prepared as usual with the exception of the spine board. When spinal immobilization is necessary, a tapered spine board should be utilized.
2. The flight team may request patient information before arrival. This is to be done after the pilot has received his or her landing-zone information. The flight nurse will contact the paramedic for an update on EMS-5. It is very important to limit the presentation to only pertinent facts, such as airway problems, hemodynamic stability, head trauma, or major bone fractures.
3. Upon arrival, the flight team will approach the scene (if it is safe to do so) or ambulance and may request a patient report or begin their assessment. A mutual respect for each professional role is encouraged. Both paramedics and nurses should work as a team in order to maximize optimal patient care.
4. Equipment used on a patient may be substituted for the flight service's similar equipment. When this occurs, this particular equipment should be returned as soon as possible. This can be returned via the operations supervisor, logistics, *etc.*
5. If the patient has not been prepared for transport by the time the flight team arrives, the paramedic may wish to have the flight nurse(s) assist with this activity.
6. If the patient is prepared for transport and the helicopter has not landed, the paramedic may choose to transport and cancel the helicopter. This is perfectly acceptable. It should be kept in mind that when the helicopter arrives at the hospital, there is a delay until the patient arrives in the emergency depart-

ment. There is an approximate 3-minute cool-down period before the patient can be safely off-loaded ("cold unload"). Critical patients, however, are off-loaded immediately ("hot unload").

7. It should be kept in mind that the flight team has the authority to utilize paralytics for intubation purposes. When airway problems arise and intubation is unsuccessful, it may prove beneficial to wait several minutes until the flight team arrives so as to attempt intubation after the necessary drugs have been given. This is especially important for patients with suspected head trauma.

CERVICAL SPINE PRECAUTIONS
SAN FRANCISCO, CA

Adult and Pediatric Cervical Spine Precautions

In general, all patients with blunt trauma, head trauma, or axial spine trauma who meet trauma triage criteria require that cervical spine precautions be taken.

I. CERVICAL SPINE PRECAUTIONS MAY BE OMITTED WHEN ALL OF THE FOLLOWING CONDITIONS APPLY:

    A. Normal neurological exam

        1. Alert
        2. Fully oriented to person, place, time, and situation
        3. Normal sensory and motor function in extremities

    B. Absence of neck and spinal pain by patient report
    C. Absence of neck or spinal tenderness elicited on palpation
    D. No evidence of intoxication or impairment by a drug
    E. Normal vital signs
    F. Patient's age is between 14 and 55 years
    G. Absence of any major painful injury that could distract the patient's ability to appreciate pain
    H. No history of loss of consciousness

II. CERVICAL SPINE STABILIZATION WHEN APPLIED MUST INCLUDE:

    A. Rigid spineboard, similar transporting device
    B. Semirigid cervical collar
    C. Lateral neck rolls or approved stabilization device such as the Headbed®
    D. Tape across the forehead and collar
    E. Straps across patient's chest, abdomen, and legs to secure patient to device and prevent movement in any direction

CODE OF ETHICS
WICHITA, KS

Emergency Medical Technicians and Mobile Intensive Care Technicians employed by Sedgwick County Emergency Medical Service shall uphold the following:

The fundamental responsibility to conserve life, to alleviate suffering, to promote health, to do no harm, and to encourage the quality and equal availability of emergency medical care

Provide services based on human need, with respect for human dignity, unrestricted by consideration of nationality, race, creed, color, status, or ability to pay

Respect and hold in confidence all information of a confidential nature obtained in the course of professional work unless required by law to divulge such information

Maintain professional competence and demonstrate concern for the competence of other members of the Emergency Medical Services health-care team

Work harmoniously with and sustain confidence in EMT/MICT associates, and the nurses, the physicians, and other members of the Emergency Medical Services health-care team

Refuse to participate in unethical procedures and assume the responsibility to expose incompetence or unethical conduct of others to the appropriate authority in a proper and professional manner.

DETERMINATION OF DEATH
FREMONT, CA

1. GENERAL INFORMATION

1.1 First responders, EMTs, and EMT-Ps do not pronounce death but rather determine death based on predetermined criteria.

1.2 Field deaths not covered by this policy **require assessment by EMT-Ps and consultation with the base hospital physician** for determination of death.

1.3 First responders, EMTs, and EMT-Ps are not required to initiate resuscitative measures when death has been determined using the criteria outlined in this policy or the patient has a valid Alameda County "Do Not Attempt Resuscitation" form. If **any** doubt exists as to whether or not the patient meets criteria, begin CPR immediately.

1.4 Once CPR has been initiated, a first responder, EMT, or EMT-P **may not** discontinue CPR. Exceptions:

1.4.1 Patients meeting criteria to **Discontinue CPR** following assessment by EMT-Ps and consultation with the base physician (see "Discontinuation of CPR" policy)

1.5 Patients with **suspected hypothermia** require full BLS and ALS resuscitation.

1.6 EMT-Ps may contact the base hospital for a "determination of death" anytime support in the field is desired. To avoid confusion, clearly state the purpose for base contact as part of your initial report (*i.e.*, "This is a request to discontinue CPR for obvious death in the field").

1.7 Multicasualty incidents are an exception to this policy.

1.8 Children 14 years old and under are excluded from this policy unless ALS personnel make base contact for consultation with the base-hospital physician.

1.9 The local public-safety agency having jurisdiction will be responsible for the body once death has been determined. The body is to be left at the scene until a disposition has been made by the coroner's bureau. A dead body may not be moved or disturbed without authorization by the coroner's bureau.

2. DETERMINATION-OF-DEATH CRITERIA

2.1 Pulselessness (*determined at two (2) sites on the body—carotid and either radial or femoral*)

2.2 Apnea, **and**

2.3 One or more of the following:

2.3.1 Decomposition of body tissues

2.3.2 Total decapitation

2.3.3 Total incineration

2.3.4 Total separation or destruction of the heart or brain

2.3.5 Multiple signs of lifelessness—apnea, pulselessness, **and** the following:

2.3.5.1 First responders without semiautomatic defibrillators:
- Total body rigor

2.3.5.2 First responders/EMTs with semiautomatic defibrillators:
- Any degree of rigor
- A nonshockable rhythm, and
- Asystole on the monitor screen for one minute

2.3.5.3 EMT-Ps:
- Any degree of rigor; and,
- Asystole on the monitor screen for one minute (documented in at least two (2) leads)

3. **TRAUMA DEATHS**—A trauma victim who does not meet the "Determination of Death Criteria" listed above *may* be determined to be dead after consultation with the trauma base hospital physician if upon arrival of EMT-Ps personnel at the scene the following criteria are met:

3.1 Pulselessness (*determined at two (2) sites on the body—carotid and either radial or femoral*)

3.2 Apnea

3.3 Asystole (*one minute of documented asystole in two [2] leads*), **and**

3.3.1 blunt trauma arrest, or

3.3.2 Prolonged extrication time (*> 15 minutes*) where no resuscitative measures can be carried out prior to extrication
- An initial rhythm assessment is required followed by at least one reassessment after 15 minutes.

3.4 "*Trauma* Determination of Death" requires assessment by ALS personnel unless the patient meets "Determination of Death" criteria, #2 above.

3.5 EMT-Ps should make base contact early in the call. The patient may only be determined dead if the patient is in asystole upon arrival or meets the criteria in 3.3.2. If there is any concern regarding leaving the patient at the scene, begin resuscitation and transport.

4. **ACTIONS** (*once the patient has been determined to be dead*)

4.1 Immediately notify the appropriate public safety agency (if not done already), and remain on the scene until they arrive.

4.2 Complete patient care report form documenting the above criteria, and leave a copy with the patient for the coroner's office.

4.3 Rhythm documentation:

4.3.1 FRD/EMT[D]—AED audio cassette tape forwarded to the FRD base hospital

4.3.2 EMT-P—EKG rhythm strips attached to the PCR

4.4 Endotracheal tube placement may be verified by the EMT-P field supervisor or senior EMT-P for patients who are determined dead in the field. The Alameda County intubation form must be signed by the verifying EMT-P, confirming proper placement. Improperly placed tubes should be left in place and reported to the appropriate personnel.

4.5 See "Search for Donor Card" policy.

DETERMINATION OF DEATH
LAS VEGAS, NV

Prehospital Death Determination

Purpose:

To provide EMS personnel with guidelines to determine if a patient has expired and requires no further medical care or if resuscitation and transportation need to be initiated.

Definition:

Death can only be "officially" declared by the Clark County Coroner's Office or a physician, but certain patients encountered by EMS personnel, as well as laymen, are obviously dead.

Policy:

I. Patients encountered by EMS personnel in Clark County that appear to have expired will not be resuscitated or transported if *all* four (4) presumptive signs of death **AND** *at least one (1)* conclusive sign of death is identified.

II. The four (4) presumptive signs of death that **MUST** be present are:

    A. Unresponsiveness
    B. Apnea
    C. Pulselessness
    D. Fixed dilated pupils

III. In additional to the four (4) presumptive signs of death, *at least one (1)* of the listed signs of death that **MUST** be present. They are:

    A. Lividity of any degree and/or generalized cyanosis
    B. Rigor mortis of any degree
    C. Damage or destruction of the body incompatible with life
    D. Body decomposition
    E. No electrical activity
    F. Arrest from primary brain injury or with no brain-stem reflexes; arrest from penetrating head or neck injury; arrest from blunt multiple injury
    G. Penetrating or blunt injury to torso

IV. When in doubt whether to attempt resuscitation, personnel are encouraged to consult with an emergency department physician via the EMS Communication Network. Personnel in doubt should start resuscitation and transport the patient.

V. Once it has been determined that the patient has expired and resuscitation will not be attempted, cover the body with a sheet or other suitable item. Immediately notify the appropriate authority. **DO NOT** remove any property from the body or the scene for any purpose.

VI. Resuscitation that is started in the field by EMS personnel **CAN NOT** be discontinued without a physician order. EMS personnel are not obligated to continue resuscitation efforts that have been started inappropriately by other persons at the scene; this includes telephone CPR initiated by emergency medical dispatchers.

VII. **NEVER** leave a body unattended, if possible. Once a responsible person (*i.e.*, coroner's investigator, police, security, or family member) is present at the scene, you may be excused.

VIII. **NEVER** transport/move a body without permission from the coroner's office, except for assessment or its protection.

DETERMINATION OF DEATH
TAMPA, FL

Blunt-Trauma Codes/Determination of Death

1. The outcome of patients who suffer cardiorespiratory arrest from blunt trauma is uniformly poor. These patients do not benefit from further intervention.
2. Any victim of blunt trauma who presents meeting criteria for blunt-trauma code can be assumed to have sustained a terminal injury. No further resuscitative measures are necessary. Any BLS intervention in progress may be stopped.
3. Criteria for blunt trauma code:

    a. Present history of blunt trauma
    b. Pulseless
    c. Apneic
    d. No palpable blood pressure
    e. No heart sounds OR no electrical activity on monitor (asystole) or wide-complex ventricular rhythm with rate less than 40/minute (agonal rhythm)

4. Documentation of the run report must include a rhythm strip unless obtaining this strip is waived in preference for delivering care at the same scene to other victims of the blunt trauma. In the instance of one victim only, a rhythm strip will be used as part of the criteria for blunt trauma code and will be attached to the chart.
5. Documentation of the run report must specifically address the above criteria.
6. Any victim of blunt trauma who in the presence of advanced life support (EMT-P) deteriorates to meet the criteria for blunt-trauma code, and in whom adequate airway control and ventilation have been accomplished, has sustained a terminal injury. No further resuscitative measures are necessary.
7. A copy of the run report must be left at the scene with the deceased.
8. All instances of declaration of death in the field will be immediately communicated to the medical director or to the 519 physician on duty. These charts will also be flagged for quality-management review.
9. The paramedic may decide to continue resuscitative efforts for any reason, including scene safety, and will then transport expediently to the nearest appropriate facility.

DO NOT RESUSCITATE (DNR)
SACRAMENTO, CA

I. INTENT:

A. To establish criteria for emergency medical technicians in Sacramento County to determine appropriateness of either:

   1. Withholding resuscitative measure, or

   2. Utilizing direct medical control for pronouncement of victims of cardiac arrest while in the prehospital setting

II. AUTHORITY:

Health and Safety Code, Division 2.5, Section 1798

III. DEFINITION:

A. Emergency medical technician (EMT) shall apply to EMT-Is and EMT-Ps.

B. "Do not resuscitate (DNR)" means no chest compressions, no defibrillation, no assisted ventilation, no endotracheal intubation, and no cardiotonic medications. This does not exclude treatment for airway obstruction, pain, dyspnea, or major hemorrhage.

C. DNR Medallion: MedicAlert® medallion which states "do not resuscitate—EMS" (or similar medallion as approved by the EMS Authority)

D. Partial DNR orders are not acceptable.

IV. PROCEDURE:

A. All patients with absent vital signs who do not meet the "determination-of-death criteria" shall be resuscitated unless the EMT is presented with:

   1. A written, signed order in the patient's medical record

   2. A completed Prehospital DNR Request Form stating "do not resuscitate", "No Code," or "No CPR"

   3. A written order stating "Do not resuscitate," "No code," or "No CPR," signed by a physician, with the patient's name and the date the order was signed

   4. The patient is wearing a DNR medallion.

B. An EMT may discontinue resuscitation after the resuscitation was instituted under the following:

   1. A written, signed order in the patient's medical record

   2. A completed Prehospital DNR Request Form stating "Do not resuscitate," "No code," or "No CPR"

   3. A written order stating, "Do not resuscitate," "No code," or "No CPR," signed by a physician, with the patient's name and the date the order was signed

   4. The patient is wearing a DNR medallion.

C. If the patient is conscious and states he/she wishes resuscitative measures, the DNR order shall be ignored.

D. The presence of a DNR order, the physician's name signing the order, and the date of the order are to be documented on the Patient Care Record (EMS form).

E. The DNR form (original or copy), DNR medallion, or a copy of the valid DNR order from the patient's medical record shall be taken with the patient.

F. If there are any questions, utilize direct medical control.

G. In the event the patient expires en route, continue to the destination hospital.

V. REFERENCES:

A. California Prehospital Do Not Resuscitate Guidelines Program and Materials (a cooperative program between the California EMS Authority, CMA, and MedicAlert®)

B. EMS Authority Guidelines for EMS Personnel regarding DNR, Directive Number 111, dated March 1993

Prehospital Do Not Resuscitate (DNR) Form

An Advance Request to Limit the Scope of Emergency Medical Care.

I,_____ request limited emergency care as herein described.
(Print patient's name.)

I understand DNR means that if my heart stops beating or if I stop breathing, no medical procedure to restart breathing or heart functioning will be instituted.

I understand this decision will **not** prevent me from obtaining other emergency medical care by prehospital emergency medical care personnel and/or medical care directed by a physician prior to my death.

I understand I may revoke this directive at any time by destroying this form and removing any "DNR" medallions.

I give permission for this information to be given to the prehospital emergency care personnel, doctors, nurses or other health personnel as necessary to implement this directive.

I hereby agree to the "Do Not Resuscitate" (DNR) order.

_____   _____
Patient/Surrogate Signature   Date

_____
Surrogate's Relationship to Patient

I affirm that this patient/surrogate is making an informed decision and that this directive is the expressed wish of the patient/surrogate. A copy of this form is in the patient's permanent medical record.

In the event of cardiac or respiratory arrest, no chest compressions, assisted ventilations, intubation, defibrillation, or cardiotonic medications are to be initiated.

_____   _____
Physician Signature   Date

_____   _____
Print Name   Telephone

_____
Address

---

*THIS FORM WILL NOT BE ACCEPTED IF IT HAS
BEEN AMENDED OR ALTERED IN ANY WAY.*

DO NOT RESUSCITATE (DNR)
ALBUQUERQUE, NM

DNR Protocol

Designation of Condition:

If the patient has a DNR order, a living will, or an advanced medical directive, the specifics of the document will be followed and care will be administered as judged appropriate by the paramedic.

- Contact MCEP
- At the scene of a cardiac arrest:
- While initiating basic life support, ask if the patient has a "living will" or "do not resuscitate" (DNR) form.
- If the patient does not have a living will or a DNR form that prohibits ACLS intervention in the event of cardiac arrest, begin the following:
  - Full ALS resuscitation efforts. If the patient remains in cardiac arrest after completion of ACLS algorithms, resuscitation may be terminated *after* MCEP contact. The scene will then be considered an unattended death/ crime scene until law enforcement and/or personnel from the Office of the Medical Investigator (OMI) arrive at the scene.

EMS COMMUNICATIONS POLICY
LAS VEGAS, NV

When EMS communication with a telemetry physician is required to request orders or report on patient status, the following EMS communications policy is to be followed:

I. *Ambulance Identification*

    A. Attendant/vehicle identification and location, *e.g.*, "Paramedic Jones on Rescue 10 at Rancho and Sahara; in the patient's home with approximately 20 minutes ETA; en route with a 7-minute ETA."

    B. Patient information, *i.e.*, number, age, sex

    C. Status or code, *i.e.*, cardiac arrest, moderate distress, critical trauma

    D. Break: Ask "Do you copy?"

Example:

"St. Luke's Hospital, this is Paramedic West on Medic 101. We're at a private home approximately 15 minutes from your location with a 68-year-old female who is in severe discomfort. Do you copy?"

II. *History*

    A. Basic problem or chief complaint, *e.g.*, auto accident, syncope, chest pain

    B. Pertinent associated symptoms, *e.g.*, vomiting blood, shortness of breath, dizziness

    C. Time course, *e.g.*, last two days, since last night, approximately 15 minutes ago

    D. Past history (only if pertinent), *e.g.*, similar problems in the past, pertinent medications

Example:

"This patient slipped and fell while getting out of the shower about 1½ hours ago. She complains of severe pain in the right hip area. She has no prior falls, takes no meds, and has no allergies."

III. *Objective Findings*

    A. General status: degree of discomfort, minor injuries, shock

    B. Level of responsiveness: responsive/nonresponsive; appropriate/inappropriate

    C. Vital signs, *e.g.*, B/P, pulse, respirations, skin signs, monitor pattern, if appropriate

NOTE: When communicating pulse rate, also communicate the origin, *e.g.*, radial pulse, monitor shows a rate of _____.

D. Pertinent localized findings, *e.g.*, lacerations, broken bones, areas of pain, neuro exam, if appropriate. Give only as much detail as necessary to direct treatment en route and prepare the ER for the patient.

E. Working impression of patient's problem

Example:

"We find the patient to be conscious but somewhat confused. She complains of severe pain in her right hip. The vital signs are: radial pulse of 110, B/P of 100/72, respirations of 20 with clear breath sounds bilaterally; skin is slightly cool and moist; monitor shows a normal sinus rhythm. There is some swelling and discoloration of the right hip; the leg is shortened and foot externally rotated. We suspect a hip (femur) fracture with possible early signs of shock."

IV. *Treatment*

A. In progress; *e.g.*, O_2, defibrillation, spinal/extremity immobilization, IVs/medications (as permitted by statute or regulations)

B. Requests: specific procedure/drug request. This may be a request to use a specific protocol.

Example:

"We have the patient on flush O_2, and a traction splint has been applied with some pain relief. Distal pulses, motor and sensory function are intact. Request permission to start an IV of normal saline and give a fluid challenge of 250 ccs; also request orders for pain medication. Copy order for IV of normal saline with 250-cc fluid challenge and morphine in 2-mg increments to maximum of 10 mg titrated for pain relief. We'll monitor vitals and have Narcan ready, if needed."

V. *Estimated Time of Arrival*

A. Identify estimated time of arrival at emergency department.

B. Indicate special circumstances that may delay transports, *e.g.*, extrication, on the 10th floor, in back bedroom of trailer.

Example:

"We have an ETA of 15 to 20 minutes. We have to carry the patient down three flights of stairs due to a broken elevator, which may cause some delay."

VI. *Special Notes*

A. Be as concise and accurate as possible. Radio reports should rarely take more than one or two minutes per patient.

B. Outstanding objective findings, *e.g.*, critical vital signs (gunshot wound to the chest) may take precedence over history and need to be reported first.

INFECTIOUS/COMMUNICABLE DISEASE PROTOCOL
DENVER, CO

Field personnel occasionally come into contact with communicable diseases. It is important that a protocol is followed so that the appropriate persons are notified. Not all diseases require immediate treatment; however, early awareness will assist those involved in taking any necessary precautions.

Contamination by infectious diseases may be minor or serious. Field personnel should take precautions to avoid unnecessary exposure. When dealing with a suspected contagious patient, attempt to avoid direct contact with the patient's blood, sputum, emesis, urine, or feces. The provider should wear disposable latex or vinyl gloves as an added precaution. *Routine practice of good hand washing and equipment cleaning may help decrease the incidence of contamination.*

The following guidelines have been provided for reference. Follow your individual agency infectious-disease-exposure policy and procedure.

A. A person with significant exposure shall report the incident to the designated infection control officer of his/her agency.
B. Agency policy, developed in conjunction with the physician advisor, will dictate procedure with regard to screening, follow-up testing, prophylaxis, and/or treatment.
C. Exposed prehospital care personnel may be counseled and treated according to the following guidelines:

INFECTION/DISEASE	MEANS OF EXPOSURE	FOLLOW-UP AFTER EXPOSURE
AIDS	Intimate contact with infected person .Contact with blood/body fluids of infected person. Needle sticks. Presence in room without contact does not constitute exposure.	Patient may be known HIV positive. Testing patient for antibodies to the HIV virus requires consent. Post mortem samples may be submitted but may not be acceptable to the testing lab. Turn around on testing is 7–10 days. Current CDC and OSHA recommendations suggest personnel with exposure to body fluids be tested within the week of exposure, and 6 weeks, 3 months, and 6 months following exposure. Testing requires consent. Results are confidential. No prophylactic treatment is known or recommended for positive HIVAB. OSHA recommends that AZT prophylaxis be considered.

INFECTION/DISEASE	MEANS OF EXPOSURE	FOLLOW-UP AFTER EXPOSURE
HEPATITIS B	Needle stick, contact with blood/body fluids of infected person	Patient should be tested for presence of Australian antigen (HAA) (also known as hepatitis B surface antigen). *If positive*, those exposed should receive hepatitis B immuno globulin (HBIG) as soon as possible postexposure and definitely within seven days. Exposure to known hepatitis B carriers require the same treatment. Postmortem blood sample may be submitted but may not be acceptable to the lab. CDC and OSHA expect all field personnel to have hepatitis B vaccination. If an individual is not vaccinated, CDC and OSHA recommend that the hepatitis B vaccine be initiated with HBIG treatment.
HEPATITIS A	Contact with blood, emesis, or feces of infected person	Exposed personnel may receive injection of gamma globulin if diagnosis is confirmed. Confirmation based on clinical and laboratory analysis.
HEPATITIS C (NON A, NON B)	Policy the same as hepatitis B	CDC and OSHA recommend consideration of hepatitis C screening and ISG administration.

NOTE: Documented exposure to patient suspected of having hepatitis and not available for blood testing may warrant administration of both gamma globulin and HBIG if patient is a member of a high risk group. Incident should be discussed with the designated infection control officer and your physician advisor.

TUBERCULOSIS TB	Contact with the infected person	Decision to treat based on skin testing of individual. Intermediate PPD administered currently and 3 months later. Any positive test suggests need for therapy. Follow-up, including medication (INH) and care, is provided free through the Denver TB clinic.

INFECTION/DISEASE	MEANS OF EXPOSURE	FOLLOW-UP AFTER EXPOSURE
HERPES ZOSTER (Shingles)	Same as chickenpox	
CHICKENPOX (Varicella)	Contact with respiratory and/or (Varicella) lesion secretions	Susceptible persons are considered to be contagious during the incubation period, the 10th–21st day after exposure. If disease acquired, they are considered to be contagious until all lesions are crusted. A titer may be obtained to determine immune status.
MEASLES (Rubeola or rubella)	Direct or droplet contact with respiratory secretions	Susceptible persons are considered to be contagious during the incubation period, the 5th–21st day after exposure. If disease acquired, they are considered to be contagious until 7 days after rash appears. A titer may be obtained to determine immune status. Vaccine recommended within the first 72 hours after known exposure. Immunization is recommended.
MUMPS	Direct or droplet contact with respiratory secretions	Susceptible persons are considered to be contagious during the incubation period, the 12th–21st day after exposure. If disease acquired, they are considered contagious for 9 days following onset of symptoms. A titer may be obtained to determine immune status. Immunization is recommended.
VIRAL MENINGITIS	Contact with feces	No specific recommendation
BACTERIAL MENINGITIS	Direct or droplet contact with respiratory secretions	Individual cases need to be assessed. Recommendation will be made based on hospital review and communicated to the physician advisor and the designated infection control officer of the agency.

INFECTION/DISEASE	MEANS OF EXPOSURE	FOLLOW-UP AFTER EXPOSURE
STREPTO-COCCAL DISEASE	Direct or droplet contact with secretions	If exposed individual develops a sore throat, culture should be done. If disease acquired, he or she is considered contagious until adequate therapy has been received (24 hours) or until strep infection has been ruled out.
SYPHILIS	Contact with blood or lesion secretions	Treatment is based on laboratory testing and presentation of symptoms. Prophylactic treatment may be considered. Testing should be done soon after exposure and repeated in 3 months.
GONORRHEA	Contact with infective discharge	No prophylactic treatment is recommended unless S/S present.
HERPES	Direct contact with exudative lesions. (Mucous-membrane contact.)	No Prophylactic treatment is recommended.
SCABIES	Transfer of parasites is by direct skin-to-skin contact and to a limited extent from undergarments or bedclothes of infected person.	Treatment based on presentation of symptoms after consult with ED physician

NOTE: All personnel must report incidents to the designated infection control officer of their agency. All personnel should be advised to consult with their private physician as well.

All health-care personnel should always practice good hygiene before, during, and after delivering patient care. Each patient contact should be considered to be a potential source of infection.

INTERHOSPITAL TRANSFER
COLORADO SPRINGS, CO

Interhospital patient transfers on an emergency basis are commonly initiated when definitive diagnostic or therapeutic needs of a patient are beyond the capacity of one hospital. The patient is potentially unstable, and medical treatment must be continued and possibly even initiated en route. Written guidelines permit orderly transfer of patients with appropriate continuity of care. COBRA has mandated such policies be established by each hospital. The following is a suggested protocol:

A. All patients should be stabilized as much as possible before transfer.

B. Paramedics or EMTs must receive an adequate summary of the patient's condition, current treatment, possible complications, and other pertinent medical information.

C. Treatment orders should be given to the ambulance personnel. These orders should be in writing. Orders given by direct verbal order from the doctor who is initiating the transfer must be recorded immediately and signed prior to transport.

D. Any patient sick enough for emergency transfer must have at least one IV in place prior to transfer. Orders for IV composition and rate should be provided.

E. Transfer papers (summary, lab work, X-rays, *etc.*) should be given to the ambulance personnel, not to the family or friends.

F. The receiving physician must be contacted by the transferring physician prior to transfer. The base physician may also need to be contacted so that appropriate radio control of the ambulance en route is assured.

G. The receiving hospital, physician, and nursing personnel must be notified prior to initiation of transfer to assure adequate space and the ability to care for this patient.

H. The personnel and equipment used to transfer a patient should be appropriate to the treatment needed or anticipated during transfer. EMTs who are not familiar with IVs should not handle emergency transfers. Paramedics should be utilized if any advanced resuscitation or treatment is anticipated. In specialized fields not ordinarily handled by paramedics (*e.g.*, obstetrics, high-risk newborns), appropriately trained personnel (*e.g.*, nurses, physicians, and/or respiratory therapists) should accompany the patient.

In order to maintain these standards, it may be appropriate for the receiving hospital to send an ambulance with more specifically trained personnel to transfer the patient. This is particularly true in the case of newborns but has also been shown to be effective in other critically ill or injured patients.

INTERHOSPITAL TRANSFER MEDICATIONS
CHARLOTTE, NC

The following medications are permitted for use during interhospital transfers. Medication orders that are communicated for patients undergoing an interhospital transport shall be followed as long as those orders are within the paramedic's level of training. If possible, the transferring physician should sign the orders. If there is any question as to the validity or appropriateness of any such order, communication may be established with either the transferring physician or medical control as stated in the On-Scene Physician Protocol. (Special Situations 4.)

1. All antibiotics
2. Whole blood or packed red blood cells
3. Any blood-component therapy, such as fresh frozen plasma, factor-8 concentrate, cryoprecipitate, platelets, *etc.*
4. Electrolytes or other additives mixed in IV solution, such as potassium, magnesium, calcium, phosphate, *etc.*
5. Nitroglycerin drips
6. Lidocaine drips
7. Heparin drips
8. Vasopressor drips
9. Thrombolytic agents, such as streptokinase, urokinase, tissue plasminogen activator (TPA), *etc.*

IV FLUID THERAPY
DALLAS, TX

Definition:

There are two types of solutions available on the ambulance: D_5W *and Ringer's lactate.*

When initiating an IV on the following types of patients, D_5W TKO should be used:

1. Chest pain
2. Any cardiac symptoms
3. Emphysema/bronchitis
4. Congestive heart failure
5. *Any* indication of pulmonary edema
6. Hypertension (except preeclampsia and eclampsia)
7. Arrhythmias
8. Near-drowning

When initiating an IV on the following types of patients, Ringer's lactate should be used:

1. All CPRs
2. Trauma of any type
3. Allergic reactions
4. Abdominal pain
5. Hypoglycemia *or* hyperglycemia
6. Gastrointestinal bleeding
7. Burns
8. Heat exhaustion
9. Infection or septic shock
10. Excessive vomiting and/or diarrhea
11. Excessive vaginal bleeding
12. Obstetrical patients
13. Any pediatric patient
14. Asthma
15. Unconscious patient/alterations in LOC
16. Overdose
17. Stroke
18. Alcohol emergency
19. Seizures
20. Drowning

This list should not be considered to be all-inclusive, and other situations may require initiation of an IV.

MCI PLAN (A-13)
WASHINGTON, DC

Any medical emergency that overwhelms the resources of the EMS Bureau is deemed an MCI. For DCFEMS, MCI is defined as follows:

A. Multiple-casualty incident—6–12 patients
B. Mass-casualty incident—13 or more patients

To facilitate the implementation of the MCI plan and to ensure that all responding units are aware that the MCI plan is in effect, the communications section will advise responding units that the plan is in operation.

A. Fire units will operate on fire channel 2.
B. EMSB units will operate on EMS channel 2.

All DC hospitals will be notified of a mass-casualty incident. During a multiple-casualty incident only the hospitals closest to the incident will be notified, as communications deems appropriate. Communications will poll the hospitals as to the number of patients they can receive from the incident. This information will then be recorded on the "MCI Hospital Status Chart." (See attachment 1.) Next, this information will be forwarded to:

A. The transportation officer
B. In the event a transportation officer has not been established, the information will be forwarded to the EMS control officer.

After it has been established which hospitals will receive patients, communications will notify the remaining hospitals that:

A. They are not expected to receive patients
B. An MCI still exists, and they may be called upon to receive patients as the situation changes

As soon as all patients are transported, the EMS control officer will notify the incident commander. Communications will then make all hospitals aware that the incident is concluded.

I. Command and Operational Structure
   DCFEMSD will utilize the Incident Command System (ICS) while operating at an MCI. The following will only represent the rescue, EMS, and staging sectors of the ICS. (See diagram A.)

   A. First arriving unit

      1. Survey, size up, and evaluate the incident.
      2. Confirm incident location and type with communications.
      3. Establish command and staging areas.
      4. Request additional help as needed.
      5. Begin triage procedures.

   After a command post has been established, all requests for additional assistance will go through the incident commander.

B. EMS control-officer responsibilities

  1. Overall EMS operations at an incident
  2. Appoints EMS sectors
  3. Notifies the incident commander as to the needs of the EMS sector
  4. Triage officer, transportation officer, treatment officer, disposition sector, EMS communications officer, and senior physician all report to the EMS control officer.

C. Triage-officer responsibilities

  1. Management of victims where they are found at the incident site
  2. Sorting and moving victims to the treatment or transportation areas
  3. Ensurance of coordination between extrication teams and patient-care provider to provide appropriate care for entrapped victims

D. Treatment-officer responsibilities

  1. Establish treatment sectors (*i.e.*, red, yellow, green, and black areas)
  2. Patient care and triage decisions of patients in the treatment areas

E. Transport-officer responsibilities

  1. Arranging appropriate transport vehicles (BLSU, ALSU, helicopter, *etc.*) for patients forwarded to him for transport
  2. Responsible for logging all transport information (see appendix 2). In a large MCI a disposition area may be established to handle transportation information

F. EMS communication-officer responsibilities

  1. Keeping the transport officer updated on hospital availability
  2. Relaying all information to and from medical control for requests not covered by protocol

G. EMS resource-sector responsibility—maintaining sufficient supplies and equipment at the staging area.

H. Staging-officer responsibilities

  1. Maintaining sufficient units and equipment
  2. Dispatching units to the transport area as they are requested

I. Rescue sector—If the situation precludes placing EMS personnel in dangerous conditions, the rescue squad OIC will assume the role of triage officer until the area is deemed safe. After scene safety has been assured, the EMS control officer will designate a triage officer to assume command of triage.

II. Triage Plan

The first-arriving EMS unit sets the stage for the MCI operation. By placing a rapid triage plan in effect, utilizing triage ribbon, the providers can rapidly identify patients needing treatment and/or transport in order. Upon entering the area, triage patients as you find them. All patients are to be tagged with ribbon.

A. Red ribbon—Patients with the following findings will be triaged red:

    1. Airway or respiratory compromise
    2. Second and/or third-degree burns, 20% TBSA or greater, who are hemodynamically unstable
    3. Uncontrollable hemorrhage
    4. Open-chest or abdominal wounds
    5. Shock
    6. Severe head injuries
    7. Cardiac problems

B. Yellow ribbons—Patients with the following findings will be triaged yellow:

    1. Second and/or third-degree burns, 20% TBSA or greater, who are hemodynamically stable
    2. Multiple long-bone fractures
    3. Spinal-cord injuries
    4. Uncomplicated head injuries

C. Green ribbons—Patients with the following findings will be triaged green:

    1. Minor fractures and wounds
    2. Burns, less than 20% TBSA, who are hemodynamically stable

NOTE: Patients tagged green are to be directed to a predetermined area.

D. Black ribbons—Patient with the following findings will be triaged black:

    1. Patients who are presumed dead by protocol
    2. Patients who have injuries so severe that they are not expected to survive

NOTE: Patients tagged black are not to be moved until MPD has given permission. This does not mean you can't rearrange these victims for means of entrance or egress.

E. After patients are triaged, they can be moved to the appropriate areas:

    1. Multiple-casualty incident—transport area
    2. Mass-casualty incident—treatment area

F. After patients are moved to the transport (multiple) or treatment (mass) area, triage tags are to be attached and completed.

III. Manpower
Manpower is the greatest resource at an MCI. Care must be exercised not to overwork personnel. It is recommended that when personnel are assigned to an area, they should not be reassigned to other sectors or responsibilities.

A. Stretcher bearers—two for every patient triaged as red or yellow. One for every patient triaged as green.

Example:

5 red, 6 yellow, 7 green
Stretcher bearers—22
Ambulatory assistants—7
Total personnel—29

  B. The treatment area must have sufficient EMS personnel to treat and attach triage tags to the patients. The situation must be closely monitored by the treatment-sector officer. Requests for additional personnel must be made promptly to ensure adequate available manpower.

IV. Identification of Sectors and Personnel

  A. Treatment areas will have color-coordinating flags located at each sector.
  B. Sector officers will wear an orange vest with the appropriate title attached with reflective scotch light letters.

V. Special Notes

  A. The purpose of the incident is to move all patients as rapidly as possible to definitive care, not from sector to sector.
  B. Communication with receiving facilities by transport units will not be necessary. Receiving facilities will be expecting incoming patients via the EMS communications officer.

MEDICAL PERSONNEL ON THE SCENE
FREMONT, CA

1. **MEDICAL PERSONNEL ON THE SCENE** *(nonphysician)*—If a bystander at an emergency scene identifies himself or herself as a **medical person**, other than a physician, the first responder or EMT-P should:

   1.1 Inform the individual that he or she may **assist the emergency response team** and/or offer suggestions but may not assume medical management for the patient.

   1.2 Maintain overall scene management.

2. **PHYSICIAN ON THE SCENE**—If a bystander at an emergency scene identifies himself or herself as a **physician**:

   2.1 The first responder shall yield medical management to the physician until the arrival of ALS.

   2.2 The EMT-Ps:

   2.2.1 Shall give the physician a *"Note to Physicians on Involvement with EMT-IIs and EMT-Ps"* card *(available at the EMS Office)*.

   2.2.2 Shall determine which option the physician has chosen.

STATE OF CALIFORNIA CMA CALIFORNIA MEDICAL ASSOCIATION	ENDORSED ALTERNATIVES FOR PHYSICIAN INVOLVEMENT
NOTE TO PHYSICIAN ON INVOLVEMENT WITH EMT-IIs and EMT-Ps PARAMEDIC)	After identifying yourself by name as a physician licensed in the State of California, and, if requested, showing proof of identity, you may choose to do one of the following:
A life support team [EMT-II or EMT-P (Paramedic)] operates under standard policies and procedures developed by the local EMS agency and approved by their Medical Director under the Authority of Division 2.5 of the California Health and Safety Code. The drugs they carry and procedures they can do are restricted by law and local policy.	1. Offer your assistance with another pair of eyes, hands, or suggestions, but let the life support team remain under base hospital control; or,
If you want to assist, this can only be done through one of the alternatives listed on the back of this card. These alternatives have been endorsed by CMA, State EMS Authority, CCLHO, and BMQA.	2. Request to talk to the base station physician and directly offer your medical advice and assistance; or,
Assistance rendered in the endorsed fashion, without compensation, is covered by the protection of the "Good Samaritan Code" (see Business and Professions Code, Sections 2144, 2395–2398 and Health and Safety Code, Section 1799.104).	3. Take total responsibility for the care given by the life support team and physically accompany the patient until the patient arrives at a hospital and responsibility is assumed by the receiving physician. In addition, you must sign for all instructions given in accordance with local policy and procedure. (Whenever possible, remain in contact with the base station physician.)
(over)	(REV.7/88) 88 49638 Provided by the Emergency Medical Services Authority

---

3. **OPTION #1**—*If the physician on the scene desires option #1:*

   3.1 The physician should assist the paramedic team or offer suggestions but allow the paramedics to provide medical treatment according to county protocol.

4. **OPTION #2 or OPTION #3**—*If the physician on the scene desires option #2 or #3:*

   4.1 The EMT-Ps should ask to see the physician's medical license unless the physician is known to them, contact the base hospital physician, and have the physician on scene speak directly with the base hospital physician.

5. **BASE HOSPITAL PHYSICIAN RESPONSIBILITY**—After speaking to the physician on scene, the base hospital physician should evaluate the situation and decide which of the available options is in the best interests of the patient. These options include:

   5.1 Retaining medical control and requesting the physician on scene to assist the paramedics and/or offer suggestions only (*option #1*); or

   5.2 Retaining medical control but considering suggestions offered by the physician on scene (*option #2*); or

   5.3 Delegating medical control to the physician on scene (*option #3*).

6. **EMT-P RESPONSIBILITY**

   6.1 Options #1 or #2:

   6.1.1 Maintaining medical control of the patient and providing medical treatment according to county protocol

   6.2 Option #3:

   6.2.1 ALS equipment and supplies should be made available to the physician. Offer assistance as needed.

   6.2.2 Ensure that the physician goes in the ambulance with the patient to the receiving hospital.

   6.2.3 Document **all** care rendered to the patient on the PCR, and ensure that the physician signs for all instructions and medical care given.

   6.2.4 If appropriate, maintain communication with the base hospital or recontact if any problems arise.

7. An EMS Unusual Occurrence Form shall be completed:

   7.1 On any physician or medical personnel on scene calls if there was a problem associated with care rendered.

   7.2 For physician on scene call if option #3 was chosen (EMT-Ps only).

NEW-PROCEDURE/PRODUCT-TRIAL PROTOCOL
NEW HAVEN, CT

Purpose:

To provide an organized system approach to suggestions from EMS coordinators, medical advisors, or field personnel for new procedures and products in a timely fashion.

1. Suggestions for new procedures, product trials, or other requests not part of current standing operating procedure must be made to the sponsor hospital program director or medical director in writing.

2. The proposal will include the following:

   Request
   Rationale
   Service or specific group to be utilized
   Written protocol for use of procedure or product
   Time frame planned: start of project, duration
   Training needs identified and training plan
   Any cost-analysis information
   Scientific evidence (bibliography) supporting proposal

3. The proposal will be placed on the agenda for the next NHSHP operational meeting. At the discretion of the NHSHP director or medical director, the person making the proposal will be invited to attend the meeting for the discussion of the proposal.

4. Action taken at the operational meeting will be detailed in the minutes and will be communicated to the requesting personnel in writing, along with the rationale for the decision reached.

5. If accepted, the EMS coordinators at each hospital will disseminate the appropriate information to the hospital staff, and the NHSHP Director will notify the appropriate service representatives.

6. A follow-up report will be made at the operational meeting within two months of the actual implementation of the proposal. The report will include:

   Incidence of use
   Positive or negative outcomes associated with use
   Recommended modifications

7. A written report will be submitted at the end of the project, or at 6 months, and will include the above information, as well as recommendations for future use.

PHYSICIAN AT THE SCENE
WICHITA, KS

Procedure When A Physician Is On The Scene

For situations in which a physician is at the scene of an EMS call, the following procedure should be followed: Such situations are divided into two types for the purpose of this procedure.

I. **Routine, normal situations**

    A. Conduct yourself with a professional demeanor and a respectful attitude at all times. The *PHYSICIAN HAS CERTAIN PROFESSIONAL AND LEGAL PREROGATIVES AND DESERVES OUR RESPECT.*

    B. Inquire if the physician is the patient's regular physician. If so, consult the physician as to the patient's history, prior treatment, *etc.*

    C. Advise the physician that we have medical standing protocols established by the Medical Society of Sedgwick County (MSSC), and request that we be allowed to continue under these standing orders.

    D. Follow any reasonable request by the physician.

II. **Problem or crisis situations**

    A. Follow the steps outlined in section I.

    B. If the physician prefers to assume responsibility for the patient, the following requirements must be satisfied.

        1. The physician must provide proof of Kansas licensure.

        2. The physician must accompany the patient to the medical facility in our unit.

        3. The physician must personally initiate any procedure that is contrary to our standard operating procedure.

    C. If, in the opinion of the charge technician, the patient's well-being is endangered or if the physician does not agree to our procedure in its entirety, a 10-89 shall be requested.

    D. The district captain shall be contacted and requested to come to the scene or meet the unit at the emergency facility.

PHYSICIAN ORDERS FOR EXTRAORDINARY CARE NOT COVERED BY MARYLAND PROTOCOL
STATE OF MARYLAND

To maintain the life of a specific patient, it may be necessary, in rare instances, for the physician providing on-line medical direction, as part of the EMS consultation system, to direct a prehospital ALS provider in rendering care that is not explicitly listed within the medical protocols.

1. All of the following criteria MUST be present in order for prehospital providers to proceed with an order under this section:

1.1 During the consultation, both the consulting physician and the provider must acknowledge and agree that the patient's condition and extraordinary care are not addressed elsewhere within these medical protocols, and that the order is absolutely necessary to maintain the life of the patient.

1.2 The provider must feel capable, based on the instructions given by the consulting physician, of correctly performing the care directed by the consulting physician.

1.3 When such an order is carried out, the consulting physician must immediately notify the State EMS Director (via SYSCOM, 800-648-3001, or 410-328-3156) of the extraordinary care situation and also forward documentation of the rationale in writing within 24 hours to the State EMS Director at the address on the cover page of this document. Attendance at a subsequent review meeting will be required.

1.4 The prehospital provider must inform the consulting physician of the effect of the treatment and notify the receiving physician of the treatment upon arrival at the hospital (if different than the consulting physician). The prehospital provider must also notify his or her ALS program medical director within 24 hours.

1.5 The public-service local EMS jurisdiction and the local ALS program medical director must then submit written notification of the incident to the regional medical director, with a copy of the State EMS Director within 7 days of the incident.

The commercial ALS company and the commercial ALS program medical director must submit written notification of the incident to the director of the state office of commercial ambulance licensing and regulation and the State EMS director within 7 days of the incident.

1.6 The State EMS director shall conduct a review conference to include when appropriate: the prehospital ALS provider, the on-line physician who provided the medical direction, the appropriate local jurisdictional official(s), the local ALS program medical director, and the regional medical director.

1.7 Reports of incidents shall be submitted monthly by the State EMS director to the State Board of Physician Quality Assurance.

2. If a prehospital provider receives an order for care that is not covered by Maryland protocols but does not feel comfortable with it or does not agree that it is absolutely necessary to maintain the life of the patient, he or she should proceed with section 1.7.2 (Inability to Carry Out a Physician's Order).

NOTE: Protocols provide a safe basis for prehospital intervention and transport and provide both prehospital ALS providers and on-line physicians with parameters for this care. Extraordinary-care situations not within the protocols may occur a handful of times over a span of years. The extraordinary-care protocol is intended to address the potential moral/ethical dilemma which may arise in unanticipated or unforeseen situations not specifically addressed within protocols. The extraordinary-care protocol is neither a carte blanche for any and all actions nor a device to avoid or circumvent protocols. In all situations, emergency health-care providers—both prehospital ALS providers and on-line physicians providing medical direction—are accountable for their actions in discharging their patient-care responsibilities.

REFUSAL OF CARE
DENVER, CO

Nontransport/Refusal of Care

(See Nontransport of patients protocol)

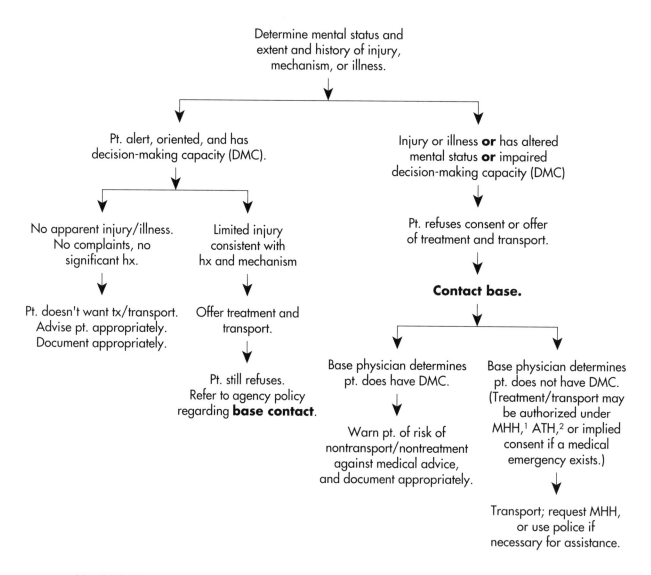

Determine mental status and extent and history of injury, mechanism, or illness.

Pt. alert, oriented, and has decision-making capacity (DMC).

Injury or illness **or** has altered mental status **or** impaired decision-making capacity (DMC)

No apparent injury/illness. No complaints, no significant hx.

Limited injury consistent with hx and mechanism

Pt. refuses consent or offer of treatment and transport.

Pt. doesn't want tx/transport. Advise pt. appropriately. Document appropriately.

Offer treatment and transport.

Contact base.

Pt. still refuses. Refer to agency policy regarding **base contact**.

Base physician determines pt. does have DMC.

Base physician determines pt. does not have DMC. (Treatment/transport may be authorized under MHH,[1] ATH,[2] or implied consent if a medical emergency exists.)

Warn pt. of risk of nontransport/nontreatment against medical advice, and document appropriately.

Transport; request MHH, or use police if necessary for assistance.

1. Mental health hold; see destination policy protocol if transporting a psychiatric patient.
2. Alcohol treatment hold

REFUSAL OF CARE
WASHINGTON, DC

Refusal-of-Treatment Protocol

A. Ensure that the patient is conscious, alert, and oriented to person, place, and time, GCS 15.

B. Unless the patient specifically refuses, do a complete physical assessment.

C. Inform the patient and/or responsible party (parent or legal guardian) of the potential consequences of their decision to refuse treatment and/or transport to a definitive-care facility (loss of life or limb, irreversible sequela), and ensure that the patient and/or guardian fully understand.

D. All measures should be taken to convince the patient to consent, including enlisting the help of family or friends.

E. If the patient continues to refuse, the patient and/or responsible party may then sign a release form. Ensure that the following information is provided:

   1. That the release is against medical advice
   2. That it applies to this instance only
   3. That EMS should be requested again if necessary and desired

F. After the release form is signed by the patient, it must be witnessed. This witness signatory should be someone other than a member of the DCFEMS Department.

G. After the signed release is obtained, other responding units may be cancelled.

H. If the patient or responsible party will not sign, this shall be documented. If available, witness signatures shall be obtained.

I. Where at all possible, patients will be left in the care of family, friends, or responsible parties.

J. Leave patient instruction sheet.

K. Patients in need of treatment who do not meet criteria in Part I or exhibit evidence of severe psychiatric disorder should be transported. MPD or EPRD services should be contacted as needed. (Refer to BEHAVIORAL EMERGENCIES PROTOCOL.)

L. Carefully document the assessment and vital sings, including all issues and circumstances indicated above.

RESTRAINTS
FREMONT, CA

1. Patient restraints are to be utilized only when necessary and in those situations where the patient is exhibiting behavior deemed to present danger to him or herself or to the field personnel. When restraints are used:

   1.1 The minimum restraint necessary to accomplish necessary patient care and safe transportation should be utilized.

   1.2 Circulation to the extremities (distal to the restraints) will be evaluated frequently.

   1.3 The restraints must be not placed in such a way as to preclude evaluation of the patient's medical status (*e.g.*, airway, breathing, circulation), and necessary patient-care activities, or in any way jeopardize the patient medically.

2. In situations where the patient is under arrest and handcuffs are applied by law-enforcement officers:

   2.1 The patient will not be cuffed to the stretcher, and

   2.2 A law-enforcement officer shall accompany the patient in the ambulance if the handcuffs are to remain applied.

   2.3 A law-enforcement officer may elect to follow the ambulance in a patrol car to the receiving facility if the patient has been restrained on the gurney by using leather restraints.

SIGNING OUT AGAINST MEDICAL ADVICE
FREMONT, CA

1. **INTRODUCTION:**

    1.1 This policy refers to those situations in which a patient refuses evaluation, treatment, and/or transportation by the prehospital care personnel.

    1.2 Persons presumed competent to make decisions affecting their medical care shall be allowed to make such decisions.

    1.3 Patients who want to be transported to the hospital should be, regardless of the severity of their medical condition.

    1.4 **First responders/EMTs** may not sign out any patient AMA if the incident involves an injury or illness but shall remain on scene with the patient until the arrival of an approved ambulance provider. A patient report shall be given to the arriving ALS personnel.

2. **WHO CAN SIGN OUT AMA?**—The patient refusing medical care must be:

    2.1 **Competent**—*able to understand the nature and consequence of refusing medical care and/or transportation,* **and**

    2.2 **Adult**—*eighteen (18) years of age or older.*

    2.3 Exceptions:
    *   An emancipated minor
    *   A self-sufficient minor
    *   A minor who is married
    *   A minor who is in the military
    *   A legal representative for the patient
    *   The parent of a minor child

3. **WHO CAN NOT SIGN OUT AMA?**—*Patients may be considered incompetent to refuse medical care and/or transportation if the severity of their medical condition prevents them from making rational decisions regarding their medical care.*
    Patients may not refuse medical care and/or transportation if they:

    3.1 Present with an altered level of consciousness, including those with a head injury or under the influence of drugs and/or alcohol.

    3.2 Have attempted suicide or verbalized suicidal intent.

    3.3 Present with severely altered vital signs.

    3.4 Are under a "5150" hold.

    3.5 Are mentally retarded or have a mental deficiency.

    3.6 Are under eighteen (18) years of age and do not qualify as an adult.

    3.7 Are clearly not acting as a reasonable person would, given the same circumstances.

    3.8 Meet **any** of the criteria in the mandatory call-in policy. This patient may only refuse evaluation, treatment, and/or transport if the base hospital physician on duty concurs. Base contact is to be made prior to the patient leaving the scene.

507

4. **IMPLIED CONSENT:**

    4.1 If a patient is determined to be incompetent, he or she may be treated and/or transported under "implied consent" *(what a reasonable individual would consent to under the same circumstances)*.

    4.2 ALS personnel should contact the base and consult with the base hospital physician.

    4.3 If it is decided that the patient should be transported and/or treated on the basis of implied consent, field personnel should use all reasonable measures, including physical restraint, to ensure transport to the hospital.

    4.4 **Exception**—If by attempting to treat and/or transport the patient, the first responder or EMT-P place themselves or others in physical danger, document the events that led up to patient signing out AMA and all steps taken to attempt transport. If possible, leave the patient with a responsible adult.

    4.5 Submit an Unusual Occurrence form to the appropriate agency.

5. **DOCUMENTATION:**

    5.1 The patient, or an individual who claims to be authorized as responsible for the patient, should sign the "Release from Medical Responsibilities" form on the First Responder form or PCR.

    5.2 If the patient refuses to sign the "Release from Medical Responsibilities" form, document the refusal to sign, and obtain a witness signature, if possible.

SPECIAL TRAUMA PROBLEMS
OKLAHOMA CITY, OK

Certain trauma situations call for assessment and treatment that go beyond the standard treatment given for the patient's presenting complaints and injury. Treatment of physical injuries should be as listed in the protocols, but the following special considerations should be noted:

Sexual Assault:

A. History should not be more extensive than necessary from a medical standpoint. Legal and psychological details are best left to persons who will be able to use that information, follow it up with appropriate actions, and provide ongoing support to the patient.

B. You can, however, help with the patient's psychological needs. Do not judge the victim, who already feels debased, worthless, and guilty, no matter how blameless. Allow the patient as much freedom of choice in dealing with the medical community as possible. Do as little controlling as you need to; let the patient control any aspects of care that he or she can.

C. Remember that the radio waves are public; particularly with sexual-assault victims, refrain from names and details.

D. There may be hesitance on the part of the victim to accept assistance from the same sex as the assailant. If an attendant of the other sex is available, it *may* be preferable to allow that attendant to treat. Be aware, however, that this can be a chance to revive faith in the other sex. Allow the patient to choose how interactive he or she would like to be.

E. You should encourage the victim to leave the same clothes on and not to bathe before coming to the hospital. This goes against a victim's instincts at the time but will help preserve legal evidence.

F. Encourage the victim to seek treatment even if reluctant to call the police and initiate legal action. There is still important medical treatment that can be offered, and the hospital staff or crisis counselor may allow the patient a better understanding of legal choices.

Child Abuse/Neglect:

A. Observe child for evidence of other injury, healing old wounds, multiple bruises. Also note relationship of child to adults, and physical and emotional relations within family unit.

B. Although some injuries such as cigarette burns are characteristic of child abuse, most abuse injuries are similar to many other injuries. Suspicious scenarios include:

   1. Injured child without obvious mechanism, injuries that do not match story or that are inappropriate to the child's age
   2. Delay in seeking treatment

3. Blame of third party
4. Multiple different stories
5. History of multiple previous episodes of trauma

C. Don't accuse or judge. Observe, and share your observations with appropriate authorities. This is an instance where your skilled powers of observation in the field and your ability to be discreet and to keep an open mind are most needed.

D. If abuse is suspected, transport the child, even if the injuries themselves do not warrant it. The same child may even be admitted for minor injuries to provide sufficient time to assess the situation and prevent serious injury or death in the future.

Pregnant Trauma Patient:

A. AVOID SUPINE POSITIONING in obviously pregnant patient. Pressure from the uterus on the inferior vena cava prevents venous return to the heart and can result in severe hypotension. Turn backboard to side, or use your hands to hold uterus off central abdominal vessels.

B. Blunt abdominal trauma is difficult to evaluate because the abdominal exam is unreliable. Deceleration forces can cause placental separation. Seatbelts should be worn, but lap belts should be low, next to the pelvis, and fit snugly. (More injuries still occur due to lack of seatbelts than are caused by them.) All obviously pregnant patients should be transported for close evaluation and observation. Note presence or absence of fetal movement.

C. Think of eclampsia as a possible cause of injury in the trauma victim with altered mental state, seizures, or *hypertension*.

D. Pregnancy alters normal vital signs, as well as response to hypovolemia. Normal BP will be lower, with pulse slightly increased. Changes with hypovolemia are often delayed. Anticipate potential problems.

E. The fetus is much more sensitive to hypoxia and hypovolemia than the mother. For this reason O_2 should always be applied, and treatment for blood loss should begin before hypotension becomes evident.

TRAUMA "LOAD-AND-GO" SITUATIONS
COLUMBUS, GA

REMEMBER RAPID TRANSPORT IS RECOMMENDED IN ALL UNSTABLE PATIENTS

This standard for trauma situations requiring immediate transport (field evaluation and care stopped—patient immediately put in ambulance and transport to trauma center undertaken without delay or any additional field time—primary survey completion and standard resuscitation efforts continued during transport) is taken word for word from the Alabama American College of Emergency Physicians Chapter Certified Basic Trauma Life Support Course (BTLS).

There are certain situations that require hospital treatment within minutes if the victim is to have any chance of survival. When these situations are recognized, the victim should be loaded immediately onto a backboard, transferred to ambulance, and transported rapidly with lights and siren. Lifesaving procedures may be needed but should be done during transport. Nonlifesaving procedures (such as splinting and bandaging) must not hold up transport.

The following are LOAD-AND-GO situations:

1. Airway obstruction that cannot be quickly relieved by mechanical methods such as suction or forceps
2. Trauma cardiorespiratory arrest
3. Tension pneumothorax
4. Pericardial tamponade
5. Penetrating wounds of the chest with shock
6. Massive hemothorax with shock
7. Head injury with unilaterally dilated pupil
8. Head injury with rapidly deteriorating condition

In addition to the above BTLS course situations,

9. Any trauma victim who is in shock and does not rapidly respond (within 5 to 8 minutes maximum) to shock resuscitation efforts also falls into the "LOAD-AND-GO" category and must be transported immediately.

TRAUMA TRIAGE GUIDELINES
SANTA ANA, CA

Although many patients with severe medical emergencies may be stabilized in the field, victims with severe traumatic injuries require immediate interventions beyond the capabilities of current prehospital care. Therefore, two general classes of trauma victims are recognized:

1. CRITICAL-TRAUMA VICTIMS: Those with obvious, immediate need for paramedic-trauma-receiving-center-(PTRC)-level care
2. MODERATE-TRAUMA VICTIMS: Those potentially needing PTRC level care

Critical-Trauma Victim (CTV):

The critical trauma victim is defined as a victim of blunt or penetrating trauma that results in any of the following alterations in vital signs and/or mechanisms of injury:

RESP < 12 OR > 30
PULSE < 50 OR > 130
SYSTOLIC BP < 80, or
Penetrating wounds to the neck, chest, or abdomen

Moderate-Trauma Victim (MTV):

The moderate-trauma victim includes all other victims of multiple trauma. Parameters for consideration of PTRC designation include:

- Mechanism of injury
- Unable to follow commands
- Abnormal capillary refill
- Age < 5 or > 65 years old
- Prolonged extrication
- Fatalities involved in the event
- Glasgow Coma Score (GSC) 10 or less

A trauma patient initially designated MTV should have frequent vital-sign checks and may be redesignated CTV if the patient's vital signs indicate a deterioration of the patient's condition. An MTV may be triaged to a PTRC or a PRC according to the judgment of the base-hospital physician.

THE FINAL DESIGNATION OF ANY TRAUMA PATIENT IS SUBJECT TO BASE-HOSPITAL PHYSICIAN INTERPRETATION.

INDEX OF PROTOCOLS BY EMS SYSTEM

SUBJECT INDEX

SUBJECT INDEX

DATE DUE

MAY 05 1997		
AP 47 '98		
OCT 08 1998		

Demco, Inc. 38-293

ISBN 0-07-069318-1

9000

9 780070 693180